SPEAKING ON STAGE

SPEAKING ON STAGE

Interviews with Contemporary American Playwrights

Edited with Introductions by

Philip C. Kolin
and
Colby H. Kullman

The University of Alabama Press
Tuscaloosa and London

Copyright © 1996
The University of Alabama Press
Tuscaloosa, Alabama 35487-0380
All rights reserved
Manufactured in the United States of America

Designed by Rick Cook

∞

The paper on which this book is printed meets the minimum requirements of
American National Standard for Information Science-Permanence of Paper for
Printed Library Materials, ANSI Z39.48-1984.

Library of Congress Cataloging-in-Publication Data

Speaking on stage : interviews with contemporary American playwrights /
edited with introductions by Philip C. Kolin and Colby H. Kullman.
p.   cm.
Includes index.
ISBN 0-8173-0796-6
1. American drama—20th century—History and criticism—Theory, etc.   2.
Dramatists, American—20th century—Interviews.   3. Drama—Technique.   4.
Playwriting. I. Kolin Philip C. II. Kullman, Colby H.
PS352.S64   1996
812′.5409—dc20
95-21171

British Library Cataloguing-in-Publication Data available

1 2 3 4 5 00 99 98 97 96

For
Susan and Ronald Marquardt,
with love

CONTENTS

PART 4
Celebrating Difference: The American Theatre since 1980   231

ACKNOWLEDGMENTS

We are grateful to many people for their help in preparing this collection for publication. First of all, we want to pay tribute to the playwrights who gave of their wit and wisdom in discussing their work for, and reactions to, the American theatre; we are equally grateful to the individuals who interviewed these playwrights. Every locution needs an interlocutor. To the many theatre companies, directors, public relations directors, agents, and photographers who aided us in crucial ways, we say thanks and more thanks. At an early stage of this project, Jackson R. Bryer at the University of Maryland gave us much wise counsel and healthy doses of encouragement, and we want to acknowledge our gratitude to him. Ralph F. Voss at the University of Alabama and Albert E. Kalson at Purdue University provided us with invaluable help about organizing this collection and planning the section introductions. All errors are our own, of course.

We are grateful to the administrators at our universities for their support and encouragement, including, at the University of Southern Mississippi, President Aubrey K. Lucas; Vice-President for Academic Affairs G. David Huffman; Dean of the College of Liberal Arts Glenn T. Harper; and Chairs of the English Department David M. Wheeler and Jeanette Harris; and at the University of Mississippi, Chancellor Gerald R. Turner; Vice-Chancellor for Academic Affairs Gerald W. Walton; Dean of the College of Liberal Arts Dale H. Abadie; Associate Dean of the College of Liberal Arts Michael P. Dean; and Chair of the English Department Daniel E. Williams. We also wish to thank Steven Barthelme at the University of Southern Mississippi and Mark Royden Winchell at Clemson University for reading early drafts of several of the introductions and giving us the benefit of their criticism. We are also grateful to Kathleen Rossman Pentecost for helping us prepare the index.

We deeply appreciate the excellent cooperation and enthusiastic support of our work from Malcolm M. MacDonald, Director of the University of Alabama Press, and the editors and staff at the Press who have worked so diligently to make *Speaking on Stage* a reality.

For their moral support, prayers, and love, we thank Sister Carmelita Stinn, SFCC, Kristin Julie Kolin, Eric H. Kolin, Fr. G. Eddie Lundin, Mannie Hall, and Cyndi Hall, all from Hattiesburg.

Finally, without the help and guidance of Susan Marquardt of Hattiesburg and Ronald Gene Marquardt, Chair of the Department of Political Science at the University of Southern Mississippi, we could have never begun or finished this collection. With gratitude and love, we dedicate this book to Susan and Ron.

Philip C. Kolin
Colby H. Kullman

SPEAKING ON STAGE

Introduction

Interviews: The New Metadrama

We live and, to a certain extent, prosper in this age of interviews. The pièce de résistance in many literary fares—magazines, quarterlies, reviews—is often an original interview with artist, poet, playwright, novelist, cultural savant, or political mogul. There are plenty of reasons why interviews are sought after and savored. For those who must have their daily dose of rationalism, the interview offers both code-establishing and code-breaking information. The interview can be revelatory; the playwright in this case confides in us, telling all. Consider, for example, Tennessee Williams's admission and glorification of his homosexuality in his interview with David Frost in 1970. Through interviews playwrights (and other icon makers and deconstructors) make the internal external. In the interview they provide information about society, family, friends, lovers, directors, actors and actresses, audiences, bêtes noires, influences, predictions, and predilections—biographically sensitive bytes that are then stored in our consciousness until the next time we read their plays or see them performed. This is one side of our fascination with interviews.

But there is another. If the interview offers revelation and light, it can also be the lens for the playwright's camera obscura. The interview is the confirmation of indeterminacy, best defined by the playwright's prized sense of otherness, not volunteering or even agreeing to be stereotyped, polarized, fixed. As an American with a distinct "American chemistry," Charles Gordone celebrates cross-cultural mixtures of race and religion in the world of his plays. He rejects being "the monkey in the tuxedo." Adrienne Kennedy also resists the designation "minority" to characterize herself or her work; as she proclaims, "I'm not a minority in the world." For some playwrights the interview is the medium through which they deny the medium as it is traditionally conceived. As Kenneth Bernard asserts, "I think the danger is in the desire not to remain the 'other,' the desire to be inside. My notion of salvation is to remain outside."

As an expression of otherness and as a manifesto of cultural independence based upon indeterminacy, the interview may reflect the playwright's engagement in the disorderly street, not his or her security in a neat library or a cushioned theatre seat. Among the many celebrated outsiders in this collection, Edward Albee, Maria Fornes, Jack Gelber, David Henry Hwang, Megan Terry, and Jean-Claude van Itallie fight in their interviews the all-too-easy shrinking of consciousness into public disclosure. There is exploitation in revelation for these and other playwrights. The other side of fascination with the interview, therefore, is provocative doubt, especially doubt engendered through the very metaphysics of interviewing. The rest is silence after all.

In many ways the interview is like the drama itself. The interview unfolds in a sense as a *metadrama*. The performative nature of drama and the process of interviewing run a close race in the illusion of life. Like a play performed before an audience, the interview offers spectacle, and a collection of interviews such as the ones in this volume is similar to the spectacle of festival. At a drama festival we are enticed into an enchanted space or recoil in alienation from a hostile (fictional only sometimes) environment. The space between the interviewer and the interviewee becomes alternatively enchanted or alienated. Thus the action between the playwright and interviewer is like the action of a play. Appropriately enough, the playwright's name and the interviewer's are marked in boldface as in a script, prefixed as characters in a dramatic exchange. The resulting *logos* is the new dramatic script, or the interview. And like the playscript we read (or see), the interview gives us dialogue, the back-and-forth exchange between the person who knows or is supposed to know and the person who wants to know or tries to know.

Each of the actors/participants in this festival of words—the interview—makes responses, supplies listening clues to the other, demands clarification, and/or inserts questions. As in the drama, stage directions occur in many interviews, and these interviews in this collection are no exception. *Laughter, silence, chuckles, pause*—such commentaries appear throughout. Stichomythia is common to these interviews, as it is to the drama; exchanges between playwright and questioner can be rapid-fire. Playwrights may, on the other hand, soliloquize. The polished arias of Edward Albee or the impassioned pleas of Ntozake Shange take on the quality of soliloquies, eloquent and refreshing or plaintive and punitive. In the interview the playwright and the interviewer are simultaneously actor, critic, stage designer, and even audience. Roles are volleyed back and forth in a verbal drama of questions and answers. The roles that the interviewer and playwright adopt are the essence of drama, the ritual repetitions of our culture, as Sigmund Freud once labeled them.

Where do we as readers fit in? We are the (re)actors and audience too—the recipients of the words in the very "delinquency of our being," as Herbert Blau characterizes us in *The Audience* (Baltimore: Johns Hopkins University Press, 1990, 42). We are also, in Blau's words, the "viewing subjects." Each of us is both listener and reader. As the "viewing subjects" for whom the interview—the drama—is intended, we are part of the process and also the subject of the reality being represented. As listeners and readers we gain information through the ears of the interviewer and playwright and also through our eyes. As Blau explains, "The word audience is the name for those whose eyes look upon what—like the gold lines of the Annunciation in a medieval painting—comes through the ears, as if it were created by the Logos. This synthetic transference, a sort of cross-breeding of viewing and voice, is part of the phenomenology of theatre . . . the audience, in short, as a figure of speech" (41–42).

As participants in the living words/drama of the interview, we exercise our power to control or decipher the representations of drama unfolding in these interviews. Paradoxically, too, we become cocreators in the ideology of revelation, or coequals in the presentation of indeterminacy. The implications of these and a great many other theoretical speculations are magnified when set inside the space of the interview. Yet, within the theoretical implications raised by the interview, the subject still matters.

We present twenty-six interviews in this collection. Eighteen were originally published in a journal we have coedited since 1986, *Studies in American Drama, 1945–Present*. In many instances the interviewers have updated their introductions and interviews as well for the current volume. To these eighteen interviews we have added eight new ones, all but one of them especially commissioned for this collection. The interview with David Henry Hwang was originally done for National Public Radio, but this is the first time it appears in print. While we certainly make no claim to include every major American playwright since World War II, we do believe that our collection is both representative of American playwrights since 1945 and responsive to the various communities that have shaped our national theatre. American theatre, like American society, is the beneficiary of an energizing pluralism. Represented here are some of America's leading playwrights who are black, Asian, gay, Hispanic, feminist, and white.

The scope of the following twenty-six interviews with these American playwrights is at once highly focused—the American theatre—and yet usefully diverse—American mythologies and cultural anxieties as they are represented by and interpreted through theatre. Our goal is to reflect the evolution of American theatre since World War II and also to chart the currents moving that theatre. After all, no theatre (or theatre company) is an island. Consequently, we have divided the post–World War II American theatre into four major periods or decades, 1945–59, 1959–69, 1970–79, and 1980 to the present.

Having said that, we readily, boldly even, admit an essential qualification. We recognize that it is difficult to divide—sequester—a living, evolving form such as the American theatre into discrete categories or decades. As Megan Terry has intriguingly said, the 1960s spilled over into 1975. But there are some watershed years—beginnings and endings that are sometimes one and the same—that help define American theatre and drama. The theatre changed radically in late 1945 with the arrival of Tennessee Williams's *The Glass Menagerie;* in 1959 Edward Albee and Jack Gelber helped to usher in the prominence of Off-Broadway, the first American wave of the avant-garde; significantly Michael Weller's *Moonchildren* arrived in 1970–71, signaling a new, different phase of the 1960s Age of Aquarius. And the 1980s and beyond gave birth to celebrating instead of denying or camouflaging difference.

This collection features interviews with some of the leading playwrights of each theatre decade. Beyond question the playwrights we have selected for each category are as impressively diverse as the drama they created. By classifying their interviews in this way we have the playwrights themselves—the ones who created the drama that is the achievement of the American theatre—help define and illustrate the theatrical milieu, the movements, the tastes of audiences and producers, the scripts and dramatic techniques, and the climate of opinion for the specific decade they helped to shape. Hence an interview with Robert Anderson sheds light on the post–World War II American theatre, especially the Broadway of the 1940s and 1950s; an interview with Jack Gelber helps readers understand what it was like to see theatre in the early 1960s; and an interview with David Mamet points to and illustrates the new, emerging theatre of the 1970s. In no way are we denying or minimizing the continuing achievements of a Robert Anderson, Jack Gelber, or David Mamet, or any of the other playwrights whose interviews form this collection. We are acutely aware of and deeply grateful for the continuing achievements of all these playwrights. All we are asserting is that American theatre/cultural history will most surely honor specific playwrights for the work they have already done to create and advance American theatre at a particular time and in a particular place.

PART 1

BROADWAY REALISM: THE AMERICAN THEATRE, 1945 TO 1959

The years between 1945 and 1959 may well have been the most influential in American theatre history: they provided both a bridge from the past and a beacon to the future. The plays written during this period look back to the works of Elmer Rice, Maxwell Anderson, Clifford Odets, Thornton Wilder, Lillian Hellman, and especially Eugene O'Neill. As C. W. E. Bigsby observes, "Those who emerged as playwrights after 1945 had, in a sense, been shaped by the assumptions of the previous decade. It was there that they found their images no less than a language of liberal possibility."[1] Building upon "this dramatic inheritance," post–World War II theatre ushered in a new, vibrant, and dazzling era. Just as Eugene O'Neill "experimented with a variety of styles that expanded the boundaries of mainstream theatre,"[2] so did the playwrights who established their careers in the 1940s and 1950s. Their experiments pushed ahead even farther than O'Neill could the nature of theatrical realism in America.

The theatre of the 1940s and 1950s was basically the theatre of Broadway, which often turned to a public exploration of our national postwar selves. Some of the greatest successes of the American theatre—our most sacred dramatic icons, in fact—date from the mid- to late 1940s: *The Glass Menagerie* (1945), *A Streetcar Named Desire* (1947), and *Death of a Salesman* (1949). It was the age of Arthur Miller and Tennessee Williams, to be sure, but it was also one of the most promising times in American theatre history in general. Even the American musical flourished, thanks to the work of Rodgers and Hammerstein, particularly their *South Pacific* (1949), *The King and I* (1951), and *The Sound of Music* (1959).

A host of new playwrights shaped the American theatre after the war. The dramatists included in this first section—Robert Anderson, Arthur Miller, Robert E. Lee, and Jerome Lawrence—represent much that was successful in and typical of post–World War II theatre. Granted, these playwrights have written across the decades and into the present, and their long, sustained careers continue to enlighten and to inspire. The first Broadway play done by Lawrence and Lee was *Look Ma, I'm Dancing* in 1948, and the two playwrights went on collaborating for nearly fifty years, until Robert Lee's death in 1994. Yet the plays they wrote for the American stage during the 1940s and 1950s are the ones for which they will probably be forever remembered. Also included in this first section of *Speaking on Stage* is an interview with Neil Simon, even though his first full-length Broadway comedy (*Come Blow Your Horn*) did not appear until the early 1960s. Beyond doubt, however, Simon offers valuable insights about the emerging modern American theatre of the 1940s and 1950s on which he was weaned. Simon's highly acclaimed autobiographical trilogy, premiering in the 1980s and comprising *Brighton Beach Memoirs, Biloxi Blues,* and *Broadway Bound,* deals with the theme of coming of age in the 1940s and 1950s.

Ultimately, each of these dramatists helps us to understand and appreciate the milieu of Broadway, then theatrical capital of America. They talk about what Broadway was—the way things were before Broadway's luster had eroded in the 1960s and 1970s, in part because of the emergence of Off- and Off-Off-Broadway and in part because of the rise of regional theatres in the late 1950s, thanks to such pioneers as Margo Jones in Dallas, Nina Vance in Houston, and Zelda Fichandler in Washington, D.C. The playwrights interviewed in this section define the Broadway ethos and give insights into what audiences were like and what producers wanted. The Broadway of the 1940s, and for much of the 1950s, was truly "boulevard theatre." Broadway plays appealed to the interests and sentiments of a formidable yet supportive theatregoing public, the mainstream middle class. Plays on Broadway were large, in both ambition and scope, and they were probing. Initially very controversial, *A Streetcar Named Desire* ran for over two years (885 performances), outpacing any other Williams play on Broadway; similarly Robert Anderson's *Tea and Sympathy* held the stage for 712 performances. Such track records are increasingly rare on Broadway today, except for a musical such as *A Chorus Line,* which remained at the Schubert Theatre for fifteen years, from July 1975 to April 1990.

The Broadway-based playwrights of the 1940s and 1950s appreciated the opportunities their theatre opened for them. Robert Anderson, for example, states uncategorically: "I am speaking as a playwright who has basically been very happy with the 'Broadway' way of doing things." What constitutes a Broadway play and what makes a Broadway playwright are central concerns of many of these playwrights. Perhaps Broadway's most successful and representative playwright has been Neil Simon. Yet Simon's sense of Broadway has itself been subjected to redefinition by a later age. Simon's *The Odd Couple,* one of Broadway's most popular plays during the mid-1960s, found success on movie and television screens, too, because of his two Broadway stars, Art Carney and Walter Matthau. Yet *The Odd Couple* was redesigned for the 1980s when Gene Saks offered a feminized version with two women playing the leading roles. Such transformations, possible and acceptable in the 1980s, would not have been likely on the Broadway stage of the 1940s or 1950s. Thus what once made for a Broadway hit, as articulated by the playwrights in this section, has been modified and in some cases radically challenged. Commenting on playwrights from a different stage tradition, Simon confidently concludes that "Sam Shepard was never a Broadway writer" and that Wendy Wasserstein's "*Heidi Chronicles* was not a Broadway play." Beginning the present collection with these four interviews provides necessary background information on the evolution of the contemporary American theatre.

The dramatists in this section also identify the themes—the central concerns of an American public at mid-century—of the Broadway decades of the 1940s and 1950s. From the mid-1940s through the 1950s many popular plays on Broadway (and increasingly on other stages, too) focused on domestic issues affecting the individual, the family, and the state. There was a perennial concern with loneliness, midlife crises, and marriage problems, or "married sexuality,"[3] as Thomas P. Adler succinctly identifies the leading themes of Robert Anderson's drama. Playwrights such as William Inge and Tennessee Williams spotlighted the loneliness that debilitated individuals who sought union or suffered isolation within cold marriages. Not surprisingly Paddy Chayefsky's television play, *Marty* (1953), about loneliness and courtship, was one of the most popular dramas of the decade, as were William Inge's *Come Back, Little Sheba* (1950) and his *Picnic* (1953), which won the Pulitzer Prize. The search for the right mate resounded through the 1940s and 1950s. Such a quest in the 1980s and 1990s has taken on different anxieties, different dramatic representations.

Domestic tranquillity was not confined to the spouse-hunting individual or to troubled families (hardly dysfunctional by 1990s standards) in the Broadway theatre up to 1959. The theatre also emphasized social problems, with impassioned attention to the individual's responsibility to the state and vice versa. The free exercise of one's conscience in the home of the free and the land of the brave was a constant idea in the works of almost all of the dramatists represented in this section. Arthur Miller's plays, for example, are steeped in moral obligations that fall on the individual and society simultaneously. The shadow of McCarthyism, with its right-wing censorship of the arts, loomed large in the early 1950s, threatening artistic integrity and the freedoms that the Constitution has guaranteed.

McCarthy's ghost lived on through the 1950s and beyond. The dramatists of the 1950s, even when responding only indirectly to his threats, did not escape the pain of his legacy. Not surprisingly some of the most popular plays of the 1950s dealt with historical events in which an extraordinary individual stands up to the petrified yet dangerous thinking of a monolithic bureaucracy. Jerome Lawrence and Robert E. Lee's seminal document in the history of unfettered thinking, *Inherit the Wind* (1955), was written, as they state here, to "rough up" the individual conscience and scrape the "moss off young minds." *Inherit the Wind* was subsequently translated into thirty-four languages. Other Lawrence and Lee plays, whether on Henry David Thoreau or on a larger-than-life character such as Auntie Mame, are bulwarks against anything that would "run over young minds or our soaring spirits." Lamentably, this first period of post–World War II drama ended with awarding the Pulitzer Prize in 1960 to a lighthearted musical, *Fiorello!,* rather than to Lillian Hellman's more serious and provocative *Toys in the Attic.* Yet this decision nonetheless reflects that the decade of the 1950s could end with the public still believing in national heroes.

The four dramatists interviewed here authoritatively talk about the ways plays were made. As C. W. E. Bigsby remarks, with a touch of irony, "Broadway plays clung to realism for reasons only partly to do with a consistent social and aesthetic position."[4] Unquestionably there is plenty of talk about "the well-made play" among these dramatists. If we can discount Bigsby's political inference, the 1940s and 1950s witnessed successes in theatre through freedom and experimentation. For some critics of the American stage these were the decades when realism in theatre reached its peak. However, the realism that ruled the day was enormously varied. Tennessee Williams's poetic realism and Arthur Miller's psychological realism are only two examples of such innovation. Williams and Miller blended expressionistic with realistic techniques to create their psychologically complex characters. Set designer Jo Mielziner helped these (and other) playwrights through his enormous contributions in what might be called the "Age of Gauze" on the American stage, referring to Mielziner's see-through scrims.[5] In retrospect the dramaturgy of the 1950s as practiced by Miller, Anderson, and Inge may seem too focused, even stilted when judged against the more self-conscious productions of the 1990s. But the strides made by the post–World War II theatre, particularly in stretching the boundaries of realism to accommodate the dramatists' increased desire to probe beneath the surface into their characters' inner selves, are still influencing our theatre today.

Notes

1. C.W. E. Bigsby, *Williams/Miller/Albee,* vol. 2 of *A Critical Introduction to Twentieth-Century American Theatre* (New York: Cambridge University Press, 1984), 1.

2. Felicia Hardison Londré, *The History of World Theatre: From the English Restoration to the Present* (New York: Continuum, 1991), 509.

3. Thomas P. Adler, "Robert Anderson," in *American Playwrights since 1945: A Guide to Scholarship, Criticism, and Performance,* ed. Philip C. Kolin (Westport, Conn.: Greenwood, 1989), 28.

4. Bigsby, *Williams/Miller/Albee,* 27.

5. We are indebted to Thomas P. Adler for calling this description to our attention.

ROBERT ANDERSON
Jackson R. Bryer

Robert Anderson (photo by Colby H. Kullman)

Robert Anderson is the author of thirteen produced plays, including *Come Marching Home* (1945), *The Eden Rose* (1948), *Love Revisited* (1950), *Tea and Sympathy* (1953), *All Summer Long* (1954), *Silent Night, Lonely Night* (1959), *The Days Between* (1965), *You Know I Can't Hear You When the Water's Running* (1967), *I Never Sang for My Father* (1968), *Solitaire/Double Solitaire* (1971), *Free and Clear* (1983), and *The Last Act Is a Solo*. He has also written two novels, *After* (1973) and *Getting Up and Going Home* (1978).

Among his screenplays are adaptations of *Tea and Sympathy* and *I Never Sang for My Father;* for the latter he received a Writers Guild of America award. His other screenwriting credits include *Until They Sail* (1957), *The Nun's Story* (1959), and *The Sand Pebbles* (1966). His screenplays for *I Never Sang for My Father* and *A Nun's Story* were nominated for Academy Awards. Between 1946 and 1952 he adapted many novels and plays for radio and television, among them *David Copperfield, Oliver Twist, Vanity Fair, The Glass Menagerie, The Petrified Forest, A Farewell to*

Arms, and *Arrowsmith.* More recently he adapted *Double Solitaire* in 1973 and wrote *The Patricia Neal Story* in 1980, both for television.

He was elected to the Theatre Hall of Fame in 1980 and was awarded the William Inge Award for lifetime achievement in the American theatre in 1985. He has served as president of the New Dramatists (1955–56) and of the Dramatists Guild (1971–73), as vice-president of the Authors League of America, and as a member of the Board of Governors of the American Playwrights Theatre (1963–79). He has taught at the Salzburg Seminar in American Studies and at the University of Iowa Writers Workshop. He also coedited a six-volume anthology for high school students, *Elements of Literature* (Holt, Rinehart, and Winston, 1988).

This interview is the result of three conversations with Robert Anderson, held on 29 January, 25 February, and 15 March 1988 in his New York apartment, on his career, his plays, the American theatre in the 1940s and 1950s, and the American theatre today. Allison Sharp helped transcribe and edit the manuscript for publication; her assistance was invaluable.

Bryer: Why don't we get started with some biographical background?
Anderson: I was born in New York City in 1917. When I was a few months old, my family moved to a suburb of New York, New Rochelle. My dad had been an orphan, a dead-end kid, but somehow he had managed to take a course in shorthand and typing at night school. He started out as a stenographer and ended up as an officer in a large copper company. He retired in 1929 and lost much of his money in the crash. I was a boy who seemed to have many talents. I was going to be a singer, an artist, an actor, a poet, anything but a businessman. My father wanted both my brother and me to have professions, because he said that in business one day someone might not like the color of your tie, and you'd be out of a job. But he didn't think of writing as a profession and often tried to warn me of its uncertainties. I went to Phillips Exeter Academy, and there I was soloist with the Glee Club and soloist with the choir and sang in Gilbert and Sullivan shows. I also played tennis and basketball and was a member of the senior council. My second year at Harvard a friend asked me if I'd like to go across the river and audition for a musical being done at a girls' school. Music and girls! I went and fell in love with the woman who was directing the play. She was ten years older than me. I met my wife and my life just like that. I sang the leads in her shows and acted in plays she produced. One Sunday afternoon during a holiday, my parents had some professional musicians in to hear me sing, to settle this matter of becoming a singer.

They listened and said, "It's a very nice voice, but not worth giving your life to."

Bryer: Had you written any plays at this point?

Anderson: Just one, at Exeter, a short play. And I received the unheard of mark of A. At that time I considered myself primarily a singer and a poet. I'd written lots of poetry as a kid and had submitted it to places like *St. Nicholas* and *Boy's Life* and *American Boy.* Never got anything published.

Bryer: So you fell in love with Phyllis—

Anderson: And my whole life changed. We more or less lived together on the weekends, and I started getting A's (I graduated magna cum laude), and I did some writing for the Christmas shows that were put on in each house at Harvard. Mine was Dunster House. I wrote the book, the lyrics, and the music and directed and acted in the shows. For a while I was dubbed "the Noel Coward of Harvard." Phyllis persuaded me that I was a better writer than an actor. So I wasn't a singer; I wasn't an actor. I concentrated on writing plays. Harvard had bid good-bye to George Pierce Baker and his famous 47 Workshop, which had been the starting point for many talented playwrights—O'Neill, Philip Barry, S. N. Behrman. He left to start the Yale Drama School. There was not much drama or theatre left at Harvard. But I turned it into a drama school. In the summers I went to summer theatres as an apprentice, built scenery, shifted sets, and played small parts. I stayed on at Harvard to get my master's and completed my course for a Ph.D. I remember my Ph.D. orals. They did it century by century, and I'd say, "I really don't know much about the novel of the eighteenth century, but could we discuss the drama?" They'd smile and say, "All right, Bob, go right ahead." I took the orals the night before I went into the navy. They passed me, I think, on the assumption that I would not be coming back from the war.

In the war I was first on a battleship and then on a cruiser in the Pacific, seeing action at Iwo Jima and Okinawa. Between engagements, while everyone else went ashore and got loaded, I sat in my cabin and wrote plays. I was much more worried about what was going to happen to me after the war than about what might happen to me in the war. I didn't really want to go on with teaching. I had worked on my advanced degrees mostly because I was married (in 1940, after my master's) and could make money assisting in English at Harvard and teaching in girls' schools in Boston. While overseas I wrote a play that won the Army-Navy Prize for the best play written by a serviceman overseas. Hallie Flanagan Davis, who had been head of the Federal Theatre Project and who was on the committee that had judged the contest, wrote to me that if I could write two other plays before I came home, she could get me a fellowship.

Bryer: You had submitted this play while you were aboard the ship?

Anderson: Right. It was called *Come Marching Home.* It was done first by E. C. Mabie at the University of Iowa. I wrote the two other plays, one called *The Tailored Heart.* I've forgotten the name of the other. So when I came back late in 1945, I had a two-thousand-dollar fellowship to write plays. By this time Phyllis had moved to New York and was with the Theatre Guild in the radio department. A few years later she became head of their play department. She was much revered and loved. Eight plays were dedicated to her, including *Come Back, Little Sheba,* which she produced for the Guild in New York. Then Mary Hunter asked me to teach at the American Theatre Wing—to set up the courses in playwriting. I said, "Mary, I've never taught a playwriting course in my life." She said, "You've taught and you've written plays. Put them together." I think by this time the Blackfriars Guild, which was one of the very first Off-Broadway theatres, had done a production of *Come Marching Home.*

Bryer: That was your first New York production of any kind?

Anderson: Yes. So I started teaching, and it was an exciting experience. If you want to learn something, teach it. I really, in a sense, taught myself. I had taken a course with John Gassner at the New School because the Rockefeller Fellowship required that I check in with a teacher. He was really my mentor in many ways. His course was not on play structure, but he talked brilliantly on drama and theatre. He was also a representative for Columbia Pictures in New York, and I used to visit his office. He'd lie on his couch and tell me, "You know, Bob, the trouble with your plays is that you're not angry enough about anything." My plays were considered slight in those days, skillful with good dialogue.

Bryer: Were you conscious, when you first started to write, of modeling your plays after any particular playwright?

Anderson: A wide variety. I wrote my undergraduate honors thesis on Maxwell Anderson (fourteen years later I became his partner in the Playwrights' Company). I admired Philip Barry, Robert Sherwood, S. N. Behrman, the Shaw of *Candida* (naturally!). I didn't care for O'Neill. I felt his dialogue was crude and his reach exceeded his grasp by too much. It wasn't until *Long Day's Journey* that I appreciated him.

Bryer: Did you read much Shaw and Ibsen?

Anderson: Shaw's *Candida,* as I said. After all, I was in love with a woman ten years my senior. I think the Ibsen came later, any real study of him, though I think I was familiar with *A Doll's House* and did see Nazimova play *Hedda Gabler.* I believe I reviewed it for the *Harvard Advocate,* where I was the drama critic for a time. As a graduate student, I assisted the few professors teaching drama, and I got to give lectures on O'Casey and Synge. So I was up on a fair amount of drama. One of the things that surprises me about young playwrights I talk to now, they don't seem to be doing any reading of the plays of the past. In those days I would read any play I could get my hands on. I was stagestruck.

Bryer: When you look back at your earliest plays now, do they seem very derivative from the plays you were reading? Or do you feel that you had achieved some sort of voice?

Anderson: No, I had no voice at the time we are speaking of. I had a skill or a touch with dialogue. I was fascinated with Noel Coward's dialogue, and Clifford Odets's. I will never forget the weekend I settled in on the side porch of my parents' home and read the Modern Library volume *The Six Plays of Clifford Odets.* The impact of that machine-gun dialogue! The vitality of the whole thing. I took to dialogue immediately. I really didn't know what a play was. In our courses at Harvard we had not studied about what made a play a play. We studied the social background of the play, its sources, the philosophy behind it, etc. I didn't discover the facts about structure, progression, and development until later when I taught the classes at the Theatre Wing.

Bryer: That was the turning point, then, both your own teaching and talking with Gassner?

Anderson: Yes, and seeing plays and more plays.

Bryer: Are you conscious that, seeing plays after you came back from the war, after having written them and after having taught and having listened to Gassner, your way of looking at plays changed and you saw more than you had seen?

Anderson: Of course. For a while, it made playwriting less fun. In my college days I didn't know that dialogue should move a story forward, develop characters, etc. I would sit down on a Friday night after classes were over and tell Phyllis, "I'm going to write a play." And I would have a play, a seventy-page play, by Monday morning. That was exciting. Thank God, I didn't know any better. If I'd known, I probably wouldn't have had all the fun of writing. Might have been turned off. I came back from the war in late 1945 and was immediately immersed in the world of drama and theatre. I was going to John Gassner's classes, I was a member of the Theatre Incorporated Young Playwrights Group, where we met and talked to each other and read our plays aloud, and I was teaching at the American Theatre Wing. In 1949 I was a member of the first group of the New Dramatists, where we met once a week and heard distinguished people in the theatre talk to us. We couldn't imagine that Robert Sherwood was having trouble with his second act, but he was, and he told us about it. Very comforting. Others were Howard Lindsay, Sidney Kingsley, Elia Kazan, Maxwell Anderson, S. N. Behrman (we also saw many plays for free).

Shortly after that I managed to get assignments writing for radio, for the Theatre Guild on the Air, where I adapted classics into one-hour scripts—*Glass Menagerie, David Copperfield, The Scarlet Pimpernel,* and many more. This really helped me to become a pro. We'd come into rehearsal on Tuesday, and Helen Hayes or Rex Harrison or Richard Burton would be looking at your script, trying out the words for sound. By Thursday you had to have a rewrite, and then by Sunday another rewrite. If at the last rehearsal you found you were somehow ten minutes over the hour, you had one hour to cut the ten minutes out of the play so that none of the actors would notice! As I said, at the same time I was teaching four nights a week. Young people now say to me, "I don't have time to write." I tell them, "I wrote plays in the morning, radio and, later, television in the afternoon, and taught at night. You'll find the time if you really want to."

I had a play of mine called *The Eden Rose* optioned several times. Gertrude Lawrence was once set to do it with Sir Cedric Hardwicke directing. It didn't happen. It ended up being done at a community theatre in Ridgefield, Connecticut. In 1951 the Westport Country Playhouse (controlled by the Theatre Guild) produced *Love Revisited.* Then Alan Schneider, who was directing plays at Arena Stage in Washington, discovered a play of mine gathering dust on my agent's shelf. It was *All Summer Long,* adapted from a novel, *A Wreath and A Curse* by Donald Wetzel. He gave it several readings, and I worked on it, and then he directed it at Arena Stage in 1952. It was a great success. Brooks Atkinson of the *Times* came down and reviewed it favorably, and producers started to take options on it. Like all my plays, it had been going the rounds for a long time. It seems that nobody has ever been eager to do my plays, the hits or the flops. And nobody is eager now. But I am used to it.

While waiting for some action on *All Summer Long,* I had written *Tea and Sympathy.* Several versions. There had been one as far back as 1948 or 1949, as I remember. Sadly my beloved agent of thirty-five years, Audrey Wood, did not like *Tea and Sympathy* and didn't think it should be submitted, but Phyllis, who was now at the Theatre Guild, said, "It's your best play. It's got to go around." Well, Audrey was almost right. It was turned down by everybody, and Audrey told me to get on with my next play, when Roger Stevens and the Playwrights' Company took it on, and Elia Kazan signed to direct it.

Bryer: Are the kinds of opportunities that you had in the 1940s and 1950s available to playwrights today?

Anderson: Not the same but different. In those days there was practically no Off-Broadway theatre. It was Broadway or bust. College and community theatres by and large were not interested in doing new work, new plays. Some summer theatres tried out new plays. *Life with Father* is one of the plays I remember was done first in Maine. But there were opportunities not available today. As I say, I cut my teeth on the Theatre Guild on the Air. Arthur Miller and Paddy Chayefsky wrote for the same program. Later there were television shows that used young playwrights (and young directors, who have subsequently become famous movie directors—Arthur Penn, John Frankenheimer). Paddy Chayefsky, Tad Mosel, Bill Gibson come to mind as the playwrights writing for television. Nowadays it is much more difficult for the new writer to get a television assignment, and the time involved in writing one is greater. I used to do eight or more hour radio or television shows in a year—and still have time to write plays. And there was the hands-on experience, at least in radio, of being very much in on the productions, hearing the lines, rewriting, revising. Also it was mostly done in New York. The playwrights were by and large in New York, and that is where the radio and television production was for the most part. You could walk out your door and turn right and be a playwright, and turn left and be a radio or television writer. It was an exciting time. But today is an exciting time too, with plays being done everywhere imaginable across the country. I think it was never so easy to get a play on somewhere, and never more difficult to get a play on somewhere so that a playwright can make enough money from it to go on with writing the next play.

Bryer: Let's talk a little about *Tea and Sympathy.* I remember seeing it in 1953 and thinking then that the whole idea of it was very avant-garde. Do you think, looking back on it now, that the reason it was successful and was a breakthrough play for you was just the luck of the draw, or do you think that it was probably the best thing you'd done to that point?

Anderson: There's no question it was the best thing I'd done. I'd matured in the skill of playwriting, and also I'd found the "passionate interest" in a subject—what Gassner had been looking for. There is so much in that play. What prompted me? For one thing I was fed up with my father's image of a man as "a top guy and a hard hitter." I wanted to say what Laura says in the last act, "Manliness is also gentleness and tenderness and consideration." The basic love story was very close to me. Phyllis was ten years older than me. I had a nostalgia for the boys' school background. Later I wrote another play with that background, *Silent Night, Lonely Night*. Also it was the McCarthy period, with the whole business of calling people names, and what could they do about it? I had a "feeling" for that period in my life. You could say that I was a reasonably "big" man at prep school. A member of the senior council, a letterman, president of the musical clubs, dormitory proctor, fraternity man, etc. And yet I was lonely and miserable and felt very much an off-horse. Phyllis used to say about that period, "Ah youth, that happy time when I was so sad." It's not a play about homosexuality. It's about manliness. It's also about responsibility. We have to give people more than tea and sympathy. It's about "judgment by prejudice." It's about the off-horse, the man who hears "a different drummer." It was an attack on the macho image, the Hemingway man. My brother, who later became dean of a great medical school, was an amateur prizefighter in those days. I was a tennis player (before the days of Connors and Borg and McEnroe). My father never came to see me play tennis. I guess the play was partly written in self-defense. At the opening night party Deborah Kerr came to me and said, "I'm having a terribly hard time keeping a straight face with your father. He's using all the lines from the play." Some of them *were* his lines. The beautiful irony in the play is that the boy would never have been in bed with the woman if he hadn't been accused of being a homosexual. They were forced into each others' arms by what the boys did to him and what her husband did to her.

Bryer: That's what makes a fairly implausible situation seem very plausible. It's a very well-made play because they're on a collision course. If you watch the way she interacts with Bill and he interacts with his peers, the inevitability of the ending is carefully plotted.

Anderson: Brendan Gill, former critic on the *New Yorker*, has a very telling comment: "Drama implies some measure of predictable progress towards a goal." I don't think audiences thought at the outset that the play was going to end where it did. But as it moved along, I think there must have been some hope that things would be righted, without knowing exactly how. And as I said, there seems to be a rightness that the abuse and pain both have gone through brings them to that lovely moment at the end.

Bryer: One of the things I like about the ending of *Tea and Sympathy,* which I think is true of the ending of a lot of good plays, is that when it ends, it's a great shock initially, but then when you think about it, you realize it's the only way it could have ended.

Anderson: I'd like to tell you a story about the famous last line. Phyllis was the first person to read the play. She liked it a lot and said, "Do they go on and have a love affair?" I was surprised that she would get that idea, and said, "No, that's the only time." She said, "Your audience is not going to know that." So I had a problem. I didn't want to go into explanations, so I had to come up with a line that would somehow convey what I meant. And that's how "Years from now, when you talk about this, and you will, be kind" was written.

Bryer: What came after *Tea and Sympathy?*

Anderson: During this whole period Phyllis was dying of cancer. It was a terrible time. She was operated on in 1951. I was told there was no hope. She was in and out of hospitals, had good periods when she could go back to work (now as an agent for MCA) and then bad periods. She died in 1956. *Tea and Sympathy* was in 1953.

Bryer: So right at the point of your great success all of this was going on in your life at the same time.

Anderson: I'm afraid it immobilized me as far as new work was concerned. On the production of *Tea and Sympathy* I was made a member of the Playwrights' Company, which at that time included Maxwell Anderson, Robert E. Sherwood, Elmer Rice, Roger Stevens, and John Wharton. The company produced *All Summer Long* on Broadway in 1954. Brooks Atkinson in the *Times* called it "a work of art," and it was generally well received, but it didn't run.

Then came the movie of *Tea and Sympathy.* Everybody in Hollywood, from Sam Goldwyn up and down, wanted to make the movie, but the Production Code watchdogs said "No!" Somewhere along the line, Kay Brown, who was an agent at MCA, came up with the idea of a prologue and an epilogue to allow for some comment on the larger aspects of the story, and MGM bought it. They said, of course, that I was not a screenwriter, so I couldn't write the screenplay. But they had some censorship problems that they invited me out to solve. When I was through, they asked me to write the screenplay. I faced the same thing before. I was not a radio writer, I was not a television writer.

Bryer: How do you feel about the movie of *Tea and Sympathy?*

Anderson: At the time, in 1955, it was a breakthrough, believe it or not. We battled the censors all the way. I would like to see it remade today without all the "adjustments" we had to make. But I can only judge its effectiveness by this story. In 1973 I represented American screenwriters at the Moscow Film Festival. The Norwegian delegation somehow "took me over." One day on a bus trip to a collective farm, I heard one of my Norwegian friends sitting behind me say *Tea and Sympathy.*" I looked around, and obviously someone from another delegation had asked who I was. For the next ten minutes people shuffled up the aisle and in one language or another looked at me and asked, "*Tea and Sympathy?*" And I nodded yes, and they smiled and shook my hand and went back to their seats.

Another story: we were about to open at Radio City Music Hall when the Legion of Decency, a Catholic panel which used to rate movies, said, "We are going to give you a 'condemned' rating." MGM sent me to the church offices behind St. Patrick's Cathedral to meet with the panel—churchmen, laymen. They said, "You've got to work in the word 'sin' somewhere." I said, "That would be a total negation of what my play is all about." They grilled me for a long time. Finally I said, "Which would you rather have, the woman commit adultery or the boy commit suicide?" They said he wouldn't commit suicide. I said, "That's for me to say, not for you to say." And we opened the next week at the Music Hall. I'm pleased with the movie, considering. I'm especially pleased to have Deborah Kerr's and John Kerr's performances recorded.

Bryer: I've always thought that, among playwrights who have had their plays made into movies, you've had two of the better experiences. *I Never Sang for My Father* and *Tea and Sympathy* are both pretty good movies and pretty faithful to the plays. After *Tea and Sympathy* and after Phyllis died, did you find it hard to get back to work?

Anderson: I think you can imagine. It had been a five-year illness. I was exhausted and more or less in despair. At this point Ingrid Bergman was about to open in *Tea and Sympathy* in Paris. It was Christmastime. Ingrid, whom I had met only once, got on the telephone and said, "I think you belong here. It would be best for you. Come for the opening." My family and friends pushed me into going, and I went. I stayed in the hotel, across the hall from Ingrid, for five months. One of the critics wrote, "Ingrid Bergman saves a play." When I left, I gave Ingrid a silver dish with the inscription, "Ingrid Bergman saves a play and a playwright."

While I was in Paris, my agent sent me the book of *The Nun's Story.* I read it and liked it very much. I was in no shape to write anything of my own, and Fred Zinnemann was going to direct and Audrey Hepburn was to play the nun. That was a pretty inviting setup. So the rest of 1957 was *The Nun's Story.* Fred Zinnemann and I did research through Belgium and France, and then into the Congo. When they started shooting in Rome early in 1958, Audrey had some questions about a page in the script, and they flew me over to confer. After that I proceeded to London to spend the winter in a flat in Berkeley Square, where I wrote *Silent Night, Lonely Night.* I had been blocked in my own writing since Phyllis's death. One day I had asked John Steinbeck's help. He said that when he was blocked, he wrote poetry as the quickest way to find out what he really cared about (art gives form to feeling). In London I started writing poetry (I had been the Harvard class poet), and of course it was about Phyllis and me. Essentially what I was trying to say in *Silent Night, Lonely Night* was something about marriage, which has been a constant theme of mine. Sick or well, she was the condition of my life. I did not use cancer. I used mental illness. The woman with whom the husband has had a one-night affair hears him talking on the phone to his wife in the asylum, when the wife is having a brief period of lucidity, and the woman walks out realizing that no matter what, his wife is the condition of his life. It tries to say something about love and marriage transcending the usual trappings of romance.

Bryer: Silent Night, Lonely Night, then, is very much a reaffirmation of your marriage to Phyllis, isn't it?

Anderson: Yes. One critic called it an elegy in a country inn. Looking back with joy and guilt. Everything talked about in the play is what happened to Phyllis and me at college and in Boston in the 1930s. I told the Playwrights' Company I wanted Fonda. But I had no director, and you don't send a play to a star without a director. Kazan had liked the play but said he didn't want to move two stars around the stage all night. He wanted something more theatrical. I'd had a failing out with Alan Schneider after *All Summer Long.* Finally I sent it to Josh Logan. He called me and said, "I love the play except for the last minute when the man goes back to his sick wife. But I know that's the point of your play." We both laughed, and he said, "Who do you want to play it?" I said, "Fonda, but I can't send it to him without a director." Josh said, "For the sake of that you can say I'm directing it."

We sent it to Fonda. I went to California to write a movie, and one day at my little rented house up in the hills there was Hank Fonda at the door. He said, "Jesus Christ, you've written the play I was meant to do. This is the play of my life. How did you know all this?" We sat down and talked, and I told him Logan had backed out. "We don't need a director. You direct it." I said I thought that would be bad business. He said, "I have never played a play on the road. I will play this play on the road. I have never played a play in London. I will play this play wherever you want me to play it. I want you to understand this is the play I was born to do." Barbara Bel Geddes joined us, and together we selected a director, Peter Glenville. A few weeks before rehearsals, Warner Brothers offered us half a million dollars for a preproduction deal. No mention was made of including Hank in the deal. I told Hank of the offer, and he said again how it was *his* play, didn't I understand? I told him to see if he could line up a deal that included him. He couldn't. I told the Playwrights' Company that I could not go into production alienating my star, particularly one who felt as strongly as he did about the play. We turned down the deal. Two days into rehearsal Hank fell out of love with the play. Hank and Barbara received great reviews, were called "the new Lunt and Fontanne." The play drew poor notices. But that's a long story. It was finally done as a television movie starring Shirley Jones and Lloyd Bridges. It's shown all over in the Christmas season (as you know, it takes place on Christmas Eve).

Teresa Wright and I were married in 1959 a few days after *Silent Night* opened, and I went through a happy time with Teresa but a difficult time writing. Blocked again, I wrote a movie called *The Sand Pebbles,* an adaptation of a novel by Richard McKenna. It was directed by Robert Wise, and Steve McQueen received an Academy Award nomination for his performance. The next play was *The Days Between,* which had the usual difficulties finding a cast and a director. I finally gave up and let it be done by the American Playwrights Theatre, an organization started by Bob Lee and Jerry Lawrence with the idea of getting new plays by "established" playwrights into the college and community theatres *before* and not after Broadway. It opened in Paul Baker's theatre in Dallas and played in fifty theatres around the country in the following year. It's a flawed play with some good scenes and one good character. It was finally done Off-Broadway in the mid-1970s.

An interesting story about that play. All plays have "interesting" stories attached to them. In the 1970s, before the play was done in New York, Gilbert Cates, who by then had produced my *You Know I Can't Hear You When the Water's Running, I Never Sang for My Father,* and *Solitaire/Double Solitaire,* told me that Liv Ullmann would like to do *The Days Between* as a movie. I met with her. I couldn't understand why she wanted to do it; I considered the play a failure. It's funny—a writer sitting in a star's dressing room and asking her why she wants to do his work. I turned it into a movie, and she loved it. It's a better movie than a play. Her agent wouldn't let her do it. She said *she* decided what work she did. Jack Lemmon was interested in playing the husband. But he wanted to do it as a television play. So we were all set. Liv and Jack Lemmon! And we couldn't get it on television.

Bryer: That's hard to believe with those two stars.

Anderson: What people can't believe is how much time it takes out of a writer's life, not just the writing, but all the planning and meeting, and discussion . . . and then, nothing.

Bryer: How did you come to write *I Never Sang for My Father?*

Anderson: It began as an original movie, which I called *The Tiger,* because I had always thought of my father as something of a tiger. Fred Zinnemann, with whom I had done *The Nun's Story,* read it and felt it was the best thing I had done. He wanted to do it with Spencer Tracy playing the father. Tracy didn't want to do it. I sent the script to Kazan, who was in Europe with a movie. He asked me if I would consider turning it into a play for Lincoln Center, which was just starting. Finally that fell through because he and Bob Whitehead felt they had no one in the repertory company to play the father. So I turned *The Tiger* into a play called *I Never Sang for My Father.* Nobody wanted to do it. A lot of people were excited about it. A lot of people wept over it, but they said, "Nobody wants to see such a shattering play." I said, "I only go to the theatre to be shattered. I want to be shattered by emotion, laughter, excitement." So I wrote *You Know I Can't Hear You When the Water's Running.*

Bryer: So both these plays were written before either of them was produced?

Anderson: Yes. It had been the same with *All Summer Long* and *Tea and Sympathy.* It's the same right now. I have two new plays I can't get produced. Anyway, nobody wanted to do four "dirty" one-act plays. Nobody in his right mind would do four one-act plays on Broadway! Finally Audrey Wood, my agent, said, "Do you mind if we send *Water's Running* to two producers who have never produced a play before?" I said, "What have we got to lose?" So we sent it to Jack Farren and Gilbert Cates. They liked it. I rejoined with Alan Schneider after thirteen years, signed on Martin Balsam and George Grizzard and Eileen Heckart, and we were off. We didn't go on the road but played previews in New York. The first preview, a Tuesday night, we sold ten tickets. That's how many people were interested in what we were doing. By Saturday night, a week before the opening and the critics, we had standing room only, and we had standing room only for two years. Word of mouth had done what no critic could have done.

Bryer: Water's Running seems to me a sort of interlude. Whatever caused you to write those four plays at the time you were writing this very shattering play about your father?

Anderson: The shattering play about my father had been written first. *Water's Running* goes back to my Harvard days, when I wrote those Christmas shows. They were funny sketches. I guess since I couldn't get *Father* on, I decided to have some fun. The idea developed rather interestingly. *The Days Between* was playing in a community theatre in Rochester as part of the American Playwrights program I talked about, and I went up to see it. Friday night went beautifully. I did not see it Saturday night. I spent the night with my brother, who was dean of the University of Rochester Medical School. I called the producer on Sunday before I left and asked how Saturday night had gone. He answered, "Well. . . . " I said, "I know, my plays don't play well on Saturday nights." I took a plane down to Baltimore, where I was to give a lecture at Center Stage, and I thought, "Why the hell don't my plays work on Saturday night?" And I remembered that John Gassner in his introduction to *Silent Night* in his *Best Plays* collection had written, "Robert Anderson is a gentleman in an age of assassins." I began to think, "Maybe you don't want to go out with a gentleman on Saturday night." So I started my lecture at Center Stage by saying that I was going to write some plays for Saturday night. In the first play a man would stand naked in the doorway of his bathroom with his toothbrush in his hand and say to his wife, "You know I can't hear you when the water's running." Everybody laughed. So I went back and settled in to write some plays for fun. They didn't "arrive" all at once. It took quite a while, one by one. But they're not all that "light." When I showed them to Kazan, I said, "A different Robert Anderson." When he read them, he said, "The same Robert Anderson, only this time they came out funny." Walter Kerr in his review wrote, "Laugh only when you want to cry." I originally called them *Four Plays for Saturday Night,* but my producers were scared of that title. People weren't interested in one-act plays in those days, and besides, audiences might think they played only on Saturday night!

Bryer: What do you think are some of the enduring concerns of your plays?

Anderson: I seem to have been concerned with the affectionate relationships between men and women. In marriage and out of marriage. My first wife, Phyllis, once said she thought I should stop writing about marriage. That was after two early plays, *The Eden Rose* and *Love Revisited.* It might also interest you to know that, after she had badgered me for months, while I was writing *Tea and Sympathy,* to tell her something about the subject matter of the play, and I finally told her, "It's about a boys' school," she said, "Not another play about a boys' school!" But *Tea and Sympathy, Silent Night, Water's Running,* and *Double Solitaire* and my novels *After* and *Getting Up and Going Home* are all very much concerned with love and marriage.

Bryer: What about the father/son motif? That's always been strong too, hasn't it, not only in *I Never Sang for My Father* but also in *Tea and Sympathy* and *All Summer Long?*

Anderson: And in *Coming Home in the Dark,* which was produced at Long Wharf in 1983 as *Free and Clear.*

Bryer: You obviously had a very ambivalent relationship with your father, didn't you?

Anderson: Yes. I'm grateful to him. My feelings about him have obviously given me a lot of material. He is also the father in *Double Solitaire.* That's a nice picture of him. He could be a very funny, witty man. He was a great storyteller.

Bryer: Family relationships mean a lot to you too then?

Anderson: Tennessee Williams said he wrote about what bugged him. And I guess family relationships have always made me ask questions. What should they be? What are they? You get this in *Father* when Gene tells his sister that when they get home they'll find their father asleep in the chair, and he'll be the very image of the Father, the old man. And then Gene smiles and says, "But then he wakes up and becomes Tom Garrison, and I'm in trouble." This is the conflict between the image— the symbol—and the real each of us is given to deal with. I think most of my plays are also disturbing. *Tea and Sympathy* certainly was. It shook people up about the image of manliness. After *Double Solitaire,* which examined a midmarriage crisis, couples went out and either didn't speak to each other for weeks or finally spoke to each other, intimately, for the first time in years. The plays raise difficult questions. A middle-aged man saw *Father* on the plane on the way to California for his father's birthday. He was so upset by the film that he couldn't go see his father till a week later.

Bryer: Are you surprised that *I Never Sang for My Father* is having a second life these many years later with the successful tour?

Anderson: I'm grateful. The play got splendid reviews twenty years ago, and Alan Webb who played the father was nominated for a Tony (Martin Balsam from *Water's Running* beat him out). But it ran only about four months. I think the excellent movie that Gil Cates made of it, starring Melvyn Douglas and Gene Hackman, has helped.

Bryer: There is something to be said for its newfound popularity in that

that kind of play about basic human emotions and basic human relationships is a rarity today.

Anderson: When I see plays and musicals now, with the sets changing and moving, I say everything's moving all over the stage all night, but in the end, nothing's *moving.* I long to be shattered.

Bryer: I'd like to talk a little bit about the theatre in the 1950s and 1960s, when you were first getting your plays produced. What was it like? Obviously it was cheaper, that's one thing, but how would you describe the atmosphere in comparison to today?

Anderson: Don't forget that I am now a seventy-year-old man looking back at a time of my more or less youth, at a time when I was struggling (of course I'm still struggling), when the whole theatre experience was new . . . what I had wanted for years. And there it was! There was great activity on Broadway, relatively little Off-Broadway or in the regional theatres. There were playwrights like Robert Sherwood and Max Anderson and Rice and Behrman and Barry and Kingsley, and Kaufman and Hart, and Van Druten, and later Miller and Williams and Inge who had new plays on year after year. There were or seemed to be more producers—the Theatre Guild, the Playwrights' Company, Whitehead, Bloomgarden, Saint-Subber, Cheryl Crawford, Shumlin, Aldrich, John Golden, Barr and Wilder. Three plays might open in one week. Productions were in competition to get the first-string reviewer. There were eight or nine newspapers!

Bryer: You're talking about sheer volume now, obviously quality too, but also a tremendous amount of activity.

Anderson: It was the place to be. It was a time when it wasn't considered quite right to go to Hollywood and write screenplays, though many writers did. To go permanently, as Odets did, was considered a sellout. Now I know only a few playwrights who can make a living solely from the theatre. I once wrote that you can make a killing in the theatre but not a living. I would certainly not still be a playwright today if I hadn't been able also to write for movies and television. All theatre people, in a sense, are subsidizing the so-called living theatre. Actors, directors, designers—most of us couldn't function without working in television or movies. This is not necessarily a bad thing, unless you get hooked. How many plays can a playwright write?

Of course, I am speaking as a playwright who has basically been very happy with the "Broadway" way of doing things. A producer optioned a play; you chose a director; you "conferred" with the director about the script; you cast the play, went into rehearsal, went out of town, and then opened in New York. Now things are quite different. First, plays get readings, readings. Then a regional theatre picks it up for a workshop production. Then if it goes well, the theatre gives it a full production. Then a producer "discovers" it and brings it closer to Broadway, possibly a tour, to Off-Broadway. Then, finally, Mecca! Many playwrights seem to be happy with this, this workshopping. I seem to remember that "in the olden days" most of us wrote our plays at our desks, and the four weeks of rehearsal and the weeks out of town seemed to be enough for us to do what we could to the play. I believe that when a conscientious playwright has given you his play, he has given you probably ninety percent of what he has to give you. Sure, there's work to be done, but if the impact isn't there, don't expect it to arrive via workshop. I was one of the first people to read *Come Back, Little Sheba* when it was sent to the Theatre Guild. And I told Phyllis that there was a lot wrong with it, but it was a powerhouse. Bill Inge never fixed what was wrong, but it was still, in production, a powerhouse. I think today perhaps the theatre has caught that television and movie disease of "developing" a "property," with many hands and minds getting involved. When I think of Sherwood, and Rice and Behrman and O'Neill . . . how would this have gone down with them?

Bryer: The money factor is, of course, much more of a consideration today, isn't it?

Anderson: That's what I hear. But believe it or not Roger Stevens found it difficult to raise the $40,000 needed for *Tea and Sympathy* in 1953. Dinners cost more now, apartments, postage stamps, but people keep buying them. Many people pay as much for a dinner on the way to the theatre as they do for the tickets and then complain about the cost of the tickets. Ask them what they ate for dinner last night, or if they happened to see a great play after dinner? For whatever reason the action has moved to the regional theatres and Off-Broadway. There is an enormous amount of creative activity, and I am pleased to say that I have enjoyed working in those theatres, these small theatres. But sometimes I get the impression that the plays also tend to be small, somehow tentative, not really defined, only approximately "there." There is some lovely work being done in these theatres, but it does seem to be different, which is fine. But sometimes I think the supposed lack of pressure, the intimacy and almost informality of the theatres, can lead to some rather loose work. I came away from one of these theatres this winter, and Teresa Wright, who was with me, said, "Next time they kid you about the well-made play, ask them about the unmade play."

Bryer: A lot of new plays are not about anything, or they're about what they're about. They're not about anything more.

Anderson: I read a lot of plays by young playwrights, and they often seem to be a series of vaudeville sketches adding up to not much of anything.

Bryer: They're television plays, too; they're sitcoms. An aspiring playwright today has one eye on *Cheers* and the other eye on the stage. In a way you can't blame them, because the way they're going to be successful is not because my theatre or your theatre does their plays. It's because someone will see something they've done and call and say, "Do you want to write an episode of *Cheers* or *St. Elsewhere?*"

Anderson: I think that's fine as long as they don't do too many episodes, and as long as when they write plays, they write plays and not pseudo-TV scripts. Many years ago when I was a happily striving but also a somewhat disgruntled young playwright, I put a sign over my desk to shut me up: "Nobody asked you to be a playwright." And that is sadly true. For most of my writing life people have been on the phone asking me to write movies or television shows, but nobody has ever called up and said, "Are you writing a play that I could perhaps read when it's finished?" As I said, nobody has ever wanted to produce a play of mine right off. My agent has always had to spend months and years submitting the play—yes, *Tea and Sympathy, You Know I Can't Hear You When the Water's Running, I Never Sang for My Father.* So why are we all still writing for the theatre? It's because for me, at least, it's the most rewarding dramatic medium. You have control in the sense of authority and control in the sense of being able to lay your hands on the work at any time during the rehearsal and production period and fix it, shape it, make it better. That's not true in television or movies. Another sign over my desk is a quote from Edmund Burke. I recommend it for all playwrights: "Never despair, but if you do, work on in despair."

JEROME LAWRENCE AND ROBERT E. LEE

Nena Couch

Jerome Lawrence and Robert E. Lee
(photo © Stathis Orphanos)

As one of the great partnerships in theatre, Jerome Lawrence and Robert E. Lee have written some of the longest running and most widely produced plays of this century, many of which have been called contemporary theatre classics. But their proudest accolade is when they are described as "the thinking-person's playwrights." Ironically, since they most often work as a team, Lawrence and Lee have been dedicated, enthusiastic proponents of the individual. This commitment to the "dignity of the individual human mind" [Jerome Lawrence, "The Renaissance Man," lecture delivered at The Ohio State University, Columbus, 5 May 1969, 2], apparent in their first Broadway success, *Look, Ma, I'm Dancin'!* in 1948, has continued to their newest play, *Whisper in the Mind,* which had its professional premiere in May 1994 at the Missouri Repertory Theatre. Be that individual a delightful and free-thinking Mame (*Auntie Mame* and *Mame*) who urges us to discover new things about ourselves and the world, a Drummond (*Inherit the Wind*) whose balancing of the Bible and a copy of Darwin shows us that the open and inquiring mind is our champion against censorship, a Countess Aurelia (*Dear World*) who proves to us that "one person can change the world," a Supreme Court Justice Dan Snow (*First Monday in October*) who fights for the light for everyone, or a Thoreau (*The Night Thoreau Spent in Jail*) who is not afraid to march to a different drummer, Lawrence and Lee have populated stages all over the world with sometimes serious, sometimes witty, but always passionately committed individuals. The playwrights are, as they say of Mame, enemies of "anything which places corsets on our minds or our soaring spirits" [draft of an article for *Queen's Magazine, London*, 3]. As Henry David Thoreau says for them, "Nobody leaves us with a smooth surface. We rough up the consciousness, scrape the moss off young minds."

Both Jerome Lawrence and Robert E. Lee were born and raised in Ohio, Lawrence in Cleveland and Lee in Elyria. Even though Lawrence went to school at The Ohio State University and Lee was just a few miles away at Ohio Wesleyan, the two did not meet until after leaving Ohio. While each has been a prolific writer in his own right, the product of their legendary partnership is astonishing. They have written plays, book and lyrics for musical theatre, screenplays, radio and television scripts, biographies and textbooks, and numerous stories and articles for a variety of publications. They have often directed their own scripts and were among the founding fathers of Armed Forces Radio Service, the Margo Jones Award, and American Playwrights Theatre. Lawrence is a council member of the Dramatists Guild and the Authors League of America, Lee is a member of the Writers Executive Committee of the Academy of Motion Picture Arts & Sciences, and both have received the Writers Guild of America Valentine Davies Award "for contributions which have brought honor and dignity to writers everywhere." In recognition of their inestimable contribution to the American theatre, Lawrence and Lee have received numerous other awards, most recently their induction into the Theater Hall of Fame and membership in the College of Fellows of the American Theatre, both in 1990. They hold multiple honorary degrees. Both men have a deep commitment to teaching and have lectured and taught extensively both in the United States and abroad.

Lawrence and Lee discussed their work in the context of the theme of an exhibition, " 'Roughing Up the Consciousness': the Plays of Jerome Lawrence and Robert E. Lee," mounted by the interviewer at The Ohio State University. The Lawrence and Lee plays quoted are available in published editions. Other materials quoted are held in the Jerome Lawrence and Robert E. Lee Collection, Library of the Jerome Lawrence and Robert E. Lee Theatre Research Institute, The Ohio State University.

Couch: I see "roughing up the consciousness" in all your plays in one way or another. What interests me particularly is what in your early lives shaped you individually and then what brought you together.

Lee: Well, originally I didn't intend to make writing my career. I was determined to be an astronomer, so I went to Ohio Wesleyan, which operated the giant telescope at Perkins Observatory in concert with OSU. Then I got interested in communications. And I began to get the feeling that somehow communicating with the stars and planets was pretty much a one-way street. So I plunged into broadcasting, which led to my meeting Jerry in New York and getting to work with him. Ironically, we had never met in Ohio, though we were both Buckeyes, born and schooled thirty miles apart.

Lawrence: I always wanted to be a writer. My father was a printer, my mother was an unpublished poet. The only deviation I had from play-writing was as a small-town newspaperman, which supplied me with masses of material for the writing years that followed.

Lee: All of our early radio writing, individually, then happily as a team, taught us to write for the ear.

Lawrence: The exhibition you mounted, Nena, was appropriately titled "Roughing Up the Consciousness" because that's what both of us have tried to do as writers from the very start.

Lee: I subscribe to that because I know as a borning scientist that nothing really adheres to a smooth surface. If you're aiming an idea at another mind, you hope it's not so slick that it won't stick. You've got to ruffle up the smoothness of that recipient consciousness, otherwise your ideas will just slide off, slip away.

Lawrence: By "roughing up" we don't mean "beating up"—we're violently opposed to violence—but "shaking up" our audiences and, even more importantly, ourselves. We've also called that "sandpapering the soul," a kind of abrasivenes that digs beneath the false surface, the gilt (or guilt) surface, and probes down there where the truth might be found.

Couch: What comes to mind immediately is the Golden Dancer speech from *Inherit the Wind.*

Lee: There's a lot of pent-up acid in that speech—to eat away the crust of complacency. Of placidity, of stasis.

Lawrence: The stand-still mind, the petrified thinking that always stays pat, never moving—even sideways.

Lee: Or shuffles in lockstep with everybody else, as in *Thoreau's* blast at people who "go along, go along!"

Lawrence: "Get along" by going along.

Lee: I think there is too much lubrication in life. I'd much rather see sparks than grease.

Lawrence: That's why we called one of our plays *Sparks Fly Upward.*

Couch: Could we go to the radio plays and talk about that experience? Bob used the words "writing for the ear." I consider your radio plays a fascinating part of your work.

Lee: Effective radio drama—and we directed most of our broadcasts— was a tapestry of words, music, sound.

Lawrence: It was theatre of the imagination.

Lee: Perhaps radio drama was much closer to theatre than motion pictures or television turned out to be. The visual media depend on the impact of spectacle. But both radio and theatre depend on *words* to fire the imagination.

Lawrence: Words and ideas made vivid.

Lee: If the quintessence of theatre is Shakespeare, he proved that the ultimate theatrical experience is primarily verbal.

Lawrence: His words create spectacle in the imagination of his audiences and readers. There are no roller skates, no cats in Shakespeare.

Lee: And very few car chases.

Couch: Bob, you once said that all audiences needed was a radio and imagination [Lee, "Lingering Thoughts about *The Railroad Hour*" (Encino, Calif., Sept. 1986, 7)]. But for the writers of a long-running show such as Lawrence and Lee's *The Railroad Hour,* it must have required a *huge amount* of imagination and ingenuity. What were some of the challenges?

Lee: To forget and never use the word "adaptation" when trying to bring to life the great musical theatre of the century. We preferred "re-creation," as if the original creators were writing and composing these works for the very first time.

Lawrence: "Adaptation" sounds like rendering lard, squeezing something down to the "handy economy size," in the manner of a *Reader's Digest* encapsulation. "Musicalization" is a more apt word in some instances, and with our *Favorite Story* and *Hallmark Playhouse* series, we always used the word "dramatization."

Lee: On *The Railroad Hour* we began to run out of great musicals, so we decided to originate new musical theatre for the air and did some sixty broadcasts in which we musicalized, with original books and lyrics, famous stories, historical subjects, legendary tales, and quite a few yarns of our own.

Lawrence: We called them "musi-plays" and several of them were later published as stage works and have been widely performed in schools and colleges.

Lee: The best example of this wedding of words and music was our blending De Maupassant's *The Necklace* with the theme melodies of César Franck's D Minor Symphony, making it a kind of mini-opera.

Lawrence: Or taking Bret Harte's *The Luck of Roaring Camp* and using the most appropriate major themes from Dvořák's *New World* Symphony, set to original lyrics.

Lee: What an education the six-year-long experience on *The Railroad Hour* was for us, particularly getting to know and even work with Sigmund Romberg, Rudolf Friml, Oscar Hammerstein, Otto Harbach, Ira Gershwin, many others.

Couch: Young Love was another of your radio shows, wasn't it?

Lawrence: I guess the point of interest here is that *Young Love* was, in effect, a "comedy à clef." Though we called the setting of this radio comedy "Midwestern University," it was based liberally on the Ohio State campus, with a little Ohio Wesleyan thrown in. And it starred Bob's wife, Janet Waldo, previously Corliss Archer and en route to being the voice of Judy Jetson.

Lee: The program was so Ohio based that we used one actual historical incident, when a cow named Maudine Ormsby was elected Homecoming Queen. We even used her genuine name.

Lawrence: Milking history for all it was worth.

Couch: Could you say a bit about your play *Jabberwock,* because that's one that is near and dear to us in Columbus?

Lawrence: The full title is *Jabberwock: Improbabilities Lived and Imagined by James Thurber in the Fictional City of Columbus, Ohio.* Thurber was, of course, the supreme individualist, the Ohio maverick, the Columbus oddball. The "improbabilities" are what gave his imagination wings. His mother, Mary Agnes (all her real-life friends called her "Mame," which, of course, we couldn't do or audiences would think she'd escaped from a couple of our other plays), was really the perpetual "Kid from Columbus," which is what we'll call the musical when we get around to writing it. Mama Mary Agnes Thurber, alias Mame, was a maverick too, somewhat of a female Walter Mitty.

Lee: I think that probably our Ohio experiences come most into focus in *Jabberwock.* And the play began at Ohio State. We convinced university authorities to name the new theatre facility the "Thurber Theatre." They agreed to do it "if Lawrence and Lee write a play about Thurber to open the theatre." And we're awfully happy we did. It's one of our most joyful adventures of all the thirty-nine plays we've written in the past near half-century.

Couch: Certainly the IDEA (that should be in capital letters!) figures in all your work—Drummond in *Inherit the Wind:* "An idea is a greater monument than a cathedral."

Lawrence: And certainly Auntie Mame, who not only opens windows but also minds!

Couch: And Guzmano, the Schweitzer-like doctor-philosopher of *Sparks Fly Upward,* who worries about the entire Western world "trading in the human mind for a computing machine."

Lee: My wife is sure the computer is Big Brother.

Couch: And there's a wonderful speech that follows: "One! . . . "

Lawrence: " . . . There is no number larger than ONE." And when they ask Senator Orton what he thinks of Guzmano, he says, "It's hard to argue with a good cello." He means that Guzmano makes a symphony of ideas, deep-sounding music out of language and thought.

Lee: I'm glad you brought that up, because in many respects *Sparks Fly Upward,* alias *Diamond Orchid,* is one of our favorite plays, partly I suppose because it's a slightly forgotten child, and we think it had some of our best work in it.

Lawrence: Most, if not all, of our plays share the theme of the dignity of every individual mind and that mind's lifelong battle against limitation and censorship.

Lee: People usually say that *First Monday in October* is about the first woman on the Supreme Court. Of course it is, but mostly it's about the real obscenity—censorship—and it attacks the kind of world controllers who want to diminish our lives, limit our horizons.

Couch: One of my favorite speeches in *First Monday* is Dan Snow's about the light: "NOBODY has the right to turn on the darkness."

Lawrence: That's it. That's the point of it. You mustn't let yourself be pushed into the empty dark. You've got to keep looking for the light. You've got to keep sandpapering things until the light shines through. It's all related. *The Gang's All Here* is the probing of the presidency, not just *a* president, but *the* presidency. And *Only in America* is tearing the scab off the wounds of bigotry and racism then applying the healing ointment of humor and understanding.

Lee: And *Whisper in the Mind* thinks aloud about the tremendously important point that even a good idea, if it is misconceived, can backfire, can be harmful. If you try to get things too well ordered, your ego shouting that you've got everything figured out, all truths saddled and ready to ride the universal derby, you're in real trouble.

Lawrence: Getting a play on paper is a long-distance marathon. It takes stick-to-itiveness to create a play, to refine it and polish it. You must have passion about your idea, in order to make your audiences think and feel and probe. There's no formula. You must travel untrodden paths, but always with open eyes and open mind.

Couch: Every one of your plays is related by this constant quality in terms of the *idea,* the *individual.* Yet each play has its own individuality.

Lee: Nena, I think that's one of the reasons we were so drawn to Norman Cousins, with whom we wrote *Whisper in the Mind,* and why we were so shaken by losing Norman. He had a quality of mind that I hope we have also: an enjoyment of life, an appreciation of the differences between people and the constructive interplay of those differences, the idea that living is a game, a contest that you sometimes win and sometimes lose. Out of that wonderful turmoil you find the real fun and laughter of living.

Couch: I think that you do have that "quality of mind." It speaks in your plays to audiences all over the world. Could you comment on some of your most memorable foreign productions?

Lawrence: Having Lillebil Ibsen, Henrik Ibsen's granddaughter, play Auntie Mame in Oslo and Bergen.

Lee: Having *The Night Thoreau Spent in Jail,* about the birth of civil disobedience, translated into Russian and performed at the Theatre of Young Spectators in Leningrad, long before glasnost.

Lawrence: And most recently, having our *Thoreau* translated into Cantonese and performed at the Hong Kong Repertory Theatre in honor of the students who died at Tiananmen Square in Beijing.

Lee: And the 1989–91, eighteen-month run of *Inherit the Wind* in Israel—

Lawrence: In Hebrew, with an Arab playing the lead. Twenty years earlier, Habimah also produced it in Hebrew. And simultaneously it was published in Arabic in Egypt. I stood on the stage of the Pocket Theatre in Cairo and said, "Here's a speech I've always wanted to read aloud from a platform in Egypt: 'An idea is a greater monument than a cathedral. And the advance of man's knowledge is more of a miracle than any sticks turned to snakes or the parting of waters!' "

Couch: There are plays of yours that many people may not even know exist, such as *The Incomparable Max* and *Crocodile Smile.*

Lawrence: And they, too, are about anomalies, eccentrics, the distinctive individualists of our world.

Lee: The odd fish.

Lawrence: But that odd fish often turns out to be a whale of a genius.

Couch: Those two plays are interesting because they're so related to the life of the theatre, theatre within theatre.

Lawrence: Our very first Broadway adventure was a backstage glimpse of the ballet, *Look, Ma, I'm Dancin'!,* with Nancy Walker as a bumbling ballerina and choreography by the incomparable Jerome Robbins. But its underlying thesis is that you'll lead a terrible life if your sole goal is to embrace what F. Scott Fitzgerald called "the bitch-goddess success," especially if you hurt people in your hacking drive into her arms. It turned into a very pleasant musical.

Lee: Please understand, Nena, we have no prejudice against success. But if success is your only motivation, you're a failure. You need more meaningful goals.

Lawrence: To live the John Donne ethic: "I am involved in mankind." Totally. And being perceptive enough to be "part of the whole," understanding it, appreciating it, transmitting that idea in your work.

Lee: What separates the quick and the dead is the ability to perceive and to process perception. When somebody can no longer react to what he perceives, he's brain-dead. But when the consciousness, the perceptive apparatus is electrified and alerted—"roughed up" if you will—then the total human being becomes totally alive.

Couch: Jerry, you once said that no one "has a platform that ultimately reaches more people" [Lawrence, "The Renaissance Man," 2] than the playwright. That's a sobering thought. How do you feel about the responsibility that places on you?

Lawrence: It's more important, we think, to be interesting than to be important.

Lee: If you're too worried about being significant, what you write will be insignificant.

Lawrence: Or being pertinent turns out to be impertinent.

Lee: And being lofty turns out being downright dismal.

Lawrence: Nena, when I was in residence in Columbus a month or so ago, I was invited to conduct seminars at a dozen high school assemblies. Most of the students seemed bright, but generally laid-back. I always read them "Grasses," the meadow scene in our *Thoreau* play: "Watch! Notice! Observe! . . . Did you ever have any *idea* so much was going on in Heywood's Meadow? I'll wager even Heywood doesn't know." And suddenly I felt they started to come awake, they were really watching, not merely keeping their eyes open, really listening. And by the end of each seminar, I sensed most of those students had begun to realize that the full life is living not just once, but a hundred times every minute, by absorbing with your pores and your souls, by daily roughing up your consciousness.

Lee: But writers who have a substantial body of work face a terrible danger—the rear-view-mirror syndrome. We want to look forward, not back. Jerry and I must constantly be interested where the creative road is going, not where it's been, so we can hope to shake up the twenty-first century, too.

Lawrence: That's why we both teach and lecture all over the world. Because we feel the surest way to guarantee just a shred of immortality is to write, to teach, to have children. Now Bob's been luckier than I have, he's done all three. I don't have any physical, rock-them-to-sleep, shake-them-awake children. But then I say, "Hey, wait a minute. All our plays are our children, too." And when our students write healthy, bouncing plays, that's like having grandchildren.

Couch: That's more than a shred of immortality.

ARTHUR MILLER
Jan Balakian

Arthur Miller (photo © Inge Morath,
Magnum Photos, Inc.)

A rthur Miller greeted me at his home in his Levi's, T-shirt, New
Balance sneakers, and baseball cap. Inside were notebooks of
Miller's play in progress, the Greek plays on the shelf (Aeschylus had
been pulled off the shelf), a computer, a typewriter, and a small cot
with a pillow saying "Arthur" on it. On the wall was a road sign pointing the way to Providence and Boston. Willy Loman would have seen
this sign driving to his New England territory. On another desk sat
copies of his new screenplay, *Almost Everybody Wins,* now called *Everybody Wins,* starring Deborah Winger and Nick Nolte.

In some ways Miller has begun a new phase in his career. His most
recent plays, with the exception of his short play *Clara* (1986), have a
different view of life that is not an overtly tragic view. With *The Creation of the World and Other Business* (1981) he wrote a comic version of
the Creation, the Fall, and the first fratricide in order to depict man's
groping for some civilized reason for his murderous feelings.

Not only has the Old Testament profoundly shaped Miller's imagination, but, as the following interview indicates, so have the depression and the culture of the thirties. He has transformed the thirties into a wonderful vaudeville in *The American Clock* (1983). Based on both his recollections of the depression and on Studs Terkel's oral history of the depression, *Hard Times,* Miller has recreated the thirties with epic exuberance; we watch America improvise its way though the calamity of the crash in a play that takes the form of a mural.

Miller moves from America in the 1930s to Prague in the 1970s for his next play, *The Archbishop's Ceiling* (1984), which he discusses in the following interview. Implicitly based on Vaclav Havel's experience in Prague, the play examines the impact of government power on four writers who sit in a former archbishop's palace, which they suspect is bugged. Like *The Crucible,* this play is about paranoia, but, as Miller points out, now he is more concerned with the elusive nature of reality, and his vision has become more apocalyptic. Miller was invited to Prague for productions of *The Archbishop's Ceiling* and *The Crucible* in the spring of 1990, and in 1991 *The Archbishop's Ceiling* had its New York debut at the Lincoln Center Theater.

In 1984 Miller's plays became more explicitly ontological. Both *Elegy for a Lady* and *Some Kind of Love Story,* published by Metheun in 1989, ask how we constitute the real and how we invent the world that we inhabit. As Miller explains, however, he can never separate the metaphysical from the social, and in *Playing for Time* (1985) he returned to his canonical concern with combating evil and celebrating the triumph of the individual spirit. Written for both television and the stage and based on a book by Fania Fenelon, *Playing for Time* grapples with the atrocity of the Holocaust, just as *After the Fall* and *Incident at Vichy* had done in the 1960s. We watch a woman's orchestra endure the Nazis of the Auschwitz/Birkenau concentration camp for whom they must play.

In two short plays included under the title *Danger: Memory* (1987), Miller probes the phenomenon of "dropping out of time" in *I Can't Remember Anything* and of a father coming to terms with his daughter's murder resulting from his liberal values in *Clara.*

The older Miller plays, however, are still alive and well. *The Price* will be playing this winter at the Roundabout Theater in New York. *After the Fall* will be in London where the black actress Josette Simon will try to free the role of Maggie from the ghost of Marilyn Monroe. A striking fact about Miller's work is that in recent years it has been celebrated in Europe more than in America.

The following interview took place on 10 July 1989, in Miller's Rox-
bury, Connecticut, home. When we spoke, he was in the process of
putting the final touches on his play *The Ride Down Mount Morgan*. In
the driveway Arthur Miller told me, "When I finish this damned play
[which he started in 1978], I'll be a happy man. I'm waiting for the
explosion." He shook my hand with an extraordinary, strong, solid, large
hand, a carpenter's hand.

Miller chose to premiere *The Ride down Mount Morgan* in London,
where he has lately had a much warmer reception than in America. His
affinity to London theatre has to do with the fact that it is not dominated by one newspaper's theatre critic and the fact that he believes
London to have a more vital theatre culture than America. Miller argues
that the play is a tragicomedy about "what it takes out of a man to get
everything he wants in marriage and life." As he has told me, this play
"views people from a tragic distance, but with a certain forbearance,
even a comic despair. But the play is still asserting that while we are
weak, the rules of life are strong. That's a tragic view, and therefore
hopeful."

Although his tragic vision is now more humorous, he continues to
be fascinated in *The Ride Down Mount Morgan* with what C. W. E. Bigsby
calls "the problematic status of the real" (afterword to *The Archbishop's
Ceiling* [London: Methuen, 1977], 93). This concern with the real, however, is not distinct from Miller's political interest. *Mount Morgan* is
about the moral depravity and narcissism of America in the 1980s. As
Miller says, "What is at issue here is the code by which we live. The
debate inside the play asks whether a moral universe really exists at all."
In the 1990s Miller continues to confront guilt, deception, betrayal, and
moral responsibility.

In 1993 Miller decided to try a new play, *The Last Yankee,* in New
York, where John Tillinger directed it at the Manhattan Theatre Club.
Set in a New England state mental hospital, it focuses on two men
who meet while their wives are being treated for depression. As Leroy
Hamilton (John Heard), a successful carpenter on the verge of middle
age and a descendant of Alexander Hamilton, sits in the waiting room
with John Frick (Tom Aldredge), a prosperous but childless businessman, they puzzle over the cause of their wives' illnesses. It becomes clear
that *they* are the cause of their wives' depressions. We then move to the
hospital room, where the wives discuss their illnesses and their marriages. According to Howard Kissle, it is also about renewal, reassessment
of values, and belief in the future in the face of disappointment ("'Yan-

kee' Explores Rebirth of Nation," *New York Daily News,* 27 January 1993, 43), a note that echoes the Clinton era. But its popularity was strong in London, where it just came off stage after eight months. Moreover, it opened in Tokyo in April of 1994. In fact, both *The Last Yankee* and *The Ride down Mount Morgan* are currently playing in a half-dozen theatres throughout Europe.

Miller is a playwright to the core, and at age seventy-nine he has just completed a new play called *Broken Glass,* written over three months and staged at the Booth Theatre on Broadway. A play in two acts, *Broken Glass* takes place in the fall of 1938 in Brooklyn. It deals with a businessman, his wife, his doctor, and a woman who has been stricken suddenly with a paralysis of her legs. Over the phone recently, Miller told me, "It is related to the situation in the world at that time."

Balakian: You have said that *The American Clock* is a play about more than just a family. It's about forces bigger than simply overheard voices in the dark, a story of the United States talking to itself. In many ways this is the most American play that you have written.

Miller: It's a historical work. The idea came out of the seventies, when it seemed that the usual amnesia had set in. I was suddenly aware that the whole experience of the depression had vanished, partly as the result of willful ignorance, people being too disturbed by it to want to recollect it, as well as people who simply had only the vaguest notions of the dimensions of that catastrophe. They thought of it in terms of what was familiar to them, that is, some small disturbance of the economy, which we've always been living with. Its revolutionary dimensions were not really known. I felt, and I still feel, that nobody alive today is unaffected by what happened then, any more than we are unaffected by the Civil War. We may not be conscious of it, but in an endless number of ways it's working on us. You see it perhaps most vividly among the bankers and Wall Street people, who are preaching optimism, but their feelers are out for the signs of a devastating collapse, which we had last October [1988].

Balakian: Nearly on the same day.

Miller: Yes. And they ran for cover, and they begin immediately to resurrect, if not consciously then unconsciously, the fear that the whole bottom had fallen out again. It's important to me because I've always felt that there is a fundamental insecurity in Americans, the fear of failing, the fear of falling out of the class they're in. In later years we have seen a whole class of people thrown out into the street. This is a whole class of people who no longer have the means to rent space in the city. There's a subliminal amount of that fear. In some people it makes them more greedy. There's no end to their desire for money. In others it works the opposite way. They don't give a damn about how much anything costs because the whole thing is falling to pieces anyway. They believe that money is losing its value all the time anyway, so they might as well spend it. Anyway, I thought it would be interesting to try to write not a problem play but direct experiences of the depression, either of my own or those that were reported by Studs Terkel.

Balakian: You based some scenes on Terkel's *Hard Times.*

Miller: The play went through various migrations. The final production was the British National Theatre's. They did it at a time when political theatre was in vogue in England. There were a good number of plays that dealt with the society, whether it be Dickens or plays about national health, etc. So they were not shy of dealing with society as such in a kind of epic fashion. With us theatre had become completely bounded by the personal.

Balakian: What about a lot of the plays Joe Papp does that tend to be political or the feminist plays that are prominent now?

Miller: Of course that's now. I'm talking about fifteen years ago. At that time I don't think it had quite happened yet. Now we're more political. I arrived at the form of *Clock* at the Mark Taper about a year earlier, with emphasis on the scope of the disaster rather than on the family. I had started out that way, and it was successful in that form at the Spoleto Festival in South Carolina. But the misfortune was that there was enough interest in it for a Broadway production, which I suspected was wrong for that play, but I didn't sufficiently resist it. It was my fault; I should have. The result was that there was a tremendous pressure to make it more familial, more domestic. And the director really had no conviction one way or the other. He couldn't find a form for it and finally fled the play in the middle of its rehearsals. Nevertheless, with all of these problems there was a full house a day or two after we opened, but the play closed because the producer didn't have money to put ads in the paper. This is life in the New York theatre. It need not have closed. This is one instance where theatre failed the play. Most of the time when a play fails, it fails. Anyway, it's as close to its form as I can make it. What it's saying is that we came very close to a catastrophic collapse, where some nondemocratic form of government could have begun. Democracy seemed on the line. Remember that it was the same time that Hitler was coming to power in Germany and Mussolini was already in power. Japanese fascists were running Japan and running all over China. So this was part of the thirties' fear, and it lay behind that play.

Balakian: When I taught this play tó Cornell freshmen, it was a complete revelation to them. They hardly knew about the depression. I ordered the play to teach and then realized Grove Press had just published a new version, so I had to reorder it. Students came to class asking, "Which one should we read?" I said, "I don't know what happened, but Arthur Miller rewrote this play, so let's read both and see what the difference is." Would you talk about the difference between the two versions?

Miller: The first emphasizes the family, whereas the second emphasizes the society.

Balakian: And the one you prefer is the one that emphasizes the society. When I think of the canon of your work, I see that so much of it is about family and how America has impacted on these families. How would you compare the tension between the private and the public worlds in this play with *All My Sons, Salesman, The Price?*

Miller: In *The American Clock* the focus is outside the family. The family is there in order to illuminate the social crisis.

Balakian: Is it because you wanted to emphasize the society that you went to what you call a mural or mosaic form?

Miller: Right. It's an attempt to deal most directly with what's happening, instead of inferring it. It's a nonrealistic form. I hope each scene gives a feeling of what living at that time was like. But the fundamental reason for the form is to throw some light on the effects of the crash. As you say, your students knew nothing about it. Well, I was assuming people knew nothing about it. It's interesting that a lot of people of my age asked, "How can you remember all of that?!" It's a shocker. Not much is remembered in general. The past for America dims very rapidly. They don't want to remember. The past is the old; the present and the future are the escape from the past.

Balakian: That's so American.

Miller: One is the pain principle; the other, the pleasure principle.

Balakian: The past is painful—

Miller: Unless it's looked back on with nostalgia. That's what heals wounds.

Balakian: The American Clock ends on an upbeat note.

Miller: Because finally, whatever anyone said about the whole thing, the people in general survived but by the skin of their teeth. Maybe, on a philosophical view, that's the way we always survive, by nearly not surviving.

Balakian: That makes me think of Thornton Wilder's *The Skin of Our Teeth,* which is about the precariousness of survival. Were you consciously thinking of that play when you wrote *The American Clock?*

Miller: No. In my play one should be left with the clock still ticking. We still don't know where we're going, and time is not standing still.

Balakian: I'm interested in the change of the narrator from the first to the second version.

Miller: I think the change had to do with my wanting to emphasize the society rather than the family.

Balakian: How would you compare the father in *The American Clock* to Willy Loman?

Miller: Moe Baum is a practical man, a realist. He has few illusions, whereas Willy is a romantic.

Balakian: Would you liken Lee Baum to Biff Loman in any way?

Miller: Biff is driven and dominated by the idea of his father. He returns home to gain his father's approval. But Lee has matured earlier, has solved those problems.

Balakian: Some critics say that the style of this play is a parody of Odets's plays and of the social dramas of the thirties.

Miller: The social plays I knew were from the Federal Theater. They were multiscene plays delivering a thesis. But this is nothing new. It goes back to the Middle Ages. Or back to *Pilgrim's Progress.*

Balakian: Back to *Everyman.*

Miller: Right. And the mural form started with religious paintings. And if you look at Bayeux tapestry depicting England being invaded by the Normans, it's like stills from a movie demonstrating the events.

Balakian: It's really Brechtian. And it's also like Renaissance paintings.

Miller: Yes. Those characters in *The American Clock* are like signs objectified. I don't want them to have a whole inner life. I wanted a cavalcade notion, so that instead of intensity you get extension. It's the difference between a portrait and a mural.

Balakian: Critics haven't understood that. They say your characters and narrative line are too diffuse. What determined the way you structured the order of events in this play? At the end time bends backward.

Miller: Basically I did it chronologically, covering a decade of time. The play starts at an equilibrium with a bourgeois family. Then an earthquake strikes, and the individual is up for grabs. It ends with the coming of World War II, which got us out of the depression.

Balakian: Why do you regard the depression as a greater earthquake for Americans than World War II?

Miller: The depression affected almost all Americans directly. It shook the value system, which the war didn't touch.

Balakian: I noticed that Grandpa in the play is based on your grandfather as you talk about him in your autobiography, *Timebends.* Did he really say, "If Roosevelt was king, he wouldn't have to waste all his time making these ridiculous election speeches, and maybe he could start to improve things!"?

Miller: Yes. FDR could have gone on forever.

Balakian: But in the play he votes for Hoover.

Miller: Right. Hoover was more reassuring for a while.

Balakian: Did this conservative grandfather really tell you to go to Russia?

Miller: Oh yes. Grandpa said a lot of things like that.

Balakian: What Lee Baum says in your first version sounds like something Willy Loman would say—that if a man was hardworking and making the right goods, he got to be well-off. That's all. Life was purely a question of individuals, in effect.

Miller: That's a paradigmatic statement. Lots of people would have said the same.

Balakian: In the play Quinn resigns as president of GE because he believes that monopolies will crush the competition that capitalism ensures. Would you talk about him?

Miller: Quinn lived across the valley here. He prophesied that monopolies would subvert democracy. And when he quit, his name was erased from the GE roster. (A German filmmaker friend of mine found the original roster with Quinn's name in it at a flea market in Manhattan. I have it here.)

Balakian: Arthur Robertson tries to tell Quinn that the populist moment is finished: "The America you love is cold stone dead in the parlor. This is a corporate country; you can't go back to small, personal enterprise again." This seems like the impersonal, corporate world that consumes Willy Loman. You wrote this as a vaudeville and have said in your introduction to the play that its "swiftness, its smiling and extroverted style, is ironic contrast to the thematic question of whether America, like all civilizations, had a clock running on it, an approaching time of weakening and death."

Miller: The vaudeville has to be done with a flair, the way it was done in London. They were able to put a whole jazz orchestra onstage. We can't afford that here. I keep saying the same thing, boring but true—we have an impoverished theatre in this country.

Balakian: And you attribute that to our lack of subsidy.

Miller: Yes. If the British didn't have subsidy, they would be in the same situation. And Thatcher is aiming at just that.

Balakian: Do you see any possibility of developing a subsidized theatre in America?

Miller: I don't see any sign of it. We have a bottom-line philosophy here: if it doesn't pay off, it can't be good. There's an old tradition of subsidized ballet, symphonies, and opera because they cannot pay their way. These are subsidized in part by the private sector and in part by the state. Somehow theatre is not allowed to be part of this because of the idea that it often can pay off. Technically it does, but there is a kind of theatre whose cost is greater than the box office will ever support, or one with a naturally limited audience.

Balakian: Just think if we took the money from one missile and used it to subsidize theatre.

Miller: Don't give it a thought.

Balakian: Getting back to the music in your play—

Miller: These popular tunes were optimistic. That was the first great age of the popular radio singers: Bing Crosby, Frank Sinatra. And those great orchestras: Benny Goodman, Stan Kenton, Glenn Miller. There were Cole Porter, Rogers and Hart. American poetry!

Balakian: The form of your play is also improvisational. Doesn't that reflect the fact that America improvised its way through the depression?

Miller: Yes. America had great improvisational resourcefulness. FDR would begin vast programs and then abandon them when they didn't work, and it seemed okay to do that. Try anything. This can only happen in a democracy. But when he began the NRA [National Recovery Act], it was considered fascistic because of the idea that the economy would be fundamentally controlled, and he backed away from it.

Balakian: The black woman is fascinating in the play.

Miller: She's out of Terkel, but I fixed her up a little. They did a production in Williamstown. There were a lot of students in it, some a bit too young for their roles, but the spirit was wonderful.

Balakian: Another wonderful scene is Edie, the Superman comic strip writer. Does Edie come out of Studs Terkel's or out of Arthur Miller's imagination?

Miller: That's mine.

Balakian: What led you to include this socialist comic strip writer?

Miller: It was typical of the left-wing rationalizations of the time. And I knew people like her.

Balakian: When Edie says Superman "stands for justice," Lee replies, "You mean under capitalism. . . . "

Miller: It was the newly discovered leftist terminology. It was all new, all fresh and full of hope.

Balakian: Edie says, "Superman is also a great teacher of class consciousness." It's difficult for me and for the students I teach to appreciate the importance of socialism at that time. It's alien to us.

Miller: What socialism meant at that time was sense. People were burning food in the West, plowing under pigs, and people in the cities were starving. It was totally irrational. People desperately needed milk, and desperate farmers were spilling it out on the highway to keep prices up. Socialism meant rational, and rational meant that people could receive what they needed and would give what they could of their labor, their skill, and their talent. That would save us from this surrealism. And that's why it was hopeful, a life of reason. When capitalism works, it's terrific. When it doesn't, that chaos is an insult to the mind. Of course one didn't know we'd end up with Poland or the Soviet Union the way it is. The idealism was so powerful. What it meant was that the big propertied interests would have to be liquidated in the name of the people. It's an old story that goes back to the Roman empire. But when you're in desperate straits, it seems to make sense. Class consciousness, of course, means that, to create this new world, people have to identify themselves with the revolutionary class rather than with the upper class. It must seem like a strange world to you.

Balakian: It's fascinating. Your play gives me a handle on a time I never knew. The yuppie freshmen had no understanding of socialism. [*Miller laughs.*] That's why this is so valuable.

Miller: I'm trying to think of what American writer they might read, besides this, to give them an idea of what that meant in those days. Maybe Steinbeck.

Balakian: I read Alfred Kazin's *Starting Out in the Thirties* to get a sense of the flavor of that period. It put a bit of the thirties in my blood. It was a very different time from the eighties. Let's talk about *The Archbishop's Ceiling.* It's a fascinating play. You have said that it's about "what the soul does under the impact of immense power, how it makes accommodations and how it transcends the power." How would you compare it to *The Crucible,* which is about the same subject?

Miller: This is probably more insidious, more sinister, this attack on the integrity of the psychological person. It's insidious in the sense that they never know whether the ceiling is bugged or not, and if it is, whether or not it's turned on. As one of them says, it's a little like God.

Balakian: A God without a moral conscience.

Miller: Yes. What interested me was the pressure of power on the way we talk to each other and relate to each other in general.

Balakian: So the archbishop's ceiling becomes a metaphor for a larger condition.

Miller: People get so used to it that they're no longer aware of cozying up to power.

Balakian: What makes this more insidious than McCarthyism or the Salem witch hunt in 1692 is the uncertainty.

Miller: You worried the phone was tapped, and indeed it was most of the time. I got a freedom of information record of my own from the government, and they blanked out eighty percent of it as they usually do. We had a dinner party at my house in Brooklyn Heights, and there was surveillance over one of my guests as he was leaving. They don't mention who or when this was. I have no idea who it was. The British are very worried about it because it turns out the government has been eavesdropping on them.

Balakian: You say the play "begs the question of the existence of the sacred in the political life of man. But now some kind of charmed circle has to be drawn around each person across which the state may intrude only at its very real economic and political peril." Would you discuss the connection you're making between the economic and political?

Miller: It's becoming more and more obvious every week now that the reason why this kind of surveillance takes place is that they don't know how to run the country. Therefore, any competition is liable to show that up and demonstrate their incompetence to hold their jobs. It's a bureaucratic thing. They're holding on for dear life. We didn't have this thing while the United States, for example, was sure of itself. When they get unsure, they begin to deprive the human being of his right to speak and think. They threaten him and make him feel he has to be careful about what he thinks and says. It's coming off the insecurity of the bureaucracy because the system is profoundly faulty.

Balakian: So in that case America doesn't seem much better than the European country in which you set your play.

Miller: Excepting that we have one major, vital difference—

Balakian: The right to protest.

Miller: We're free to protest, and we're free still to elect our own representatives independently of the government. And that's a big difference. For them there was simply no way out. The Poles, in effect, had to bring down the government. They made it impossible for the government to survive economically. The government had to bring in solidarity in order to carry it on at all with any authority. And that's a confession that is simply crucial. What I'm saying, as far as the similarity is concerned, is that there's no mystery about it. J. Edgar Hoover went about blackening the name of anyone who had the slightest tendency to oppose him, spreading rumors about him, writing lies about him. There was the head of the largest apparatus. The guy was nuts but untouchable, very nearly sacrosanct.

Balakian: It seems to me that, as C. W. E. Bigsby says, the question you're presenting in *The Archbishop's Ceiling* is that when performance becomes a personal and political necessity, how can morality be constructed?

Miller: Right.

Balakian: Bigsby has also noted that your present concern with life as theatre—with the coercive power of private and public fictions, with the nature of the real, and with the necessity to reconstruct a moral world in the ethical void left by the death of God—seems to be an extension of your earlier plays. Would you say that now your mood is more apocalyptic, that moral certainties are under greater pressure than they were in *Salesman, The Crucible, Incident at Vichy, The Price*?

Miller: It is, because this is the last stage. This is the end. After this is truly the void. If people don't overthrow this or struggle against it, they've ceased to be people anymore. They've literally vacated their identity. There is no such thing as an individual anymore.

Balakian: Are these writers in the play under greater pressure than John Proctor?

Miller: It's a different kind of pressure. John Proctor, in the last analysis, is accused of plotting with the devil, personifying pure evil. In the seventeenth century the oppressor was still righteous and couldn't conceive that he was doing evil. The oppressor in Czechoslovakia is far more cynical than that. He would know that he himself is replaceable and hardly sublime. He might well end up, as many of his predecessors did, on the other side of the bench. It's all a very cynical operation of power. It's just pure power now. There's no cloak of religion, no cloak of moral values. It's just "I'm in and you're out, and as long as I'm in, I'm not going to let you push me out."

Balakian: I question what Bigsby has to say about the bug. He says, "To be bugged is to be violated but it is also to have one's existence confirmed. The alternative to submission to invisible power is freedom and abandonment. Are we really free if we act outside of man and God? It takes more courage to act in privacy." But it seems to me that your play says that the bug does not confirm one's existence, but rather that it robs one's identity. As you say, "The 'I' becomes 'we.' "

Miller: What he's driving at is that in the event of the struggle with that bug (up to a certain point there is a struggle before they give up), they glimpse their identity even if only to kiss it good-bye when they give up.

Balakian: I thought he was saying that the fact that they're being listened to confirms their existence. And that troubles me.

Miller: [*Laughs*] Maybe it's a temporary confirmation until they're squashed. As long as they're being listened to, they have some importance. They only have the importance of people who are about to be crushed. They wouldn't bother crushing them if they weren't important.

Balakian: Are you also saying that if we do inhabit a world of competing fictions in which our task is no longer to distinguish true from false but to generate fictions that assert rather than deny human values, then the role of the artist becomes central? Doesn't that place the writer in an extremely important position?

Miller: It does. You can talk a lot about that, because we've been living through the bankruptcy of politics, the moral bankruptcy. You can hardly find anybody anywhere now who hasn't a certain amount of suspicion of, if not contempt for, politicians and a certain despair about political programs as being efficacious in curing what ails us. I just read in the paper yesterday that they can hardly find priests anymore, or ministers. It's difficult to staff the church anymore. The younger generation is not passionately interested in practicing organized religion. So what is there for creating a moral image? Literally there's nothing except art. From whence can an individual get any idea of what he's supposed to be? A young person gets his economic image from business, but it doesn't take him long to find out that this is not the whole of life. Even a dumbbell knows that, even after he's moderately successful. The routine begins to appear. He needs more than that. Man doesn't live by bread alone. Where's he going to get that wine? I think it's the arts that are the only place left.

Balakian: Yes. In *Salesman* Charley says, "No man only needs a little salary." We're talking about the sacredness of art and of the writer, but in your play Adrian, the American novelist, seems exploitative. You have created a writer who must be watched.

Miller: Sure. He's a snoop. He's a gossip.

Balakian: But that doesn't nullify his value.

Miller: He has to do that in order to create his images. He has got to be listening to people.

Balakian: So the writer is like the bugged ceiling.

Miller: [*Laughs*] He's doing the same thing. But the purpose is something else.

Balakian: Your play asks whether we lose sincerity when we suspect we are being overheard by an omnipotent ear. Are you saying that ultimately the only sincere one can be the writer of fiction?

Miller: As writer, perhaps. He throws his whole heart into his writing. As person, it may be another story.

Balakian: Like *Elegy for a Lady*, *The Archbishop's Ceiling* and *Some Kind of Love Story* ask, "What is real?" But they deal with this question in very different ways. Whereas *The Archbishop's Ceiling* is both political and metaphysical, the other two are not political.

Miller: *Some Kind of Love Story* is dealing with a parallel question on a personal but also on a social level. As you'll see in the film—

Balakian: Is it possible to read the script?

Miller: It's being published. [*He goes to his studio to get a copy.*] You'd have to wait until October to get it. You can read this.

Balakian: Would you discuss the question of reality that you raise in both this screenplay and in *Some Kind of Love Story*?

Miller: When you say "what's real," it's what you commit yourself to as being real. There are different aspects to the same problem. In other words, in the relationship between a man and a woman, each person has to believe in some reality, unless it's a purely sexual, glancing encounter. And when somebody is a fantasist, as she is . . . yet there's something terribly actual about her.

Balakian: Maya in *The Archbishop's Ceiling* also raises the question of what's real by saying that *Vogue* magazine is real. She learns English by *Vogue*, models her hairstyle after those in *Vogue*. She comes right out and says, "Everything in *Vogue* is true." Something is terribly wrong if she believes that this magazine truly depicts America.

Miller: Look, the biggest chunk of American culture abroad is *Dallas* and *Knot's Landing*. I saw *Knot's Landing* in Cairo.

Balakian: Do you see the time when the archbishop's palace actually functioned as an archbishop's palace as a moment that was more favorable than the one you depict in your play? One of your characters says, "There was never much mercy in that plaster anyway."

Miller: The only thing positive about it was that the archbishop probably believed in himself as the archbishop. He believed that he was carrying through some basically useful, good order of the universe. It's been taken over by cynicism, and there's just the power. There's no sublimity anymore. It participated somehow in the sublime, one could assume, even though there never was much mercy up there. But the authority, the validity, the authenticity of the real we could assume existed.

Balakian: How do you interpret the government's return of Sigmund's manuscript? Is it simply a bribe to get him to stay?

Miller: It's both a bribe and a measure of their laughter. He's a mouse they're playing with. They're just showing him who's boss.

Balakian: Would you discuss his decision at the end to remain on home ground in order to write? Do you see it as completely self-serving? After all, his writer friends have tried to help him escape, and then Sigmund subverts their good intention.

Miller: It's paradoxical. On the one hand he's refusing to be saved. On the other hand he's going to be saved his own way. And his own way is to remain a rooted artist rather than the refugee, which would menace his artistic life and therefore make him useless to the future. He sees himself as being instrumental in bringing the future about. It's a rather heroic act, even though it does represent his egoism, too. But heroes are, generally speaking, egoistic people with great pride, overt or concealed.

Balakian: You say that "even Sigmund, with all his vitality, in the end must desperately call up a sanction, a sublime force beyond his ego, to sustain him in his opposition to the state's arrogant treatment." Would you discuss that?

Miller: What he's calling up is the great tradition of literature. That's the sanction.

Balakian: You have also said that "including the bug in the baggage of one's mind dulls the resistance, and when resistance to its presence is finally worn down to nothing, something like the naked soul begins to loom, some essence in man that's unadaptable, ultimate, immutable." [*Miller's burglar alarm starts chirping. He goes to reset it and finds his ninety-three-year-old mother-in-law has done it. He laughs with amazement.*] But it seems to me that when resistance to its presence is at its greatest that the naked soul would loom.

Miller: You're right.

Balakian: Do you finally see Maya and Marcus as government agents, or are we never to know?

Miller: They probably are. That means he's been at one time or another compromised. And once they get their fingers on him, it's hard for him not to give them a little here and there.

Balakian: Why does Adrian describe the people in this Eastern European country as "embalmed in a society of amber"?

Miller: Nothing is allowed to change. It's fixed. It can only go on repeating itself.

Balakian: Are you pointing your finger at Western hegemony in this play? You have the American hotel causing all of the phones to ring and Adrian returning to "repossess" this Eastern city.

Miller: I wouldn't generalize too much from that. The Americans bring their own problems. It's another great power. It's another big monolith to deal with, and you won't have these problems, but you'll have other ones.

Balakian: In *Timebends* you discuss *Elegy for a Lady* by saying that this is an "attempt to write a play with multiple points of view, one for each character, plus a third which is of the play itself. It's a work without a first person angle, like the neutrality of experience itself. At moments the proprietress seems actually to be the dying lover herself." You also say that "it's a play of shadows under the tree of death, like an Escher drawing in which water runs uphill, a reminder of how our brains have created the objective physics of our lives."

Miller: You see, that play is quite close to pure feeling. The one thing you can hang onto in that play is the feeling of grief for a loved one. *That* is the play. If that can be generated onstage, that's the play. Incidentally they managed pretty well in England to do that with two wonderful actors: Helen Mirren and Robert Peck. Metheun just published it.

Balakian: I have the one by the Dramatist's Play Service.

Miller: [*He hands me another book.*] This is something else. [*He hands me a newly published copy of* The Golden Years *and* The Man Who Had All the Luck.] It just came out. You can have it.

Balakian: Thanks! The only copy I could find of *The Man Who Had All the Luck* was in the Lincoln Center library.

Miller: *The Golden Years* will be on stage in London next year [1990]. *The Man Who Had All the Luck* opens at the Bristol Old Vic in May 1990, and an American TV version of it is in the works.

Balakian: *Elegy for a Lady* is also about commitment.

Miller: The mourning for the lack of it in the face of death.

Balakian: Would you talk about being caught between two theatres, the one that exists and the one that doesn't, as that relates to this play?

Miller: That play is unique in my work because of the fact that it's like a dream. I didn't want to reduce its dreamlike quality or to superrationalize it. I wanted to deliver up that feeling as purely as I could.

Balakian: What strikes me about your later work is your interest in relationships and in the question of reality, as opposed to the social statements that characterize your early work. Is that safe to say?

Miller: That's probably true.

Balakian: You have said that *Some Kind of Love Story* "concerns the question of how we believe truth, how one is forced by circumstance to believe what you are only sure is not too easily demonstrated as false." And you say that, like *Elegy,* it's "a passionate voyage through the masks of illusion to an ultimate reality. In both the unreal is an agony to be striven against." So these plays are closely linked.

Miller: They were written roughly in the same period, the same year.

Balakian: You weren't thinking of Pirandello, who is also interested in voyages through the masks of illusion to a reality?

Miller: Not consciously.

Balakian: This crazy woman holds all of the significant facts.

Miller: That's the irony of it.

Balakian: It makes me think of Pirandello's *Henry IV.*

Miller: Well, it's like it.

Balakian: The woman assumes the personae of a prostitute, a little girl, and a bourgeois woman. Why did you decide on those?

Miller: It's pure instinct. There's nothing programmatic about it.

Balakian: Catholicism is an issue in this play.

Miller: It's just that that's what she is and what he is, but I suppose you could say it's the lost order that has crumbled. They're left high and dry. They can only find reassurance in each other, if that.

Balakian: In *Playing for Time* I was struck by the whole issue of nationalism as you present it. What Fania is adamantly opposed to is nationalism. She says, "I'm sick of the Zionists and Marxists; Jews and Gentiles; Easterners and Westerners; Germans and non-Germans; French and non-French. I am a woman, not a tribe!" Yet at the end she sings that very moving French nationalistic song. What do you say about that paradox?

Miller: She's finally united with some culture. She isn't alone. In the camp she's despairing of any survival even. Since the tribe is of no aid to her there, and on the contrary it's part of the accusation against her, she refuses this false hope of being part of the tribe. But once she's out and free, I guess, she wants to belong to something other than just herself. It's a paradox.

Balakian: The other paradox, which is so striking and is one that you grapple with in *Incident at Vichy,* is that these Nazis value art and music. The Nazis kill the conductor, and yet Mengele wants to preserve her conductor's baton and gloves.

Miller: It's art without value, art as sentimental escape.

Balakian: It's incomprehensible to have art without value.

Miller: It is finally, because their idea is pure kitsch and worshiping the tradition—

Balakian: As opposed to the real thing. So it's not a paradox.

Miller: It's the mockery of art that comes from such minds—they are moved by their attempt to seem refined.

Balakian: There's also the paradox of these women who "play for time," who entertain Nazis by playing in this orchestra in order to save their lives but know that they are hated by the other Jews who are being slaughtered. Do you think they are justified in their decision to join the orchestra?

Miller: I suppose there's no way to hold judgment over them.

Balakian: Thank you so much for your time.

NEIL SIMON
Jackson R. Bryer

Neil Simon (photo by Jackson R. Bryer)

A critic has described Neil Simon as "relentlessly prolific." By virtually any accepted standard he is the most successful playwright in the history of the American theatre. In thirty-three years his twenty-nine Broadway shows (including revivals of *Little Me* and *The Odd Couple*) have played a total of well over fifteen thousand performances. When *The Star-Spangled Girl* opened in December 1966, Simon had four Broadway productions running simultaneously. Despite this popular success and general critical approval, Simon did not win his first Tony Award for Best Play until 1985 (*Biloxi Blues*), although he had won the Tony for Best Author of a Play for *The Odd Couple* in 1965. *Lost in Yonkers* won both the Pulitzer Prize for Drama and the Tony Award for Best Play in 1991.

Simon's Broadway productions include the plays *Come Blow Your Horn* (1961), *Barefoot in the Park* (1963), *The Odd Couple* (1965), *The Star-Spangled Girl* (1966), *Plaza Suite* (1968), *Last of the Red-Hot Lovers* (1969), *The Gingerbread Lady* (1970), *The Prisoner of Second Avenue* (1971), *The Sunshine Boys* (1972), *The Good Doctor* (1973), *God's Favorite*

(1974), *California Suite* (1977), *Chapter Two* (1977), *I Ought to Be in Pictures* (1980), *Fools* (1981), *Brighton Beach Memoirs* (1983), *Biloxi Blues* (1985), *Broadway Bound* (1986), *Rumors* (1988), *Lost in Yonkers* (1991), *Jake's Woman* (1992), and *Laughter on the 23rd Floor* (1993). He has written the books for the musicals *Little Me* (1962), *Sweet Charity* (1966), *Promises, Promises* (1968), *They're Playing Our Song* (1979), and *The Goodbye Girl* (1993). Besides the adaptations of several of his plays for the movies his screenplays are *The Out-of-Towners, The Heartbreak Kid, Murder by Death, The Goodbye Girl, The Cheap Detective, Seems Like Old Times, Only When I Laugh, Max Dugan Returns, The Slugger's Wife,* and *The Marrying Man.*

Born, as was George M. Cohan, on the Fourth of July, in 1927 in the Bronx, New York, he grew up there and in the Washington Heights section of Manhattan with his only sibling, his brother Danny. He early received the nickname "Doc" for his ability to mimic the family doctor. When their parents, Irving (a garment salesman) and Mamie (who often worked at department stores to support the family during her husband's frequent absences), divorced, the two boys went to live with relatives in Forest Hills, Queens, and Simon attended high school there and at DeWitt Clinton in Manhattan. After brief military service at the end of World War II, he worked for several years with his brother as a comedy writer for radio and television. In 1953 he married Joan Baim, a dancer, who died of cancer in 1973. His second wife was actress Marsha Mason; he is now married to Diane Lander. He has two grown daughters and a stepdaughter.

This interview was conducted on 23 January 1991, in Simon's suite at the Willard Hotel in Washington, while he was preparing *Lost in Yonkers* (then playing at Washington's National Theatre) for its Broadway opening. The interview was transcribed by Drew Eisenhauer.

Bryer: You always say that very early on you knew you wanted to be a playwright.

Simon: I wanted to be a writer very early on. It's not quite true about the playwriting thing. I started writing the first play when I was thirty and got it on when I was thirty-three, so that's fairly old to be starting as a playwright.

Bryer: Most young people want to write poetry or want to write novels. When you knew you wanted to be a writer, was it always writing plays that you wanted to do?

Simon: I started out with different aims and ambitions. I grew up in the world of radio, so the first couple of jobs I had were in radio and then television. I think I was setting my sights for film. I'm not quite sure when I decided to do plays. I know when I actually did so, which was after years of working on *Your Show of Shows* with Sid Caesar and *The Bilko Show,* I said I didn't want to spend the rest of my life doing this—writing for someone else—I wanted to do my own work. So I started writing the first play, *Come Blow Your Horn,* and it took me almost three years to do the twenty-some complete new versions before I got it on. When I did get it on, I said, "My God, three years!," and I was exhausted. I had only taken other little jobs just to make a living, since I had a wife and two children. But once the play hit, *Come Blow Your Horn* subsidized the next one, which was a musical, *Little Me,* and that subsidized writing *Barefoot in the Park,* and then I was making enough money so I could do this full-time.

Bryer: So in a sense your playwriting grew out of writing for TV and radio, in that writing for TV and radio was basically working within a dramatic form? That's what really led to the playwriting.

Simon: Right. I started off just writing jokes for newspaper columns and things and then working on *Your Show of Shows* and *Bilko. Your Show of Shows* was writing sketches, and *Bilko* was like a half-hour movie. So I was learning the dramatic form. Then I worked for about two years with Max Liebman, who was the producer of *Your Show of Shows,* doing specials. It was a very good education for me because we were updating pretty famous musical books of the past—*Best Foot Forward* and *Knickerbocker Holiday.* We would throw the book out completely and use the score. We would sort of follow the story line but use our own dialogue. So I was able to step in the footprints of previous writers and learn about the construction from them.

Bryer: What was the purpose of those? Were they for television?

Simon: Yes. We did about twenty of them, two shows a month. One show would be a book show. A couple of them were originals. One was *The Adventures of Marco Polo,* and we used the music of Rimsky-Korsakoff. So I was really learning a lot about construction. I had made a few abortive attempts to write plays during that time—one with another writer on *The Bilko Show*—and it was going nowhere. I always had my summers off because in those days we did thirty-nine shows a year on television in consecutive weeks, and you had something like thirteen weeks off in the summer, in which I would try to write plays. And I would say, "Wow, this is tough!" Finally I went to California to do a television special—for Jerry Lewis of all people. I had quit *Your Show of Shows*—it had finally gone off the air—and so I was freelancing. I went out there for six weeks. In about ten days I wrote the whole show, and I said to Jerry Lewis, "What'll I do, I've got all this time?" He said, "I've got other things to do. Just do what you want until we go into rehearsal." And I started to write *Come Blow Your Horn,* which was almost a satirical or a farcical look at my upbringing with my parents. I was on the way, but it took three years to do that, as I said.

Bryer: As a child and as a young adult, did you read plays and did you go to the theatre?

Simon: I went to the theatre. I read quite a good deal. I went to the library. I used to take out about three books a week, but they weren't about the theatre. It wasn't until I was about fourteen or fifteen that I saw my very first play, *Native Son,* the Richard Wright book and play.

Bryer: A strange thing for a fourteen- or fifteen-year-old to go see, wasn't it?

Simon: There was a local theatre in upper Manhattan, in Washington Heights, where I lived. It was called the Audubon Theatre. It used to be a movie house, and then they used it for acts—sort of vaudeville acts, but I wouldn't really call it vaudeville. They started doing that all over New York at the time when the theatre was truly flourishing. You not only played Broadway, you could go to Brooklyn and Manhattan and the Bronx, and there were theatres that did their versions of plays that had closed on Broadway. So I went to this local theatre and saw *Native Son* and was mesmerized by what the theatre could do. I had also acted in plays in public school and in junior high school, so I had a little glimpse of that. But acting is a lot different from writing. I think that slowly, as my parents started to take me to the theatre more, mostly musicals (I remember seeing *Oklahoma!* It was—for its time—so innovative and so original), in the back of my mind I thought about that. But all during those years I was working with my brother, and I thought that the only way to write a play was to do it by yourself, because one needed an individual point of view. Even if we were to write about our own family background, his point of view would be completely different from mine, and so it would get diminished somehow and watered down. When I wrote *Come Blow Your Horn,* I never even told him about it. It meant that I would have to make a break with him after ten years of writing together. The break was pretty traumatic. It was worse than leaving home, because one expects that, but this was breaking up a partnership that he started because he was looking for a partner. He doesn't like to work by himself, and he always noticed and encouraged the sense of humor I had. I didn't have a sense of construction. He had that, and I was wonderful with lines and with the comedy concepts. Finally, when I did *Come Blow Your Horn,* I knew I had to step away.

Partly I think it had to do with my being married. I began to feel my own oats and wanted the separation.

Bryer: Can you speak at all about plays or playwrights that impressed you, influenced you, early or late?

Simon: Well, it was any good playwright. I didn't have favorites. In terms of comedy I guess maybe Moss Hart and George S. Kaufman. A play that neither one of them wrote, Garson Kanin's *Born Yesterday,* I thought was a wonderful comedy, and I liked *Mr. Roberts* too. But I was as intrigued by the dramas as I was by the comedies. It wasn't until sometime later that I decided what I wanted to write was drama and tell it as comedy. I was such an avid theatregoer, especially when I first married Joan. You could go to the theatre then twice a week and not catch the whole season on Broadway and even Off-Broadway. *Streetcar Named Desire* probably made the greatest impression on me, that and *Death of a Salesman.* These are not comedies. Although I knew I was not up to writing a drama as yet, I thought when I wrote something it would be from a comic point of view.

Bryer: If you could have written one play that was written by somebody else, what would that play be?

Simon: The question has been asked a lot, and I generally say *A Streetcar Named Desire.* I have a certain affinity for that play—so does everyone else in America for that matter, I think. *Death of a Salesman* I thought was maybe the best American play I've ever seen—but it lacked humor. The humor that I saw in *Streetcar Named Desire* came out of a new place for humor. It came out of the character of Stanley Kowalski saying, "I have this lawyer acquaintance of mine" and talking about the Napoleonic Code. It was the way he talked that got huge laughs, and I knew that this was not comedy. It was character comedy, and that's what I aimed for later on. If I were able to write a play, an American play, I would say it would be *Streetcar.*

Bryer: The same quality is present in *The Glass Menagerie,* too. That play also has some very funny moments in it, but they grow very organically out of Amanda and out of her situation.

Simon: Yes. Even in Eugene O'Neill, who really lacks humor, I found humor in *Long Day's Journey,* in James Tyrone's meanness with money—turning out the lightbulbs all the time and being so cheap. That was a play that I said to myself when I saw it, "I could never write that, but I would love to write like that," to write my own *Long Day's Journey.* I have an oblique sense of humor. I see comedy—or humor, not comedy (there's a difference)—in almost everything that I've gone through in life, I'd say, with the exception of my wife's illness and death. Humor has become so wide open today that it's almost uncensored on television. It's all part of the game now. As I said, *Long Day's Journey* impressed me very much early on, and the writings of August Wilson impress me very much today. There's great humor in them and great sense of character and storytelling. It's almost old-fashioned playwriting, in a way. There are not many playwrights who write the way he does.

Bryer: I think some of the humor in O'Neill comes from the Irish quality in those plays, the whole Sean O'Casey tradition of Irish drama, where the humor and the seriousness are very closely juxtaposed. And I wonder whether there isn't something similar in the Jewish idiom, with humor coming out of serious situations. Do you feel that is a factor in your own plays?

Simon: I'm sure it is, but I find it a very difficult thing to talk about because I'm unaware of anything being particularly Jewish. This present play, *Lost in Yonkers,* is about a Jewish family, but rarely is it mentioned or brought up. But the humor comes out of the Jewish culture as I know it. It's fatalistic—everything bad is going to happen. In the opening scene the father talks about his troubles with his wife dying, being at a loss about what to do with the boys and so worried about how they're going to look well and be presented well to the grandmother. It's all out of fear. There's no sense of confidence, because he knows what he's up against. The mother is, I think, more German than Jewish, because she was brought up in Germany, and her culture is German. So one doesn't ever get a picture that she was brought up in a Jewish home in which they paid attention to the services. I would doubt very much if they were Orthodox Jews. But it's there someplace, and it's so deeply embedded in me and so inherent in me that I am unaware of its quality. When I write something, I don't think, "Oh, this is Jewish." At one time I thought I did, that I needed Jewish actors, but I found that people like Jack Lemmon or George C. Scott or Maureen Stapleton were equally at home with my material and that they gave great performances. I rarely work with Jewish actors now. There are very few of them in *Lost in Yonkers.* However, in making the film of *Brighton Beach Memoirs,* when we did not get Jewish women to play the mother and the sister, it didn't sound right. Blythe Danner and Judith Ivey, as wonderful as they are, did not sound right. To the gentile ear it may not sound wrong, but still the audiences are aware that something is not quite organic. They don't know what it is. They can't name it. The difference came when Linda Lavin played in *Broadway Bound* and was right on the button and had the sense of truth. I think it's true too with O'Neill. He doesn't have to have Irish actors, but Jewish actors playing O'Neill would have to have a very wide range to be able to do it well.

Bryer: You have always said you stopped writing for TV because you wanted control, because you wanted to be on your own, not to have network executives and ad men running your creative life. But didn't the same sort of thing start to happen after a bit when you started to write for the stage, where producers like Saint-Subber wanted you to write a particular kind of play?

Simon: Saint used terms that no longer exist—they come from the turn of the century. He talked about "the carriage trade," those people, not necessarily Jewish, maybe New York society or wealthier people, whom we wanted to appeal to as well. When I wrote *Barefoot in the Park,* I think in an earlier version I made them a Jewish family without saying so. Saint said, stay away from that because we were going to miss the carriage trade, so to speak. So maybe I was aware of it. Certainly it was in *The Odd Couple,* with Oscar Madison, only because Walter Matthau played it. I was aware of that in the beginning and then gradually got away from it until I got specifically Jewish when I was writing the autobiographical plays. In *Chapter Two,* something made me lean toward an actor like Judd Hirsch, playing the leading character, George, because I knew the cadences and the attitudes came from me. So I thought that character had to be Jewish, but I didn't call him Jewish. In these plays—I'm talking about the trilogy (*Brighton Beach Memoirs, Biloxi Blues,* and *Broadway Bound*) and about *Lost in Yonkers*—they are Jewish families, you can't get away from it. Some plays are just not. *Barefoot in the Park* was not necessarily at all. *The Odd Couple* has proven not to be because it's the most universal play I've written. They do it in Japan as often as they do it here now. It's done all over the world constantly because it is such a universal situation. Two people living together cannot get along all the time, and it made it unique that it was two men. It seemed like such a simple idea that you thought surely someone would have written a play about it, but no one ever had up until that time. It was the idea or concept that made it so popular and then the execution.

Bryer: Which of your plays gave you the most trouble, and which was the easiest?

Simon: Rumors gave me the most trouble because of the necessities of farce. One has to get the audience to dispel their sense of truth, and they must believe in the premise even though we know it's about three feet off the ground. It has to be filled with surprises, and it has to move at a breakneck pace. People have to be in jeopardy constantly. The minute the jeopardy stops and they can sit back and relax, it's like a train that runs out of steam. And it has to be funny every minute. It was like constructing a murder mystery, an Agatha Christie mystery in which you are kept in suspense, only it had to go at a much greater pace than any of Agatha Christie's stories. I wanted to do it because I wanted to try the form. In a sense I was buoyed by watching an interview with Peter Shaffer, whom I respect enormously. I think he's a wonderful playwright. *Amadeus* is one of my favorite plays, again a play with a great concept—an original one—about professional jealousy. The interviewer said, "Why did you write *Black Comedy?*" And he said, "Well, it was a farce, and everyone wants to write one farce in his life." I had tried bits and pieces of it. The third act of *Plaza Suite,* with the father and mother trying to get the girl out of the locked bathroom, is a farce. But it only ran for thirty minutes, and it wasn't a full-blown piece, so I wanted to try that. That was the most difficult. None of them come easy.

What happened with *Brighton Beach* was interesting. I wrote thirty-five pages and stopped and put it away for nine years. And when I came back to it, somehow the play had been written in my head over those nine years without thinking of it, so I wrote it completely from beginning to end without stopping. But that's only the beginning of the process. You can never say any play is written easily, because you write it once, and then you write it again, and then you write it again. Then you have a reading of it, and then you go into rehearsal, in which you write it ten more times. So they all present their difficulties. But I can't think of any one play where it was really easy, where I didn't have a difficult time with it.

Bryer: Have your writing methods changed over the years? You say you wrote *Come Blow Your Horn* twenty times. Is that still true, that you write a play over and over again, or do you find that you're getting better at it?

Simon: If I do write it over and over and over again, it means that the play has some serious flaw. I wrote *Jake's Women* seven times, almost from beginning to end, before I put it on the stage, so I never really corrected the serious flaw. With this play, *Lost in Yonkers,* the first version was fairly close to what we have now. I did two more versions before we went into rehearsal, but I had less trouble with the construction of the play. It just seemed to lead to the right thing. It has to do with the beginning of the play, with how each of the characters is introduced and how each of them has his own problem. Manny Azenberg, our producer, has always said that if I reach page thirty-five, it is almost always a "go" project. Sometimes I get to page twenty-five or so, and I start to look ahead and say, "What are you going to write about? What else could possibly happen?" I've come up with some wonderful beginnings of situations and don't always know where they're going but sort of know what they're going to be.

Billy Wilder, the director, once said to me (he was talking about a film, but I think it applies to a play as well), "If you have four great scenes, you've got a hit." He says that if you don't have those great scenes, then you're not going to make it. When I wrote *The Sunshine Boys,* the whole play came to me at once in a sense. Since I fashioned it somewhat (even though I didn't know them) after the careers of Smith and Dale, and got the premise that they had not spoken to each other in eleven years and then they were being offered this job to work together and didn't want to speak to each other, I said, "Well, they've got to get together." That's the first funny interesting conflict, then the rehearsal, then the actual doing of the show on the air. I knew that they could cause great conflict and problems with each other, and then there would be the denouement of finally getting together. I said there are those four scenes. I don't think about that all the time, but that time I knew where it was going—there was a play there—so I sat down with some sense of confidence.

Others just unfold themselves. When I was writing *Lost in Yonkers,* I knew I had these four characters in my mind. I had witnessed somebody who has this dysfunction of not being able to breathe properly, and I never thought about using it. But it suddenly came to mind in this dysfunctional family, which the mother has created. When you write, you're always trying to catch up with your thoughts. They're ahead of you, like the carrot in front of the rabbit or the horse. If it's always there ahead of you, then you know that each day that you go to work you will be able to write something. It's awful when you are writing a play and you get to page forty and you come to your office in the morning and say, "Well, what do I write today? Where does it go?" I want to leave it the night before saying to myself, "I know what that next scene is tomorrow," and I look forward to the next day.

Bryer: How do you get started on a play? Do you usually start with an idea or with a character?

Simon: First it starts with a desire, to write a play, and then the next desire is what kind of play do I want to write. When I finished *Broadway Bound,* I said, "I do not want to write another play like this right now." I've done a play that in degrees develops more seriously, because I thought that *Broadway Bound* dealt more truthfully with my family and with the kind of writing I wanted to do than anything I had done in the past. I did not have an idea for the next one, and so sometimes I just play around with an idea. I said I wanted to write a farce, and I just sat down and thought of the opening premise. It literally started with how it looked. Most farces are about wealthy people. They're not about people who are poor, because their lives are in conflict all the time. They must be satirical—you want to make jabs at them socially. These were all fairly prominent people, and I wanted them all to show up in black tie and their best gowns, because I knew, whatever it was that I was going to write, they would be a mess at the end of the evening—either emotionally or physically—with their clothes tattered and torn. I thought of it as a mystery. I had no idea where it was going. The host had attempted suicide and was not able to tell them what happened, the hostess wasn't there, and there was no food. That's all I knew. I had read (I read a great deal of biographies of writers and artists) that Georges Simenon wrote most of his murder mysteries without knowing who was going to be murdered and who the murderer was. He picked a place, a set of situations, just something that intrigued him. I think almost anyone can sit down and write the first five pages of a murder mystery because you don't have to leave any clues. You just think of some wild situation that sounds interesting. It's only the really great mystery writers who know where to take it. *The Thin Man* is one of the most complicated books I've ever read. I don't think Dashiell Hammett is given enough credit. That's really literature, that book. What was your original question?

Bryer: How you got the ideas for plays.

Simon: I never really can remember the moment, maybe with a few exceptions. *The Odd Couple* came out of watching my brother and the man he was living with at that time. They had both just gotten divorced, had decided to live together to cut down expenses, and they were dating girls. I said what an incredible idea for a play. *Barefoot* came out of my own experiences with my wife. Strangely enough, *Barefoot in the Park* started in Switzerland. The first version of it—this really happened— was when my wife and I went on our honeymoon to St. Moritz, Switzerland, met an elderly couple, and decided to go hiking with them. My wife then—Joan died in '73—was a wonderful athlete, and she and the older man were practically jumping up this mountain while his wife and I staggered behind, and I was angry at Joan for being able to jump like a goat up this mountain. Then I realized that it had too exotic an atmosphere, and I wanted to locate it in a place where one could relate to it more. I thought about that tiny apartment that we actually lived in that was five flights up and had a shower and no bath. It had a hole in the skylight in which it snowed. So I used all of those things.

You don't know that when you're sitting down to write it. It's an adventure. It's really jumping into this big swimming pool and hoping there's going to be water when you hit.

Bryer: How has the experience of writing musicals and writing films been different, and why do you continue to do them when you don't need to? Why have you continued to write in collaborative situations and seemingly against the whole idea of wanting to be independent?

Simon: I do it because I think I have to keep writing all the time. Each year I want to be doing something. I wouldn't know how to take a year off and do nothing. I would feel it a wasted year of my life, unless I did something else productive that I love—but I haven't found anything. I think that even at this age I'm still growing and that I want to do as much as I can before I can't do it anymore. Again, I think, what do you want to do following what you have just done? I was about to start another play that I had in mind, but I still haven't quite licked where it's going, and I'm not ready to do it. It's not that I won't have anything on next year, but I won't have anything to work on. So I'm toying with the idea of doing a musical now, which is like a breather, even though the musical is a much more collaborative and a much more debilitating effort than anything else in the theatre could be. The movies have been in the past—some of them—such good experiences that I was usually eager to do one again. The movie industry has changed enormously. I did ten films with Ray Stark. Nine of them were successful and one was terrible. But for all of them Ray Stark was the producer. He always got me a good director, always got a good cast, and was really the blocking back for me, the runner, with the studio. I almost never had to deal with the studio. This last experience I had, *The Marrying Man,* was enough to make me say I never want to do a film again.

I did have good experiences doing *The Heartbreak Kid* and *The Goodbye Girl,* even *Murder by Death. Murder by Death* is not a great work of art, but it's great fun. In my reveries I used to wish that I had been older in the thirties and in the early forties and could write for Cary Grant and Humphrey Bogart and Jimmy Stewart. One of the great thrills I had in Hollywood was when I met some of these people, and they said, "Gee, I wish I could have done a picture with you!" When Cary Grant said that to me, I said, "Wow, what I've missed!" Those actors who were, I think, in some ways (the best of them) superior to some of the actors we have today, carried none of the weight that the actors do today. Now even a small star, a starlet, has something to say about the picture. I will deal with the director always, with the producer seldom but sometimes, the studio hardly ever, and with an actor never. I will listen to an actor's inabilities to find what he needs to accomplish in a part and try to accommodate that, but not because he wants to be portrayed in a certain way. On the stage Manny Azenberg and I must have fired eight to ten actors over the years because we found they were not fulfilling what we wanted. An actor's training is mostly with dead playwrights, so when they do the classics they don't expect any rewrites. I want them to feel the same thing. I rewrite more than anybody I know—I just do it over and over. I'm still giving pages and new lines on *Lost in Yonkers* and will do it until we open. But they'll always come to you and say, "I'm having trouble with this line. Can you think if there's another way of me saying it that makes it more comfortable?" I'll say, "I'll rewrite it if it makes it more comfortable for the character, not for you." When they understand that then we can find a way to do it.

To give you a really good example of the difference between films and plays for me, a director of a play will come to me and say, "What do you think about this section? I'm not so sure that this is working. Do you think you could find something else?" And I'll either agree with him or disagree with him and write it or rewrite it, but he does nothing about it until I rewrite it. He'll even come to me about a sentence or a couple of words. That play is sold to the films, and he becomes the director. He shoots the film and then invites me to the first cut, and three major scenes are missing. I say, "What happened to those scenes?" He says, "They didn't work for me." It now has become his script—it's not mine anymore. And the only way to control that is to direct your own films, which I don't want to do. I'm not a director. I don't want to spend all that time. I love writing. I hate directing. I hate hanging around the rehearsals. I do it when I'm working and I need to do something, but just to stand there and watch—I don't want to do it. So I do the films, but I'm not really very happy with them. Musicals are something else, because when you work with some of the best people (I worked with Bob Fosse a number of times, and I thought he was really a genius. I worked with Michael Bennett a few times, even a little bit on *Chorus Line*), that's great fun. That's like being invited to the party, so you just do it.

Bryer: You talk about rewriting. When you're readying a play like *Lost in Yonkers* and you're doing the rewriting, to whom are you responding when you do the rewrites? Is it purely your own responses when you're in the theatre? Or do you also respond to critics, or the director, or an actor?

Simon: All of them. Not an actor so much, a director yes, a critic sometimes. If a critic says something that's valid, and especially if it's backed up by another critic who hits on the same point, I say, "I've got to address this." When you're writing it over and over again and then you're in rehearsal and you're out of town and you start to try it, you've lost all objectivity. Now you need the audience to be objective for you (and they are totally), and you listen to them. Sometimes the actor will come to me and say, "This line isn't getting a laugh." And I say, "I never intended it to." They assume that everything they should say when the situation is comic should get a laugh. I say, "No, no, no, this is character. It's pushing the story ahead." That never happens in any of the dramatic scenes in *Lost in Yonkers.* Very few of those lines were ever changed because they don't have the difficulty in expecting a reaction from the audience. I rewrite just watching what it is that I hear wrong. And sometimes I can watch a play, and after about eight or nine performances, I say, "I don't like that." There was a producer who once said to me, "Only look at the things that don't work in the play. The good things will take care of themselves, don't worry about that. Don't say, 'I know this stuff doesn't work, but look at all the good things I have.' " He said, "The bad things'll do you in every time." So I concentrate on the bad things. And after I get whatever I think is unworthy of the play out, then I start to hear it more objectively. I stay away for two or three performances and come back and say, "We need something much better than that." When you first see that play up on a stage for the first time in front of an audience, all you care about is that the baby is delivered and is well and has all its arms and legs and moves. Then you say, "Okay, now starts its education."

Bryer: I teach a course in modern American drama, and many of the playwrights in the course, people like John Guare and Beth Henley, are considered by the "establishment" to be serious playwrights who write plays that contain comic moments. Neil Simon, on the other hand, is considered a writer of funny plays that are occasionally serious. That strikes me as unfair because, especially in the most recent of your plays, like the trilogy and now *Lost in Yonkers,* the proportion of humor to seriousness is, if anything, less comedy than in, say, *Crimes of the Heart.*

Simon: Crimes of the Heart is a comedy.

Bryer: Yes, but Henley is considered a serious playwright.

Simon: I don't consider it necessarily unfair. I just think it's inaccurate. Unfair means that I'm being picked on for not writing serious, which is better than comedy, which I don't hold to be true. For the most part I think I have written, with the exception of *Rumors* and the musicals (starting even with *The Odd Couple*), a serious play that is told through my own comic point of view. There are no serious moments in *The*

Odd Couple, but when I first sat down to write it, naive as this may be, I thought it was sort of a black comedy, because in most comedies up to that point, there were always women in the play and a romantic relationship. Here there were none—the relationship was between these two men. *Plaza Suite,* with a husband and wife getting a divorce after twenty-three years, was basically a serious play that had comedy in it. The audience at that time was so trained to laugh at what I wrote that, in Boston, Mike Nichols and I kept taking out all the funny lines in the first act—and they found other places to laugh.

I write with a sense of irony, and even with lines that are not funny, sometimes the audience senses the irony, when they are sophisticated enough, and they see the humor. That's why I always need really good productions for the plays to work. I once met a woman who said, "You know, I've never been a fan of yours," and I said, "Oh, that's okay," and she said, "Now I'm a big fan!," and I said, "What happened?" She said, "Well, I come from"—it was either Wyoming or Montana—and she said, "I've only seen dinner theatre productions of your plays, in which they would play all the plays on one superficial level. They played it all as comedy, and then I read the plays, and I said, this isn't comedy at all." I remember people walking out of *Prisoner of Second Avenue* confused, because some would say, "This wasn't funny." I didn't mean it to be funny—I thought it was a very serious subject, especially at that time. It was the beginning of people being so age-conscious, with the man of forty-eight years old losing his job and finding it very difficult to start all over again, which is true even today. That to me was a serious play that had a great deal of comedy.

I use the comedy in a way to get the audience's attention and then sort of pull the rug from underneath them. That's how I view life. Things are wonderful, things are going along just great, and then a telephone call comes and just pulls the rug from under you. Some tragic thing, some tragic event, has happened in your life, and I say if it can happen in life I want to do that in the theatre. It took a long time to convince audiences and critics that one could write a play that way. I remember reading Lillian Hellman saying, "Never mix comedy and drama in the same play; the audiences won't understand it." They say to me, "What are you writing?," and I'll mention something, and they say, "Is it a comedy?" I say, "No, it's a play." They say, "Is it a drama?," and I say, "It's a play. It has everything in it."

Bryer: When you look back over your career to date, how has Neil Simon changed as a playwright? In other interviews you've mentioned the idea of the tapestry play, that you're now writing about more than two people as the focus of the plays. I assume that's one way, but are there other ways that you see your plays changing?

Simon: Well, in a glacier-like way. They move slowly. I don't make sudden overnight changes. I think back to *Chapter Two,* which was the story of the guilt a man feels who has lost a spouse and who feels too guilty or is made to feel too guilty by his children or other relatives to go ahead in another relationship. There were people who spent the next fifteen or twenty years or the rest of their lives never moving on with it. In my own case I was encouraged by my daughters to move on when I met somebody else. But still you get that kick of guilt, not a high kick, a kick in the gut, of guilt much like the survivors of the Holocaust, when those who lived felt guilty all their lives. So the man in the play was not able to give himself the enjoyment and the latitude of exploring this new relationship without always pulling in the guilt of being alive and his wife being dead. Around that point it's what I started to look for in almost every play. I think if there's any change, its that way. It's not necessary for me to be conceived of as a serious playwright, because the word is so bandied about I think that it gets misinterpreted, "serious" meaning the intention is lofty. It isn't any loftier than comedy can be, but I don't write a pure comedy anymore, with the exception of *Rumors,* where I intentionally did. I try to write plays about human emotions. I don't write plays about society. I find I can't. They become very current plays, and I like plays to be able to last for fifty or a hundred years or so. These are plays that contain serious subject matter. *Lost in Yonkers* is very well disguised, not that I meant it to be, but I couldn't open up the play showing the tragic side of Bella. It only came out when she was confronted with this chance to better her life and she didn't quite know how to do it and didn't get the permission of her mother, who was the one who stunted her growth in the first place. That has to be built to, and I see how the audience is taken by surprise as it goes on. If they leave after that first act, they say, "It's nice, it's funny, it's cute." And then the second act just hits them so hard. It's what you leave the theatre with, not what's going on in the beginning of the play, that's important.

Bryer: Perhaps this analogy will seem far-fetched to you, but one could say that it took O'Neill almost his whole creative life to write a play like *Long Day's Journey,* where, as he said, he "faced his dead at last." He had started to do it with *Ah, Wilderness!* in a more lighthearted way. *Ah, Wilderness!* and *Long Day's Journey* are really the same play, but one is weighted toward a comedic treatment and the other toward a more tragic approach. It seems to me that you could say the same thing about

Brighton Beach Memoirs and *Broadway Bound. Brighton Beach Memoirs* is your *Ah, Wilderness!,* and *Broadway Bound* is your *Long Day's Journey.* You started to confront your family directly in *Brighton Beach,* particularly through Eugene's narration in a comic way, and then in *Broadway Bound* you did so much more seriously.

Simon: There was a really valid reason for that. With *Brighton Beach* my mother was still alive, so she could come and enjoy it and *Biloxi Blues* as well. She died after that, so she never saw *Broadway Bound.* I would not have written *Broadway Bound* if my parents had been alive. I couldn't have put them up on the stage that way. I don't think I put them in an unsympathetic light certainly, but in a truthful one in a way. I was probably harsher on my father than I was on my mother. At that time in our lives, I really think she was the one who caused the anguish in the family. But I have more of an understanding of him now, having lived through some of the same things myself.

Bryer: So you think it was basically the death of your mother that enabled you to write *Broadway Bound* when you did?

Simon: It freed me to do it. I reveal things about her, her inability to be close and emotional. I don't remember ever being hugged by my mother as far back as being a child. I always knew that she loved me, but she was unable to show emotion. I did talk about something that happened to my mother personally, that she was burned in a fire. The grandfather talks about that. I don't go into it in *Broadway Bound,* but it must have affected their marriage very much—how she was scarred. She was actually scarred on the front, not on the back, as in the play.

Bryer: And you never could have done that if she'd still been alive?

Simon: No, I couldn't. When O'Neill wrote *Long Day's Journey,* he put it in a drawer and said it couldn't be done until twenty-five years after his death, which didn't happen of course. His wife had it done. I sort of felt that way. *Chapter Two* was cathartic for me. It helped me get rid of my own guilt by sharing it with the world. But *Broadway Bound* was not cathartic. It was an attempt to try to understand my family and my own origins. It's a play of forgiveness, and I didn't realize it until somebody associated with the play—the set designer or a costume designer—said after the reading, "It's a love letter to his mother." I had a very up-and-down relationship with my mother. I used to get angry at her very often, and I loved her too, but there was no way for either one of us to show it—and so there it is on the stage. I remember in real life once I gave a surprise birthday party for my mother—she really was surprised—and we brought out the cake. She couldn't smile or say, "This is wonderful." She just looked at me as she was about to cut the cake and said, "I'm still angry with you from last week when you did such and such." It was the only way she could deal with it. So when I wrote the play, what I had to do after listening to the first reading when I didn't have that scene about George Raft, I said, I've got to show the other side of my mother, show her when she was happy. I like that when, in the second act of a play, you begin to show what really is information that happened way before that, to give it late in the play.

Bryer: Do you have a favorite among your own plays? The last one you wrote?

Simon: Yes, it's generally that. It suddenly becomes the one that you're working on. But when I think of my favorite, I think about what my experience was when I wrote it and put it on. Was that a good time in my life, in my personal life and in doing the play? With some of the plays I had terrible times doing the play yet the play came out very well. Other times it was great fun doing it. I think the greatest kick I got on an opening night—when I knew I was sort of catapulted into another place in my life—was the opening night of *The Odd Couple.* It was accepted on such a high level by everyone. It was what you dream about—Moss Hart in *Act One*—the hottest ticket in town. That night was a terrific night!

Bryer: What about as a craftsman? Which of the plays are you proudest of as a piece of writing?

Simon: Structurally I like *The Sunshine Boys,* and I like this one structurally.

Bryer: The Sunshine Boys is my favorite Simon play so far, because of the integration of comedy and seriousness and because of the organic nature of that integration. Maybe it's an accident of the subject matter because you're dealing with comedians.

Simon: You're dealing with comedians, which gives you license for them to be funny. But the seriousness in the play was inherent too. It wasn't always written about because you knew that they were old, you knew they couldn't deal with things. One was really fighting for his way of life to continue; the other was quite satisfied to be retired and live in another way. So there was something classic about it. It just seems to hark back to another period in time. That play is done by more national theatres in Europe—in England or even Germany—because they relate to it in some part of their own culture, to the old vaudevillians and what's happened to them. They've died out. That's another play that sat in the drawer for six months after I wrote twenty-five pages of it, until I had lunch with Mike Nichols and said, "I'm kind of stuck. I have a play." I started to tell him the idea, and he said, "That sounds wonderful!" That's sometimes all I need—that's like a great review. "You really like that, Mike?" "Yes." And I went ahead and wrote the whole thing. *Bryer:* Can you think of plays that exceeded your expectations and plays that you had great expectations for that never reached them once you saw them on stage?

Simon: That's an interesting question because I think I always know what the reception is going to be. I'm rarely surprised. Sometimes I write a play knowing it's not going to succeed. There's a psychological subconscious will to fail after writing four or five hits—you don't deserve that much. I pick a subject matter that is so far out—something that I would not do right now. Not one that's more dangerous and that's taking more of a chance with an audience, but one that's almost guaranteed not to be commercially successful (not that I always know when it's going to be). *The Odd Couple* and *Barefoot in the Park* fooled me because they were so early in my career. I didn't know what to expect. When they were both such big hits, I was really shocked. But a play that I knew I wanted to write for a reason other than artistic or commercial success was something like *God's Favorite.*

God's Favorite was my way of dealing with my wife's death. It was *Waiting for Godot* for me. I could not understand the absurdity of a thirty-nine-year-old, beautiful, energetic woman dying so young. It was railing at God to explain to me why He did this thing, so I used the *Book of Job.* One critic cried on television in his anger: "How dare you do this to the *Book of Job!*" Yet there were critics like Walter Kerr, a devout Catholic, who loved it, just adored it. And so I wasn't too surprised that we weren't a major success, but I learned in hindsight that it was not a Broadway play. It should have been done Off-Broadway, as *Fools* should have been. *Fools* I did in a way like *Rumors.* Again it was farce in a sense. I just loved the premise. It's almost Hebraic culturally, like the towns written about by Sholem Aleichem in which there were stupid people (without ever going into the reasons why), and I had a curse in my town. I thought it was good. Mike Nichols came up and did it. We had a good time. If we had done it in a small theatre, it would have been fine—Playwrights Horizons or something like that—but not with the expectations of a Broadway audience, paying whatever it was at the time, expecting a certain kind of play.

I remember when we did *The Good Doctor,* which was another play written during my wife's illness, when they discovered that she would not live. I was just sitting up in the country, and I wanted to write to keep myself going, and I read a short story by Chekhov called "The Sneeze." And just to kill time I dramatized it. And I said, "Gee, this would be fun, to do all Russian writers and do comic pieces—or non-comic pieces—by them." I couldn't find any, so in order to give unity to the evening, I decided to do Chekhov, because he had written so many newspaper pieces where he got paid by the word. And I found as many of them as I could. Then when I tried them out of town, some of them didn't work. So I wrote my own Chekhov pieces, and some of the critics pointed them out and said, "This one is so Chekhovian," which wasn't his at all! I don't mean that as flattery to me but as not knowing by some of the critics. I remember a woman in New Haven coming up the aisle, and she said to me, "This isn't Neil Simon." So I asked, "Do you like it, or do you not like it?" She said, "I don't know. It's just not Neil Simon." I have to overcome their expectations of me so that they don't get to see what they want to see. It's like going to see Babe Ruth at a baseball game. If he hits two singles and drives in the winning run, it's not a Babe Ruth game.

Bryer: How do you feel about the current relationship between the theatre and film and TV? It's a cliché that television is ruining the theatre, that we are a culture of filmgoers not theatregoers. Do you feel those are valid kinds of observations? You once said you thought the biggest obstacle to theatre was the price of theatre tickets. Do you think it's really that?

Simon: That's one of them. It's only one of them. No, there's enough money around, I think, for people to go to Broadway theatre. I think we've lost the writers more than anything. David Richards of the *New York Times* recently said to me, "Do you realize you may be the only one left around who repeatedly works for the Broadway theatre?" And I said, "Well, they're all gone." Edward Albee hardly writes at all. Arthur Miller has grown older and writes occasionally for the theatre but rarely for Broadway—it's usually for Lincoln Center or someplace else. David Mamet now would rather direct and write his own films. Sam Shepard was never a Broadway writer. There are no repeat writers—the Tennessee Williamses, the George S. Kaufmans, or even Jean Kerr in terms of comedy. You talk to anybody today, especially in California, and they will use writing as a stepping stone to becoming a director. They want to be directors. It has to be about control. Even a promising young writer like John Patrick Shanley has a big success with *Moonstruck* after he had small success in the theatre. We had said this is an interesting playwright. He does *Moonstruck* and then he wants to direct—so he does *Joe Versus the Volcano,* and I'm sure he just wants to keep on directing. Nora Ephron writes a couple of movies that are nice, and now she wants to direct. I have no desire to direct at all. I see the soundness of it, in terms of movies. As I said before, I have no control over what goes on up on the screen or what's cut later. Between the director and the actors you lose all of that.

It's almost a mystery as to what's happened in the theatre. I think it's just changing. It's becoming regional theatre, and the plays are in a sense getting smaller, not necessarily in their scope. *Six Degrees of Separation* is a wonderful play. I really like that play. I'm not so sure, if it had opened on Broadway at the Plymouth Theatre, that it would have gotten the kind of attention, the demands for seats. It's viewed from a different perspective when it's presented in an off-Broadway atmosphere. You see what happens when they transfer plays. One of the few that transferred fairly well was *The Heidi Chronicles,* but even when you're watching *The Heidi Chronicles,* you say this isn't really a Broadway play. That could be a misnomer too, because it makes it sound crass and commercial, but *Amadeus* is a Broadway play, and I think it's a great play. I think most of Peter Shaffer's plays are wonderful plays: *Five Finger Exercise* and the one about the Incas, *The Royal Hunt of the Sun.* Tennessee Williams didn't write Off-Broadway plays except at the end of his career when the plays got smaller in their scope. *Cat on a Hot Tin Roof* is a beautiful play, but it's got size to it, and there is no one around who does that anymore. It's changed, I guess maybe the way painting has changed. I don't know who the great portrait painters are anymore, if they exist at all. I think it's economics that changes it. In the theatre now they are catering to an international audience. Who comes to America now but the people who have money—the Japanese or the Germans? They don't all understand English, but if they go see a musical like *Cats* they don't have to. Even *Phantom of the Opera*—if you don't understand it you can still enjoy it. If a play runs two years, it is amazing. Most musical hits will run ten years now. You can't get *Cats* out of that theatre. *Phantom* will be there forever. It will be interesting to see what happens with *Miss Saigon,* because it has this amazing anti-American number. When I saw it in London, you could almost cheer it, but if, when it opens in March, this war [the Gulf War] is still going on, there may be some repercussions.

Bryer: One of the things that occurred to me when I was watching *Lost in Yonkers* the other night is that you're one of the cleanest playwrights I know, even though you write about very intimate things.

Simon: You write to what fits the play. There are all sorts of four-letter words in *Rumors* because these are very contemporary people. In *Lost in Yonkers* you're dealing with the 1940s, and you're not only trying to emulate a play that might have existed in that time, but certainly what life was like at that time. And that kind of language, street language, I at least didn't hear that much. I never heard it at home, except maybe in a violent argument between my mother and father. It's interesting to watch playwrights like Tennessee Williams and Arthur Miller who never resorted to that language but found another language that was more potent. In doing *The Marrying Man* with Kim Basinger and Alec Baldwin, which was just an awful experience, she did this scene in which she was sitting in a box at the opera in Boston. She used to be Bugsy Siegal's girlfriend but is found by this guy who's a multimillionaire, and they get married—they're forced to get married through no intention of their own. Later on they fall in love and get remarried. She's sitting in Boston, and a man in the box is annoying her as she's sort of kissing the ear of Alec Baldwin. He keeps shushing her, and she says, "Oh, come on, this opera isn't even in English, you can't understand it." And it goes on, and finally she ad-libs, "Oh, go fuck yourself." And I said, "Wait, you can't say that." It had nothing to do with my thinking that the language is offensive, but it's so wrong for the character and for the tone of the movie. It's a movie that takes place in 1948. It's okay when the Alec Baldwin character and his four cronies are in the car. They use all sorts of language, but for her to use it in that place seemed so wrong for me. So it wasn't being prudish about anything. You've just got to use it where it's got some weight. Sometimes I would use "fuck you" or whatever it is once in a play, and it has much more impact than just using it all the way through. I like it when David Mamet does it sometimes, as in *American Buffalo.* It is said so often that it is no longer offensive. It bothers some people I know—they don't want to hear it. But it never bothers me. I think he writes in such wonderful rhythms and cadences that the language is so important, so precise.

Bryer: Linda Lavin once said apropos of *Last of the Red-Hot Lovers,* in which she was then appearing: "People come to the theatre to see their lives verified. They haven't been offended. The life they lead hasn't been challenged, it's been reaffirmed." And I think you once said, "recognition" is what you'd like to see your plays be all about. Let me be a devil's advocate and say that one should come out of the theatre upset, as Edward Albee insists. I don't mean necessarily emotionally upset, but something should have changed. You shouldn't have been patted on the head, you should have been disturbed. *Lost in Yonkers* can be a very disturbing play in that way.

Simon: Oh, absolutely.

Bryer: Do you think you've changed in that respect?

Simon: Yes. I remember that when I did *Plaza Suite* and I wrote the first act about the husband who's having the affair with the secretary, the general manager for the play read it and said, "You can't do this play." I said, "Why not?" He said, "Do you know how many men come from out of town and meet their secretary or somebody and come to this play. They'll be so embarrassed." I said, "Good, that's what I want to do. I want to shake people up." So I don't think I was trying to reaffirm middle-class values. In *Last of the Red-Hot Lovers* the man was trying to have an affair. I found him sort of a pitiful character, not even being able to break through that. I saw him in a way as an Everyman who finally had the courage to try to break out but didn't know how to do it. Sometimes those labels stick with you. But as I said, it's a glacier. It moves along and it changes and it pulls along the debris with it. I don't think I write that way. I think why I get bandied about a lot by critics is because of the success ratio. There must be something wrong when it appeals to so many people around the world. They hate it that I've become a wealthy person from the plays.

Bryer: You can't be any good if you're wealthy!

Simon: Yes. I remember at the time reading about Tennessee Williams's wealth, which was relative compared to today's market, but he was a fairly wealthy man because he was so successful. But he also took such chances with plays like *Camino Real.* He was a poet, and he made his reputation on plays like *The Glass Menagerie* and *Streetcar Named Desire.* It's because I do write plays that for the most part are so popular. I never mind a bad review from a good critic who has liked some of the work in the past and then says, "No, you didn't do it this time." I say that's valid, and I can accept it. I don't expect a rave from Frank Rich. Frank Rich always will find fault. He's tough to figure out, because he'll write a very middling review of *Brighton Beach* and talk about its faults and at the end of it say, "One hopes there will be a chapter two to *Brighton Beach.*" He finds fault with the play, yet he wants to see a sequel to it! I had no intention of writing a trilogy, I just wrote *Brighton Beach.* When I read his notice, I said, "Well, I'll do another play." You still don't think about a trilogy, because if the second play fails, who wants to see the sequel to a failure? So I wrote *Biloxi Blues,* which he loved. It won the Tony Award, and so I did the third one, which he again then finds fault with by saying, "I missed it being a great play." He gives it a negative sounding review by saying it almost reaches great heights but doesn't.

You have to steel yourself. You become very thick-skinned after a while, because you're out there naked and they are writing about you personally. They don't write about your work as much as who you are in the reviews. In a way I think the theatre has been changed a lot by critics who are now looking to make names for themselves. It bothers me that critics are hailed as personalities. Siskel and Ebert, good critics or bad critics, it makes no difference to me, I hate that they are celebrities and have such power. Fortunately there are so many people who write reviews for films, and people generally make up their minds to go see a film before they read the reviews. Not so with the theatre. The reviews mean everything. If you get a bad review in the *New York Times,* you can still exist, but you've got to overcome it.

Bryer: No, that's not exactly true. *You* can still exist. Neil Simon can still exist. A lot of other people can't with a bad review in the *Times.*

Simon: Well, it depends on the play. There have been a few that have existed without it, but it's very hard. Rich loved *Biloxi Blues,* and the first day after *Biloxi Blues* opened, we did an enormous amount of business, twice what we did on *Brighton Beach Memoirs.* But *Brighton Beach Memoirs* ran twice as long as *Biloxi Blues.* The audience seeks out what they want, and *Brighton Beach,* next to *The Odd Couple,* is played more than any play I've ever done. There is something about the idealization of the family in that play that we all dream about. They know it's an idealization. It's like looking back on your family album and seeing it better than it was.

Bryer: But it's not *Ah, Wilderness!* It's not that sappy.

Simon: Well, those were sappier days.

Bryer: There's a lot of what happens in *Broadway Bound* underneath the surface of *Brighton Beach.*

Simon: Oh, yes—the mother's hurt when she finds out that the father has had this heart attack and that the boy has lost all the money.

Bryer: What do you think you've done differently in *Lost in Yonkers?* What would you say has inched the glacier forward with this play?

Simon: I've written about much darker people than I ever have before. I've written about normal people in dark situations before—the death of spouses, the break-up of marriages (tragedies in proportion to their own lives at that time, as in *Brighton Beach*), anti-Semitism and antihomosexuality in *Biloxi.* But in this play I really wrote about dysfunctional people and the results of a woman who was beaten in Germany and who, in order to teach her children to survive, teaches them only to survive and nothing else. That's much further than I've gone in any other play, so it's deeper. It's why I want to do a musical next year, because I need really sure footing to go on to the next place. That doesn't mean I need to write about people even more dysfunctional, but as a matter of fact the play that I've been working on and haven't been able to lick quite yet is about two people in a sanitarium who have had breakdowns and find solace in each other almost more than in the doctor. I've written about thirty pages of it, and I've had it there for two years, and I'm anxious to write it. But each play comes when its time is ripe. Who knows? If at some point I lose faith in the musical I'm working on, I'll probably go back and start to write that play. Right now all I want to do is get out of Washington, go home, rest, come back, do the stuff in New York. Then I'll forget all about *Lost in Yonkers*. They all become a piece of the past for me. I've learned from them, and then they only come up in interviews like this, when you talk about them. I don't think of the plays. I don't try to remember or go back or ever read them and see what I've done to see how I could do that again. I want to go to some other place. I'm just hoping that there'll even be theatre enough around for people to want to go see these plays.

PART 2

ANXIETY AND ALIENATION: THE AMERICAN THEATRE, 1959 TO 1969

The years 1959 to 1969 marked a new era in the American theatre. Its starting point was as historically significant—and as seminal— as 1945 had been for an earlier generation of playwrights and directors. A radically new kind of drama emerged in 1959 with Jack Gelber's *The Connection,* an improvisational play in which jazz musicians on heroin sound a musical score attacking middle-class morality and happiness, and with Edward Albee's *The Zoo Story,* where a beatnik named Jerry validates the absurdity of life as he commits suicide to prove that relationships can be possible. A new generation of playwrights guided the American theatre in a bold yet brilliant new direction. It might be fairer to say that these playwrights did not so much reshape the American theatre as they reinvented it.

The American theatre was blessed with a wealth of new, talented playwrights in the 1960s, with first plays by a generation of unestablished, previously unproduced playwrights. During the 1950s it appeared as if the same playwrights kept recycling Broadway—Williams, Miller, Inge. The post-1959 generation of dramatists included women and other marginalized individuals such as Hispanics and blacks, as well as white males, the first two groups in significantly larger numbers than had ever been represented in the American theatre before. Consequently the American theatre experienced a democratization that it has progressively built upon and now can boast about.

The six playwrights interviewed in this section fairly represent the most significant dramatic activity of the 1960s. Beyond doubt, pride of place goes to Edward Albee who, as C. W. E. Bigsby rightly acclaimed, "dominated the American theatre of the 1960s." Bigsby clearly explains why: "His brilliantly articulate calls for a reinvigorated liberal humanism, his dramatic parables of the need for the restoration of human values on a public and private level struck just the right note for the

Kennedy years, as did his hints of a threatening apocalypse."[1] The plays for which Albee likely will be best remembered captured the New York stage in the 1960s: *The Zoo Story* (1959), *The American Dream* (1960), *Who's Afraid of Virginia Woolf?* (1962), *Tiny Alice* (1964), and *A Delicate Balance* (1964), for which he won his first Pulitzer Prize, and the strikingly Beckettian *Box* and *Quotations from Chairman Mao* (1968). Though central to an understanding of the theatrical experience of the 1960s, Albee and his work did not monopolize or preclude other kinds of drama. As Terrence McNally happily acknowledged in an interview included later in this collection, Albee "was an influence on any writer of my generation. He had to be. His stories were this startling explosion of language. . . . "

Of the women playwrights whose interviews appear in this section, Albee directly advanced the career of one of them, Adrienne Kennedy, and helped to shape the theatrical environment that encouraged the work of two more, Megan Terry and Maria Irene Fornes. In a sense Albee was Kennedy's mentor. In 1962 she was a member of Albee's nonprofit Playwright's Workshop, during which time she continued to work on her *Funnyhouse of a Negro*, which was produced as part of that workshop at the Circle in the Square Theatre. Two years later Albee's production company sponsored *Funnyhouse* at the East End Theatre, where Kennedy's play opened on 14 January 1964. When Kennedy won an Obie for *Funnyhouse* in 1965, Albee must have rejoiced with her. Kennedy's continuing gratitude to him is recorded in, among other places, the acknowledgments in her autobiography, *People Who Led to My Plays* (1987).

Kennedy's own voice, her anxiety, of course, are far different from Albee's. "My plays are meant to be states of mind,"[2] asserts Kennedy, whose haunting works are feminized, surreal nightmares of pain and punishment. Expressionistic fantasies of a black woman's psychic history, documented through rape and victimization, Kennedy's plays explore what it is like being a black woman in America. Her *Funnyhouse*, *The Owl Answers* (1963), *A Rat's Mass* (1967), and *A Lesson in Dead Language* (1968) confront issues of split personalities and cultural repression, heritage (white and black), gendered identity, and the central concerns of the struggle for justice and freedom in America during the 1960s.

Other women playwrights in this section also shaped the drama of this turbulent decade. Megan Terry, one of the founders of the Open Theatre, wrote the first American rock musical, *Viet Rock* (1966), a cry for liberation (from oppressive dramatic forms), for a society languishing in hypocrisy, and for women's rights. Similarly, the works of Cuban-born Maria Fornes contributed significantly to a highly political, alternative theatre in America during the 1960s. As Bonnie Marranca claims, Fornes is "one of the last real bohemians among the writers who came to prominence in the sixties."[3] Her plays into the 1990s continue her contributions to feminist aesthetics, audience interaction, and dramatic experimentation.

The theatre of the 1960s was aggressively experimental. For many historians it was America's most avant-garde theatre decade yet—highly revolutionary, radically absurdist, and aesthetically skeptical. The name of one of the major theatres founded in 1965, the Open Theatre, reflects the liminal (experimental) approach so many dramatists of the decade took. The dramatists of the 1960s were open to explore new dramatic forms and techniques to publicize the faults of a self-destructive America. Profiting from some of the most experimental work of the previous decade, such as Tennessee Williams's *Camino Real* (1953), the playwrights of the 1960s assaulted and discarded traditional, realistic notions of character and plot. In Megan Terry's plays, for example, characters blend into and are transformed by each other, dissolving the strictly codified boundaries of what individuality is (or is not). Similarly in Adrienne Kennedy's *The Owl Answers* one character becomes many others, such as "She who is Clara Passmore who is the Virgin Mary who is the Bastard who is the Owl"; in Kennedy's *Funnyhouse* Sarah the Negro reveals her fragmented selves through the Duchess of Hapsburg, Queen Victoria, Jesus, and Patrice Lumumba. The linear, realistic plots of an earlier generation, with an emphasis on causality and resolution, were rejected. In their place came the plotless plots or recursive plots of Jean-Claude van Itallie or Kennedy, where satisfying resolutions are impossible in the chaotic, surrealistic world of the 1960s. Even a seemingly realistic play such as Albee's *A Delicate Balance* ends with an existential nightmare, as the unnamed terror that afflicts Agnes and Tobias's friends, Edna and Harry, threatens to engulf them as well.

Finally, the theatre of the 1960s reveled in a great deal of role playing and games. Appropriately enough the title of act one of Albee's *Who's Afraid of Virginia Woolf?* is "Fun and Games," an accurate descriptor of what happens in so many plays of the decade. Yet the fun and games are intentionally deceptive, hiding a canker in the state and in the trauma of a character that particularizes the plight of the state. In *Virginia Woolf* Albee's childless couple, George and Martha, quarrel, destroy, and strip away all idealism, a "sad, sad" commentary on the national legacy of the Washingtons. Offering a frightening insight into the effect of Albee's attack on our national pride, Geri Trotta sardonically claimed it was "rather like finding a live tarantula at the bottom of a box of Cracker Jack."[4]

New theatres emerged to meet the needs of experimental plays and performance pieces in the 1960s. As the 1950s drew to a close, Broadway became much more conservative and costly; accordingly, producers opted for politically and socially safe plays that would attract a growing, upward-aspiring middle class who could afford theatre tickets. What Broadway shunned, Off-Broadway and Off-Off-Broadway welcomed and perfected. Though started before World War II, Off-Broadway theatre flourished in the late 1950s outside New York's Times Square theatre district on the lower East Side where the houses were much smaller than those of Broadway (150 to 200 seats) and the price of tickets far less expensive, thanks to lower rates sanctioned by Actors Equity. Theatres such as Circle in the Square, the Phoenix, the New York Shakespeare Festival, Roundabout, and Chelsea Theatre Center offered noncommercial, experimental plays to literate, usually liberal audiences. Off-Broadway theatres premiered the early works of many major dramatists of the decade, including Edward Albee's *The Zoo Story,* which had its American premiere on 14 January 1960 at the Provincetown Playhouse, where it ran for 582 performances, and Jack Gelber's *The Connection,* which opened at the Living Theatre on 15 July 1959 and stayed for 722 performances.

As an even greater contrast to Broadway commercialism and the courtship of the status quo in the 1960s, the Off-Off-Broadway effort supplied alternative, nonprofit theatre where politically radical (left-wing and anti-Vietnam War) plays appealed to the bohemian lifestyles of New York's Greenwich Village. The Off-Off-Broadway movement began in the late 1950s when Joe Cino founded Caffe Cino; and shortly afterward, in 1960, Ellen Stewart established La Mama, where Jean-Claude van Itallie was introduced to New York audiences with *War* in 1965. Al Camines spearheaded Judson Poets' Theatre, where Maria Irene Fornes got her start in 1965 with *Promenade,* a work on which she collaborated with Camines. Required reading about this theatre movement is Albert Poland and Bruce Mailman's *The Off Off Broadway Book: The Plays, People, Theatre* (New York: Bobbs, Merrill, 1972), which vividly describes the ethos of these theatres: "The places were small, nontheatrical facilities, makeshift theatres in cellars, bars, lofts, storefronts and coffeehouses. The tightness of the space forced the playwrights to work within stringent limitations" (xi). Poland and Mailman offer the following succinct definition of both the plays and the audiences typical of the Off-Off-Broadway theatre culture in the 1960s:

> The plays of Off Off have a common language that is built on a set of new symbols. The new symbols are a function of the new audience, for Off Off is an audience-oriented theatre. Not since the great age of the American music hall and the melodrama has there been such real audience devotion and interaction. The audience participates; they boo, they cheer, but most of all they *enjoy* the plays and they attend the theatre because the new symbols are as familiar to them as they are to the playwrights. One need only be familiar with general American sociology to understand the new syntax: the movies on Saturday nights, popcorn, Cokes, the radio, TV, comic strips, drugs, etc. (xi)

This new theatre was as right for the times as the times were right for it. The drama of the 1960s reflected and was sensitive to the changes transforming American society. It was a decade of cataclysm and change, socially and politically, at home and abroad. America was turned inside out. The Vietnam War accelerated in the early 1960s and by the end of the decade had split the country into warring camps, threatening to destroy the flower of a generation. Within five years three legendary American leaders had been assassinated: John Fitzgerald Kennedy in 1963 and Martin Luther King, Jr., and Robert F. Kennedy within two months of each other in 1968. Crises were normal occurrences. The Cuban missile crisis in 1962 armed America for what surely was thought to be Armageddon. In mid-1965, United States troops were sent to the Dominican Republic to put down a revolution by Communist-backed rebel forces. Racial tensions raged. In the streets violence erupted in Watts, Harlem, and elsewhere. In July 1967 President Lyndon B. Johnson sent federal troops into Detroit to quell the worst rioting yet. Other hydra dangers reared their heads, too. McCarthyism, the old enemy of the liberals of the 1950s, was supplanted by a new juggernaut, the industrial-military complex, which just as cruelly demanded human sacrifice. One of the most significant political events of the decade, the inauguration of John Fitzgerald Kennedy as the thirty-fifth president of the United States on 20 January 1961, took place on the day before one of the more important events in the theatre, the premiere of Edward Albee's *American Dream* at the York Theatre, a play whose groundbreaking effect might be compared to that which Arthur Miller's *Death of a Salesman* received over a decade before.

Great hope existed alongside poignant and potential despair, in the drama and in the state. As Thomas Adler observes about American society and drama: "*Death of a Salesman* [is a] drama as much about the decline of the American Dream as about the demise of Willy Loman. The works that follow in its path might be seen as variations on Miller's *Dies Irae* for the American Dream."[5] The titles of some of the leading plays of the 1960s underscore the theatre's worry over national myths about success, happiness, and colonization. Jean-Claude van Itallie's bitter *War* (1965) and his *American Hurrah* trilogy (1966), Megan Terry's *Viet Rock: A Folk War Movie* (1966), and Arthur Kopit's satire against genocide, *Indians* (1969), are manifestos of alienation and anxiety, testaments to the failure of the American dream. Interestingly enough George in the last act of Albee's *Who's Afraid of Virginia Woolf?* (1962) intones the *Dies Irae* litany for the dead, as much for the death of his imaginary son as for an American, indeed Western, civilization falling into dangerous decline.

Notes

1. C. W. E. Bigsby, *Williams/Miller/Albee,* vol. 2 of *A Critical Introduction to Twentieth-Century American Drama* (New York: Cambridge University Press, 1984), 327.

2. Adrienne Kennedy, *People Who Led to My Plays* (New York: Theatre Communications Group, 1987), 127.

3. Bonnie Marranca, "The Real Life of Maria Irene Fornes," *Performing Arts Journal* 8, no. 1 (1984): 34.

4. Geri Trotta, "On Stage: Edward Albee," *Horizon* 4 (September 1961): 79.

5. Thomas Adler, *Mirrors on the Stage: The Pulitzer Plays as an Approach to American Drama* (West Lafayette, Ind.: Purdue University Press, 1987), 103.

EDWARD ALBEE
Jeffrey Goldman

Edward Albee (Susan Johann Photography)

It was perhaps *the* most appropriate environment in which to interview Edward Albee: the rehearsal set for the Los Angeles production of *Who's Afraid of Virginia Woolf?* (1962). At center stage a chipped wooden coffee table wobbled in front of a faded green couch. Upstage right sat the play's ever-present bar, stocked with a variety of bourbon and whiskey bottles. As the rehearsal broke up and actors John Lithgow and Glenda Jackson exited the room, the Pulitzer Prize-winning American playwright took a seat on the tattered sofa.

Albee was preparing *Who's Afraid of Virginia Woolf?* for the opening leg of a tour that would take the play from the Doolittle Theatre in Hollywood to Houston to London and beyond. This was the second time Albee had directed *Virginia Woolf*—the first being the much-heralded 1976 Broadway production with Colleen Dewhurst and Ben Gazzara—and by the time the show left southern California, it had garnered mixed reviews: an enthusiastic *Newsweek* announced that "the play hasn't lost its power to shock," while the lukewarm *Los Angeles Times* complained that *Who's Afraid of Virginia Woolf?* "only stings us this time around, where once it stunned us."

But then again Albee has always had a precarious relationship with American theatre critics. Revered for such modern classics as *The Zoo Story* (1959), *The American Dream* (1961), *A Delicate Balance* (1966), *Seascape* (1975), and, of course, *Virginia Woolf,* he has also been vilified for writing *Malcolm* (his 1966 adaptation of James Purdy's novel), *The Lady from Dubuque* (1980), and *The Man Who Had Three Arms* (1982). The critical reaction to *The Man Who Had Three Arms* was highly representative. After a favorable response from the public in Miami and Chicago and during its preview engagement on Broadway, the play opened to hostile reviews and closed soon after. Subsequently it went on to win a significant award and wide accolades at the Edinburgh festival in Scotland. Such is the life of a playwright who refuses to pull any punches with his potential critics.

The following interview took place on 19 September 1989. Albee was dressed in a simple black shirt, grey pants, and black Reeboks. He had salt and pepper hair, a moustache, and glasses, but his otherwise extraordinarily youthful appearance belied his true age of sixty-one years. The soft-spoken Albee offered intense, measured responses throughout the interview, although his infamous wry and subtle humor surfaced frequently. In the background the stage hands broke down the set, while a photographer snapped photos of the playwright, who is generally considered to be one of the finest American dramatists of the past three decades.

In the five years since this interview was done, Albee has repeatedly demonstrated that he is among America's most significant and celebrated playwrights. His *Marriage Play,* which has been compared and contrasted with *Who's Afraid of Virginia Woolf?,* received its American premiere in 1992 at both the Alley Theatre in Houston and the McCarter Theatre in Princeton, following its world premiere at Vienna's English Theatre in 1987. In 1994 Albee received his third Pulitzer for *Three Tall Women,* a play that also had its world premiere at Vienna's English Theatre. In addition to winning the Pulitzer, *Three Tall Women* garnered the Drama Critics Circle, the Outer Critics Circle, and the Lucille Lortel awards. With this play Albee seems also to have received something none of his other works has. In a short interview with Steven Samuels ("Yes Is Better Than No," *American Theatre,* September 1994, 38), he observed, "*Three Tall Women* is the first play that has gotten almost unanimously favorable press in the United States." Albee continues to direct his and others' (for instance, Beckett's) works, to teach classes in playwriting (at the University of Houston and elsewhere), and to chair the Edward F. Albee Foundation to assist artists and writers.

Goldman: What are the primary ways the theatre has changed since the 1962 premier of *Who's Afraid of Virginia Woolf?*
Albee: The theatre. Define what you mean by the theatre.
Goldman: Okay, the American theatre.
Albee: The American theatre. What do you mean by that?
Goldman: Well, how about Broadway?
Albee: There is more interesting theatre going on in the United States than you would ever know about if you only went to Broadway theatre. I mean, the best regional theatre, the experimental theatres, the university theatres too—very, very interesting new work. I'm absolutely convinced that Broadway could vanish from the face of the earth and the American theatre as an art form would not be hurt at all.

And Broadway has become infinitely more difficult for valuable, useful, serious plays to get produced. When we first did *Who's Afraid of Virginia Woolf?,* we brought the play in, and it cost $45,000 to get it open, and ticket prices were $7—that was 1962. When we did a revival in '76 on Broadway, it cost $300,000 to open it, and ticket prices were up to $20. If we did it on Broadway this year, it would probably cost $800,000 or $900,000 to open it, and ticket prices would be up to $45. In the past producers and theatre owners were more willing to take chances on tough, serious plays and bring them right onto Broadway. Now, almost always, a serious play has got to prove that it is both serious *and* commercial. Being serious is no longer enough.
Goldman: Is this due to economic considerations?
Albee: Part of it has to do with the economical—the value of real estate, taxes, etc.—and part of it has to do with the fact that an audience that is paying $50 for a theatre ticket does not want to be hit over the head with ideas. They want *entertainment.*
Goldman: Do you think that the influence of Hollywood has anything to do with this?
Albee: Maybe audiences want our theatre to be more like television and film. I'm convinced that our society wants less social and political engagement and more entertainment.
Goldman: Is there a difference between European and American audiences?
Albee: This is a generalization, but European audiences tend to go to the theatre more regularly, are probably educated more in terms of serious theatre, and are more interested in theatre as an art form than as

merely entertainment. But that's shifting—European audiences are probably getting just as lazy as some of our American audiences!

Goldman: Why do you think critics often say that your work has a European feel to it?

Albee: Well, I'm not a regionalist, like Tennessee Williams or Sam Shepard or David Mamet. I guess my plays seem to translate very nicely into other cultures. But they *are* set in America, and I'm *clearly* an American writer, and my characters *are* American. But they're not regionalized, they're not that locale-specific.

Goldman: How have you changed as a playwright since the premiere of *Virginia Woolf?*

Albee: Apparently, considering the fact that I run into so much trouble, I haven't changed enough.

Goldman: Trouble with . . . ?

Albee: Oh, trouble with critics, management, audience. I suspect that I haven't accommodated the way I am supposed to. I've always just written whatever's been inside my head, whatever came naturally.

Goldman: Do you think that the initial popular support of *Who's Afraid of Virginia Woolf?* made the critics suspicious and even hostile toward your work?

Albee: I don't know what made those who became hostile hostile. Maybe they just disliked me, disliked the instant success, or maybe it was just dismay over things I was saying.

Goldman: How do you deal with the reaction to, say, *The Man Who Had Three Arms,* which was lambasted by the critics when it first appeared on Broadway in 1983, but which went on to win a prestigious award at the Edinburgh festival? Do you just laugh off the initial reaction?

Albee: Oh, you have to in order to protect your sanity! If you know that the work you do is good and is unintentionally or intentionally misunderstood or shot down for reasons that have nothing to do with the quality of your work, then naturally there's nothing you can do except just to go about your business and assume that in a more rational time people will say, "Gee, I wonder why the critics behaved so irrationally about that play?"

Goldman: Did this attitude take a long time to develop?

Albee: Not really. I've never been surprised by the reaction to plays of mine. I've been disappointed sometimes. Sometimes a play hasn't been allowed to reach the audience I thought it should. But if you know you've done your job properly you can't worry about it too much—you'd go crazy if you did.

Goldman: What do you think about all of the talk about Los Angeles becoming the major cultural and theatrical center of the United States—and possibly the world—within the next decade or so?

Albee: When I see as many good plays coming from experimental theatre out here as I see in New York, I'll be more convinced. Though I must say I am more pleased with Los Angeles than I am with other large cities. But I still think that going to the theatre is somewhat of an unnatural occurrence out here. It is not like New York, where going to the theatre is as natural as breathing.

Goldman: Why is that?

Albee: I don't know! It's not a theatre town! It's a film and television town! And most actors I meet out here complain about the fact that they are really being pushed into film and television and do not have the opportunity to do live work on the stage.

Goldman: Do you direct differently in Los Angeles than when you are staging a play in a theatre town?

Albee: No, I don't think so. You have to direct the play to know its intention. Trouble comes with too much accommodation. I would never cut a play of mine to make it more tolerable for an audience. You must make the assumption that an audience will come to the play and is interested in being in the theatre, interested in seeing the play, immersing themselves in it, and maybe even having a complex experience.

Goldman: You've directed work by such playwrights as Sam Shepard, Lanford Wilson, and David Mamet. Do you find directing your own work easier or more difficult than directing other playwrights' work?

Albee: It's probably a little easier directing my work because I know a little more about what the playwright had in mind. I have to invent a little bit more if I'm directing somebody else's work.

Goldman: What do you think about the school of thought that says a playwright shouldn't direct his or her own play?

Albee: Well, I don't think anybody should direct a play unless they are a competent director. I've learned how to be a competent director. Lots of playwrights have directed their own work—besides Shakespeare and Molière. In the twentieth century Brecht, Beckett, Gelber, Anouilh, Pinter, me. Lots of us direct our own work.

Goldman: What do you consider to be your greatest play?

Albee: I don't know whether *any* of them are great.

Goldman: How about your most satisfying?

Albee: I find this is to be true with every single one that I do. As I go on, I find that the next one is always more interesting than the previous. You know, it would be an awful, terrible thing to think that you've done your best work. I like to think that maybe it's three plays down the line.

Goldman: Who would you cite as your major influence outside of the theatre? For instance, I've read that you collect art.

Albee: I've been influenced by everybody, and I'd be a fool if I weren't. I don't think that anybody in the creative arts can be a well-rounded, well-informed person unless they're conversant in all the arts. A playwright who doesn't know painting and sculpture and classical music—especially classical music, since composing music and writing for the theatre are so closely allied—and doesn't know what's going on in fiction and poetry is probably not an educated man and will put terrible limits on himself. All of the arts feed on each other, all of them influence each other, and it's very valuable and useful to know everything that you can.

Goldman: Do you have a deep interest in classical music?

Albee: I wanted to be a composer when I was thirteen, but I didn't become one because I was incompetent. So I started studying music on the phonograph, and I would dare say that I've probably listened to—very conscientiously—more classical music than anybody who is not a composer.

Goldman: You mentioned the similarity between the theatre and music, between dramatic structure and musical structure. Can you explain this to me?

Albee: Well, a string quartet is a performed piece that is heard and seen—so is a play. There are great similarities—structural similarities, psychological similarities. There are voices speaking, instruments speaking . . .

Goldman: Does it primarily have to do with the language of the play?

Albee: No, it's in the psychology. A good piece of music has a structure that gives it a psychology, proper duration, whereas a bad piece of music doesn't end where it should—it goes on too long, ideas run out. The relationships are very complex and intertwined. A composer and a playwright use notation in very much the same way—rise, soft, fast, slow—it's a profound relationship.

Goldman: Have you ever written a play with a particular piece of music in mind?

Albee: No, but I am aware sometimes when I'm writing a play that this section is a passacaglia, for example, or a theme and variation.

Goldman: Can you describe the process you go through when writing a play? For instance, do you, as Pinter has said he does, begin with two characters in a room?

Albee: Doesn't everybody? Didn't Shakespeare, didn't—

Goldman: Well, I don't know. Is that the germ? Or do you pick up ideas from something you read in the newspaper?

Albee: No, I've never—with the exception of *Bessie Smith*—never known where it came from. Everything starts coming into focus at the same time—the environment, and the characters, their relationship to each other—it just starts coming into focus.

Goldman: Do you use an outline?

Albee: No. I will think about a play for quite a while before I start writing it down. The best way for me to lose interest in a play is to write it down.

Goldman: You have said that the unconscious is the most efficient part of your mind. Why is that?

Albee: It must be since my conscious mind is very inefficient! I seem to come to lots of creative and dramatic conclusions which I inform myself of, so obviously I am moving from the unconscious to the conscious. I rely upon the unconscious mind for creativity, just as most people do. And the conscious mind is a kind of translator.

Goldman: Do you believe that there is such a thing as the perfectly made play?

Albee: In which there is nothing missing and no excess?

Goldman: Yes.

Albee: Oh, I've seen a few of them I think.

Goldman: Care to name names?

Albee: A couple of Beckett's plays, one or two of Chekhov's. I see them now and again.

Goldman: Do you still believe that, as you've once said, "a text is never dependent on performance and that no performance is as good as the performance the author saw when he wrote the play"?

Albee: I was talking about a good play. Now, a bad play . . . most performances are better than the play. For most good plays the performance does not add anything to the play, it merely brings the play to its own life. You see, the better the actors you have, the closer the author's intention will be achieved. A great play is not *improved* by a performance, it is *proved* by a performance. The best actors in the world aren't going to make a Chekhov play any better than it is. Or a Beckett play. They're first rate! It's the responsibility of the actors to try to prove that they're as good as the play. In a lousy play the actors have got to be compensated for the fact that the play is lousy.

Goldman: Do you think there are many actors out there who would agree with you?

Albee: Yes. The professional and intelligent ones.

Goldman: You once said that it was one of the responsibilities of playwrights to show people how they are and what their time is like, in the hope that perhaps they'll change it. Do you still believe this?

Albee: Sure.

Goldman: What other responsibilities does the playwright have?

Albee: Oh, to write as well as he can, to tell as much of the truth as he knows—as clearly and as honestly as he knows it. Not to lie, not to deal in half-truths. You see, all art is useful. There's no point if it's merely decorative. Art tells us who we are, how we live, our consciousness. The whole concept of metaphor is so important to the human animal, and that's what art does—deals in the metaphor. And so all good art is useful! And that's why the merely decorative, the merely escapist, is a big waste of everybody's time.

Goldman: But you're not a great fan of social realism are you?

Albee: The only problem I have is that it limits its scope to accommodate the problems it addresses. I had a problem with a lot of the agitprop plays that were written in the 1930s—they just weren't very good plays. I have no objection to a first-rate play of social realism. But I don't think that you can justify writing a bad play just because it deals with social realism.

Goldman: Do you see yourself as a social critic or as a writer interested more in metaphysical issues, interested in penetrating, as George in *Virginia Woolf* says, "the bone and the marrow"?

Albee: I don't see how you separate the two.

Goldman: Really?

Albee: I mean, most of my plays do deal with people in the context of relationships, which is a microcosm and a macrocosm. If the play doesn't transcend what it is specifically about, it doesn't resonate and therefore isn't any good. It's got to be about not only how these couples live, but how we live as a society.

Goldman: As a playwright what do you think are the major issues confronting America today?

Albee: Too many people don't live their own lives, they pass through their lives half-asleep. I think that's a great waste of time. Most people do not wish life to be an adventure, they wish it to be a nice, slow descent. Most people are far more interested in comfort than they are in adventure, in escape rather than engagement.

Goldman: What about on a purely social level?

Albee: How—how do you separate these? A society is made up of people who run their society based upon their own needs and how they wish to participate. If we have people who do not wish to be living in an adventurous society, we end up with reactionary know-nothing dodos, which has been happening for quite a while in this country. You can't separate the two; they're desperately related!

Goldman: What are your feelings on the current war on drugs in America? Are you interested in writing about this subject?

Albee: I'm less interested in addressing specific things than I am in addressing the kind of people we are that permit certain things to happen. Now, for example, there would be no drug problem in the United States if people did not want to take drugs. Right? So, really the way to address the drug problem is to create a society in which people do not want to take drugs. The people who take drugs are the people who are affluent and the people who are very poor. Right? People with money and people without money. That seems to be the division in our society, there being no middle ground anymore: people have money, people don't have money. People are enfranchised, people are disenfranchised in this society. You have to make the people who have the money, who do drugs on a social level, want to participate so much in their lives that they don't want the escape of the drugs. Now, the people who are poor and desperate and are using drugs because reality is too hideous to tolerate—you've got to create a society in which they don't have to live in those conditions. If you accomplish both of those things there'd be absolutely no drug problem in this country.

The drug program the Bush administration has put forward, as I see it, is spending infinitely too little money on alleviating the poverty in this country. You can take care of the drug problem in this country by creating a society in which you don't have so many desperate, disenfranchised minority poor. The Bush administration gives the impression that they are much more interested in solving the drug problems of the upper-middle-class white kids. And it strikes me as being ultimately, if not phony, then certainly badly misdirected.

Goldman: Let me ask you this, since I think it ties in to what you've just said in a roundabout way. Your characters, versus those of a playwright like O'Neill or Williams, are always aware of the illusion they are creating around themselves. They admit that they invent an illusionary life. Do you think it is sometimes better to live life as a self-inflicted illusion rather than survive the day-by-day realities of it?

Albee: Well, obviously I prefer that people not have false illusions and that they participate completely in their own lives! The majority of my plays are about people who are deluded—consciously or unconsciously, in one way or another. And I want to say, "Do it!" Shake 'em. "Stop it! Do it!"

Goldman: Do you have any comments or predictions about the future of theatre and your role in it?

Albee: Oh, I don't know. I'm not a crystal ball gazer.

MARIA IRENE FORNES
Una Chaudhuri

Maria Irene Fornes (photo © Harry Heleotis)

In Maria Irene Fornes's recently published libretto for an opera entitled *Terra Incognita*, a character remarks: "Just because I am in Spain, I think people are speaking Spanish to me when they are as plain as day speaking English. Doesn't that happen to you all the time: that after a while you don't know what language you are speaking?" Fornes's theatre exists to bring us to the recognition that our lives are a constant negotiation between what we think and what is there before us, "plain as day." Having begun her artistic career as a painter, she composes her plays meticulously to reveal that the complex coordinates of real life contain, direct, and illuminate our apparently illogical actions, our relentlessly paradoxical emotions.

The real life that gives every Fornes play its rock-solid foundation is a seamless amalgamation of cultural patterns and biological experience. It inscribes itself within the bodies and beings of her characters, making them extraordinarily present, inhabiting their social roles—roles of class, of gender, of nationality, of generation—in a way that far exceeds current theoretical notions of performative identity, while always escaping the reductiveness of traditional essentialisms—biological, psychological, moral.

It is tempting to locate this conceptual feat—this achievement of a dramatic world that is both compellingly specified yet existentially unfettered—in Fornes's own biography. Having left her native Cuba at the age of fifteen to immigrate to the United States in 1945, she spent the first three years of her artistic career in the early 1950s living and painting in an international community in Paris. After her return to America in 1957, she became a playwright almost by accident, with only the most minimal formal knowledge of theater. Her first play, the astonishing *Tango Palace,* outlined the terms of an original and sophisticated theatrical imagination, in which such fundamental life experiences as birth, death, love, and domination were inflected through the performative modes of speaking, reading, moving, and acting.

Her next few plays put her at the heart of the then-burgeoning Off-Off-Broadway movement, whose energy and commitment to experimentation ideally supported her innovative yet nonprogrammatic dramatic vision. The movement, with which Fornes strongly identifies herself even today, rejected the values of commercial theatre and encouraged constant experimentation in form and subject. In such plays as *The Successful Life of Three* (1965), *Promenade* (1965), and *Molly's Dream* (1968), the Fornes method began to emerge: an endlessly surprising mingling of whimsical invention with the intense rhythms of people living and loving. Perhaps nowhere is this mixture better seen than in the musical *Promenade* (1965), which tells the story of two escaped convicts, identified simply by their numbers, 105 and 106, as they make their way through a fantastic social scene, peopled by characters with names like Miss I, Miss O, and Miss U. Complementing her irreverent attitude to society's shibboleths, a sophisticated political vision emerged in her plays of this period, exemplified in what is perhaps the most fiercely felt anti-Vietnam war play of the sixties, *A Vietnamese Wedding* (1967). While revealing Fornes's deep affinity with the central gestures of the sixties avant-garde (the play is a simple ceremony in which the audience is asked to participate), *Wedding* also adumbrates the terms of a dramatic vision, which, like few others, survived beyond the culture of radical experimentation that gave it birth: a politics of experience rooted in a sense of the vibrant continuity between public issues and private lives.

After a fallow period Fornes returned to the theatre in 1977 with her masterpiece, *Fefu and Her Friends.* To the delicate sense of structure and lucid action that had distinguished her earlier works, *Fefu* added a whole new palette of emotion: the darker, more violent, and more disturbing strata of the psyche seeped onto the still-luminous Fornes stage. A more political and historical imagination could now be seen undergirding her ongoing theatrical meditations on the psychocultural anatomy of the present, on its vulnerability to nuclear destruction (*The Danube*, 1982), to poverty and ignorance (*Mud*, 1983), and to political and sexual violence (*The Conduct of Life*, 1985).

Today, at the age of sixty-three, Fornes remains as active as she has been for the last three decades, writing, directing, and teaching. She was awarded the Obie Award for Sustained Achievement in 1982, *Terra Incognita* was performed at Yale in 1993, and she is at work on several other projects. This interview took place in October 1993 in the Greenwich Village apartment she shares with her mother.

Chaudhuri: People who write about you often point out the fact that, despite your long and unbroken career in the American theatre (you are widely cited as being one of the few "survivors" from the experimental avant-garde of the 1960s and 1970s), your work remains largely unrecognized by the mainstream of American theatre. In spite of the ever-increasing critical attention and acclaim your work receives, in spite of the many Obie awards you've garnered, you remain decidedly on the fringe. In his *Village Voice* article in 1986, Ross Wetzsteon theorizes that the reason for this is that your constant experimentation in form and style—the very thing that has kept your work so alive and made your career so interesting—has made it hard for people to get a "fix" on you. "There's no Fornes 'signature,' " he writes, "to capture the attention of either the casual theatregoer or the middlebrow critic." However, after discussing your plays, he concludes that "there is . . . a Fornes signature after all—emotional complexity conveyed through ruthless simplicity, moral concern conveyed through a wholly dramatic imagination." Now, rather than ask you whether you agree with this, I'd like to ask you what you think about this whole issue of an artistic "signature," and what the general idea of cachet means to you personally, as an artist.

Fornes: Well, I think an artist should not work on an artistic signature any more than a person should work on a personal style. If a style results from your effort, that's fine, but the moment you concern yourself with creating an image, you cease to concentrate on your work. And the work demands all your concentration.

The changes in my work are always of great value to me, even when the first manifestations of that change have not been artistically successful. Each change has represented a new courage, a new knowledge.

And if I have courage and I trust it, it has always yielded something interesting.

Chaudhuri: So you're never interested in seeking some sort of security or stability in an ongoing artistic identity?

Fornes: No, not at all. The moment you concern yourself with any kind of security, you are doing something detrimental to your work. Quality is achieved by constant search, and sometimes by dangerous search. You follow your artistic curiosity and your artistic impulse. There are times when you say, "I don't know what I'm doing. This feels so strange to me. I am interested in doing this, I want to do it, I am driven to do it, but it feels so peculiar, I don't know if it's good, I don't know if it makes any sense." But you still have to do it. If you really are concerned with the quality of your work, you have to do it. That is how you develop your craft and a sensitivity to your medium. This must be your constant concern.

Chaudhuri: So what concerns you most is not the play you will end up with but rather keeping the artistic process as alive and open as possible.

Fornes: That is how you will produce the best work. Part of the search is to analyze the process. There are times when we do something and we don't know how we did it. So we need to analyze the circumstances when it was coming out right, and then we begin to discover technique and creativity—technique for ourselves. We need to acquire the craft and the knowledge of the medium that is theatre. There are many craft secrets that I don't know yet, so the process continues. People think that because theater is as old as life, we know all about it. But we don't. We can see this very clearly when we have someone like Robert Wilson, who dared to plunge into the theatre in a way that was almost like committing suicide. Now we can say, "But of course! It's so good, therefore he knew exactly what he was doing and what he was saying." Well, that is so, but he went out on a limb. He could have crashed and destroyed his possibility of working. But he didn't. And it's quite clear now that what he was doing is theater. It's just theater that, as far as we know, had never been done before. Wilson understood that there is a way of doing theater that had not been done before, and he knew how to do it. And that's what's exciting. What's exciting is to have a relationship to the art itself, to the craft itself, and to be honest, to work very hard, not to be arrogant or self-conscious, but to have that relationship with the art. Not to wonder if people are going to like it or not.

The concern has to be with the work itself. It's the artist and the work who know. It has to be the artist who knows; it cannot be the public; otherwise the art doesn't grow. Whenever I say that, people think that I'm elitist and that it's undemocratic to say something like that, but that's how it is. Any new development in art or science or politics has to come from a single mind, from someone who is dedicated to that work. Years later the public will begin to catch on.

Chaudhuri: Among the things you are known for are your unorthodox compositional strategies. A number of interesting and delightful stories have been told about how you get started writing, such as the story of how a Hungarian language lesson record led you to write *The Danube.* How does your writing happen? Where do your plays begin, and how do they develop on the page?

Fornes: Well, basically I do think that what drives me to write is an investigation. When I am writing, I feel I am making up something, and I am deciphering it at the same time. I think I am investigating something. And in order to investigate something, it has to begin to exist. So, I do writing exercises. I start writing simply to put something down, not because I think it's going to become a play, but just because it is something that is in my mind. And then I examine it. I cannot write a play just because I think I have an interesting story. If I start that way, I can't write. I get paralyzed. So there's an exercise or a warm-up. Then sometimes an exercise like this stays very vividly in my mind, and those characters and that world keep coming back to me, so I keep writing more of it until it becomes a play.

Chaudhuri: Although you are known primarily as a playwright, your work in the theatre extends beyond writing. You have had a long career as a director, both of your plays and others', and as a teacher of playwriting. How does your work as a director and as a teacher connect to your playwriting? Do you regard directing as a final stage of writing? Can you tell me about some specific instances where your directorial work has changed the text you began with?

Fornes: Any play that I write has many drafts. And I'm sure every playwright, no matter how clear they are at the outset, shapes their plays as they go along. Playwrights usually don't start with a very specific idea. Rather they become interested in a set of characters, or a theme, or a situation, but how they are going to work on it is not clear to them. They start writing, and they continue writing, and then they do a lot of editing. Plays are changed and molded all along. There are writers who start with an ending in mind—as soon as they start, they know how their plays are going to end. So there is a beginning and an end, but the middle has to be molded. I don't know any playwright who doesn't go through a number of drafts and rewrites. Even after the rehearsals start, they are rewriting.

When I direct a play, the first time is usually a workshop, so I do a lot of revisions. And then if the play is going to be done again, or if the play is going to be published, I do more revisions. If I find something that could be improved, something I hadn't noticed before, I keep revising it. So that with every single play of mine, on the first production, the changes are incredible—endless changes, on every single one of my plays, without any exception.

People have the idea that theatre is something that can be completely planned, and fortunately it's not. I say "fortunately" because, to me, that's what's interesting about theater. It's not like making a building, where you make a plan, and you visualize all its details and make drawings that are exactly the way it's going to look. Theatre's not like that. No matter how much you plan it, when it's on its feet, you discover all sorts of new things.

Chaudhuri: And what are the major sources of this transformation? The actors' special qualities? The space?

Fornes: Sometimes. But for the most part it is the play itself. That's the nature of theatre. It is the same as if you get a recipe for a dish, and you cook it according to the recipe, and it doesn't taste right. Only the people who have cooked it before would do it right. A friend of mine, Willa Kim, is a very good cook. She was asked to do a Korean dinner for one of the "home" magazines. Now, the process was this: they asked her to send in the recipe, and they cooked it themselves according to her recipe and asked her in to look at it and taste it. Well, it wasn't right. She had left out many important details—how long should the garlic be cooked? how hot was the oil when the garlic was put in?—very important little things that were not there in the written recipe. Then they asked her if she would come in one day and cook it in front of them. She cooked it, and they watched and wrote everything down, and then they cooked it according to the new recipe. This time, when she tasted it, it was right.

In the theatre this doesn't happen only when the director is someone other than the playwright. It also happens when the playwright is directing the play. There are things that you take for granted when you are writing, and then you have to figure out how they should be done. When you write a play, you have the recipe, but you don't have the performance. And in rehearsal you notice how many details were left inconclusive. It isn't that somebody misunderstood the play. It is that the play was dealing only with the reality of the imagination and not yet dealing with material reality. The more you know about theatre, the more you see how many things are left out, how many things are not clear, and how many things could work better. So you make the changes.

Chaudhuri: That's a wonderful analogy. The best I've ever heard for the relationship between text and performance. How do you experience your plays when they have gone through the hands of another director? Is it illuminating, surprising, depressing?

Fornes: I have to say that I have seldom enjoyed watching a play of mine directed by somebody else. I seldom get anything out of it. This is not surprising. The first time I direct a play, even a play I wrote, I'm just putting my feet in the water. The second time I direct it, the play begins to take shape, and the third time is when I feel that I know the play directorially. Now, how could somebody who is coming from nowhere do something good with it the first time they try it? I feel that even though I wrote the play, I don't know it. So how can somebody from the outside come and do something spectacular? Not likely, unless this person is spectacular.

Chaudhuri: What is the role of teaching in your life? How does your teaching relate to your writing?

Fornes: I like to share my own discoveries about writing, because that's what teaching is, to show the students some possibilities. Or even to give them the desire to find their own way to go about writing.

Chaudhuri: Are you saying that one can't really teach writing, that one can just help start the process in other writers and just get them connected to their own process?

Fornes: Getting them connected to their own process is teaching writing.

Chaudhuri: I mentioned the Hungarian language lesson record that led to *The Danube,* especially to the bilingual device you employ in many of the scenes of that play. Many other of your plays include foreign language snippets, often translations of dialogue already delivered in English. What is your relationship to languages (plural), and how much of it do you think is determined by the fact that, like many writers of this century, you have always written in what is essentially a second language?

Fornes: Yes, I'm sure that has a lot to do with it. There is a very special and very wonderful experience in learning how to name things in a foreign language. It is both humbling and godlike, because you possess things when you name them. When you learn a foreign language you learn to think differently. This also happens when you move to another country or another city, even if they speak the same language. Things don't mean exactly the same.

Chaudhuri: A number of your plays involve the figure of reading: characters will read out things, often in a way that draws attention to itself as a reading. Mae in *Mud* reads out an amazing paragraph from a book on the life of a starfish. *Molly's Dream* begins with Molly reading out a story with dialogue from a magazine. She then gradually begins to perform the dialogue. This seems in some way linked to the central device of your first play, *Tango Palace,* in which Isidore reads many of his lines from cards, which he then discards ostentatiously, implying some kind of ambivalence between speech and writing, speaking and reading. In *Fefu and Her Friends,* the women gather to rehearse a presentation, the centerpiece of which is a reading of a section of "The Science of Educational Dramatics" by Emma Sheridan Fry. How do you think of this whole issue of reading what is written and its relationship to speaking and performance?

Fornes: It is beautiful to see someone read to another person onstage, in the same way that it is beautiful to see people playing music and singing for one another. In films of the thirties and forties a way of depicting a sense of well-being at home was to have someone singing while someone else accompanied that person on the piano, to have a duet of violin and piano. It is theatrically beautiful and useful to represent harmony and to let the audience rest a while.

Chaudhuri: Your plays are now increasingly included in college courses and anthologies. Do you think your plays can be enjoyed and engaged just as well, if differently, by readers as well as by spectators? Are they "readerly" works as well as works for the stage?

Fornes: I think they are, but you would know that better than I, since I have never read them without knowing what's in them. I would say they are, because on a first reading actors seem to be able to make sense of them, and people have a sense of what is happening.

Chaudhuri: This brings up the whole question of production as interpretation. What you just said suggests that you regard your plays as having quite stable meanings, meanings that are encoded in the text and can be recovered from it and put onstage. Are you ever surprised to find that the meanings that emerge in production are different from what you felt were contained in the text?

Fornes: I am surprised, sometimes pleasantly and sometimes unpleasantly. Some willful interpretations of a play violate something of value that is contained in the play. If something of value is violated, whether in a play or in anything else, it is objectionable.

Chaudhuri: Your people, your characters, seem, on first acquaintance, strange and unfamiliar. This is because they do not behave the way dramatic characters usually do: they do not explain themselves or furnish coherent and extensive accounts of their inner and outer lives. Instead, to an extent unmatched by those of any other playwrights—including playwrights known for their antipsychological characterology, such as Beckett and Ionesco—your characters simply speak and act as they please. One has to take them as one takes people in real life, with all their contradictions and enigmas. Do you feel you know these people "better," in the sense of more thoroughly, more coherently, than we can? What is your relationship to your people, and what relationship do you want your spectators to have to them?

Fornes: I experience my characters as real people. I don't think they are so strange. They may be unfamiliar, but I don't see this as being strange. Most characters in dramatic literature are unusual. Not even in soap operas are characters familiar. And if you go out into the world, you may find that what you think is usual may be strange to others. When my characters start behaving in a one-key or automatic manner, I feel that I have lost touch with them and that the play has gone flat.

Why should theater be limited to the rules that some people without imagination created so that they could write about it? If you have imagination, you can write about things with imagination. I am so amazed when people say—and they say over and over and over—that in spite of the fact that I didn't seem to be following any of the rules, my play was very moving. What do they think the theatre is? A baseball game? I don't even know what rules they are talking about. I think that if I had known those rules, I may have never written a play.

Chaudhuri: One of your best-loved plays is *The Successful Life of Three.* The title of that play points up one of the characteristics of your dramatic worlds, namely, that in them relationships are rarely contained or negotiated between two people. One important exception to this is *Tango Palace,* which is in some sense a play about nonrelationships, about the consequences of an almost insane level of narcissism and solipsism. How do you think of all these triads that people your plays? Is the only successful life a life of three?

Fornes: I would say three or more. For the stage two is just not a good number. It locks in. I would say that one is better than two, as hard as one is. *Mud* started as a two-character play. I wrote the first two scenes of *Mud,* we started rehearsing at the Padua Hills. After a couple of days I thought, "I don't want this to be a two-character play. I can't stand two-character plays. I have to get another character." Then I thought, "Okay, Mae has a father." And there was an actor in the company who was old enough to play Mae's father. So I asked him, and he said, "Could

I see the script?" And I said, "Well, there's no script yet." And he said, "Fine. I'll do it." Then two days later he said that he was sorry he couldn't do it, that he'd said yes because he wanted to work with me, but that he was already overworked with technical work besides acting in another play. So I asked John O'Keefe to play the part. I thought, "He's not old enough, but if I put gray on his hair he'll look old enough." Then I started writing, and, without knowing how, there was no father but another man, Henry. Had the other actor done the play, there would have been a father, and the play would have been entirely different.

Chaudhuri: You have often spoken about the whole vexed question of your relationship to feminism and your reaction to feminist critics. In an article you wrote for *American Theatre* back in 1985, you said that you are more interested in the experience of women as "female organisms" than in the cultural or social coding of gender. Does the "female organism" call for a female dramaturgy? Is there a female aesthetic?

Fornes: Aesthetics is a feminine thing. When a man has an aesthetic sense, that is thought of as the feminine side of him. I'm trying to think of a male playwright who has a more of a female sensibility. I would say that Chekhov has more of a feminine sensibility than other playwrights. There is something about the way Chekhov looks at his characters and at the world, and the way he laughs at the whole sense of conventional structure, whereas others take conventional structure very seriously. Brilliant men like Ibsen have been quite satisfied to follow conventional structure, but Chekhov just laughed at it. You can see that he knows very well what he is doing—it isn't as if he had never heard of it. He just laughs at it, and he structures his play in manners that are a lot more complex, and the structure is very solid.

Chaudhuri: So disrupting or departing from conventional structure would be one sign of a female sensibility?

Fornes: To say departing would suggest that that which is conventional is basic and primordial. Conventional structures appear to be strong and fundamental when they are reigning, but when you look at history, you see they are ephemeral. Structure is essential to art, but I don't think any particular form is designed by a higher order. Look at dwellings. Structure is necessary to create a pleasant and practical living space. But look how the shapes of dwellings change according to time and culture and weather and economic and social class and individual imagination.

Chaudhuri: But you seem to be saying that there is such a thing as "male" structure and such a thing as "female" structure and, so far, that "female" structure tends not necessarily to observe these convenient, conventional patterns. But beyond that, can we describe it?

Fornes: I would rather say that there is individual structure. Each individual has his or her own sense of structure, which may or may not be relinquished in favor of something more conventional. Each person has an innate preference for certain rhythms, certain tones, cadences, and all of that ends up forming personality, a style, a sense of structure. An artist should never relinquish this. An artist should not speak with a common voice but with a singular voice. How could this singular voice continue being singular if it succumbs to common principles? Only in theatre do we have the notion that the writer should have a common voice, a common vision, a common concern to appeal to every one of us. Some works do, but that is not achieved by speaking with a common voice. On the contrary it is achieved by a very singular genius. None of the other arts do. Maybe this is because there are so many hands involved in making it. As if the specifications must be basic and simple, in the same way that instructions for do-it-yourself merchandise have to be kept simple, so all kinds of hands can put it together. In a sense so everyone can play.

Chaudhuri: Fefu and her Friends is also one of the greatest examples I know of what is now a kind of subgenre, the community-of-women play. Would you comment on this aspect of the play? What does Fefu mean when she says that if women were to recognize each other, "the world will be blown apart"?

Fornes: What she means is that women who try to ingratiate themselves to men socially and intellectually, and who do not recognize the importance of other women in the presence of men, behave as if the world would be blown apart if they recognized other women. And what she means by "the world being blown apart" is that they feel that if they did, men would feel dethroned and would leave them for women who would put them back on pedestals so that they would feel again smart and on top of everything. That is what she means. That women play up to men's egos shamelessly, or they used to. They don't so much anymore, but they did when the play was written.

Chaudhuri: For many people Julia's hallucinatory monologue is the interpretive key to *Fefu and Her Friends.* But I have always been most arrested by another speech, the one in which Fefu tells Emma how she feels. She says, "I am in constant pain . . . I can't describe it . . . it's as if normally there is a lubricant . . . not in the body . . . a spiritual lubricant . . . and without it, life is a nightmare, and everything is distorted." I think this is a very strong speech. Am I right in reading this as an account of what is nowadays called clinical depression?

Fornes: I suppose it is, in its early stages.

Chaudhuri: Is Fefu's condition related to Julia's nightmare—is it a more commonplace version of it? Is she experiencing what normal women experience, but that Julia sees in a more intense way, and is that why she has to kill Julia?

Fornes: Fefu's experience is more common. It is a painful and distorted sense of reality, but it is a common and recognizable experience. In a sense it is an early stage of Julia's condition. But Fefu doesn't kill Julia; she kills a rabbit out of frustration and pain. The judges use her violent act to kill Julia. In the same way that they used the violent act of the hunter as a physical medium to wound Julia. The judges have to use an earthly physical violence to destroy someone, because they are not physical.

Chaudhuri: And Fefu's fear of being contaminated by Julia?

Fornes: When you're feeling vulnerable, you need to be among people who are wholesome and strong. People who are unsettled can, in a way, contaminate you. They can make you nervous. Fefu gets nervous, and she wants Julia to get up and walk. Julia refuses, and in frustration Fefu kills the rabbit.

Chaudhuri: Another frequent element in your plays is the idea of work, especially domestic work. For example, one of the most revealing things about Fefu, it seems to me, is her pleasure in fixing the plumbing. And in *Mud* Mae, who spends much of her time at an ironing board, says, "I work. See, I work. I'm working. I learned to work. I wake up and I work. Open my eyes and I work. I work. What do you do! . . . I work, jerk." One critic has argued that your plays stage domestic chores as ritual activities, suggesting that there is some sort of spiritual salvation to be gained for women from performing traditional "female" tasks of housekeeping.

Fornes: Well, everybody works; at least, in this country, most people work. Work is part of everyone's life. Except in plays. In plays people only work when the play's set in an office, and then they only do a little bit of work. But usually plays have more to do with people's emotional relationships and problems with each other. And I find that this becomes kind of tedious and stagnant, when every confrontation in a play has to do with an emotional thing, a want, a demand. And just to see people working is a physical relief. It supports the reality and the life of the characters. In a way, yes, work is redeeming, and I think, indirectly, that's why the work is there in my plays: because it's redeeming to the play, as well as to the characters.

Chaudhuri: Fefu is also widely regarded as being one of the most challenging and searching explorations of the meaning and effect of theatrical space. Please discuss the structure of the play: two traditionally staged acts sandwiching one in which everything is in motion, actors, spectators, fictional space. What issues or ideas was this unique spatial arrangement a response to? What was the problem that this choice helped to solve (or to clarify, or to complicate)? How does the fragmentation of the audience in the middle act and the repetition of the actions in it relate to the thematic concerns of the play?

Fornes: Well, if I tell you how that part of the play got there, you would be totally frustrated, because you won't be able to build a theory on it.

Chaudhuri: Don't worry. I'm getting used to that!

Fornes: I'm glad you're getting used to it. Still, let me give you an example to say what I feel about theories. If a painter goes out to the park to paint, he or she will paint what he or she finds there. The painter is not going to be able to paint a giant bird sitting on top of a hill if the giant bird is not there, he will paint what he finds there. If there are children, he will paint children, and if there's a tree, he will paint a tree. He will choose what to paint of the things that are there. How the painter paints the bird or the children is more important than why he decides to paint the bird or the children. How you start choosing things and discarding things along the way is often based for no other reason than because it is interesting, because it is beautiful, because it is time to have something lovely here, something more active to wake up the audience, and maybe that is the reason why two characters have an argument. Of course the audience may make of it what they want, but why would anyone want to think that everything is there for a symbolic reason? Why not give some value to timing, color, shock, sweetness, violence? Not because it means something other than what it is. A dance is there because it's entertaining. People playing because it's fun. Someone crying because it's moving. The audience moves from room to room because it's interesting to walk into the rooms and because you can feel you are closer to the characters if you walk into their place. I chose to do it that way because we were looking for a place to do the play and we answered an ad for a performance place that was a loft with some partitions and a little office and a kitchen. And I had just finished the first scene, so I said, I'm going to do it here and use all these rooms. Because I thought it would be interesting.

There is always an element of chance. Once a writer starts writing, it all happens. *It* happens, rather than the writer making it happen. I spend a lot of time editing and rewriting. But the editing and rewriting is the same as the original writing. I follow it. I sense it. I analyze it to death. But the solutions come by inspiration, not by reasoning.

Chaudhuri: Was the third part then in some ways affected by the fact that you had split up the second part in that way? Because in the third act, they all come back—

Fornes: Yes, of course. I hadn't made a plan for the rest of the play, so I don't know how I would have proceeded. I had already written most of the speeches that are in the play today. Julia's hallucination speech, Paula's speech about a love affair and her speech to Cecelia, Cindy's dream, Emma's speech about lovers in heaven, Fefu's speech about her depression were already written. But the setting and the moment when each occurred would have been different. I think some of those monologues would not have been in the play. You have to limit the amount of speeches in a play if you want the play to move along. But the short, close-up format of the middle scenes invited the monologue. On a stage scenes need a different kind of energy. Too many monologues can make a play topple over. Another thing is that, in the rooms, because of the closeness to the actors, the scenes had to take on a more filmlike quality, not a climax to the scenes, not an end. These scenes would not work on a main stage. I waited until I had sat there with them in the rooms to bring in the scenes, to adjust them to the intimacy of the place. The acting had to be brought down a lot. At that distance if the actors would act the way they acted on the stage, it would just seem histrionic.

Chaudhuri: That's a better story than any theory about the play could ever be. Although most of your plays tend to be ahistorical, a few of them, including *Fefu* and *The Danube,* specify a historical setting: both take place in the 1930s. Your recent play *Terra Incognita* makes explicit use of historical documents and events and, indeed, seems to be squarely confronting the meaning of History with a capital H. To what extent is your thinking informed by historical concerns? How does the historical past come into the lives and situations you dramatize?

Fornes: The past comes into every one of my plays. I think this is because I feel a longing for it. There are things about the present that I could not live without, but the past is always with me.

Chaudhuri: Some of your characters express concern about how modernization is changing the way we live our lives. Henry in *Mud* says, "Soon everything will be used only once. We will use things once. We will need to do that as our time will be of value and it will not be feasible to spend it caring for things: washing them, mending them, repairing them." What social change—changes in the way we live our daily lives—do you find most alarming? What are the changes that you've seen in your own lifetime that you worry about or are pleased about? Do you feel the world is radically different now from what it was when you were a girl, and how do the changes affect you?

Fornes: Remember Henry is an innocent. He looks forward to innovations that will give ordinary people possibilities they never had before. He is not a sage who knows how it's all going to turn out.

The most alarming change is violence. The second is dishonesty, the belief that it's all right to lie about anything just to grab a little more, to feel a little more on top of things, that you can violate anyone and anything to feel a little more powerful. That's what's most alarming.

Chaudhuri: Can you comment on the waiter's speech in *The Danube* on "the lightness of Americans"? Would the world be safer if America and Americans somehow felt "heavier," had more "weight"?

Fornes: Well, I don't know if "heavier" is the solution. We are not rooted, and we seem to be going around senselessly and insanely. Older people try to imitate their crazy children. They like what their children like. They act like their children and dress like their children.

Chaudhuri: As a person of Hispanic background who has been writing in this country for so long, you must be a little amused by all the recent excitement about multiculturalism? What do you think about this issue? Do you think it's important for writers from backgrounds other than the Anglo majority to identify themselves as such? Do you think of yourself in terms of these ethnic categories?

Fornes: Writers have to speak from their own visions. And they have to fight the temptation to be assimilated, whether the assimilation consists of giving up the creative self or the native self. The awareness of the diversity of cultures, races, and nationalities that constitutes this country is long overdue. How long can you ignore the fact that this is not an Anglo-Saxon country? We speak English, but that's because we have learned English. The excitement or emphasis on multiculturalism may stop people from assimilating too quickly and from throwing out the baby with the bathwater in the effort to lead a dignified life.

Chaudhuri: But more politically do you identify yourself as a Hispanic-American artist? Do you think of yourself as belonging to a Hispanic-American tradition or movement?

Fornes: I am a Hispanic American, more so than other Hispanics who were born here. You are what you are. I am a minority because I am a Hispanic, and I am a minority because I am an artist, and I am a minority because I am a woman, and being what I am is primary. But I may not be primarily writing about those things.

As for tradition, if you can call plays like *Ubu* and *Woyzeck* and writers like Beckett and Ionesco and Genet a tradition, that is the tradition

I belong to. I belong to the Off-Off-Broadway movement, which was the idea of doing art. And doing something that we loved doing. And doing something that reflected our thoughts. And we were not thinking of careers. We did theater because we needed to do it.

Chaudhuri: Actually I think one of the greatest intercultural plays ever written in this country—if we define interculturalism as an exploration of the encounter between cultures—is *The Danube.* But of course the cultures staged there are the American and the Eastern European, not the Hispanic. How much are you interested in this whole topic? I would think that, as an immigrant, you would consider this a major issue in your life, the issue of cultural dialogue, cultural conflict, cultural interchange.

Fornes: I never thought of it that way. I thought of the play as being about the destruction of things that are lovely and ancestral. Like a young man meeting a young woman, falling in love, and getting married. That they are from different parts of the world gives the play color, but it's not relevant to the main thought of the play, which is that a young and simple couple cannot lead a normal, simple life because the world around them is falling apart. It could have been a boy from Alabama and a girl from Nebraska.

Chaudhuri: What is your perspective on the current state of the American theatre? How do you regard the present form of the movements you have been so much a part of, Off-Broadway and regional theatre? Are they, as we always hear, dead or dying? Should we care?

Fornes: I'm not part of the Off-Broadway theatre nor a part of the so-called regional theatre. I'm a part of the Off-Off Broadway theatre and the equivalent, the smaller theatres throughout the country, which, unlike the "regional theatres" are so underfunded that they can hardly pay anything to the people who work there out of a devotion to art. Anyway, yes, we should care. The American theatre is going through a bad period. And I think the bad period has to do with the direction the funded theatre took, which was to dedicate itself to an audience that didn't have a real need for the event. It would have to start all over again and dedicate itself to something better.

Chaudhuri: Do you see any signs of hope? Any places where things may be reborn?

Fornes: Sure, there's always hope. We hope there'll always be people who love the theatre.

Chaudhuri: You are exceptional for writing exclusively for the theatre. Have there been times when you have questioned the form of theatre and its limitations? At this point what does the theatre mean or represent to you—the theatre as a form, as a medium, not this institution? Has its feasibility and significance changed for you?

Fornes: No. Theatre represents happiness for me. Maybe even religion.

Chaudhuri: What is your relationship to the whole institution of dramatic criticism, both journalistic and academic? Is any of it of interest to you? Do you find anything stimulating for your work in what people have written about it? Are there critical discussions of your work that you find particularly annoying or wrongheaded?

Fornes: Generally what bothers me about dramatic criticism is that frequently there is a very slim connection between it and the subject it speaks of. A person's work is personal. And if someone talking about you says that they saw you in a restaurant and you were wearing an ugly red dress and you were having dinner with so-and-so, you don't mind their saying the dress was ugly, because they are entitled to their own taste. But if the dress was green and you were with someone else, you feel weird, as if you don't exist.

Some critics seem to think that the author just puts out raw material. That you say these things, but that you don't know what they mean, and that you need somebody to analyze it and to tell you what you're saying. I think I know what I'm saying.

Chaudhuri: What about interviews, of which you've generously given a large number, including, of course, this one? Do interviews like this force you to discuss your work in ways you prefer not to think of it? Is there an unfair pressure on you to create a coherent narrative about your life and career, and does this ever affect the direction that life and career take? Do you like talking about your work?

Fornes: The answer to the first question is, no, it has rather indulged me to blabber about myself. To the second, I never noticed a pressure, and, no, it has as yet not affected my career. And to the third, yes.

Chaudhuri: Since this interview will appear in a book of interviews with American playwrights, perhaps I should ask you how you see your position in the tradition of modern American drama.

Fornes: I have no idea. I'm looking at it from the rubble, on my knees.

JACK GELBER
David Sedevie

Jack Gelber (courtesy of Jack Gelber)

Jack Gelber, born in Chicago in 1932, is a prize-winning playwright, a novelist, poet, screenwriter, director, and an educator, but most important Jack Gelber is a theatrical innovator. Gelber, along with Edward Albee and Jack Richardson, was the voice of the new American theatre of the 1960s. Gelber's first and most famous play, *The Connection,* was hailed by Ruby Cohn as "a clarion call for the theatre of the 1960s" (*New American Dramatists: 1960–1980* [New York: Grove Press, 1982]: 48). *The Connection* opened 15 July 1959 and was produced by the Living Theatre, the influential leader in American avant-garde theatrical experimentation founded by husband-and-wife team Julian Beck and Judith Malina. Gelber's play shook the theatrical foundations of its time, running for 722 performances from 1959 to 1963. C. W. E. Bigsby labeled the Living Theatre's production of the twenty-seven-year-old Gelber's play as a crucial event for the American theatre, "not merely because it signalled a renewed interest in the work of young American dramatists but because it raised fundamental questions about the nature of theatre, the role of the actor and the substance of reality" (*A Critical*

Introduction to Twentieth Century American Drama [Cambridge: Cambridge University Press, 1985]: 3:73).

The Connection is a play within a play, centered on the heroin subculture. Eight junkies are assembled onstage and are to follow the directions of a playwright (Jaybird) and a producer (Jim Dunn). They are to improvise on the themes of Jaybird but instead improvise in their own directions. Jaybird and Jim continually interrupt the action onstage, trying to coax the performance. The characters, waiting for their heroin supplier, their "connection," interact with the audience and in doing so sabotage Jaybird's and Jim's ideas. While the play leads audiences to believe they are watching an improvisational documentary, they in fact become a part of a carefully crafted play whose theatrical illusion is that it appears to have no theatrical illusion.

The Connection developed a cult following, not only showing audiences a world they had never seen, but also taking itself directly into the audience's consciousness and physical space, "connecting" them to a theatrical experience many had never before witnessed on an American stage. In his introduction to *The Connection* British theatre critic Kenneth Tynan said the play "became, in short, a cultural must" (London: Evergreen, 1960, 7).

Gelber has written many plays, including: *The Apple* (1961); *Square in the Eye* (1965); *The Cuban Thing* (1968); *Sleep* (1972); *Barbary Shore* (1973), adapted from the novel by Norman Mailer; *Jack Gelber's New Play: Rehearsal* (1976); *Starters* (1980); *Big Shot* (1988); *Magic Valley* (1990); and an adaptation of *Venice Preserved,* the Thomas Otway play, which Gelber entitled *Rio Preserved* (1993). Gelber and Michael Roloff translated the Francis Xavier Kroetz play *Farmyard* (1975). Gelber has also written a screenplay of *The Connection* (1962) and a novel, *On Ice* (1964). He was twice a Guggenheim Fellow (1963, 1966) and also received grants from the Rockefeller Foundation (1972) and from the National Endowment for the Arts (1974). Gelber is currently working on a play about Whitaker Chambers.

Gelber has directed several of his own plays and many plays of others, including the world premiere of Arthur Kopit's *Indians* in London in 1968, and in New York *Seduced* by Sam Shepard in 1979 and José Rivera's *The House of Ramon Iglesia* in 1983, having won Obie awards for the direction of *Seduced* and also for *The Kid,* which he directed in 1974.

Gelber received his bachelor's degree in journalism from the University of Illinois in 1953. He has taught at Columbia University, City University of New York, Yale University, and currently Brooklyn College, where he has been professor of English since 1972.

Gelber and *The Connection* influenced the style of many American playwrights—Sam Shepard comes immediately to mind because of his presentation of previously unseen subcultures and his use of music as setting and form in *Tooth of Crime*—opening up dramatic possibilities previously unrealized. Though none of Gelber's plays has been as successful as *The Connection,* Gelber's place in theatre history is secure based on the enormous and influential changes he helped initiate, redefining the conceptualization of theatre and the American stage.

Gelber lives in New York City with his wife of thirty-six years, Carol. The following interview took place on 17 December 1993 from Gelber's home in Manhattan.

Sedevie: What kind of theatre background do you have? Did you have training in classical theatre?

Gelber: No. None whatsoever. My background in the theatre was like many of the playwrights of that generation, as well as a number of playwrights who followed. Many came from outside theatre work to find a vehicle in the theatre to express themselves. Some remained in theatre and some went on to other things, other forms—movies, novels—and some stayed. Most people I knew that were writing came to the theatre, some as fans, because of a need to use the form, as opposed to being trained in the form. This is the principal difference, I think, between American theatre and what I later observed in England in the early 1960s. Most playwrights of the English theatre were actors or directors or people in theatre with wide experience in practical theatre work, whereas most of the playwrights I knew in America—Edward Albee, Jack Richardson, Arthur Kopit, Rosalind Drexler—had almost no theatre experience. Most of the Off-Broadway movement was characterized by playwrights with very little experience in the theatre before they got their feet wet. They just jumped in, as I did, and learned as they went along.

Sedevie: You and the playwrights you mention did not have irreverence for classical theatre, but you did have different ideas regarding theatrical conventions from those of some of the other American dramatists who preceded you. What are some of the differing attitudes you held?

Gelber: That's definitely true—we took a different approach. We were not like the playwrights of the 1930s who had a political or social platform. We made up the rules to fit the function of what we needed to say. The Louis Sullivan adage—"Form follows function"—was very much a part of my thinking. To shape a play as a writer—and I was very conscious of this while writing *The Connection*—after a play is done once, no matter how fresh and extemporaneous it might appear, it's a known quantity to both actors and audiences. So the problem becomes how do you keep the play fresh the second, third, hundredth, or five hundredth time you do it. You begin to find out what makes it alive, and what makes it exciting, and what makes people want to turn the page or stay in their seats for another act. It's one of the things I had to learn while I was writing. Specific to *The Connection* I looked at the whole atmosphere of studied improvisation or extemporaneity. I had people breaking into the fourth wall, people coming in from the audience, people making mistakes backstage with the lights, people interrupting each other—these were techniques I thought would stand in good stead and keep the play fresh no matter how many times people saw the play.

Sedevie: Describe how you came to write *The Connection.*

Gelber: In 1957 I went on a trip with my wife, intending to do some writing. It was the first time we were out of the country. We were both young. It was July. We got a lift to Florida and took a little airplane from Key West to Havana. We were in Cuba for about two weeks and then took a night plane from Santiago to Port-au-Prince, where I had the name of a painter on a Fulbright. He was dead broke—he had a place but no food, and we had some money but no place. We stayed with him for about three weeks, and in those three weeks I took my notes for a bunch of short stories that I was trying to write that weren't coming out right, and I sat down with my portable typewriter every morning above the city of Port-au-Prince, above Kenscoff, and wrote *The Connection.* It came very, very fast, and it was a good experience and a heady experience.

Sedevie: Had you always intended the play to take the form it did?

Gelber: I had been thinking about how to do this in terms of a play for a very short time. I had been getting letters from friends on the West Coast, where my wife (she comes from the [San Francisco] Bay area of California) and I had been in 1953 and 1954, telling me about the Allen Ginsburgs and the certain kind of freewheeling dada events that were happening at art galleries and various other spaces in San Francisco. That kind of anarchistic, surreal energy attracted me very much. I tried to take that and use it in kind of a free-flowing way in my work and in writing this play. There were a number of things going on in the popular arts that were very upsetting to someone who liked jazz. Jazz was always a second-class citizen as music. There were many people who looked at jazz musicians only when they got arrested, which was about the only time you ever heard of them. In 1957, in New York, I started to put on some jazz concerts with friends—I wasn't a musician, I just tried to organize them in a small studio theatre that put on small plays by Lorca and others. It was a small, intimate theatre that held about sixty people. I helped paint some sets. I got the idea that theatre didn't have to be large scale, but that it could be chamber pieces, smaller in scale.

Sedevie: The Living Theatre and *The Connection* seem to have been a perfect match. How did the production come about?

Gelber: It was. When I wrote *The Connection,* I didn't think I was writing it for the ordinary theatre audience. I hadn't seen anything like it in my travels, and as any young playwright, then or today, I had no idea what to do with it. I read in the *New York Times* about a woman who produced interracial plays, and since *The Connection* had both blacks and whites in it, I sent her the work, and she sent it back, saying it was filthy, vile, and portrayed blacks in a ghettoized, criminal way, and she wasn't going to be part of that. I called some serious theatre places, one of which, the Phoenix, told me they were only doing Nobel Prize–winners that season. I was at my wit's end when I ran into a fellow I knew, Norman Solomon, who was an onlooker into the art and dance world, and he asked me what I had been doing. I told him about the play, and he read it. He came to my apartment about a week later and told me that, about six or seven years earlier, he had been in a production of *Desire Caught by its Tail,* a Picasso play done by the Living Theatre at the Cherry Lane Theatre. He thought they would very much like this work. I called them and told them I would like to deliver my manuscript. They were very polite. I went to their apartment, and they showed me a scrapbook with pictures and reviews of productions they had done. It all looked interesting.

Sedevie: When you say "they," you're referring to Julian Beck and Judith Malina?

Gelber: Yes. They were the Living Theatre. They were mainly interested in poets and had spent a lot of time doing Auden, Ezra Pound, John Ashbery in the late 1940s and early 1950s. They were interested in language elevating the truth of theatre work. Doing the poets was a symptom or extension of their anarchistic philosophy that they could undermine the sentimentality of Broadway. The idea being that even though they were friends with Tennessee Williams and many others who appeared on Broadway, they really were philosophically dead against the kind of emotionalism, the soap opera quality of the dialogue, and the quality of issues that were being presented on Broadway. They were very antiestablishment. In the middle 1950s, before I met them, they did a whole series of plays in which they were politicized. Not only did they want to do this in the abstract, but they also became involved with political movements, such as protests against the nuclear bomb. They protested against atomic bomb drills and were thrown in jail. Back in the 1950s we had mandatory bomb drills. Judith and Julian refused to go inside during a drill and were thrown in jail for ten days, where they met drug addicts and other people and so by the time I got to them in the spring of 1958, they had seen a little bit about the life of drug addiction and were receptive to the idea of this play. I called them up after a week. They said they were redoing a space into a small theatre, downtown at Sixth Avenue and Fourteenth Street on the second floor of what used to be Hecht's Department Store. They said they were going to do William Carlos Williams, another poet, in the fall of 1958 as their first play, and they wanted to do my play just after that, and indeed, they did, and I began working with the Living Theatre.

Sedevie: How was the Living Theatre managed and organized?

Gelber: Julian designed the sets and ran the theatre in terms of the management, and Judith did the directing. Both selected plays, and other than that, everybody did everything. I learned just about everything I know about theatre from working with the Living Theatre—sweeping up the floors, doing the lighting, directing, auditioning. They would say, "We don't know very many black actors. Jack, go out and find some." I had no idea how to go about doing that, so I just did it.

Sedevie: The Connection opened to hostile reviews, yet still had a very long and popular run. What do you think accounted for its success?

Gelber: There were twelve papers in New York at the time, and most of them reviewed the play. The *New York Post* thought I ought to leave town. The *New York Times* called it a "farrago of dirt." I had to look up "farrago." It was the middle of the summer, July 15, 1959, when the play opened, and so it was mostly second- and third-string critics that reviewed it. I left town about the first of August, thinking the play was a complete disaster. My wife and I, with our little baby, drove to California to visit her parents, stopping in Chicago along the way to see my parents. After that a couple of things happened. The British theatre critic Kenneth Tynan became one of the foremost promoters of the play. I had never met him and hadn't even known he had come to see the play. Apparently under his contract with the *New Yorker* he wasn't allowed to review an Off-Broadway play, but he kept sending people down to see it. And then, sometime in October or November, three very positive reviews appeared in prestigious weeklies. One in the *New Yorker* by Donald Malcolm, another in the *Saturday Review* by Henry

Hewes, and a third in the *New Republic* by Robert Brustein. Those reviews, combined with one in the *Village Voice,* which wasn't very big in those days, seemed to get people interested in the play, and from there it just took off.

Sedevie: How did you support yourself before the Living Theatre production of *The Connection?*

Gelber: I had worked at the United Nations for two years as a mimeograph operator, which was a very good job for me, because it gave me a lot of time to roam around New York. The royalties from *The Connection* were just barely enough to do another play, so I wrote another one for the Living Theatre, *The Apple,* which opened there on December 7, 1961. When *The Connection* got rolling in November or December of 1959, it literally became a play that was being done all over the world. Money started coming in, not the way money comes in these days, but enough to feed the baby and keep on going, allowing me to write. I also worked on screenplays from 1960 to somewhere into the 1970s.

Sedevie: In his introduction to *The Connection* Kenneth Tynan said it was a play that pervaded the consciousness of its audiences and developed a loyal following. What was the social context of *The Connection* that you think made it pervade the consciousness of its followers?

Gelber: Yes, it did develop quite a following. The play treated the theatre as a type of total experience in which very realistic acting portrayed very human characters in a context that altered the way people thought theatre could be done. Not only did the play present a kind of authenticity, but the production values reflected that. I think our breaking the fourth wall and not separating the audience from the proceedings onstage was one of the first times our audience members had ever seen anything like that. I didn't invent any of these things, but I wasn't aware of who did what before me either. It seemed that most people had never been in an experience like this. They had never felt so much of the total theatre experience. The play really did have a deep, penetrating psychological effect. For example, in the four years *The Connection* ran at the Living Theatre, hundreds of people fainted, hundreds. They fainted when Leach turns on onstage—the only scene in the play where a needle goes into an arm. It happens very late in the play, during the overdose. When he did that, and people looked at him doing that—it was done so realistically—essentially just the men, very few of the women, fainted. We had to hire a nurse to be in attendance.

Also, at that time people didn't really know about drugs. Today we're inundated with information about drugs by documentaries, written material, television shows. Sometimes in a horribly sentimental way, sometimes in a demonizing way. Then it was only demonizing with very little understanding—*Reefer Madness*—the mentality where you were told that one puff on a marijuana cigarette would ruin your life. There was a lot of dread and a lot of ignorance. People knew about these things, but it wasn't part of the mainstream consciousness.

Sedevie: Was *The Connection* a political statement?

Gelber: Some people thought so. I thought it made ripples, but I'd have a hard time pinning down what they were around the world. We have this in the theatre all the time. We get something new, and people from other countries jump on it and see something in it they can focus on. It certainly was a bit of thumbing our nose at the establishment, breaking down what was then the staid conditions of life around us.

Sedevie: Was that your intention going in?

Gelber: No. Absolutely not. I didn't have an agenda about what the results would be. I didn't know a particular stimulus would produce a certain result, nor did I try to do that. What I tried to do was to describe as accurately and as interestingly and as theatrically as I could a certain situation that I knew about. I had a certain amount of anger in me, to correct the record. Also, in *The Connection* there is an emphasis on waiting and the nature of waiting. This was not because I had read *Waiting for Godot.* I'd never even heard of Samuel Beckett at that time. It was just very much a part of what I saw going on at the time—people waiting for the next thing to happen.

Sedevie: How have the different productions of *The Connection* over the years, both in this country and abroad, changed your ideas about the play?

Gelber: I don't really know what I think about the play after all these years. About three years ago, some people here in New York wanted to do the play and gave me some money to take a look at the script and see what, if anything, had to be done to the script to be able to do the play again. I found myself enjoying the play, but I also found myself wondering about the major differences between our times and the time of *The Connection.* There is much more separatism today than then. It was my idea that the black and white roles were interchangeable, an integrationist point of view that doesn't seem as prevalent today. Also heroin addiction is not necessarily a central metaphor for other times. It's hard to substitute LSD or cocaine as the drug of choice in the play, and I'm not sure I would want to.

Sedevie: Have you thought about directing a revival of *The Connection?*

Gelber: No. I don't think so. I think you need a young person to direct the play. Funny enough I just had this conversation. I gave a copy of the play to a young theatre group here in New York, and they asked me to direct the play. I told them I didn't think I should be the one to direct the play. With this play you need someone who isn't tied down to the old way of doing things.

Sedevie: You mentioned you worked as a screenwriter for many years. What happened to the screenplays you've written?

Gelber: They never got done. I did two versions of *Midnight Cowboy* which were not used by the producers. I didn't get screen credit, but I still feel I did a lot of the work that was never recognized. I did get paid. I worked with Louis Malle on a script about Jelly Roll Morton that was never done. I had about thirteen or fourteen screenplays that I got paid for but were never done.

Sedevie: What are some of the differences you see between the American theatre of the 1960s and the 1990s?

Gelber: Theatre work in the early 1960s was terra incognita. Most of the work was done on unmarked, uncharted ground, that is, the work done by the people not in the ordinary theatre stream. There was the establishment theatre stream uptown, but there was also our thing going on downtown that was very chaotic, very lively, very sporadic. It contained all kinds of people and theatres—Caffe Cino, La Mama, the Living Theatre, people who wanted to do very good productions of classics and couldn't do them uptown. It was very heterogeneous, but difficult to pin down what all of those people had in common.

Sedevie: Would it be fair to say the whole Off-Broadway movement was difficult to pin down, and therein lies what it was?

Gelber: That may be. It certainly was the beginning of a reaction against the established order. There is no doubt about that. That is not going on now in the 1990s. Most of the people I see and teach want to be part of the establishment. Often the things that were done in the 1960s now have become the established way of doing things. Today the avant-garde is the establishment.

Sedevie: Was it a reaction against the established order of the theatrical establishment or social establishment?

Gelber: I would say both. For example, we're talking about the Eisenhower years and the beginning of the Kennedy years. We had all lived through the 1950s and the red scare, the conventions of *Father Knows Best.* I wouldn't call my theatre work doing battle against the established order—more like skirmishes. It was like Ethan Allen and the Green Mountain Boys, as opposed to joining up in the militia.

Sedevie: What was it that made you want to engage in these skirmishes?

Gelber: I really didn't know what place I had in the world, which, I think happens to every young person, and the working out of that is what I think are the skirmishes.

Sedevie: Your fourth play, *The Cuban Thing,* closed after its first night. Why do you think that happened?

Gelber: I don't really know why. There are a number of my plays that have not met with a favorable initial response, but I was very disappointed that *The Cuban Thing* was one of them, because it's always been one of my favorites among my plays. There was a bomb, a tear-gas bomb, set off during the previews and an angry anti-Castro group that threatened a bomb scare every night. The FBI and Secret Service were calling and trying to get the show stopped. They felt they couldn't protect the actors and the audiences during the show. There was a lot of pressure from all sides not to do the play. The pro-Castro forces did not want people to see the treatment of homosexuals that had occurred during the revolution. In terms of the ideological left and right, neither one was very happy with what I had to say. *The Cuban Thing* was my attempt to show the radicalization of the middle class.

Sedevie: What trends do you see playing themselves out in the American theatre of the 1990s?

Gelber: I see a continuation of fractured theatre. Instead of a wide diversity of appetites, there will be more single-issue theatre. I think eventually the pendulum will swing back toward a broader view of ourselves and our world.

Sedevie: What scares you the most about American theatre today?

Gelber: One of the most frightening things I see today is the great number of people in the theatre who have nothing to do. There are too few outlets for the multitudes of talented people. We have trained and encouraged a couple of generations of theatre workers without giving them any place to work. The regional theatres, which were supposed to be such a vibrant part of theatre life—I don't know if they have fulfilled that dream. The Reagan years took a lot of funding away and left a lot of people in the arts high and dry and without outlets for their talents. I don't really know the solution or even really have an overview on the topic. Probably because I'm still in the forest.

ADRIENNE KENNEDY
Elin Diamond

Adrienne Kennedy (courtesy of Adrienne Kennedy)

Born in Cleveland in 1931, Adrienne Kennedy began writing seriously in her mid-twenties after moving to New York City with her husband and first child. A long stay in Ghana inspired her first plays, the Obie award–winning *Funnyhouse of a Negro* (1964) and *The Owl Answers* (1965). In these short texts the Kennedy aesthetic emerges: female consciousness as a collage of history and fictional biography; swiftly changing scenes marked by temporal and spatial distortion; terrifying surreal images, both verbal and material; an astonishing linguistic range, from self-descriptive prose to poetic incantation.

While she rejects the simpler clarities of psychological realism, Kennedy has proved to be one of the most articulate writers of black American experience. In *Funnyhouse of a Negro,* the protagonist's personal history of miscegenation, rape, and madness subtly encodes a social history of racial oppression. In *The Owl Answers* and *A Lesson in Dead Language* (1970), reverence for the Western classics of white culture mingles complexly with, respectively, images of spiritual anguish ("I call God and the Owl answers") and bodily guilt ("I bleed, Teacher,

I bleed"). In *A Movie Star Has to Star in Black and White* (1976), Kennedy explores the fantasy incursions of movie stars and scenarios into the life of a young black woman, named (as in *The Owl Answers*) Clara. Sharing with earlier American dramatists—Elmer Rice, Sophie Treadwell, Clifford Odets, Tennessee Williams—a fascination with film technique, Kennedy goes beyond occasional reference: her cast list calls for actors who resemble the stars in *Now Voyager*, *Viva Zapata*, and *A Place in the Sun*, as well as actors who resemble family photos. "Real" life and cinematic "life" are interwoven, movie stars adopting the rhythms of their film roles but uttering words that provide us with fragmentary knowledge of Clara's history. Familiar Kennedy themes—psychic pain, guilt, family trauma, isolation—mingle with allusions to earlier Kennedy texts as (the playwright informs us) *"[Clara] lets her movie stars speak for her."* The effect is both disturbing and compelling.

Awarded a Guggenheim in 1967, Kennedy has received commissions from Jerome Robbins, the Public Theater, Julliard, and the Royal Court. Her plays have been produced in New York, London, Rome, Paris, West Africa, and South America, although in recent years, as she somewhat ruefully notes below, her work has appeared more in university syllabi than in the theatre. It is all the more fortunate, then, for theatre scholars as well as practitioners, that the University of Minnesota Press has issued *In One Act* (1988), collecting for the first time *Funnyhouse of a Negro, The Owl Answers, A Lesson in Dead Language, A Movie Star Has to Star in Black and White,* along with *A Rat's Mass* (1966), *Sun* (1968), and two adaptations from the Greek, *Electra* and *Orestes*. She is one of five playwrights included in the third edition of the Norton Anthology of American Literature.

Kennedy has recently published a stylistically innovative autobiography, *People Who Led to My Plays* (Knopf, 1987, hardcover; Theatre Communications Group, 1988, paper), a work, says Kennedy, designed to answer the question that students and directors most frequently ask: who or what influenced you to write the way you do? An informative yet elusive portrayal of family, friends, political leaders, cultural idols, and other artifacts, *People Who Led to My Plays* positions written text alongside beautifully reproduced photographs from Kennedy's own collection. And as with *A Movie Star Has to Star in Black and White,* personal reflection becomes cultural collage. The sensibility here, though Kennedy never uses such terms, is postmodern—distinctions between subjectivity and social formation, foreground and background, history and fantasy, word and image are slippery or continually displaced; the texture of the text admits gaps, silences, refuses closure, so that no unified reading of Kennedy's life is possible or even desirable. A writer in residence at Stanford University in the fall of 1988 and visiting professor of English at Rutgers, New Brunswick, in the spring of 1989, Adrienne Kennedy still resides in New York City, where she raised her two sons. In 1988 she participated in the Pen-Faulkner readings at the Folger Library and later that year received the Manhattan Borough President's Award for Excellence in the Arts. In June 1989 Kennedy attended the first reading of a new work, *She Talks to Beethoven,* at River Arts Repertory in Woodstock, New York.

I had the pleasure of meeting and interviewing Adrienne Kennedy in her New York apartment on 25 August 1988. Our conversation ranged widely but began with, and returned to, the experiences and ideas that led to *People Who Led to My Plays.* However, since this interview was conducted, several important events have occurred in Kennedy's life. From January to March 1992 the Great Lakes Theatre Festival in Cleveland (Kennedy's hometown) held the first Adrienne Kennedy Festival. The "centerpiece" of that festival was the world premiere of Kennedy's *The Ohio State Murders,* a work she was commissioned to write for the occasion. Later in 1992 the University of Minnesota Press published Kennedy's *The Alexander Plays,* which included *The Ohio State Murders* as well as *She Talks to Beethoven,* two plays in which Suzanne Alexander, Kennedy's protagonist, plays a central role. In 1995–1996, the Signature Theatre Company mounted an Adrienne Kennedy Season at the Joseph Papp Public Theater in New York City.

Diamond: I would like to ask you about *People Who Led to My Plays.* There are things that intrigue me enormously about this book. When you say "people" you are covering a whole range—people who are family members, world leaders, faces on playing cards, movie stars. The very first italicized title of the text is "People on Old Maid cards" and later you refer to Humpty-Dumpty, Little Bo-Peep, and say that people did illogical things. Could you say more about this word "people"?

Kennedy: First of all I should say that I started to read when I was three years old. Apparently I made very little distinction between fictional people and real people, dead people and living people. When I was three years old, four years old, Humpty-Dumpty was terribly real to me. I don't think I was really aware of that until many years later, when I had accumulated photographs of all these people and someone said to me, "Well, a lot of these people are dead!" The point is, if I'm reading a book about Beethoven in July, Beethoven is definitely more real to me than members of my family at that moment. (By the way, I used to have a statue of Beethoven on my desk, but I don't have it anymore.) I don't know why this happens. People on Old Maid cards were as real to me as my brother, whom I was playing the game with. I remember my editors at Knopf wanted to publish the book for that reason, because of the sensibility that ties all these people together.

Diamond: There's a voice in this book, a beautiful voice, but I wonder where it's situated. Is it situated in the mind of a mature, now-famous writer, or somewhere between those amazing fantasies of childhood and the present moment? In other words, in your plays there are many voices, or many pieces of one voice, but here there's only one. A calm, reflective, affectionate voice that moves away from . . . or that presents certain scenes without letting them unfold. For example, there's a wonderful moment when you and Cornell [the playwright's brother] return home from your grandmother's, and you have a movie magazine—*Modern Screen*—which your mother disapproved of. When I reread the book last night, I thought, now she could have gone into this scene, but she seems to be avoiding it—could you talk more about that?

Kennedy: I know exactly what you're saying. Remember, I am fifty-seven, and I wrote this book when I was fifty-four, fifty-five. I have always wanted to just take a moment—that's what this book really is— and honor the people that I think contributed to my development. I really wanted to do that. The anger, the darkness that's in my plays . . . that's me, certainly. But over the years I really felt that I had never taken a moment to honor certain people in my life. It started with real people. With my mother, my teachers, my father, and that I think is what is in that voice. I would be sitting, say, on the Berkeley campus and thinking about my piano teacher and how great she was. I don't know how to analyze it, I can't analyze it, but this voice definitely stems from knowing that I had great teachers and that there's a lot of greatness in both my parents and my grandparents, and I wanted to put it all down before I died. There was a period about three or four years ago when I knew several people who died, and that may have had a tiny impact on me; I wanted to put it down before I died. I felt that I had shortchanged them, especially my parents.

Diamond: How did you shortchange them?

Kennedy: By not really talking about what they had done for me.

Diamond: Do you mean that in your plays the mother and father are imagined violently?

Kennedy: Yes, but that's the playwright speaking. I just wanted to write about what these people had done for me. [*Pause*] This is something I discuss very often with my black friends who are my age. We feel that people in that photograph [*gesturing toward a framed photograph, reprint-ed on page 48 of People*] they're in their eighties now if they're living—who went to southern schools like Morehouse and Spelman and Tus-kegee—those people were dedicated to us, the ultimate of parenthood. They were usually double-income families, the women were teachers and social workers. Those people were in their twenties, their mid-twenties, around the depression, and they were determined [that we should go] to college. They made a lot of sacrifices for us. Plus, I don't know, maybe it's utterly sentimental, but I really do believe that teachers were great in those days—not that I'm taking anything away from cur-rent teachers—but teachers in public schools were at that time so in love with their subjects. When they talked about Shelley—

Diamond: They made Shelley important, vital?

Kennedy: Yes, and for twenty-five years, maybe longer, I wanted to write something about those teachers. I had millions of notes. I might just write a line in the diary about my third-grade teacher, but I didn't envision a book. I had written a short autobiography about sixteen years ago, and it made the rounds in New York. People said it was just too fragmented.

Diamond: Was it in the format of *People Who Led to My Plays?*

Kennedy: No. It started when I was about twenty-two, and then I tried to go backward. It didn't work. In any case from time to time I would read parts of it and try to understand why it failed, and that's . . . I was frustrated. I was always frustrated by that book. It was only about ninety pages long, and I couldn't understand what was so wrong with it. Then that summer, about three years ago, I was looking at parts of it again and suddenly it . . . well, it also started with that question that people always ask me, who influenced me, and that seemed to open something. That's why the book has integrity for me, because these two things came together: the influence of all those great teachers, and then the failure of this other autobiographical work that I always wanted to fix somehow.

Diamond: What is so terrific about the book is that there is really no answer to the question of who influenced Adrienne Kennedy.

Kennedy: I never answer it?

Diamond: No, I don't think so, that's the pleasure of it! It's Elizabeth Taylor, it's Chopin, it's Langston Hughes, your mother, and Gene Kelly. Ishmael Reed is absolutely right about this—you have created a way of speaking about a life. That's what this book is to me. It's a way of thinking about memory, and it performs the very things that you refer to in the little passages of text. When you say, for example, that every song has a secret inside it that only adults can unlock, in a sense every passage has a secret that can't be unlocked. The book doesn't answer the question of influence; it provides a context for the question.

Kennedy: That's fascinating. It doesn't answer the question?

Diamond: You give us an immediate sense of a certain kind of cultural experience; you make culture real for us. I noticed this line when re-reading the book: "Sometimes I think I see life as like my mother's red scrapbook" [of photographs, *People,* 91].

Kennedy: Right, yes, and I have to credit my editors with that. They wanted the book to be like my mother's photograph album, and they wanted it to be red. They were very concerned about making it a red book.

Diamond: Was it you who wanted to include the photographs?

Kennedy: I put them on the manuscript. I photocopied the photographs because I wanted them to see what I had in mind. I have hundreds of photographs, but some are in storage, so I used the ones I had here in the apartment. And I like books with photographs.

Diamond: I was just looking at one of the sections, this passage about Cornell. He ran away for a few hours when he was ten, and it was snowing. That's a little biographical fact about Cornell; there could have been a thousand more, but you chose that one.

Kennedy: Yes.

Diamond: And you say no more about it except for the comment, "And I know there was an unseen sadness in him" [*People,* 12]. A conventional autobiography would explore that, would have dealt with your feelings about Cornell, stopped time to develop that relationship. By not doing that, by moving right on to whatever it was—to the Wolfman, to Fred and Ginger—what happens is that Cornell rises to the surface of the reader's consciousness and sort of swims around with the flotsam of American culture, and in that way, to me, Cornell becomes more real than he would in a realist narrative. Did you intend that, did you feel that this is how you wanted it done?

Kennedy: No.

Diamond: You didn't work it out?

Kennedy: No.

Diamond: This is the critic's observation?

Kennedy: I don't know. Suddenly, right in this room, and certainly walking around the neighborhood, but also right in this room, I'd suddenly wake up at three o'clock in the morning, and for at least seven or eight months these images all came back to me. It was a wonderful experience. I started it in July, and in the fall I was teaching at NYU and had to go down to Princeton one day a week, and I wrote all the time. On the bus, everywhere. I had yellow pads everywhere. And by February 1st, these images just flooded out, I was unable to stop them, and I just used the ones that came to me. Fortunately Knopf let it alone.

Diamond: There was no rearranging?

Kennedy: My editors were wonderful, they just let it alone.

Diamond: And the images came in that order?

Kennedy: Yes. [*Pause*] I'd been—I don't want to use the word "haunted"— but there were things that had been pressing on my mind for years and years and years. There were things that I'd thought about many, many times. I'd thought about my brother running away in the snow, sitting in the garage. We opened the garage door, and there he was, sitting. I thought about that hundreds of times. So I think, I'm not sure, but I think that these are the things that ended up in the book. It was a release for me.

Diamond: And yet you don't finish that story. I mean, you're telling me you found him in the garage. But that's not in *People*.

Kennedy: It's the main image. I was censoring, obviously. I guess I do that all the time. I was so eager to get these things down. I couldn't linger too long on Cornell. I couldn't linger too long on anyone.

Diamond: How did you get to Knopf? Did your agent suggest . . . ? [*Laughter*] You don't want to say?

Kennedy: Oh no! I laugh when you say "agent." No, really, in retrospect everything I've ever really done, I've done on my own. Also, I love Knopf books, and so one rainy afternoon in October, I took it—what I had finished up there. I didn't know anyone at Knopf—I knew Bob Gottlieb was the editor, but really it was just one of those instinctual things. I had seventy pages and just went up and left them for him. When I got there, I didn't know it at the time, but they were redesign- ing some of the offices, and the floor and tables were loaded with manu- scripts. And I smiled [and thought] to myself, "Well, your manuscript will just sit there on the floor or the desk." I didn't realize they were redesigning the back offices. They called me up in about a couple of weeks.

Diamond: Wow.

Kennedy: And that has to go down as one of the most important mo- ments of my writing career. I picked up the phone, and Alice Quinn [formerly at Knopf, now at the *New Yorker*] said that they liked my book and asked if I could meet with them. It had to be in the realm of miracle. It makes up for all those manuscripts that we send out and nothing ever comes of that. I've certainly had my share of those. But the editors at Knopf liked it. They asked only whether I would be able to finish it; they couldn't imagine where it was going. I said I didn't know. But you see, even then I knew that a certain part of my life ended when I came back from my trip to Africa. And I had *Funnyhouse.* My life did change after that.

Diamond: How?

Kennedy: There was this idealistic person who wanted to be a writer.

Diamond: She became a writer, didn't she?

Kennedy: Well, she became a playwright, which is more difficult than I had ever anticipated. I'm not even sure I was cut out for that. You know. Getting your plays on. Going through the rehearsals. That was very, very difficult. I enjoyed writing my plays, but that part I never enjoyed.

Diamond: This brings me to a question. Just before going to Africa, you write about Kazan, Williams, Brando, and ask, "Will I ever be part of an artistic brotherhood like this?" [*People*, 95].

Kennedy: That was a dreamer who wanted to be part of them.

Diamond: Have you ever been part of that? Or of an artistic sisterhood?

Kennedy: I don't feel that. I think I'm too . . . [*pause*] I identify with writers—dead writers, living writers, men and women. That's given me a tremendous sense of security, coming from what is referred to as a minority—a word I hate because there are more people of color in the world than white. I feel an identification with writers. I can go to any city and look up writers, try to meet them, and I can read about writers, you know, and that gives me a great sense of security. [*Pause*] The theatre, in my opinion, is so tiny. I was most comfortable, in terms of being in the theatre, with the label "Off-Broadway playwright" or "Off-Off-Broadway playwright." I'm not comfortable when it's broken down further.

Diamond: Why not?

Kennedy: Because a playwright is a person who wants to be a part of a theatre movement. I mean I want to get my plays produced. I'm a black writer who is an Off-Broadway playwright. I'm comfortable with that.

Diamond: You know history gets into this speaker's voice in subtle ways. We get used to a modulated, loving, sensitive female voice. And then there's something like, on page 33, "I hated . . . the dirty Jim Crow car."

Kennedy: Yes.

Diamond: Cornell crying on your shoulder.

Kennedy: He was crying because he was leaving my mother.

Diamond: But when you say that Cornell cried as you rode south on the train, you leave the impression that he was anxious not just about leaving his mother, but about the environment of the Jim Crow car.

What comforted you was your movie magazine with a picture of Clark Gable dressed in an army uniform on the cover.

Kennedy: Well, one was making the other tolerable.

Diamond: I guess that the irony here is just another feature of mass culture, how it comforts us all in the most contradictory ways. In your case you were enamored of the movie icon, Gable, in the role of the white American male patriot, when it's white male culture that has produced the Jim Crow that is making you and Cornell so miserable.

Kennedy: Well, that's very savvy. But don't you think that these magazines did that, offered comfort and illusion? I mean, it's a little embarrassing, but I'm sure I spent the rest of the summer, many, many hours, in a Clark Gable fantasy.

Diamond: Imagining him kissing you?

Kennedy: Imagining him kissing me.

Diamond: So did I. Of course.

Kennedy: In the summer in that little Georgia town, that *Modern Screen* would have been with me every day. But at that time, in the thirties and forties, no man or woman, not even Clark Gable, was in the strata of glamour of Lena Horne.

Diamond: On page 61, you have a picture of her.

Kennedy: Yes, in her MGM pose, that 1940s pose.

Diamond: And she reminded you of your mother?

Kennedy: Sure. My mother had a lot of friends, and they all seemed to look that way. They were from the South, those women, they had that look.

Diamond: At this point in the book you put *Negro* in quotation marks, but later you don't. Were you pointing to something specific there?

Kennnedy: Lena Horne has no peers, even today, 1988. She was in the MGM movies, something that, to me, no one, no black woman, has attained. I don't know why. I once saw her in a stage show at the Palace Theater in Cleveland. So, not only was she in MGM movies, but I had actually gone to the Palace on Saturday and sat in the balcony and watched Lena Horne. And my mother's friends worshiped her; we all did. They would say, people like my mother, who were maybe in their forties and fifties, she's the only Negro woman that was this, she's the only Negro woman that was that. She's the only Negro woman in Hollywood. She's the only Negro woman who is doing that well. There was so much pride about Lena Horne. I would go to those MGM movies and say, "Look at her dress."

Diamond: It's true, those movies created demigods. Did that have something to do with the use of the quotation marks?

Kennedy: I'm not sure why I used quotation marks. Did I use them sometimes?

Diamond: More in the first sections.

Kennedy: I'm not sure; you have to remember that this stuff comes out of the dark. Maybe I wanted to indicate sarcasm. That irony you talk about. [*Pause*] But I can explain it in terms of Lena Horne. In her case it was an adjective of pride. "She's a *Negro* woman." But I think, too, there are meanings of which I'm not definitely aware. *Negro* is the word we used; we referred to ourselves as Negroes. I think that probably someone could analyze how I'm using it at any given moment—sarcasm, darkness, pride. It has many meanings. I definitely used the word *black* in the 1960s.

Diamond: I thought it was an unwillingness to give up your own history. But a student asked me after class whether you now felt self-conscious about the word *Negro* in *Funnyhouse*.

Kennedy: Oh no. All those people, Lena Horne, Paul Robeson, Marian Anderson, all those people were Negroes, and I was very proud of those people. My father gave a lot of speeches because he was a "Y" secretary, and he talked about the NAACP and the Negro College Fund. When I wrote *Funnyhouse of a Negro,* that was the word I used. That was the word I grew up with. And of course Negroes were also the people not allowed to eat at Schaefer's.

Diamond: I wonder then, where is the anger when you informed Miss McCreary, your journalism teacher in junior high, that you wanted to be a journalist, and she said that "she didn't think, because of my color, that it was realistic for me to pursue that thought" [*People,* 45].

Kennedy: There is not a lot of anger. But you see, we are talking about a person in her mid-fifties now. Anger will always be a part of my personality, but race, and the history of race and the part race plays in world politics, is something now that is very real to me. Hatred, you know, is a very ordinary thing—hatred, wars, racism—I've come to grips with that.

Diamond: Could you say a little more about this?

Kennedy: I've come to grips with it. I think this is the way human beings are—they seem to hate one another. That's why I don't like the word *minority* because I'm not a minority in the world. I hate the phrase *third world.* What's the first world? As you grow older, you realize how much hate is a part of the world. You just have to come to terms with that hatred. It doesn't mean that there isn't a tremendous residue of anger. I can be offended by a salesperson and become extremely angry, but I have some perspective.

Diamond: Still, it's no coincidence that *Funnyhouse* and *Owl Answers* were released in you after you'd lived in West Africa.

Kennedy: Oh, sure. Unquestionably.

Diamond: When you talk about the colors in Ghana and compare them to your remembrances of Georgia—

Kennedy: Yes, that's right. And that was one of those accidents. I had nothing to do with going to Africa. Joe [her former husband] took me to Africa with him. To see how beautiful West Africa was changed my entire life. And to be there, at that moment, when they were getting their freedom from the British, it was just one of those accidents. Those plays wouldn't have existed if I hadn't gone to West Africa.

Diamond: Another part of that landscape was Kwame Nkrumah. You write on page 122, "To see a man and to see a statue of him in the same space of time broke through boundaries in my mind. Statues were of real people." I wonder how this jibes with other cultural constructions like movie stars, characters in your favorite novels.

Kennedy: When I saw Nkrumah come off the plane, and he stood there and gave a little talk, and we sat very close together—the Accra airport was so tiny—I knew there was something very different here.

Diamond: Which makes me think of the statue of Queen Victoria that you mention in *People* and the bust of her in *Funnyhouse,* with all its hideous connotations.

Kennedy: But you have to understand that the person who sees the statue doesn't know that it's arousing that kind of rage, doesn't know that she is going to write about it—in that case in less than six months. [*Pause*] I think that is very much a part of my personality. I really do not know that these things are affecting me. That's something I would never, even as a little girl, admit.

Diamond: But that's actually the speaker's strength in the autobiography. She's not judging even as she's selecting, as you said earlier, "the main image." I mean, there's a sort of deception going on, a gap between writer and the persona of the speaker.

Kennedy: I think there is a gap there.

Diamond: That's an important—

Kennedy: But that gap is very much a part of—

Diamond: Of you.

Kennedy: Yes.

Diamond: That's the safety valve.

Kennedy: Exactly. I think it's something I learned in my crib [*laughter*].

Diamond: Tell me, what is it about our mothers?

Kennedy: What is it about our mothers?

Diamond: What is it about their stories, their dreams that's so attractive?
Kennededy: I remember—it's a very early memory—my mother was always holding my hand and telling me stories. She didn't go to work until I was eleven, and so I became her companion.
Diamond: You became a listener.
Kennedy: I became a listener. My brother was born, he was almost three years younger—I don't know what he would say if he were alive—but when very early on people said that I was smart, my mother definitely grabbed hold of that. My father went to work at about eight o'clock in the morning, and she got books to teach me to read. Sometimes we sat in bed, sometimes we sat in the kitchen. She made me into her confidante, told me her feelings. In fact, it's not in the book, but when I went to kindergarten, the teacher was very worried about me because I didn't like being separated from my mother. My mother had to go and discuss the matter with the teacher. Remember we're talking about 1935, 1936, 1937. My mother was a college graduate, and she hated being a housewife. She talks about that even now.
Diamond: She's still alive?
Kennedy: Yes. Oh. Extremely. A very powerful person. She had a degree then, and she thought she should be teaching.
Diamond: Yes. Well, that was the idea of the middle class, even the struggling middle class, wasn't it? Well-educated women who were mothers were not supposed to work.
Kennedy: She said, maybe a couple of years ago, she said, I used to stand by the window all the time and think, "Is this all my life is going to be?" Finally she went to work in a war plant.
Diamond: Which one?
Kennedy: Fisher Body. My father almost died! "You're going to work in a war plant?" She said, "You know, I could make a lot of money." And I think that's how she went to work. My father was always sullen about that. But she was so proud of her paycheck. I remember her showing it to me. And I remember that there was a difference in my mother's demeanor. She would put on those slacks and this thing you had to wear over your head. Anyway, that's how they bought their first house. But my father never recovered from that.
Diamond: A strange thing happens with material you supply in *People* that almost works against the aesthetic of your plays. Works against because you deliberately undermine the operation of truth in your drama. There's no linear time, as in realism, and you refuse the social referent, except in certain cases, say, Raymond in *Funnyhouse*. But now your readers will be tempted to fill in what your plays deny. I've found my-

self wondering if Wally [*Movie Star*] is based on Cornell, or if Miss Rosebaugh was anything like the White Dog [*A Lesson in Dead Language*]. On the other hand if what I said earlier applies, then the autobiography just gives us another Kennedy text, no more true than the plays. But the temptation is there to fill in, especially because there is so much psychic pain in the early plays.

Kennedy: I can understand that. I don't know what to do about that. My plays are the product of my imagination, but there are people who literally want to make me Sarah [*Funnyhouse*]—they think she has my background. [*Pause*] It's important to remember that I grew up in an immigrant neighborhood but was also a product of black middle-class culture, and I always tried to make sense of that. Tried to balance that. To understand where I fit into that world. I mean I feel intensely that white American culture always, always, always is trying to diminish black Americans. In ways that are subtle and ways that are not so subtle. So that I always had to be a fighter. I feel that very much. The six o'clock news shows nothing but blacks being arrested for drugs, when everybody is being arrested for drugs.

Diamond: Yes.

Kennedy: Or, going back to that salesclerk that you know about. I'm always fighting. I'm always fighting not to be diminished by the so-called majority culture. Whatever that is.

Diamond: Let me ask you something about your collected plays, *In One Act*. Are your plays being produced now as often as they were?

Kennedy: No, but they're being taught now in all sorts of college curricula—in women's studies and in black and American studies courses. Ultimately—and I understand this—my plays appeal to only a small group of people, both black and white, who are sympathetic. My work has never made it into the mainstream. It appeals to college students, college professors. And I have come to terms with that. They're still—my plays—abstract poems. That's what they are, abstract poems. [*Pause*] There is a group of women who are my mother's friends, who are in their late seventies or eighties, who have tried for years to get various theatres in Cleveland to do my plays. These were very powerful women. They tried for years because they were proud.

Diamond: And?

Kennedy: My plays make people uncomfortable. So I've never had a play done in Cleveland, never. One of my mother's friends, who also is a very good friend of mine, told me these plays make them feel uncomfortable.

MEGAN TERRY
Felicia Hardison Londré

Megan Terry (courtesy of Megan
Terry © 1991)

From her days as a founding member of the Open Theatre in New
York (1963–67), to her current activities as resident playwright and
literary manager of the Omaha Magic Theatre, Megan Terry has used
the stage to tell the truth for and about the communities in which she
worked, while her innovations in theatrical form have emerged from
the creative process itself. The community of seventeen actors and four
writers that made up the Open Theatre provided the impetus for *Viet
Rock* (1966), her best-known play of the Vietnam War period. Today she
draws upon the concerns of the Midwest communities that the Omaha
Magic Theatre visits on tour, demonstrating in her plays the possibility
of change through "creative action."

Megan Terry is the author of over sixty plays and the recipient of
numerous awards, including the Stanley award, an ABC-Yale University fellowship, two Rockefeller grants, an Earplay award, a Creative
Artists Public Service grant, and a Guggenheim fellowship.

Terry's way of creating a script by "playing with the elements of theatre" actually pioneered certain techniques that we associate with theatre of the 1960s, some of which have been absorbed into standard theatre practice: the involvement of actors in shaping a work for performance; the expansion of American musical comedy form to include rock music; borrowing clichés of the mass media; having actors leave the performance space to interact with audience members; and using "transformations." Terry's work is emblematic of the 1960s, a decade in which many idealistic young talents turned their backs on the commercial theatre and devoted themselves instead to exploring alternative venues and forms. In the explosion of activity—happenings, street theatre, guerilla theatre, the work of Joseph Chaikin and the Open Theatre, the Bread and Puppet Theatre, the San Francisco Mime Troupe, the Living Theatre, the Performance Group, and many others—perhaps the only common characteristic was the breakdown of traditional Aristotelian dramatic structure. Terry's transformations may be considered one of the more successful alternative forms that appeared in that heady era.

Terry developed her transformational technique and honed the script for *Viet Rock* through her work with members of the Open Theatre in a series of all-day Saturday workshops devoted to exploring the subject of violence, particularly as manifested in the war that was dominating the media. During that six-month process in 1965–66 she used improvisation as a tool to explore the group's confusion, anger, fears, and hope (for the optimistic Terry, there is always hope). *Viet Rock* actualizes her experimentation with constructing a dramatic action composed of brief sequences that are suddenly transformed into different sets of characters and circumstances. Exploring the social ramifications of the war from multiple points of view, the rock musical opens with the actors playing children's games, which segue into the inevitable cops and robbers, cowboys and Indians; these build to the sounds and actions of real war. An explosion cues their transformation into mothers cuddling their male babies. The "babies" are stripped to their shorts, and this transforms them into draftees lined up for an army physical, for which the women play the doctors. In the course of the play the same actors become senators, war protesters, Vietnamese, and various other characters. The use of transformation, as opposed to a motivationally connected narrative, allows for greater compression, rapid pacing, freedom to digress and to comment through counterpoint, and unlimited perspectives on the topic.

Viet Rock opened at Cafe La Mama on 21 May 1966, was taken to New Haven that fall to open the professional theatre season at Yale University, and had a sixty-two performance Off-Broadway run. Terry recalls that "one of the best things *Viet Rock* did was bring a lot of very bright people into the theatre" (David Savran, *In Their Own Words: Contemporary American Playwrights* [New York: Theatre Communications Group, 1988], 249).

Viet Rock illustrates another of Terry's abiding concerns: the role of language in human power struggles. According to Phyllis Jane Rose, the play was "meant to be a catalogue of clichés, conscientiously chosen to demonstrate the disparity between the reality of war and contemporary American attitudes toward it, attitudes expressed in habitual media-propagated language" ("Megan Terry," *Twentieth-Century American Dramatists, Part 2: K–Z,* ed. John MacNicholas *Dictionary of Literary Biography* [Detroit: Gale Research, 1981], 7:284). The sergeant drilling his GIs repeatedly calls them "girlies," as if to reinforce his authority by verbally reducing his recruits to the lowest status he can conceive. Indeed, sexism in language became the subject of an entire play, *American King's English for Queens* (1978). "English can be like bullets," Terry told David Savran (250). That work then led to *Goona Goona* (1979), a play about family violence arising from violence in language. As Terry observed, "Roles and attitudes toward the self are shaped within the family by how one is spoken to" (Kathleen Betsko and Rachel Koenig, *Interviews with Contemporary Women Playwrights* [New York: Beech Tree, 1987], 387).

A feminist perspective came to the fore in Terry's dramatic biography of Simone Weil, *Approaching Simone* (1970), which won an Obie award for the best play of 1969–70. Terry's move to Omaha in 1974 to join Jo Ann Schmidman's Magic Theatre signaled the growing importance of theatre outside New York. "In the seventies, maybe our style scared people, but now we find people are beginning to crave it," Terry has said. "I think that the more our culture gets fragmented, the more people want a feeling of community and contact." Thus her current work, as she explains in the following interview (conducted on 21 March 1989 and amplified in January 1994), grows out of the needs she perceives in her adopted community and the surrounding region.

Londré: To start with something biographical, could you tell me a little about your work at La Mama and how you arrived at your transformational technique?

Terry: Ellen Stewart let me do a play a month at La Mama, and that led to *Viet Rock*. We did *Magic Realists, Comings and Goings,* and opened

Viet Rock on Armed Forces Day in May 1960. *Magic Realists* was the only play that didn't grow out of workshops with Joseph Chaikin and the Open Theatre. Regarding the transformation, a lot of things came together. I was trained in creative dramatics at the University of Washington and worked a lot with children. I ran a playschool in Canada for two years, and I learned a lot about transformations from them. Another influence on transformations comes from American stand-up comedy—the impressionists, people who can switch from one character to another—plus the cartoons—Bugs Bunny and Tom and Jerry. Then there was Gertrude Stein and the cubists, the collagists. Put them all together! The first transformations were done in New York in *Calm Down Mother.* Then we, the Open Theatre, did a double bill of *Calm Down Mother* and *Keep Tightly Closed.* There were influences from Joseph Chaikin, who had worked with Nola Chilton, who had been influenced perhaps by Viola Spolin.

Londré: Are you still using the technique?

Terry: If the material demands it. At Omaha Magic Theatre we develop one or two pieces a year that have no set characters. In plays like *Sea of Forms* and *Walking through Walls,* which I wrote with our artistic director Jo Ann Schmidman, the actors constantly transform, because those plays develop themes rather than characters—themes like the unity of all forms or how to break down internal or external barriers.

Londré: Is it important to you as a playwright to work closely with actors?

Terry: I like it because I was brought up in the theatre. I love actors and the social interaction. I have my typewriter down here, and I like to work here. I find that actors stimulate me very much. I adore actors, and I adore the art and craft of acting. I love to be up close.

Londré: Does your method of working combine the typewriter and the cassette recorder?

Terry: No. No, I really don't record what they say. But I see *how* things work. What's interesting about actors is their souls. When they find their gestures, you can see how much they can do, and then see how many lines or speeches I can cut. I learned to edit from watching actors. What they can do is a substitute for words. I find, when I'm judging a lot of playscripts in a contest, that many writers haven't the foggiest notion about editing their work. The plays are overwritten.

Londré: What do you look for in a new playwright?

Terry: A voice. A clear, fresh voice or point of view that really wakes you up, something that only that one writer knows and can convey and that makes you understand things in new ways. I look for theatrical power, hypnotic energy, and the psychic news. We have a bias toward avant-garde work.

Londré: I understand you have something called a community-problem play. What is that like?

Terry: Well, we listen to community concerns. This is what's supporting our art. It supports all the rest of the work we do. It's the opposite of what they taught me in playwriting class in college, for example, that "art and politics don't mix." But actually what has supported us for the last fifteen years are plays like *Babes in the Bighouse,* which deals with women in prison, and *American King's English for Queens,* which shows how children are socialized by the way adults speak to them, how gender roles are developed through the way children are talked to and how they internalize pronouns. We talk a lot, at great length actually, about the play in every community where we play, on the road or here in Omaha. We have a discussion afterward to get the audiences thinking. Out of that kind of work came *Goona Goona,* which deals with spouse and child abuse. Out of the discussions after *Goona Goona* performances came *Kegger,* which deals with young people drinking and driving. In those discussions the audience said, "The reason we drink is because we can't talk to one another," and out of that discussion came *Dinner's in the Blender,* which deals with impossible and possible ways for families to communicate. It's just moved on like that. The production of *Kegger* supported our company for three years. We even had to organize a second company to deal with the demand. And now that it's been published, it's being done all over the country. It's been done in Maryville, Missouri, in Los Angeles, and by Dallas Children's Theatre and will be done by San Francisco New Conservatory Children's Theatre and the Virginia Children's Theatre.

Londré: Is there any difference in audience response between Omaha and the small towns you visit on tour?

Terry: The difference is that on tour the whole town comes, unless there's a basketball game.

Londré: Is the script adapted for different communities, or is it pretty much set after the Omaha performances?

Terry: We toured our version around the Midwest, so it was the same in Iowa, the Dakotas, Nebraska, Kansas. What they did in Dallas was change the slang to keep up with the local language, and they changed certain place names. Also I encouraged them to go out and listen to the music that their young people listen to. Then I encouraged them to rearrange the music to carry the local beat. Our Midwest rock translated perfectly into rap music for Dallas. They put it to a Spanish beat for L. A. We prepare study guides and send them out. We get a lot of help in developing the plays and study guides from humanities scholars, some from Nebraska and some from Iowa. We take scholars with us on the road, and they help with the discussions after the show. It is an interdisciplinary project during the development of the play. Then we take scholars from different disciplines with us on tours. For instance, one scholar is a historian and talks with the community about the history of alcohol, which is fascinating! We hear how alcohol developed because grain was rotting and they needed to do something with the grain to create another cash crop, so they invented alcohol. Then they had to invent corks so alcohol could be transported from one place to another without evaporating. It's just so amazing, the things we learn. At other places we've had a neurosurgeon, a neuropsychiatrist, who explains what happens to you physiologically. We've also learned about alcohol in prisons, because every time we played a college or community center we played a local prison too. And that's where we got firsthand testimony. Prisoners would say, "You know, I started drinking when I was eleven or twelve, and so emotionally I'm still eleven or twelve." I think this kind of arrested emotional and intellectual development is so tragic. The quest for the self arrested by drugs and alcohol is a sad and tragic state for a person to be in. It's another kind of stunted prisoner.

Londré: You say you perform inside the prisons?

Terry: Yes. We started doing that with the Open Theatre. And we perform on Indian reservations, in community centers, colleges, halfway houses, high schools—we play a lot of gymnasiums.

Londré: Would you describe your work as "political theatre," or is there another term for it?

Terry: I'd call it "social action theatre," because it's a catalyst for a community to talk together about how to solve a problem. For instance, one town decided that, instead of having a senior prom where all the kids drank, as they usually did, they would buy up tons of red paint and let the kids paint the town red.

Londré: What did they paint!?

Terry: They painted the whole town. All the exteriors. It was a very small town.

Londré: And this was your doing?

Terry: We were just the catalyst for it. They figured it out for themselves.

Londré: Do your local reviewers see your work as art or politics?

Terry: They don't care—it's just a play. It doesn't matter whether it's art or politics. It's a catalyst for the community. Some communities were able to get together and create halfway houses and safe houses for battered women and abused children after we played *Goona Goona,* for instance. Now we're doing a piece called *Head Light,* which deals with literacy. I've done a lot of research for it, worked with the literacy council. And again scholars will help with leading audience discussions after the performance and help us to develop and finalize a good study guide for schools and communities and literacy councils to use in conjunction with our visit.

Londré: How do you begin your work on a play like that? Does the research come first?

Terry: First there's the stimulus from audience discussions, accounts by honest eyewitnesses, or people who are involved in helping people in trouble, or the victims themselves. When I find that the same themes keep coming up, that's when I get going and start my research.

Londré: At what point do you know you are ready to sit down at the typewriter?

Terry: When the shape of the play takes place in my mind. When I can see that shape or when the characters start talking to me, when they take on a life of their own—then I can write the play. I revise it during rehearsals and also on the road. Some plays start out twice as long as they end up. So I subtract. Then I add materials stimulated by the audience. It's a process of adding and subtracting. Mostly subtracting.

Londré: Why is music such an important element in all your plays?

Terry: I love to have music around me. I come from a very musical family. Every time we had a family party, everyone sang and played and even sang in five-part harmony. We have many wonderful young composers here. You know, Kansas City and Omaha are the homes of jazz. So I can have any combination of soft jazz or hard rock and roll. There are a lot of very creative composers here. We have composers ranging from a Charles Ives disciple to a synthesizer/industrial rock musician to a reggae musician. According to the feeling of the piece, we can call on anywhere from one to six composers. We have five on *Head Light.* It's plain fun to have music in a play.

Londré: I've noticed this upbeat, positive attitude of yours that comes through in other interviews, like the one with David Savran in *In Their Own Words.* Does your optimism ever hamper you from really grappling with problems in your plays?

Terry: Gee, I don't know. I want other people to be as happy as I am, I guess. I get upset when they don't get the chance. There are quite a lot of young people depressed these days. People in their twenties. I can't understand being depressed in your twenties. But I see a lot of it in my travels.

Londré: How do you keep your optimism while dealing with the serious problems you confront in your work?

Terry: I don't know, maybe it's because of my pioneer background. I feel very close to a pioneer culture. My people went from Illinois, Minnesota, Iowa, Nebraska, to the West Coast. And before that they came across the seas from Ireland. So I know that you can keep moving forward to get where you want to go. I still feel very close to that. I was lucky enough to know my great-grandparents. They lived into their nineties. So growing up hearing all the stories they could tell—going against the elements, going through the Civil War, coming West, and surviving, and then establishing themselves there—it's just all part of my environment. Knowing that is very important. I mean, many people have no idea who their grandparents are. You know, our so-called affluence has created this modern mobility, but people don't know who they are. The extended family has been decimated by the automobile and upward mobility. It really disturbs me to see young people floundering, because I knew what I wanted to do at an early age. I was lucky enough to live three blocks from a great theatre. A theatre that took me in as a young teenager and taught me theatre arts and crafts and a respect for our field.

Londré: Do you separate your personal life from your professional life, or are they totally integrated?

Terry: They're totally integrated. I think of our theatre as extended family. I like to have people of all ages around me. We have people from high school age to a sixty-seven-year-old sculptor working on our shows. When people come to the Magic Theatre, they always marvel at the cross section of ages—onstage *and* in the audience.

Londré: Do you ever crave to work with the classics?

Terry: Oh, I love the classics. The Greeks, the French, the Irish, the Scandinavians, the Russians.

Londré: But your theatre doesn't produce them?

Terry: Everyone else does though. We might get around to it one day, but there's so much good new work to do. We've been presenting plays from the 1960s along with fresh, new work.

Londré: Describe what you believe were the most significant changes between the American theatre of the 1950s and the theatre of the 1960s.

Terry: The 1960s marked an explosion of playwriting styles. One reason for this was because at least thirty-five strong playwrights arrived and began to show their work in New York within the same time period. It was the kind of creative combustion that hadn't been seen since Greek and Elizabethan times. Sheer numbers of challenging writers with many different points of view were in the same geographical location. I believe this could take place because of some excellent teaching that had gone on in the universities by the people who had fought in World War II. They came back to their students with a global view and a new sense of American power and energy in the world. Before this playwrights seemed to arrive in the national consciousness one at a time. But this new group of playwrights realized they were a group. Some realized this because they literally received energy from one another, and others, because their audiences were telling them it was so. And yet others hated to hear it from people who were then starting to write about the theatre, the way they had previously written about politics. It was like sport to show our work to one another and almost play "can you top this" with each new play.

Another physical fact that made this possible was that our theatres were literally within walking distance of one another. When I say that playwrights arrived one at a time, it seems sometimes that it was true and at other times that the people who were writing about the American theatre of the 1950s and before could only see or hear that one person at a time. They didn't seem to be able to hold more than one writer in their consciousness, that is, one O'Neill, then one Tennessee Williams, then one Arthur Miller, etc. There were other people writing at this time, but then a writer had to make a big, big Broadway impression to take up enough psychic space to be able to be hailed as *the* American playwright. In the 1960s we realized we weren't welcome on Broadway, but we had confidence. We started our own theatres and found directors and actors of like minds, colleagues, who would work in collaboration, in groups where the actor was treated as a cocreator, not as an employee or interpreter. This attitude or practice made for a completely different dynamism in performance. The 1960s audiences responded to this, and we were off and flying. Our work and ideas took over the decade, and soon American theatre production ideas and playwriting seemed to be leading the world. These ideas cross-pollinated with many other cultures.

Londré: What influences do you see the 1960s having on theatre of the 1990s?

Terry: I feel now in the 1990s much of this early interaction is now coming to a new fruition. Evidence is already on our stages, on world stages with more on the horizon. I believe the American theatre of the

1950s was the culmination of European influence on American playwriting. For instance, I believe the American theatre of the absurd is the end of that cycle, not a beginning. Many important playwrights are represented in an excellent collection, edited by Poland and Mailman, *The Off-Off Broadway Book*. Here you will find the work of many strong writers who are still at work today: John Guare, Rochelle Owens, Maria Irene Fornes, Ronald Tavel, Rosalind Drexler, Kenneth Bernard, Jean-Claude van Itallie, and myself among many others. Recently we produced double bills of plays by many of these writers. One written in the 1960s and one written in the last two years. We didn't tell our audiences which were which, and we found they couldn't tell the difference. Each of the plays seemed fresh to them; all seemed to them to have been written that morning. This tells me that it's time for a reevaluation of all of the work of these writers and that a concerted effort should be made to bring their work to wider audiences. We try hard to get the news of the writers we admire out to others who may be interested in producing this exciting work. We have published a book to help with this, *Right Brain Vacation Photos: Twenty Years of Omaha Magic Theatre Productions*. It is our hope that the production possibilities shown in the photos and samples of text will stimulate more productions for these productive 1960s writers, as well as the new writers we have been producing. Included in the book are instructions and addresses for contacting the writers. At our theatre many Ph.D. candidates come from all over the world to visit, to observe our work, and to pore over our archives. In time they will get the word out, and there will be more productions of the works of this fecund period, as well as productions of the many subsequent works of these writers. Nearly all are still writing, and many are writing now at the top of their form.

Londré: In what ways were the playwrights of the 1960s distinctly American?

Terry: The 1960s writers and the 1960s productions have a distinctive American voice. I should say "voices," because there are many Americans, and the 1960s began to demonstrate this fact. The cultural diversity of our country and our heritage began to become known then. These ideas have been taken up by all the other media and most of our social and political institutions.

Londré: How would you characterize 1960s contributions to directing and acting?

Terry: There were great advances made in direction, acting, and production design in the 1960s. A synthesis and cross-pollination from discoveries in other media and art were coming into the theatre. You can see fruition of these seminal ideas in much of the performance art of the last ten years and now on Broadway in productions such as *Tommy,* as well as in opera and the new wave festivals at the Brooklyn Academy of Music, that is, [in the work of] Robert Wilson, Laurie Anderson, and Karen Finley and in the current work of the Omaha Magic Theatre. Ideas from the last hundred years in art and design have come into the theatre. Some of these ideas are amplified, modified, and expanded by the use of electronic media and by the application of image projection possibilities on a large scale. Now you can see that the designer, too, has been brought to join the creative, producing team as a cocreator who makes as strong a statement about the theme or ideas of the play as the playwright, director, and performer. Sometimes one person may wear all these hats, sometimes a creative team, but all work together to bring new power into our field and thus more enjoyment to the audience that makes the effort to go out to the theatre and join in with the creative interaction possible in this evolving art form.

Londré: How would you evaluate theatre of the 1960s in light of your work and interests of the 1980s and 1990s?

Terry: The theatre of the 1960s—the energy of it and the ideas of it—the plays themselves, the productions, many of which I saw, are still in my mind. I know that I was privileged to be alive then and to be a part of it and to have it embroidered into the fiber of who I am. Not a day goes by that some young person doesn't come to our theatre to ask me what the 1960s were really like—to sit with me, to hear the stories of those who were the shakers and movers then but are putting it down now. I believe there will be an entire reevaluation of that period and that the positive discoveries will be given their proper honor in our formal histories. The 1960s will always be with us. That decade, which I believe is one of the longest decades in history, wasn't really over until 1975, when the Vietnam War was stopped. That war marked the fact that we live in a global village, and it brought about the rediscovery of the facts that we truly are, not only our sister and brother's keeper, but that we had only a short time to relearn to be the stewards of our planet.

Londré: Over the last several years what have been your major goals for the Omaha Magic Theatre? How have your roles as director-playwright-producer helped you fulfill those goals?

Terry: These past several years have been crucial ones of trying to survive. Our funding has shrunk, not only from public and private entities, but colleges and universities also have barely enough funds for their own arts programs. To secure touring dates takes ten times the effort that it did in the mid-1980s. We have to keep our company going, and we have to make new work for our audiences. And we feel a strong desire to keep growing as artists. We feel an obligation to serve our field through outreach and education, to share with the young and with other artists some of what we have learned. We are seeing theatres folding across the nation. It takes everything we've learned and more hours than we can count anymore to do the work to keep OMT alive. But we've managed to live into our twenty-fifth year as a theatre that produces *only* new work. It doesn't get easier. What sustains us is that we know that in the 1960s we created a new theatre, and that through this theatre we made worldwide friends for our theatre and for our country and ourselves. We still have these friends, and we are adding new ones all the time. We must be doing something right, because there is a steady stream of young artists and seasoned scholars coming to our door. We have managed to build a touring and residency season for our new collaborative works. We keep going by building new works that will challenge and refresh our company and our audience. We use every skill we have and borrow, through advice, those we don't possess. In some ways theatre is an ideal situation because one must constantly learn to keep doing it at all. The brain and body get maxed out every day. Theatre is not only an art form, it is a form where to stay alive you have to constantly solve new problems, and that is the fun of it and the head-banging part of it. I am privileged to work with very great and generous artists and colleagues, like our artistic director, Jo Ann Schmidman, and our designer, Sora Kimberlain, and an expanding team of young and mature artists. Theatre is still fun, and it is still the hardest thing that there is to do. We create something out of nothing, we artists. We don't use up resources; we recycle and rearrange and thus create new resources, self-renewing, to fire ourselves and warm the souls of those who are dedicated to serve and/or take sustenance from this art form.

JEAN-CLAUDE VAN ITALLIE

Alexis Greene

Jean-Claude van Itallie (courtesy of
Jean-Claude van Itallie)

Belgian-born Jean-Claude van Itallie has been closely associated
with the Off–Off-Broadway theatre. In fact during the 1960s van
Itallie was one of the more iconoclastic playwrights working Off–Off-
Broadway. His *America Hurrah* (a trilogy of one-act plays, including *Interview, TV,* and *Motel,* done in 1965–66) explores the sterile conven-
tionality of America during the Vietnam War. *Motel,* for example, is a
daring image of apocalypse in the nuclear age. Using fractured language, actors costumed as grotesque puppets, intense white light, and
blaring sound, van Itallie turned a room in a conventional American motel into a metaphor for the destruction of Western civilization
and in so doing created a piece of theatre that was both poetic and
socially critical. In the early 1960s van Itallie also became the principal
writer for Joseph Chaikin's Open Theatre and collaborated with that
ensemble on *The Serpent* and a number of briefer pieces, lending the
Open Theatre both his spare but rhythmic language and his alertness
to society's ills.

After the Open Theatre dissolved in 1973, van Itallie seemed to be searching for new forms for his theatrical imagination. In addition to writing plays, he adapted a number of works by other writers, notably Chekhov, Euripides, and Mikhail Bulgakov. In 1979 van Itallie's play *Bag Lady* opened in New York City to a generally favorable response. The play is both a poignant study of a woman living on the streets of New York and, as with the earlier *Motel,* a highly theatrical metaphor for disintegration in our time.

In the 1980s two major plays by van Itallie, *Paradise Ghetto* and *The Traveller,* displayed a vein of realistic writing. *Paradise Ghetto,* produced in the fall of 1987 at the Actors' Alley in Los Angeles, is set in the Nazi detention camp at Theresienstadt, where a number of inmates create and perform cabaret sketches as a means of emotional survival. *The Traveller,* first produced at the Mark Taper Forum in Los Angeles in March 1987 and then in Leicester, England, and London the following autumn, is about a composer who suffers a stroke and must regain his ability to speak. The central character is based on Joseph Chaikin, who suffered a stroke during heart surgery in 1984. Both plays demonstrate a fresh turn in van Itallie's playwriting, a mingling of nonrealistic styles with what van Itallie calls the "Chekhovian" side of his writing. *The Traveller* and *Struck Dumb,* which van Itallie has written with Chaikin, are additionally valuable as documents of the continuing relationship between two groundbreaking artists of the 1960s.

Two important works by van Itallie in the 1990s deserve mention. In March of 1990 van Itallie's *Ancient Boys,* a play dealing with an artist who has AIDS, premiered at the University of Colorado at Boulder, and in June 1993 his *Master and Margarita,* based on Mikhail Bulgakov's 1938 novel, opened at the Theater for the New City. In the latter play van Itallie captures the satiric thrust of Bulgakov's story about the devil visiting Moscow.

Throughout his career van Itallie has been vitally occupied with the faults and power of language. He recently told William Harris, "In the 1960s language was suspect because we were always being lied to by religious leaders and politicians. I'm constantly trying to re-find the route of the word, to speak from the heart rather than from the head" ("Plays Are for Questions, Not Answers," *New York Times,* 23 May 1993, sec. 2, p. 5).

The following interview with Jean-Claude van Itallie took place several years earlier, on 5 February 1988, in New York City's Greenwich Village, in an airy, peaceful loft apartment that van Itallie had designed and once owned. The interview took place during the late afternoon and lasted a little over an hour.

Greene: When did you begin to write *Paradise Ghetto?*
van Itallie: I'm not good at dates. About six or seven years ago.
Greene: How did you come to write the play?
van Itallie: I was commissioned by a Broadway producer named Alvin Cooperman. Alvin and his partner at the time, Judith DePaul, had interviewed a great many ex-inmates of that concentration camp who lived in Israel. It wasn't a concentration camp in the sense that everybody was killed, as in the other camps, but rather a detention camp where the Czech artists were sent and then rich German Jews. It was somewhat unique in that the Czechs were asked to run the camp themselves. When the war was turning against Hitler, the Nazis wanted to use the camp as their showplace for the International Red Cross, and they actually commissioned the artists there to write an opera, *The Emperor of Atlantis.* I don't think the opera ever did get performed, but some of it got written. That basic story seemed very dramatic to Alvin, and he came to me with the title *Paradise Ghetto* and commissioned me to do it. He didn't produce the play, for various reasons, partly because I created a large cast. It really does need about eighteen people, and that's not a Broadway play size. But it took me about a year and a half to write. I went to Theresienstadt, got arrested for taking photographs by the Czechs, who didn't want anyone to know that the Russians had a military camp there—it was very strange to be arrested there. And then I worked on the play dramaturgically with a woman who had directed my play *Bag Lady,* Elinor Renfield. Then Alvin didn't produce it, and I put it away. And last year Jordan Charney, an actor and producer of the Actors' Alley Theatre in Los Angeles, and an old friend, asked me if I had any plays he could produce, and I sent him this, and he liked it. At which point I went through and cleaned it up and tightened it a bit. But that was the first time I had looked at it in a while.
Greene: Was this the first time you had written a play that could have a historical basis?
van Itallie: Yes, for the theatre. For Public Broadcasting I wrote a documentary on Pablo Picasso called *Picasso: A Writer's Diary.* I like history a lot. When I was at Harvard, I majored in the history and literature of Russia, France, and England, 1850 to 1950, whatever that was. And my grandfather got me started on history when I was in my early teens. He used to pass me all his books on Napoléon and Louis XIV. But in relation to *Paradise Ghetto* it's very hard to be faithful to such a mountain

of material. There were a tremendous number of tapes made with inmates and records and some drawings, and to try to boil that all down to something manageable was not easy. The whole business with Eichmann is completely invented. He had something to do with the camp, but that's all we know.

Greene: In the play there seem to be two threads that you follow: the day-to-day events in the lives of the camp inmates and then the cabaret pieces that some of these inmates create. The cabaret skits become more grotesque and satirical as the play progresses. What is the function of that side of the play?

van Itallie: It's a play that comments on itself, and I like plays like that. It's also a play about artists, which is not easy to write. So it's the events, plus the events as seen through the eyes of the inmates, which give you a second lens. I based the cabaret a little bit on feelings about the Open Theatre, because that bunch of actors was the bunch of actors that I was most familiar with. If it had been the Open Theatre that had been locked up in Theresienstadt, how would we have gone about making our comments? That part of the play wrote itself most easily.

Greene: I feel it's also the most vital side of the play.

van Itallie: Could well be. I'm quite fond of the scenes between the mother and son. I like that kind of writing. I feel that in my writing there are two big streams, and one is the stream that started with the Open Theatre, breaking ground, dealing with a reality other than the more concrete, usual everyday reality, and the second stream is that concrete, usual everyday reality. The exploration of the second stream started for me when I was doing the new Chekhov versions. A lot of my interest now is to create plays where all of these come together. Because we do live in more than one reality at once.

Greene: Would you discuss the end of *Paradise Ghetto?* What do you intend the audience to go away with?

van Itallie: I'd like the audience to feel the power and goodness of the spirit of the people who were in the camp. I don't want any message to go out about whether people resisted. People didn't resist. Some people did resist, and some didn't. But there was a powerful live spirit from these people. They were human beings, and in some way they continue. Even in this worst of all possible situations, there's still something about the human spirit that is triumphant, and that is what I'd like to have the audience feel at the end.

Greene: Is there any further writing you intend to do on this play?

van Itallie: No. I would love to have more productions of it. I'm glad it finally did get to see the light of day.

Greene: In 1987 you were working on *The Traveller,* which is about Joseph Chaikin's experience of having and recovering from a stroke, and the subsequent impairment of his ability to speak. When did you begin to work on *The Traveller?*

van Itallie: Dates again. Joe had his stroke in May of 1984, and I think we began working the following September—no, probably around January 1985. We worked on it with a few actors for a few weeks, and that didn't seem to lead anywhere. I finally wrote it by myself, sitting up in the country, in what must have been the summer of 1985. And then continued to rewrite it. That play has more drafts than any play I've written. It's a post–word processor play, so drafts are easy enough to grind out.

Greene: When you say "we," do you mean that was a creation of yours and Mr. Chaikin's?

van Itallie: No. First of all I didn't correct you because it was close to the truth, but you said this was a play about Joe's experiences recovering from a stroke. It's *partly* about Joe's experiences, it's partly fictional, and it's partly about my experiences being very close to him during that time. So it's not simply standing outside objectively, observing something and transforming it into a play. But what happened was that I was driving Joe up to the hospital a couple of months after his stroke, for some postoperative checkup or something, and he was reading aloud from an illustrated edition of Dante's *The Inferno.* First I was thinking that the captions were very nineteenth century and that I'd better rewrite them if he was going to learn to reread that way, and secondly I thought that it would be terrific to make a piece in which we made an analogue between the Dante material and Joe's operation. We could maybe use Joe's voice as a voice-over—I was looking for a way to pull him back into work.

So that was the idea. And we brought in friends: Robert Woodruff, director, a friend of Joe's; Rosemary Quinn, actress, friend of mine. And we sat around the table, and we talked about what such a piece might be like. And then in the winter Ellen Stewart gave us some space at La Mama, and Joan McIntosh and a few other actors came in, and we began playing around with this idea. I sort of would feed them some facts. It was the first time that Joe had been able to sit around with actors since the stroke and begin to express something, and so it was wonderfully productive from that point of view. But it became very clear that a piece about Dante wasn't nearly so interesting as a piece about Joe or somebody that was like Joe recovering from a stroke, and so Dante sort of went. There's a bit of Dante left in the surgery sequence, but the rest doesn't matter. We only had about four or five meetings with actors. Then I wrote it. It took me a couple of months during the summer. When I sat down to write, the Traveller was still a woman. It was originally written for a woman, because we were working with Joan McIntosh, and I wanted Joan to play it. The Traveller became a man because Gordon Davidson agreed to produce the play in Los Angeles, and Joan's young son was having some need for her presence in New York, and she felt she couldn't go to Los Angeles. And also Joe kept showing the script to friends who said, "Well, you're a man, why shouldn't it be a man?" Anyway, since we couldn't have Joan, I changed it to a man. My original idea was that the play was going to be for a woman, and the Friend was going to be a woman, and then I changed the Traveller to a man, and the Friend remained a woman. I have kept thinking that the Friend should really be a man if the Traveller is a man.

Greene: Why?

van Itallie: It seems to ring truer to me. I think the dynamics of the relationship ring truer if that's so. I don't feel violently and strongly about it. If we were able to do a production in New York with Morak Hood, the wonderful actress who played the Friend in England, I'd be perfectly happy for the character to be a woman. But if we couldn't have Morak, I'd like to see it happen with a man.

Greene: Would the relationship remain a romantic one?

van Itallie: Still romantic. But it's a relationship that's ending—not ending, transforming. I think *The Traveller* is not only about the main character. I hope it's also about the travels of the two secondary characters, of the Brother and the Friend. I mean, it keeps getting rewritten so that the Friend has more and more to say. At the end it's not that she's left him completely, but that she's left the needy part of the relationship. And she wouldn't have had the strength to do that unless he had the strength to go through what he was going through. So it should properly be called *The Travellers.* But obviously the main traveling is through the emotional levels of the main character. I think originally the part of the Friend was underwritten, and I think that came from the fact that a lot of it is based on me. And it is very hard to write something that is based a lot on yourself. But I think it's okay now. I've added more to it.

Greene: Is *The Traveller* more personal than other plays you've written?

van Itallie: I think so. And so more dangerous to write and so more exciting to me. I'm closer to *The Traveller* than I am to *Paradise Ghetto,* for instance. In *Paradise Ghetto* what's most personal is in fact those mother-son scenes, because they're the closest to my experience of myself when my mother was dying—not in a concentration camp, but nonetheless. On the other hand I am at least three-quarter Jewish, and I did have to flee the Nazis, and some of my family did get put in camps, and that theme has arisen for me from time to time. It came out in *Bag Lady* and, of course, in *Paradise Ghetto*. So in that sense *Paradise Ghetto* certainly was personal. But *The Traveller* is much closer in terms of the actual memory of events happening to me. It's based specifically on incidents in which I took part. I wrote a journal during that time when I was helping Joe to go through—I went through all three of Joe's open-heart surgeries with him. As the people in *The Traveller* do, I was waiting around and kind of sending him good vibrations. I was present during the entire hospital stay, from the beginning until the end—for all three.

Greene: During the actual stroke incident?

van Itallie: During the actual stroke incident nobody remembers or acknowledges anything. I came into his room after the operation, and like the character of the Friend in *The Traveller*, I noticed that he was speaking funny. And the doctors weren't saying anything. Now that it's happened, the doctors talk about it as if he had had a stroke, but there was no moment afterward when they announced that. I'm a health fiend, and I've spent a lot of my life working very hard not to be in a hospital. I eat healthily and I diet and I exercise, and I just don't believe in doctors. I'm not crazy about them.

Greene: What stages has the play gone through, prior to the production in Los Angeles and since then?

van Itallie: Well, the question of the sexes of the characters, which is still not totally resolved in my mind. The play has refined itself. It's shorter now than it was in Los Angeles. In the second act in Los Angeles there was a back and forth to the hospital, which we cut, so that now the Traveller returns home from the hospital once. There were a lot of simplifications like that. There were even a couple of minor characters: an agent, a woman, who was very funny, extremely nervous and extremely flamboyant, but relative to the rest of the play, it was fairly cheap and really needed to go. Each succeeding script has become more modest in its production requirements. In Los Angeles we spent mountains of money on screens and slide projections, and I think it just weighed the play down. In England we did it without any projections. The production in Los Angeles had seventeen people. The production in England had eight and was done in a much more ensemble fashion, because the actors had to switch roles. I think an ideal number would be nine. I think there was a little too much switching. I feel everything that is extraneous to the words and the relating of the human beings should be absolutely minimal. I don't know why I hadn't learned that lesson a long time ago, but at least I'm learning it now.

Greene: You said that *Paradise Ghetto* was about artists on some level. I feel that about *The Traveller* as well.

van Itallie: I think it is about that. One wonders, what is an artist? A professor of psychology at Sarah Lawrence once told me they had brought famous artists to a seminar and questioned them, and the only common denominator was that all the artists felt they had grown up out of context in some way. Either they were not really at home when they were growing up, or they grew up in two languages or with the feeling that they were really the son or daughter of some prince. I think that being an artist has to do with that kind of perspective. I had the good fortune to grow up in a couple of languages, and I think that makes you realize that no single language contains reality, that words are always an approximation of reality, that language and even thought are perspectives on reality, not reality itself. I don't know if there's a definition of an artist, but I think that's a possible definition. And that definition may pertain to these plays, where reality is not an absolutely solid, palpable thing. You have to deal with it in the everyday world, but at the same time it shakes and wobbles, and you see it from upside down and downside up.

What interests me is the relationship between realities. I'm a Buddhist, and of the Tibetan variety, and they talk about the *Bardo.* One translation of the Bardo is "the in-between place." It's dreaming, it's that moment when you sneeze or have an orgasm, moments when reality no longer has the sharp rectangular edges. If you follow the *Tibetan Book of the Dead,* it's what goes on at the moments before dying, and it goes on most strongly between death and rebirth. It's a very exciting concept. I think laughter is a kind of acknowledgement of a leap from one reality to another. Suddenly she slips and falls and is splattered all over the pavement. Before that she was the dignified lady walking down the street. It's a leap.

Greene: You said in an interview in Los Angeles, during the production of *The Traveller,* that *The Traveller* brought together some of the forms you explored in the Open Theatre, as well as more traditional forms. Could you be specific?

van Itallie: The play starts out in "real" reality—whatever you want to call that, Chekhovian reality or high-pressured New York reality. And then the Traveller begins to get drugs and anesthetic, and his mind begins to fuzz a little. The conceit of the play is that at this point he goes down into the inferno world, and he's in a dream reality, a very profound dream reality. That's what I relate with Open Theatre techniques, because the Open Theatre was working to find ways to express perceptions of that kind of reality. The play has a kind of parabolic shape. It goes down at that point, and then you start coming back up, and as you surface, you come back into the more Chekhovian reality. But there are still some leftovers: when the Traveller sees the horse neighing or when he has hallucinations. And so then there are juxtapositions of realities. But more and more as he deals with people and has to find a new language to do that, is reborn into the world really, there is more of the Chekhovian reality.

I think the Open Theatre part for me is the old, and it's the easiest. I think what's new for me about *The Traveller* is that it is as personal as it is. I feel I've been let free, let out of the nursery in some way. Out to the big world. I, too, can deal with everyday reality.

Greene: Then the leap for you here is the realistic side of the play?

van Itallie: What I would call the more personal part. I need to express my Chekhovian part more, my personal part. I think Chekhov deals with home and family, as well as homelessness and lack of family. And I'm interested in those themes.

Greene: You've also been working with Mr. Chaikin on *Struck Dumb.*

van Itallie: Yes. It's about to go into its first production in Los Angeles, at the Taper, Too, which is the sibling of the Mark Taper. Robert Woodruff is directing it. It's being done with a shorter play that Joe wrote with Sam Shepard, *The War in Heaven*. It opens in March.

Greene: How did this piece evolve?

van Itallie: Well, I was in one hotel and Joe in another in Santa Monica, about a block away from each other, during the production of *The Traveller.* Joe was hired as the consultant on *The Traveller*, because, indeed, who could have consulted better? Joe is now able to read aloud from the stage rather than act without a piece of paper in front of him. He can read anything, but he can't remember words to string them together. So he and Sam Shepard had this short play, and people would ask him to read that some place, and I thought it would be real good if he had something to go with it, so that he could tour with it. That would be his performance piece for the next few years. The Mark Taper kindly said it would commission the piece. So there we were living on the coast in California, and I thought, "Well, what would be better than to write about a character who lives on the coast in California and is sort of a waif." So Joe and I went out and walked by the sea, and Joe made some comments about the sea, and then I would sort of interview him as the character, and then we went for a trip to the zoo, and Joe made a few comments about the zoo, and I would make a few comments about the zoo, and then we would edit them. We also had Bill Coco out there, who's been dramaturging a lot of the work that I've been doing recently. So there was this team to write this play. It's structured so that it takes place in the space of a day, and there is an actual journey that is made.

Greene: It seems like a stream-of-consciousness piece in some respects.

van Itallie: Well, it's very edited and very shaped. It's not really stream of consciousness, because some of it comes from me, and much of it comes from Joe, but it had to be really pulled out of him. If you mean by stream of consciousness that that's what the audience is supposed to take away from it—yes. But somewhat theatrical too, because he does take in the audience, sometimes he looks at them and talks to them.

Greene: Is there an avant-garde in American playwriting today?

van Itallie: Oh, gosh. I don't know. I don't like the word avant-garde. I feel that's sometimes the box I'm shoved in. I feel that there's good theatre and bad theatre, and there's very little good theatre and a lot of bad theatre. Maybe I'm rear-guard, but I want to be moved. I was tremendously moved by Lily Tomlin. I thought she was just fantastic. I was also tremendously impressed by the last piece I saw Charles Ludlam do, *Irma Vep.* But this minimalist, heartless, technically beautiful theatre, which appears here and there—it has no interest for me at all. If it's just appealing to the head, or to the eye and the head, to me it's cold. Just as, if you appeal only to the heart, it can get terribly sentimental, and if it's only in the gut, it can get too angry, and if it's only the genitals, it's pornography. It has to be the whole thing. It doesn't often happen. It did for me in *The Mahabharata.* I loved *Mahabharata.* I thought, "Oh, this is really great, tell me more fairy stories." I feel that if art or theatre doesn't have some sort of sacred intent, it's not of interest to me. It's meant to heal in some way, maybe by bringing out something that's in the collective dreaming or the collective unconscious, that we wouldn't have recognized otherwise.

Greene: What would you like to explore as a playwright, as an artist, in the immediate future?

van Itallie: I've never liked thinking of myself as purely a writer or purely even a playwright. I'm enjoying working on a dance piece that Nancy Spanier is choreographing. It's a piece about aging. I've been doing Sufi dancing and Yoga work for many years, and I find that my body is able to move in a way that's not shameful, so it's a great pleasure for me to get into something that is more toward performance. I want to direct a bit, and next fall I'm directing my translation of Jean Genet's *The Balcony* at New York University, where I also teach. I may want to write in forms that are not purely play form. I have for years had this idea about science fiction. Aside from that I want to explore a kind of Chekhovian reality with a few other overtones, but in a subtle way, something that looks more like a conventional play.

Greene: That is interesting to me, coming from you, who started as a playwright who was breaking down barriers of form and content.

van Itallie: I think and I hope that I'm still breaking down barriers, but I'm breaking them down in myself as I want to break them down in my work, and that seems to me completely parallel if not identical. But they're barriers against feeling. I'm trying to break down the barriers of feeling. Now you could say that's a function of age and that maybe I've come full circle. I don't know. But I feel more and more alive as I get older. I feel more and more vibrant and want to feel more—I'm greedy for it. And I feel that we are extremely cut off. And that's a theme I stated twenty, twenty-five years ago. I was very impressed by R. D. Laing's *The Politics of Experience*—the idea that if we don't acknowledge certain of our feelings, even our uglier and our more aggressive feelings, our sexual feelings, they are out there doing violence by themselves. So I am still interested in breaking barriers, but they are barriers of feeling. And in some sense I was interested in that even when I was writing *America Hurrah,* although at that point I was saying, "Look, there's a war going on in Vietnam. It has to do with our feelings of violence." It seems to me I'm still interested in expressing the same things; only it's taking a different road.

PART 3

RECOVERY AND REGENERATION: THE AMERICAN THEATRE OF THE 1970s

L ooking back on the New York theatre of the 1970s, Samuel Leiter
found that

> The period was enormously rich in controversies, developments, and
> talents. The avant-garde was stretching the boundaries of the theatre
> to places it had rarely been before; new theatres were being built on
> Broadway for the first time in half a century, and venerable ones were
> being threatened with destruction; the musical theatre was being
> redefined; the city's production loci were being expanded; widespread
> institutionalization and subsidization were replacing the traditional
> producing methods; the commercial theatre was experiencing a star-
> tling turnaround from near death to vibrant life; numerous new ideas
> for selling shows were being created; with the rise of regional theatres,
> New York was becoming a showcase for new works rather than an
> originator of them; exciting young actors, directors, and designers
> were lighting up stages in every corner of the city; and fascinating
> and important changes were being made in every corner of the pro-
> fession.[1]

Leiter's book *Ten Seasons: New York Theatre in the Seventies* is an invaluable guide to the American stage of this decade. Each of Leiter's
generalizations above receives a chapter, but the changes in the 1970s
that have the most significant implications for later decades include the
growing importance of the avant-garde, the rise of regional theatres,
and the transformation of Broadway into "a showcase for new works
rather than an originator of them." The playwrights whose interviews
appear in this section corroborate and extend the importance of Leiter's
observations.

   In many ways the changes begun in the American theatre of the

1960s became even more prominent and powerful in the 1970s. Off-Broadway, Off-Off-Broadway, and regional theatres once too new or too small to compete with Broadway became center stages producing some of the most important plays of the 1970s. What was once marginal theatre gave the nation its mainstream plays by the end of the decade. By 1975 there were over 150 Off-Off-Broadway theatres, though not all of them survived into the 1980s. Sam Shepard's work of the decade originated from the Open Theatre, where it was promoted and in some cases cowritten by director Joseph Chaikin; Albert Innaurato's two most important plays of the period, *The Transfiguration of Benno Blimpie* (1975) and *Gemini* (1976), started Off-Broadway at the Playwright's Horizons and then arrived on Broadway. The latter play was "one of the longest running non-musicals on Broadway."[2] David Mamet got his start at the St. Nicholas Company in Chicago, where three of his 1970s plays, *Sexual Perversity in Chicago, Duck Variations,* and *American Buffalo,* captivated audiences before moving to Off-Broadway; Mark Medoff premiered his Obie-winning *When You Comin Back, Red Ryder?* at Off-Broadway's Eastside Playhouse; Marsha Norman's poignant *Getting Out* was performed by the Actors Theatre of Louisville in 1977; Samm-Art Williams (*A Love Play,* 1976) and Charles Fuller (*A Soldier's Play,* 1981) wrote for the Negro Ensemble Company; in the early 1970s David Rabe launched his career with the help of Joseph Papp at the New York Shakespeare Festival ("arguably the most important producing organization of the postwar era"[3]), and from there his *Sticks and Bones* (1972) went to the John Golden Theatre on Broadway.

But it was Ntozake Shange's *for colored girls who have considered suicide / when the rainbow was enuf* that perhaps best represents the theatrical versatility of the leading playwrights of the 1970s. Shange's "choreopoem" first was performed in San Francisco. It was then staged at Studio Rivbea in the East Village, and from there moved to 120 performances at the New York Shakespeare Festival, and finally reached Broadway's Booth Theatre, where it ran for 742 performances from September 1976 to July 1978.

The 1970s also witnessed the steady rise of regional playhouses, which decentralized the American theatre. Gordon Davidson aptly claimed that the "decentralization of the American theater is the most challenging and enduring transformation of the last three decades."[4] No longer was there one main American theatre center, as Broadway had been in the 1940s and 1950s. In the 1960s several regional theatres were established, including the Actors Theatre of Louisville, the

Guthrie Theatre in Minneapolis, Trinity Square Repertory Company in Providence, Rhode Island, and the American Conservatory Theatre in San Francisco. The 1970s saw the arrival of the American Repertory Theatre in Cambridge, Massachusetts, the Seattle Repertory, the Indiana Repertory Theatre in Indianapolis, and the Wolf Trap Company in Vienna, Virginia. Thanks to the regional theatres across America, opportunities for new playwrights multiplied. Regional theatres encouraged and underwrote daring innovations, launched more effective ways to attract audiences, and offered more chances to increase both private and public funding. Fleeing New York City in 1974, Megan Terry journeyed to Omaha, Nebraska, to join Jo Ann Schmidman at the Omaha Magic Theatre, which continues to develop dramas challenging the status quo and shaking up our national conscience and consciousness.

What was true of the plays, of course, was true of their creators, the dramatists of the 1970s. Of all the playwrights who began their careers in the 1970s, perhaps none was to be as prominent or prolific as David Mamet. Mamet's career-building plays of the 1970s included *Duck Variations* (1972), *Sexual Perversity in Chicago* (1974), *A Life in the Theatre* (1977), *The Water Engine* (1978), and *American Buffalo* (1976), the last hailed as "a classic of the American theatre."[5] Beyond doubt *American Buffalo,* a key play of the 1970s, has entered the pantheon of American cultural history. Written in Mamet's jabbing, pulsating language (an innovative blend of street poetry, Muzak, and verbal epilepsy), *American Buffalo* depicts an America transformed into a junkshop, where the American dream has been perverted into sordid business dealings and petty thefts. While Mamet's staccato style contrasts with Edward Albee's polished prose, Mamet nonetheless carries on the venerable/vulnerable tradition of satirizing American values and norms, a tradition that established Albee's reputation in the 1960s. Through his plays and screenplays of the 1980s and 1990s, Mamet continues to capture an America hustling from one ethical perversion to another.

The 1970s were also a time when black, ethnic, and women playwrights were rightly valorized as major voices in America. Some black playwrights were, of course, prominent before 1970. In 1959 Lorraine Hansberry's *A Raisin in the Sun* opened at the Ethel Barrymore Theatre on Broadway and ran for 530 performances. The 1960s launched the work of James Baldwin, Baraka, Ossie Davis (*Purlie Victorious*), Adrienne Kennedy, and Ntozake Shange; the canons of the latter two playwrights, as we shall see, expanded greatly in the 1980s–1990s. In 1970 Charles Gordone became the first black writer to receive a Pulitzer Prize for drama for his *No Place to Be Somebody.* Other black play-wrights, such as Ed Bullins, Charles Fuller, and Samm-Art Williams, also commanded much-deserved attention for their work in the 1970s.

An interesting corollary to the success of black playwrights in the theatre of the 1970s was the dramatization of Alex Haley's *Roots* on ABC, which attracted one of television's biggest audiences in 1977. Like Haley, black playwrights such as Kennedy, Shange, Hansberry, and others tapped their African roots for plots, characters, and myths. Building upon such a heritage, Shange, for example, was passionately committed to the idea of creating "new rituals and new mythologies for people of color." Yet Shange, Adrienne Kennedy, Charles Gordone, and many other playwrights of color were also explicit in their attempt to break down racial and gender stereotypes.

Ethnic playwrights also contributed significantly to the American theatre of the 1970s. Albert Innaurato captured the Italian-American community with comic brilliance. Luis Valdez, who founded the Teatro Campesino in 1965, wrote and produced at least ten plays during the 1970s, becoming America's leading Chicano playwright. Native American playwright Hanay Geiogamah, who founded the Native American Theatre Ensemble in the 1960s, wrote *Foghorn, Body Indian,* and *49* during the 1970s to attack the stereotypes and injustices perpetuated against Native Americans by the white establishment. Significantly in 1981 Geiogamah published "the first collection of plays by a native American playwright."[6]

Reflecting the world of his regional heritage, Romulus Linney wrote plays about the South in the 1970s. As illustrated by such plays as *Tennessee,* which was written in 1979 and won an Obie in 1980, Linney clearly situates himself and his work in that region: "Faulkner, of course, explained my childhood to me long before analysis or therapy."

Women's achievements in the theatre need to be seen alongside their expanding roles and rights during the 1970s. In 1971 the National Women's Political Caucus was formed to break down barriers women faced in attaining elected office. In 1973 the Supreme Court legalized abortion in the highly controversial case of *Roe v. Wade.* In 1976 women were finally admitted to the formerly all-male United States military academies.

Many feminist theatres and women playwrights got their start in the 1970s. Susan M. Steadman's useful *Dramatic Re-Visions: An Annotated Bibliography of Feminism and Theatre 1972–1988* appropriately begins with the early 1970s.[7] The effect of the women's liberation movement on the theatre was profound. Feminist theatre played a vital, activist role in American culture during the 1970s, and beyond. The political theories of Simone de Beauvoir (*The Second Sex,* 1961), Betty Friedan (*The Feminine Mystique,* 1963), and Kate Millet (*Sexual Politics,* 1970) energized women directors and playwrights, both established and new. Megan Terry, Adrienne Kennedy, and Maria Irene Fornes, whose careers began in the 1960s, continued their work through the decade. Similarly Alice Childress, the first black woman to have a play professionally produced (in 1952), had her *Wedding Band,* about a doomed love affair between a white baker and a black schoolteacher (played by Ruby Dee), staged in New York in 1972. These established women dramatists were joined by such new writers as Marsha Norman (her *Getting Out* won the Gassner New Playwright's Medallion in 1979) and Wendy Wasserstein (whose *Uncommon Women* was produced in 1977 at the Phoenix Theatre in New York). Emily Mann, currently the artistic director of the McCarter Theatre at Princeton, shaped the theatre of testimony in the 1970s with her *Annulla Allen, The Autobiography of a Survivor* (1977), based upon the life of a remarkable woman who survived the Holocaust. One of America's most talented political playwrights, Mann reconstructs historical events to deconstruct their multiple, often contradictory meanings.

But despite their enormous achievements in the American theatre or the effect their works have had in the political arena, the women playwrights included in this volume defy neat categorization. It is important that we do not fall into the essentialist traps that feminist scholars have been warning us about. Women playwrights do not all write the same; Kennedy's style and voice are very different from Tina Howe's or from Ntozake Shange's, for that matter. Moreover, though women have been cast in subservient roles by a dominant patriarchy, women's writing about such experiences varies immensely. An African American, Latina, or other woman of color will have experiences vastly different from those of a white woman.

Not only politically but also militarily the 1970s were a time of transition. The Vietnam War, which had raged for more than ten years, was winding down. Contrasts between the 1960s and 1970s emphasize the far-reaching significance of this pullout. In late December 1969 almost five hundred thousand American forces had been stationed there. Three years later there were barely twenty-four thousand troops in Vietnam. A cease-fire went into effect on 27 January 1973, and in May 1975 President Ford officially ended the war. The conflict in Vietnam took over fifty-eight thousand American lives and cost $110 billion dollars.

While the war was ending slowly and tragically, it became the subject of many plays that were first produced during the 1970s; Vietnam and the failures of American mythologies of course still continue to occupy diverse theatres and playwrights. David Rabe's Vietnam trilogy, *Sticks and Bones* (1969, 1971), *The Basic Training of Pavlo Hummel* (1971), and his award-winning *Streamers* (1976), swept across many stages, from Broadway to college campuses, in the 1970s. In March 1969 the Living Theatre performed Kenneth Brown's *The Brig,* one of the most grisly testimonies to the brutality of the era; in November 1970 El Teatro Campesino presented *Vietnam Campesino;* and in 1975 Tennessee Williams, a Vietnam War protester himself, wrote *The Red Devil Battery Sign* to satirize the military-industrial complex that fueled the war. Almost all of the plays included in Theatre Communications Group's widely used anthology *Coming to Terms: American Plays & the Vietnam War* date from the period: Tom Cole's *Medal of Honor Rag* (1975), Rabe's *Streamers,* Amlin Gray's *How I Got That Story* (1979), and Emily Mann's *Still Life,* written in 1978–79 and first produced in 1980.[8] These and other Vietnam plays helped the 1970s not only come to terms with but also to reflect upon the agonies of the 1960s.

Notes

1. Samuel Leiter, *Ten Seasons: New York Theatre in the Seventies* (Westport, Conn.: Greenwood, 1986), xi.

2. Linda McDaniel, "Albert Innaurato," in *American Playwrights since 1945: A Guide to Scholarship, Criticism, and Performance,* ed. Philip C. Kolin (Westport, Conn.: Greenwood, 1989), 209.

3. Don B. Wilmeth and Tice L. Miller, eds., Introduction to *Cambridge Guide to American Theatre* (New York: Cambridge University Press, 1993), 15.

4. Gordon Davidson, Foreword to *Famous American Plays of the 1970s* (New York: Dell, 1981), 9.

5. C. W. E. Bigsby, *David Mamet,* Contemporary Writers Series (New York: Methuen, 1985), 85.

6. C. W. E. Bigsby, *Modern American Drama, 1945–1990* (New York: Cambridge University Press, 1992), 333.

7. Susan M. Steadman, *Dramatic Re-Visions: An Annotated Bibliography of Feminism and Theatre 1972–1988* (Chicago: American Library Association, 1991).

8. *Coming to Terms: American Plays & the Vietnam War,* introduction by James Reston, Jr. (New York: Theatre Communications Group, 1985).

CHARLES GORDONE

Susan Harris Smith

Charles Gordone (photo: Susan Kouyomjian)

Currently a distinguished lecturer in the department of speech communication and theatre arts at Texas A & M University, Charles Gordone is best known for his play *No Place to Be Somebody* (produced 4 May 1969, Shakespeare Festival Public Theatre; Indianapolis: Bobbs-Merrill, 1969), for which he won the Pulitzer Prize, the Drama Desk Award, and the Los Angeles Critics Circle award in 1970. At the time Walter Kerr hailed Gordone as "the most astonishing new American playwright to come along since Albee" (*New York Times,* 18 May 1969). Other reviewers, stirred in part by Kerr's effusiveness, were deeply critical of the play's mix of melodrama, surrealism, and harsh social vision. Gordone himself heightened the ensuing debates with his refusal to be narrowly pigeonholed as "black." Repeatedly he has defined himself as an American concerned with what he calls "American chemistry," the cross-cultural mixture of races and religions. Translated into several languages and produced all over the world, *No Place to Be Somebody* ran for two years on Broadway and for three years on national tours.

Gordone, who began his career as an actor, appeared in the original Off-Broadway production of Genet's *The Blacks* and toured with the show for four years. He also has extensive credits as a director. Recently he has been working with Susan Kouyomjian, the artistic producing director of the American Stage in Berkeley, a theatre company designed to break through apartheid on the stage. Together they created a multicultural theatre where actors of different ethnic origins were integrated into traditionally "white" roles without losing their unique identities as Latinos, blacks, or Asians. The aim was to dramatize a critical aspect of American society, that it is not simply multiracial or multicultural but, more significantly, cross-cultural.

At the time of the following interview, which took place by phone from Gordone's home in College Station, Texas, on 10 January 1988, he was working on two projects: a new play, *Roan Browne and Cherry,* which will reflect his concern for America's cultural diversity, and a television pilot called *Heart and Soul,* a "dramedy" set in Harlem.

Smith: Nearly twenty years ago you won the Pulitzer Prize for *No Place to Be Somebody.* How did winning the prize and being the first black man to do so affect you?

Gordone: I have a history of being "the first," and I understand what that means. The news of my being a man of color seemed equally as important as my work. Therefore, it was less of a distinction for me, and more of an insight as to how limited American theatre had been up until the seventies.

Smith: You have not been a prolific writer, and yet you spend a great deal of time on each work. Could you describe your methods of composition?

Gordone: *No Place* was my first work, and winning the prize interrupted any creative momentum I had. You see, most writers, take Mamet and some of the other writers, have written plays and gotten some momentum before they won any prize. This was my first, and everybody leaped on it, and I was taken off the typewriter for quite a while. I directed two or three national tours [of *No Place*], and so there for seven years, 1970 to 1977, I was very much preoccupied with directing this play. It takes time to start a play, and so I give it a great deal of thought.

Smith: No Place has been translated into several languages. How has the play been received abroad?

Gordone: In some instances not very well. They love the gangsterism in it because that's what they hear about, but they find it hard to understand. There's a great disparity—the play has to be interpreted out of their stereotypical idea of what they know about American blacks. Someone has to interpret it, because it completely destroys what they know about American blacks. They're very curious about it, and they love to discuss it.

Smith: Has it gone over better in some countries than in others?

Gordone: In Italy, France, and South America. It's a question of mixed bloods—a problem of mixed bloods. In France they're up on Franz Fanon and Genet.

Smith: If you were to rewrite *No Place* today, how would you change it, if at all?

Gordone: Oh, you don't change it at all, but you will direct it for today's audience, and I had this experience in Los Angeles with the recent revival at the Matrix in Los Angeles [17 July 1987]. You can't do a sixties interpretation because the play, underneath, is a play about the relationships among human beings. It's also a play about people who have no place to be. The conservative mind today doesn't know the sixties and the early seventies and does not respond to that kind of theatrics any more. You have to present your problems in a much more human way. We have the same problems as the sixties today, but we have to address them from our time.

Smith: You have cited Genet as a formative influence on you. Can you expand on this?

Gordone: Genet's *The Blacks,* which I acted in for six years during the sixties, created onstage the reality that was beginning to alter America outside the stage door. So as we performed this ritual each night, it became a way of comprehending through drama the rapid changes.

Smith: On you as an artist? On you as a director? On you as a playwright?

Gordone: On all of it. I'm not just a writer for the theatre; I do it all, so it just affected me, the person.

Smith: What other writers have influenced you?

Gordone: Oh, I couldn't say. I don't know of any, because I don't recognize any of my style, or whatever, because I don't write specifically from a soapbox attitude. So I don't recognize it in any other writer.

Smith: What writers are you conscious of having influenced?

Gordone: No Place has had sort of a cult following, but I don't know of any particular writer that has openly admitted that I have had an effect upon him.

Smith: You resisted the critics who narrowly defined you as a black playwright by repeatedly insisting that you are a black playwright writing about America. Has this stance had either negative or positive consequences?

Gordone: Because I'm a playwright of color who does not write black plays, I've experienced some isolation. I don't write exclusively about blacks. The scholars who put together anthologies don't know what to call me, but that's their quandary, not mine. I personally see that not to be categorized is an advantage for any playwright. If I've been made to pay a price or experienced any negative consequences, I must also say there is a tradeoff in not belonging to either that makes it possible for me to talk to all. As a consequence I'm able to create characters from a whole spectrum of American people. It's been an essential part of my work.

Smith: Recently you have had some trouble with the critical reception of *The Last Chord,* your play about con artists in the black church. Given the current flap over the PTL [Jim and Tammy Bakker's Praise the Lord ministries] fiasco, your subject seems quite timely. Are the critics still insisting on seeing you as black first and a writer second?

Gordone: Yes, that is racist. And also, when a black writer writes about anything—if it has any kind of scope to it—once they learn he's a black, they begin to work from there. So you're always a black first. Yet we should look at the writer writing a full spectrum. I try to write about all people—and we are a country that's very diverse—and to say I have a black point of view is putting me in a corner.

Smith: Do you think that other writers, say Chicano or Chinese, have the same problem?

Gordone: Yes, I think that Luis Valdez has this problem.

Smith: What about women writers?

Gordone: Yes, I think so, too. It applies there, too.

Smith: How do you assess the state of the American theatre today?

Gordone: I think it's a sensitive field. We are still bound up in a racist tradition. Many folks in the theatre have seen things a certain way for so many years that it's difficult to integrate a lot of my thoughts and ideas because traditions are in the way. It's very slow. I know there are many parts of the country that are behind, behind socially, and the children did not experience any of the civil rights movement or know much about it—they're just ignorant no matter what color they are. The answer lies with the playwright: every problem does not have to be a Caucasian one.

Smith: Have you spotted any up-and-coming new playwrights?

Gordone: No, I haven't. *The Color Purple* and *Fences* fit the establishment pattern and are very popular. I think that the eighties have reinstated a stereotyped image of blacks.

Smith: You travel about the country a great deal. Do you think that regional theatre is strong? Are some parts of the country healthier for theatre than others?

Gordone: No, I think it's more political than anything else. The attitudes seem to be so provincial. They're not taking a look at what's going on in other parts of the country, so I don't see regional theatre as doing much of anything.

Smith: Even theatre in Los Angeles, which is focusing on cultural plurality?

Gordone: There is some movement in Los Angeles, but nothing strong enough to have an effect on the national scene. I think college theatre has largely been ignored because of academic influences, but I think that's where movement will come.

Smith: Do you follow what the critics and scholars have to say about you? If so, how do you process their observations?

Gordone: Most of them are not familiar with the subculture.

Smith: What about the black critics who write about you?

Gordone: Critics are critics, and they write about what they think their audience wants to hear. They have a tendency to roll with the idea. They're offended by the fact that I paint such a bleak future for blacks. I think what they're getting is the significant realization—which I reexamined in *No Place*—that, if blacks walk willingly into the mainstream without scrutiny, their identity will die or they will go mad, and we cannot embrace that from which we instinctively retreat. So we have to, in my estimation, reinvent or transcend, and that presents a challenge that they have to reexamine. You know what some people say about the black bourgeoisie: a monkey in a tuxedo is still a monkey. So they find it hard put to understand that they're all scrambling to move into the society and become the very same thing they have been trying to avoid. They take on—they move in the same guise—they will have to. There's no way to change it once one's in it, and that's infallible. They can only be something else; they lose their identity, and of course, you see, what happens in *No Place* is that they either kill themselves or they go mad.

Smith: Do you look for a different kind of society in which white and black are united?

Gordone: It's inevitable, but it has nothing to do with white and black.

It has to do with the communication of culture to people. You know, as Thoreau said, that's man's destiny, the adventure that has yet to be answered. If we keep talking black and white, in those terms we can never emerge. It all gets back to people. It's the humanness.

Smith: Is your kind of theatre going to help us understand our humanness?

Gordone: I believe so, and I believe, as we come up in the nineties, they will be ready to listen—that's my sense—because of greater awareness of cultural diversity and ethnic groups, especially since we're made aware of it every day in one form or another. It's a question of "if I know who I am, I know where I'm going." See, if I don't know who I am, and I embrace your values, we both suffer.

Smith: How did your experience teaching in the Cell Block Theatre program in the New Jersey prisons influence you as a playwright?

Gordone: It taught me a lot about my own criminal tendencies, but I enjoyed that, and I loved them and they loved me. They hated to see me go, but I knew where they were at. If you want to know what the country is all about, and if you really want to know social problems in the country and where they lead, you work in a prison, you see the eruptions—and we have eruptions, as we talk, all over this country. Somebody's doing something, and he doesn't do it for no reason, and he's just pointing to a lot of unfairness, to a lot of terrible, terrible things that happen. I could see this in one of the most realistic ways in prison. I could see these young boys, who had committed murders and were dealers in dope, had lived in a code you would cringe to know. And how, when they're rehabilitated, that's an act. They still have the same thoughts and feelings because the social situation has not changed. Someone else will rise to take their places.

Smith: Would you describe your new play, *Roan Browne and Cherry?* Does the appropriation of a true story mark a new direction in your writing?

Gordone: *No Place* was based upon a real story, a true experience, so *Roan Browne and Cherry* is no different. I write out of my own experience and observation. I've always done that. I can't sit down and make up a story. That would turn out to be sort of pamphleteer, that comes out of observation and that would come too close to journalism and reporting. You have to write on a gut level. I've had four or five different rewrites of *Roan Browne and Cherry,* and it's still in process. I'm still wrestling with the question of identity.

Smith: Since 1977 you have been working with Susan Kouyomjian at the American Stage in Berkeley. Though some innovative theatres have

been exploring the possibilities of "blind-casting," you have been util-
izing the actors' ethnicity, what you call "seeing-casting," in challenging ways. How has this been received, and does this herald a change in
American theatre?
Gordone: Yes, it does, when people begin to look at it with new eyes.
Once they see it, they'll think, "Oh, it's so simple, why didn't I think
of this before?" The minute you say, "We're going to have blind-casting"—well, you know, we don't walk around blindly. The other ethnic
groups in this country are extremely visible. We rub elbows with them
every day. Why in the arts do we suddenly switch gears and make the
change and continue on in our usual tradition? This is a country of
extreme diversity, with people of all races, colors, and creeds. We have
to begin to look at this American experience as an American theatre.
The current situation in which all sorts of "American" theatres have
only WASPs has got to change, and even though we have high visibility
of "minorities" on television, it hasn't happened in the theatre. You could
have a play that uses all whites or all blacks, but let's think historically,
logically, and socially. Let's have something that has a social conscience.
Smith: Of the plays that you did in Berkeley, were there some that went
particularly well in terms of "seeing-casting"?
Gordone: Yes, there were. Some were received better than others. It was
a matter of trial and error, of defining and redefining this business of
cultural backgrounds of each actor, of each character. You can't just go
and say, "Well, now we'll have a blonde playing the mother, and a kid
the color of your shoes playing her child." You can do that in the theatre for a certain kind of elite audience, you know, these liberals who
are saying, "Oh, isn't that wonderful, we don't pay any attention to
color!" You could do that somewhere like Milwaukee, but people are
not going to accept that. People are going to accept just what they see
every day. You can take a play and adapt it, or you can take a play and
not adapt it. You take a play like *Night of the Iguana,* and you cast the
part of the minister as a black man. You don't see those kinds of black
men; we just see black men screaming and hollering and carrying
on, but if you cast him as a Harvard or Yale divinity school graduate, who is in just as much a state of turmoil or, in fact, more, the question of identity comes in more, and it enhances rather than takes away.
Most people think that that kind of experience is only limited to
whites. In *Streetcar Named Desire* we cast Stanley Kowalski as a mulatto who is part French and Creole. Here's a case of logical casting coming out of social background. There are damn few Polacks
in New Orleans, particularly in the French Quarter. It enhances the

struggle between Blanche and Stanley when she sees her sister married to this man out of the jungle, a mulatto who couldn't pass for anything else.

Smith: The critics have praised your ear for language, for the rhythms of individual speech. Can you discuss the function of unique voices in your plays?

Gordone: My mother was great with dialect. I grew up with that kind of ear. Most of the people in my family had that kind of ear. I came out of a diverse, racially mixed family. Diverse ethnic groups will have a tone, a pitch, a timing all their own. They have their own style, their own meter. They still think, though unconsciously, in their own native language. I don't care how well they speak the English, somehow their ethnicity will come through. When you're paying attention to that, if all your characters only spoke the standard English and came out of the same social background, then you have nothing to do but to talk about the problems of that sort of narcissism, you have no scope, you're limited with the kind of story to tell. So you will stay with sex and violence, because that's the only dramatic thing that comes out of your daily experience. There are more dramatic things than sex and violence.

Smith: Some writers see themselves as storytellers, others as shatterers of illusions, others as social reformers. How do you describe your function as a playwright?

Gordone: I would say all of the above, but not consciously. If it happens, it happens. I don't want to be on a soapbox. I just tell a story. I will have some awakening, something I want to talk about. Something will occur to me, and out of it a story will emerge. I don't sit down to write about a particular thing.

Smith: People in the theatre fall into two groups; either they love reading plays and going to see theatre, and seeing what other writers, directors, and actors are doing, or they do their own work and they stay completely away. Which camp do you fall into?

Gordone: I don't go to the theatre very much. When people recommend things to me, I go, and I'm usually disappointed. I eventually get around to reading things. When Sam Shepard has a new play out, I don't care to go see it because I know what Sam Shepard writes about. He's not writing about me. I try to write about Sam Shepard, but he's not interested in where I'm coming from. I don't go to see David Mamet because he's not writing about me. He doesn't even hang out in the places where I hang out. You see, theatre has a way of gobbling you up, and it just takes you right out of life, and the first thing you know, you're writing about it, or about Hollywood or something. I have a whole lot of other things going. I have a life outside of theatre. You can't reinvent sex, and you can't reinvent Hollywood. You can't turn and write about the very thing that you're in. The sun cannot define the sun. I can tell you pretty much where I'm at today, but I don't know where I'm going to be tomorrow.

Smith: Okay, where are you today?

Gordone: Well, in what way, mentally, spiritually, or physically?

Smith: What about all three?

Gordone: I'm in good shape (*laughter*).

DAVID MAMET
Matthew C. Roudané

David Mamet (photo © Brigitte Lacombe)

The interview with Mamet took place 4 December 1984. The conversation was originally scheduled to be held at the playwright's Cabot, Vermont, home, a renovated farmhouse near Montpelier. However, last-minute changes prompted Mamet to fly to New York City, where *Glengarry Glen Ross* was playing at the John Golden Theatre. So we met at the Players, a club for actors, playwrights, and others committed to the theater. Located next to Gramercy Park, the Players was an ideal setting for our conversation. When Mamet entered dressed in a dark suit, I was struck by his physical presence: crew-cut hair, thick neck, solid shoulders, stocky frame. No wonder, I thought, he was a wrestler in his Chicago high school days at Frances Parker. Today Mamet looks much the same, although he exudes a quiet confidence that well complements his fame.

Over coffee Mamet voiced his opinions, not only about his plays and personal experiences in the theater, but about the state of contemporary American drama as well. He spoke directly, looking eye to eye across the oak table. I had interviewed other writers, and they all spoke constantly. Not Mamet. He gave precise, almost blunt answers, followed by what seemed to me long, awkward pauses, Havana in hand. But what he did say made for an important statement from one of our leading dramatists. I noticed immediately his Chicago accent, which at times made him sound like many of his characters that I first saw in the 1970s at the St. Nicholas Theatre Company.

Although Mamet has granted many interviews since our conversation, he seems to be much more guarded with his time. Perhaps after *Glengarry* had won a Pulitzer Prize in 1984, Madonna had played Karen in *Speed-the-Plow* in 1988, or *Oleanna* in 1992 had raised questions about sexual politics and harassment, Mamet decided to keep a lower profile. Or maybe his increasing involvement with Hollywood leaves him little time for an interview. He has written screenplays for *The Postman Always Rings Twice* (1981), *The Verdict* (1982), *The Untouchables* (1985), *House of Games* (1987), *We're No Angels* (1989), *Ace in the Hole* (1990), *Deerslayer* (1990), *High and Low* (1990), *Hoffa* (1990), and *Glengarry Glen Ross* (1993).

Despite his work in Hollywood and his collections of essays (*Writing in Restaurants, 1986; Some Freaks,* 1989; and *On Directing Film,* 1991), however, Mamet's reputation lies with his stage work. Mamet is an ethicist. From the initial plays, *Camel* (1968) and *Lakeboat* (1970), to those pivotal works that first brought him notoriety, *American Buffalo* (1977) and *Sexual Perversity in Chicago* (1978), from *Glengarry Glen Ross* (1984) to *Speed-the-Plow* (1988), Mamet appropriates the stage with a singular vision. This unity of vision most often finds its expression in terms of an implicit social critique of a contingent and decidedly ambiguous universe: a world from which Mamet eviscerates any moral balance between public virtue and private self-desire. From such a theater of disruption has grown Mamet's unique, and disturbing, cultural poetics. His wit and comedy seem obvious, but beyond the comedic witticisms lie darker visions. Mamet's ideographic backdrop often concerns the near-complete separation of the individual from genuine relationship. Mamet replicates human commitments and desires in demythicized forms: commodity fetishism, sexual negotiations and exploitations, aborted or botched crimes, brutal physical assaults, fraudulent business transactions enacted by petty thieves masquerading as businessmen, and human relationships whose only shared feature is the presence of physical sex and the absence of authentic love.

A playwright of poetic idiolect, Mamet spectacularizes his stage, above all, through language, a riposte that lexically as well as psychologically shapes his cultural poetics. Mamet's evolving oeuvre spotlights not only the texture of his characters' language, but, too, the quality of human relationships defined (and confined) by that very language. Within his junk shop or trashed office settings Mamet places his characters, whose predicaments and responses to their lives define a postmodernist world in which loss, betrayal, and ethical perversity dominate.

These are the kinds of issues that Mamet addresses in the following interview.

Roudané: The myth of the American dream seems central to your artistic vision. In *American Buffalo, The Water Engine, Lakeboat, Mr. Happiness, A Life in the Theatre,* and *Glengarry Glen Ross,* a whole cultural as well as spiritual dimension of the American dream myth is present. Could you comment on why this myth engages you so much?

Mamet: It interests me because the national culture is founded very much on the idea of strive and succeed. Instead of rising with the masses, one should rise from the masses. Your extremity is my opportunity. That's what forms the basis of our economic life, and this is what forms the rest of our lives. That American myth: the idea of something out of nothing. And this also affects the spirit of the individual. It's very divisive. One feels one can only succeed at the cost of someone else. Economic life in America is a lottery. Everyone's got an equal chance, but only one guy is going to get to the top. "The more I have, the less you have." So one can only succeed at the cost of the failure of another, which is what a lot of my plays—*American Buffalo* and *Glengarry Glen Ross*—are about. That's what Acting President Reagan's whole campaign is about. In *Glengarry Glen Ross* it's the Cadillac, the steak knives, or nothing. In this play it's obvious that these fellows are put in fear for their lives and livelihood. For them it's the same thing. They have to succeed at the cost of each other. As Thorstein Veblen in *Theory of the Leisure Class* says, sharp practice inevitably shades over into fraud. Once someone has no vested interest in behaving in an ethical manner and the only bounds on his behavior are supposedly his innate sense of fair play, then fair play becomes an outdated concept: "But wait a second! Why should I control my sense of fair play when the other person may not control his sense of fair play? So hurray for me and to hell with you."

Roudané: What are your thematic concerns in *Glengarry Glen Ross?*

Mamet: If there are any thematic concerns, they must be blatant. The play concerns how business corrupts, how the hierarchical business system tends to corrupt. It becomes legitimate for those in power in the business world to act unethically. The effect on the little guy is that he turns to crime. And petty crime goes punished; major crimes go unpunished. If someone wants to destroy Manhattan for personal gain, they call him a great man. Look at Delorean. He completely raped everybody in Northern Ireland with that scheme. He made a car that wasn't worth the money—and that wasn't enough. He started dealing in cocaine—and he walked. He walked away because he had "suffered" enough.

In *Glengarry Glen Ross,* it's interesting to watch Aaronow. He's the one who comes closest to being the character of a *raisonneur,* for throughout the whole play he's saying, "I don't understand what's going on," "I'm no good," "I can't fit in here," "I'm incapable of either grasping those things I should or doing those things that I've grasped." Or his closing lines, "Oh, God, I hate this job." It's a kind of monody throughout the play. Aaronow has some degree of conscience, some awareness. He's troubled. Corruption troubles him. The question he's troubled by is whether his inability to succeed in the society in which he's placed is a defect—that is, is he manly or sharp enough?—or if it's, in effect, a positive attribute, which is to say that his conscience prohibits him. So Aaronow is left between these two things, and he's incapable of choosing. This dilemma is, I think, what many of us are facing in this country right now. As Veblen, who's had a big influence on me, says, a lot of business in this country is founded on the idea that if you don't exploit the possible opportunity, not only are you being silly, but in many cases you're being negligent, even legally negligent.

Roudané: At the close of *American Buffalo,* I sensed a felt compassion, some sense of understanding among all three men, but especially between Don and Bobby. However, at the close of *Glengarry Glen Ross,* I sensed little compassion, no resolution, little sense of redemption. Could you talk about these two plays in light of this?

Mamet: Glengarry Glen Ross is structurally a very different play from *American Buffalo. Buffalo* is a traditionally structured drama based on tragedy, whereas *Glengarry,* although it has aspects of tragedy in it, is basically a melodrama—or a drama. Endings in tragedies are resolved. The protagonist undergoes a reversal of the situation, a recognition of the state, and we have a certain amount of cleansing. This is what Don experiences in *American Buffalo.* But this doesn't happen in *Glengarry Glen Ross.* So the structure is different. It's not as classical a play as *Buffalo,* and it's probably not as good a play. But it is the structure of each that affects the characters and the endings.

Roudané: What engages your aesthetic imagination in *American Buffalo?*

Mamet: I was interested in the idea of honor among thieves, of what is an unassailable moral position and what isn't. What would cause a man to abdicate a moral position he'd espoused? That's what *American Buffalo* is about. Teach is the antagonist. The play's about Donny Dubrow. His moral position is that one must conduct himself like a man and that there are no extenuating circumstances for supporting the betrayal of a friend. That's how the play starts. The rest of the play is about Donny's betrayal of the fellow, Bobby, whom he's teaching these things to. The same is true to a certain extent of Levene in *Glengarry Glen Ross.* Throughout the play Levene is espousing the professional doctrine of technique. What he's saying is that I am therefore owed certain support because of what I've done, because of who I am. And at the end of the play Levene betrays himself.

Roudané: I think one of your major contributions to the stage is your "language." Clearly you have an ear for the sounds, sense, and rhythms of street language. Could you discuss the role of language in your plays?

Mamet: It's poetic language. It's not an attempt to capture language as much as it is an attempt to create language. We see this in various periods in the evolution of American drama. And when it's good, to the most extent it's called realism. All realism means is that the language strikes a responsive chord. The language in my plays is not realistic but poetic. The words sometimes have a musical quality to them. It's language that is tailor-made for the stage. People don't always talk the way my characters do in real life, although they may use some of the same words. Think of Odets, Wilder. That stuff is not realistic; it is poetic. Or Philip Barry. You might say some part of his genius was to capture the way a certain class of people spoke. He didn't know how those people spoke, but he was creating a poetic impression, creating that reality. It's not a matter, in *Lakeboat* or *Sexual Perversity in Chicago* or *Edmond* or my other plays, of my "interpretation" of how these people talk. It is an illusion. It's like when Gertrude Stein said to Picasso, "That portrait doesn't look like me." Picasso said, "It will." It's an illusion. Juvenile delinquents *acted* like Marlon Brando in *The Wild One,* right? It wasn't the other way around. It was life imitating art! So in this sense my plays don't mirror what's going on in the streets. It's something different. As Oscar Wilde said, life imitates art! We didn't have those big pea-soup fogs until somebody described them.

Roudané: Despite your social exposures of human folly, one could argue that you're a playwright concerned with existentialist themes. That is, you seem fixed on objectifying certain crimes of the heart: the failure to communicate authentically with the self and the other. Possible? What do you think?

Mamet: Concerning ourselves with the individual's soul is certainly the fit province of drama. I really never understood what existentialism meant. I've tried a long time. It has something to do with sleeping with Simone de Beauvoir, but other than that I'm kind of lost. But I suppose my plays are about the individual's inner spirit. I think that's what it's about. The purpose of the theatre, to me, is to examine the paradox between the fact that everyone tries to do well but that few, if any, succeed. The theatre concerns metaphysics, our relationship to God, and ethics, or our relationships to each other.

Roudané: Whereas many contemporary playwrights create antimimetic plays, you seem to rework a more classic, Ibsenesque dramatic form, the well-made play. Could you discuss the dramatic form of your work?

Mamet: I'm sure *trying* to do the well-made play. It is the hardest thing to do. I like this form because it's the structure imitating human perception. It is not just something made up out of old cloth. This is the way we perceive a play: with a clear beginning, a middle, and an end. So when one wants to best utilize the theatre, one would try to structure a play in a way that is congruent with the way the mind perceives it. Everybody wants to hear a story with a beginning, middle, and end. The only people who don't tell stories that way are playwrights! Finally that's all that theatre is, storytelling. The theatre's no different from gossip, from dirty jokes, from what Uncle Max did on his fishing trip. It's just telling stories in that particular way in which one tells stories in the theatre. Look at *Sexual Perversity in Chicago* or *The Duck Variations.* To me recognizing the storytelling dimension of playwriting is a beginning of a mark of maturity. That's why I embrace it. Nobody in the audience wants to hear a joke without the punch line. Nobody wants to hear how *feelingly* a guy can tell a joke. But we would like to find out what happened to the farmer's daughter. That's what Ibsen did.

Roudané: Has your cinema work—the screenplays for *The Postman Always Rings Twice* and *The Verdict*—helped your playwriting technique?

Mamet: My work in Hollywood has helped me very much. The good movie has to be written very clearly. The action has to be very clear. You can't take time out to digress to the highways and the byways of what might happen. You've got to tell the story. And I am trying to do this in my plays. I mean, I wrote a lot of plays about feeling slices of interesting life. Nothing wrong with that—I just didn't know any better. I'm talking about my earlier plays, *Lakeboat,* for example, and others with those episodic glimpses of humanity. Those were fine, but now I am trying to do something different.

Roudané: What's the effect of Hollywood and mass media on the theatre today?

Mamet: It ain't good, but it doesn't make any difference. They're flooding the market with trash. The taste and the need for a real theatrical experience, which is an experience in which the audience can come to commune, not so much with the actors but with themselves and what they know to be true, just increases. Everyone's palate has been dulled to an extraordinary degree by the mass media. But that's just the way it is. Television, of course, isn't an art form. It might be, but nobody's figured out how to make it so. It's not even a question of doing good work on television, which happens once in a while. It's that nobody seems to understand the essential nature of the medium. I certainly don't.

Roudané: Could you elaborate on the actor's relationship with an audience?

Mamet: The young artist has to get better every year, the audience doesn't grow just numerically. It's not even a question of growing spiritually. What happens if the audience doesn't grow is that everything deteriorates. You don't have enough funds coming in to support the artists. So you start having to appeal to a larger and larger audience, which means you start getting worse and worse. This is exactly what happened to Broadway. You have to take advantage of people. Rather than appeal to a native constant constituency, you're appealing to people who ain't never going to come back, who don't really have any expectations but know they better get something for their forty-five dollars. So we show them a hundred people tap dancing onstage instead of *Death of A Salesman.*

Roudané: You've said that acting has nothing to do with emotion but with action: "stick to the action" and "practical aesthetics." What do you mean?

Mamet: The action is, what *is* the character doing. That's what the actor must do. Acting has absolutely nothing to do with emotion or feeling emotional. It has as little to do with emotion as playing a violin does. You have to study emotion. People don't go to the theatre to hear the emotion; they go to hear the concerto. The emotions should take place in the *audience.* It just doesn't have to be dealt with from the actor's viewpoint.

Roudané: How might you answer the charge that your plays tend always to focus on the negative, cynical side of experience?

Mamet: I've never heard that charge, so I say that's interesting. But it's easy to cheer people up if you lie to them. Very easy. Acting President

Reagan says he's not going to raise taxes. Of course he's going to raise taxes, he has to raise taxes. Although it's easy to cheer people up by lying to them, in my plays I'm not interested in doing that. I'm not a doctor; I'm a writer.

Roudané: In *A Life in the Theatre,* Robert and John undergo a role reversal: John's career rises, Robert's declines. What were you suggesting about the theatrical world in this play?

Mamet: The play is not so much about the theatrical world, although that's the metaphor. The play concerns how youth and age talk to each other. John and Robert show something about our inability to communicate experience. While this notion isn't really present in *The Duck Variations* because George and Emil are the same age, it's there to a certain extent in *American Buffalo* and in *Lakeboat.*

Roudané: Could you talk about the way in which form and content coalesce to generate the creative process within your plays?

Mamet: My real concern always is with the play as a whole, with writing the play. There's a curious phenomenon that happens when you compose a play or movie. The creation very quickly takes on a life of its own. I have no idea why; it's just words on paper. But the art I can compare it to in my experience is carving wood. You start to carve wood, and very quickly the thing takes on a life of its own. Part of the wisdom of wood carving is to realize when the wood is telling you where it wants to go. Obviously it's going to be a duck if you start out to make a duck, but the kind of duck it's going to be is largely dictated by the kind of wood. And there is a similar phenomenon in writing drama. You start out with an idea, it becomes something else, and part of the wisdom is learning to listen to the material itself. Much of the material, of course, is in the subconscious.

Roudané: What is your artistic response to what some may call a "business-as-sacrament ethic" in America?

Mamet: One has to learn something that can't be taken away: you have to learn your craft. As Sherwood Anderson said, a man who has a trade is a man who can tell the rest of the world to go to hell! If you want to become a commodity, which is what most actors and actresses tend to become, then you have to rely on the goodness of others, not only for your bread, but for your happiness. That's not very much fun.

Roudané: As a writer you're confronted with a universe that is largely hostile, even absurd. Flux, struggle, the precariousness of existence itself is the norm. Given this reality, what is your artistic response to such a world?

Mamet: My response is always the same thing; it's never any different.

Tolstoy said it's a mistake to think that human nature ever changes. This is the only world that I live in, so (a) it would be silly for me to say something else because it isn't something else, and (b) I am part of it. So the ability to perceive the problem doesn't necessarily mean that one is not part of that problem. Of course I am part of the problem. It's the same thing as people driving home from the country on Sunday night. Look at all these assholes driving, getting in my way! It's modern life. I *am* one of those assholes.

Roudané: Do you see yourself, as a writer, as one who shatters illusions or as some kind of truth-teller?

Mamet: No. I am just a storyteller. Keep in mind that playwrights—O'Neill or Albee or myself—know as little about what we do as anyone else. We're just storytellers, that's all. It just so happens that society rewards some of us in extraordinary ways because the society is desperately betting that one of us is going to say something that might offer some comfort. Our job, as writers, is to do our jobs. I was thinking the other day. I have trouble sometimes finishing a lot of plays. But then I always try to remind myself it took Sophocles eighteen years to write *Oedipus Rex.* That's also because he wasn't trying to write *Gigi.*

ALBERT INNAURATO
John Louis DiGaetani

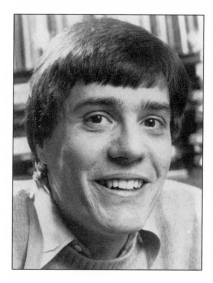

Albert Innaurato (photo: Christopher Little)

Albert Innaurato was born in Philadelphia on 2 June 1948. He earned a bachelor of fine arts degree from the California Institute of the Arts in Los Angeles in 1972 and a master of fine arts degree from Yale drama school in 1974. In New York he has been playwright in residence at the Playwrights' Horizons Theatre, the Public Theatre, the Circle Repertory Theatre, and the New York Shakespeare Festival.

His first staged play was *Urlicht* (1971), followed soon afterward by the highly successful *Gemini* (1977), which ran for over three years on Broadway and won an Obie award. Innaurato also won an Obie award for his play *The Transfiguration of Benno Blimpie* (1975), staged Off-Broadway. His *Passione* was staged on Broadway in 1980; others were *Ulysses in Traction* (Off-Broadway, 1977) and *Urlicht* (Off-Broadway, 1983). In addition spring of 1985 saw his *Coming of Age in Soho* staged at the Public Theatre in New York. For his plays Innaurato has won two Obie awards, a Drama Desk citation, a Guggenheim fellowship, and a Rockefeller fellowship.

Innaurato has also written scripts for television. He was an Emmy nominee for *Verna: USO Girl,* directed by Joseph E. Levine and broadcast on PBS. For Aaron Spelling and Douglas Cramer, Innaurato wrote *Coming Out,* which was televised on ABC. For Jane Rosenberg he wrote *Matter Between Friends,* broadcast on CBS, and with Mort Lauchman he wrote *Just Plain Folks* for Stu Blumberg, Reeves Productions, broadcast on ABC. Innaurato, who lives and writes in the Chelsea section of New York City, recently has devoted most of his energies to journalism.

I spoke with Albert Innaurato in New York City on 2 August 1986 in a restaurant across from Lincoln Center to discuss his career, his plays, and the condition of contemporary theatre.

DiGaetani: Mr. Innaurato, one of the things I like about your plays is the Italian theme you sometimes use. Italian culture has not had much of an effect on serious theatre in America.

Innaurato: Well, the basic thing they always say in creative writing courses is "Write about what you know," though I don't think that all my writing is autobiographical or based solely on my own experiences. Nonetheless I have written my plays especially about what I know, which is basically Italian-American customs in a very Italian-affiliated neighborhood in Philadelphia, and then dealing with a different world. This world is not really inimical all the time, but it is alien to some degree to the culture that both you and I knew growing up. And I especially, because I went to prep schools and an Ivy League college, experienced a very different kind of culture from what I'd known. Sometimes it was funny, and sometimes it was embarrassing. And then from that tension theatrical situations can arise, and it's a handy way to get a drama or a comedy going.

DiGaetani: You also dramatize the problems of being overweight.

Innaurato: I am overweight, so I know. It's terrible in this society, the way fat people are treated, or people who just simply don't conform to what is a very rigid view of the human anatomy. What I've become aware of as I've aged is the discrepancy between the things we read and the reality. For example, in the *Times* recently there were all these articles about how even slight amounts of overweight are dangerous. There was a whole series about how life insurance companies were reducing the weight charts. But in fact I subscribe to something called *The Human Brain and the Human Anatomy,* a medical journal. The latest research there indicates a wide range of body weights that are natural, and there is not one body weight that is natural for all people and all situations.

DiGaetani: You present overweight in some of your plays as a form of suicide. For example, in *The Transfiguration of Benno Blimpie* the main character is eating himself to death.

Innaurato: Well, he is literally eating himself. He's chewing on his bones, his flesh. I mean, he's consuming himself. Blimpie is meant to be a vision or a version of a certain kind of artist who burns out and dies into his art. Blimpie is a failed artist who is unable to make any of the connections that you need to make in order to survive in a career. And what happens when your art meets a dead end? You either give up entirely or you start becoming your art, you start consuming, you start becoming your art to the point that your art is consuming you, and that's really what he does. His death becomes his final work of art, and I think it's a vision of an artist in a dying art form, in a society that has contempt for art as we understand it, or whose use for art is a commercial use—that is, to make money and buy prestige. With that there will be many more artists who fall through the cracks, who aren't socially useful, in the way that Shakespeare was socially useful, in the way that Mozart and Beethoven were, however much their misery and poverty have been glamorized and distorted, because neither was as badly off as our playwrights would have us believe. But nonetheless they were socially useful artists. Their art filled a social purpose—for entertainment, for intellectual pursuits—and they have a large audience. But I think Benno Blimpie is in a way a version of our twentieth-century art form, with no audience and no support and no civilization supporting him, who had no option but to die. And the weight becomes a symbol of the outside or the person who is instantly recognizable—somehow a failure in our society. In a society as obsessed with cosmetic appearance as ours is, anyone who does not adhere to the norm is immediately seen as a freak.

DiGaetani: Well, just being interested in writing or being interested in art is seen as rather freakish in American culture. That's not what normal people are supposed to be interested in. You make a point in the introduction to your collected plays, *Bizarre Behavior,* that theatre has really become a minority, elitist art form. Normal people don't go to the theatre; it's the artsy-craftsy bunch.

Innaurato: Even the artsy-craftsy bunch don't go anymore. Now they'll go to performance art. Yuppies have incomes, a lot of leisure time, and some kind of arts awareness, and you'll find that most of them don't go to the theatre. They'll go to an event. It's usually a performance by Laurie Anderson or Robert Wilson. There's a real trendiness, and there is not that solid middle-class, core audience that simply loves the art form and that goes out of a desire to have that connection with art that our grandparents or great-grandparents had with the theatre or the opera or symphonic music.

DiGaetani: I don't know that my grandparents had that, coming from poor southern Italy. They talked a lot about Caruso, but they didn't really go to the opera. One of the points you make in your plays that I found very true is that most Italians in this country hate opera.

Innaurato: Most Italians—period—hate opera. I mean most people in the world are not interested.

DiGaetani: And in southern Italian culture the worst thing you can call someone is a "fruit," and in *Gemini* Francis begins to dread that homosexuality may be part of him. Am I reading the play properly?

Innaurato: Oh yes, I think so. I also think that there are many strands in Italian culture, and most cultures really. I mean Italians in my experience, real Italians, are very tolerant so long as they don't know about it, and even if they know about it, as long as you don't confront them with it, they don't care. And I think that's true of most cultures about sexual secrets of all kinds. So long as you're not out in the open about it, it's fine. There is, however, an American need to be totally honest— gay lib is an American phenomenon and an American need. It's part of American culture. Maybe it's a curious inversion of the Puritan ethic— to admit, to live openly, not to pretend. It's a very European trait for the homosexual to marry and have children but then carry on a very open sexual life with other men, but that seems uncomfortable for Americans. And I think that in *Gemini* that's reflected in Francis. He goes to Harvard, and the play takes place at the end of the sixties, which was a big decade of turmoil for gay lib, for all kinds of liberationist politics. For Francis there's this need not to hide, not to want to hide. And he doesn't want to have a girlfriend just to comfort his father because he feels that's not ethical for the girl. He doesn't want to use the girl in that way, and at the same time he has some attraction to the girl, so that's the clash. I mean an Italian would want to hide it, to be macho. The American middle-class drive is to be open and call a spade a spade. Meanwhile there's the person. In all my plays I deal with the person who doesn't really fit into any kind of prefabricated identity, either a gay identity or a straight identity. Francis is genuinely attracted to this woman and is bisexual.

DiGaetani: He's genuinely attracted to her brother Randy as well.

Innaurato: At the same time, because he's probably bisexual, you see. And there's very little tolerance in our society for that. Gay people are often hostile to bisexuality and refuse to believe it exists, but in fact it does.

DiGaetani: What makes your plays distinctive? What do you think you've contributed to the American theatre?

Innaurato: I don't think I've contributed anything to the American theatre. But I can tell you what people don't like about my plays, and that may be what I've contributed. In *Coming of Age in Soho,* for example, people were really shocked that parts of the play were almost burlesque in their humor, and then there was a demand made on the audience to take the characters, despite the humor, very seriously and to try to get people to see a life-or-death seriousness beating under them and their eccentric behavior. You see, television has made it impossible for some Americans to understand that you can be flamboyant, peculiar, or very eccentric and be human. That underside of reality is rarely presented in our popular art form, and even our most intellectual critics watch much more television than they go to the theatre or even read, so that almost subconsciously they've adopted a TV aesthetic, which has to be very straightforward. In my plays there's a lot of grotesquerie, a lot of eccentricity, and a lot of flamboyant behavior, but I never see the people as cardboard or as zanies.

DiGaetani: Yes, I think one of the things you contributed most is your form of humor. You do use comedy to make very serious points, which is nothing new, but you do it in a new way. Also I like your use of language. The combinations of the American English and southern Italian dialects are interesting. One of the things I don't like much about television is that the use of language there is generally so tedious.

Innaurato: Well, it's often very ordinary. It's a deliberate shutting down. You see, as in sexual experience, I don't believe in limits. I don't believe experiences are black or white. I don't believe in the small screen in life since I think life is not a small screen. I don't believe there is *one* sexual feeling. I think that in the course of a lifetime we all have many sexual feelings, though we may or may not choose to act on them.

DiGaetani: That's like Thomas Mann's *Death in Venice,* when an apparently heterosexual artist all of a sudden falls in love with a fourteen-year-old boy, much to his woe. Is life full of these ugly surprises?

Innaurato: I don't think they're ugly, they're just life! Life isn't a twenty-four-minute TV drama interrupted by commercials every six minutes. Or maybe a change is more typical now, or at least in America people are more willing to pursue these things and not immediately reject them. And I also think that some people have much more decided and rigid notions of what is acceptable and what isn't. For example, one of the critics who reviewed my play *Passione* said, "Oh, Innaurato is an Italian and can't really write about American southern women." Well,

I spent fourteen years of my life, every summer, in the South because my mother had friends down there, and her best friend had a farm about forty miles out of Knoxville in the Great Smoky Mountains. It was really very rural and countrified, and I heard that speech every summer for fourteen years, day in and day out. And I have very good ears. So the speech those two southern women speak is absolutely accurate, not exaggerated, not false. Yet this man assumed it had to be false. And many more people read and believe reviewers than ever see a play, and that has become a reality of our times, especially if it's in the *New York Times.* What amazes me is that it is so. corrupt, and this is why I sometimes think art is dead in our times, why I think the theatre is dead.

DiGaetani: You say the theatre is dying? Then why do you write plays?

Innaurato: With *Coming of Age in Soho* I worked very hard. I worked twenty hours a day for about four months, because I wrote the play in process. We started with one version of it, and then for a lot of factors—some of which had to do with the actors available—I rewrote, though I actually liked the play we started with very much. It opened and got some good reviews and some bad reviews, typically. It had a respectable run, and I made three thousand dollars. And now it's going to be published, and it took a lot to get it published. There's no reason to write another play, because most serious plays in recent years on Broadway have not had much of a run. *Glengarry Glen Ross* won a Pulitzer, got the kind of reviews you dream about, and ran eight months. Yet it rarely sold out—even at half-price. You can read the *New York Times* and assume that there's a big revival of Sam Shepard and that he's got millions of audiences, but in fact his plays are playing in 130- and 180-seat theatres and often aren't selling out either. You can't have a public art form, and the theatre is a public art form, without an audience. If there's no audience, there's no play! And I don't see an audience anymore. I really don't.

DiGaetani: It's Off-Broadway. I think serious plays are going to have short runs Off-Broadway, though your *Gemini* ran for three years on Broadway.

Innaurato: Well, I don't think that's possible anymore. I think even in that short time since *Gemini* closed, I really think it's not possible anymore. I don't think you need necessarily an enormous audience or an extremely long run, but any writer needs to feel there is some base with the public.

DiGaetani: One of the things you imply in *Ulysses in Traction* is that if theatre is dying, the university theatre has destroyed it.

Innaurato: Oh, I don't think you can say that! I think the pathos is that the institutional theatres in this country are basically run by intrigue and terror, and there's constant money trauma. Undeniably university theatre provides many people with a hands-on experience they can't have in the professional theatre. And obviously of all the people who work in the university theatre there are some very talented, very sophisticated people. Also talent is talent! There are people who are perfectly content teaching college and who are very talented, who are better directors than some of the people who make a lot of money directing extravaganzas like *Cats*, but the point is I believe in audience. When you don't have an audience, when you have some kind of protection in the form of a subsidy, whether it's the university paying your bills or the state, then you're in a less real world.

DiGaetani: To get back to your plays, I really like their allusions to music, especially to opera—for example, *Urlicht*, with the references to the Mahler song and the Mahler Second Symphony, and all the operatic allusions in *Gemini*.

Innaurato: Well, I'm a passionate opera lover.

DiGaetani: Which of your plays do you like the best?

Innaurato: I often don't like them, and I'm often disappointed in them. I rarely feel that I've achieved very much or as much as I wish I had or wanted to when I started. At the same time, when time has elapsed and I go back and read them, I'm often surprised at what I did. There are moments in *Gemini*, and even in a relatively weak play like *Ulysses in Traction*, that have a kind of spontaneity. I'm a very intuitive writer, and that's bad in a way. I think my writing has a kind of stream to it, and it's very spontaneous and very intuitive, and I think there's an unevenness when that's the case.

DiGaetani: Tell me about your work habits.

Innaurato: I'm lazy and self-indulgent, but I have had experiences in the theatre, and I have been through rewrites and all that pressured stuff.

DiGaetani: In the introduction to your collected plays you state that you feel your plays lack action. Could you elaborate on that?

Innaurato: Yes. I think you need an action in plays. I mean plays shouldn't be static, shouldn't just sit there. You need something to be happening. You need a motor, and I have trouble finding a motor.

DiGaetani: There is a lot of action in *Gemini*. I kept wondering what would happen at that birthday party.

Innaurato: Well, a more successful example of that occurs in several of my other plays. I'm also speaking in terms of the continuum, and I just think that I tend to operate in terms of character and in terms of emotion, not really in terms of an underlying action or underlying story.

DiGaetani: One of the recurrent tensions I see in your work is the conflict between the happy, comic, jolly versus the sad, depressed, suicidal, and of course this is a conflict in most people. I think part of the source for this conflict may be that Italian culture is very negative about the homosexual element in people, and Catholicism exacerbates that. I think this engenders in some creative people a kind of self-hatred or a suspicion that they are really frauds, that success is not really theirs.

Innaurato: Well, I think that's accurate. I think that in many artists, or many people who try to be artists, there is a suspicion that it's all a joke or a fraud. That's why I keep talking about audiences. You need some kind of external check, some way to say, "Well, I've achieved that," or "I've achieved this," and if you don't have that, it's hard, after a time, to believe the talent is real. No one that I know can lock himself in a garret and say rejection doesn't matter. It does matter enormously if one is very sensitive to being dismissed, to being mocked, to being shrugged off, to being ignored. I don't know how anyone, anyone, can ignore that, and I don't know that anyone has. I mean, from what I know of James Joyce and Virginia Woolf, they had a terrible sensitivity to rejection. I mean no matter how arrogant in other respects these artists may have been, or however tough they may have appeared, there was a great sensitivity to bad reviews and perceived rejection.

DiGaetani: The artist's life, the freelance life, unless you have an independent income, is very difficult.

Innaurato: I know some British playwrights, and the level of their income is low. It's not as if they're living very well, but it's true that if you get into that circuit of writers who get produced, there are subsidies that do allow people to have some kind of security. It may be modest, very, very modest by American standards, but it's something. What happens in America is it's all or nothing. You either are doing so well that you live like an upper-middle-class person, or you have nothing. And there is very little support. It's a capitalist system, so you can get lucky. It's like playing the lottery, you know. And regional theatres either don't want to do new plays or they want to do only what's hot, what will get them the maximum coverage, as opposed to what's good and ought to be supported.

DiGaetani: So you had better keep writing.

Innaurato: Yes.

ROMULUS LINNEY
Don B. Wilmeth

Romulus Linney (photo © Susan Johann, 1991)

The first part of this interview with Romulus Linney occurred in early April 1986; the final questions were posed to Linney in October 1993. Linney, born in Philadelphia but reared in North Carolina, lives in New York City and oversees the playwriting program at Columbia University (and also teaches at the University of Pennsylvania). He places great hope in the not-for-profit theatre and has frequently directed his own plays for major regional and small theatre companies in New York. In 1991–92, for example, he was the first resident playwright at the Signature Theatre Company in New York, where five of his plays were presented, including revised revivals of plays, four of which he directed or codirected, as well as the premiere of a new play, *Ambrosio.*

Linney is the author of three novels, thirteen long and twenty-two short plays (as of early 1994) produced on, Off-, and Off-Off-Broadway, in repertory theatres of Great Britain, Canada, Germany, and Austria, and in resident theatres throughout the United States. Among his critically acclaimed plays are *The Sorrows of Frederick* (1967), *The Love Suicide at Schofield Barracks* (1972), *Holy Ghosts* (1976), *Childe Byron* (1978), *Tennessee* (1979; Obie 1980), *Laughing Stock* (1984), *Woman Without a Name* (1985), *Sand Mountain* (1986), *Three Poets* (1989), *Unchanging Love* (1991), and *Ambrosio* and *"2"* (both 1992).

Linney's topics and themes have been diverse. As Gerald Weales noted in the *Georgia Review* (Fall 1981), he is a "writer who deals in complexity whether he is working in a literary vein—*The Sorrows of Frederick, Childe Byron*—or dealing in the apparent simplicities of the rural South, as in *Holy Ghosts.*" Indeed he seems equally at home with folk plays such as *Sand Mountain* or with contemporary commentaries on the human condition such as the three short plays grouped under the title *Laughing Stock,* singled out by *Time* magazine as one of the best plays of 1984.

Linney, in his early sixties, was termed by Martin Gottfried several years ago "one of the best kept secrets of the American theatre, a playwright of true literacy, a writer in the grand tradition," while Richard Schickel in *Time* magazine described him in 1984 as "one of the American theatre's most mysteriously buried treasures." This reputation as a slighted, unknown writer seems to be on the wane, for in 1993 alone, following the success of the season with Signature, two collections of his plays appeared (*Romulus Linney: Seventeen Short Plays,* Newbury, Vt.: Smith and Kraus; and *Six Plays,* New York: Theatre Communication Group). In 1984 he received the Award in Literature from the American Academy and Institute of Arts and Letters, and in 1992 he was awarded an Off-Broadway Obie for sustained excellence in playwriting. In his semiautobiographical play *Childe Byron* Linney not only creates a theatrical piece that reflects his considerable theatrical imagination, honed by his own training as an actor and director (at the Yale School of Drama), which he discusses in the interview, but it demonstrates most successfully his approach to history as a springboard to drama, one of several subjects explored in this interview. The Linney of the 1990s, however, seems to be moving into a slightly new phase. Instead of just filtering himself through the past or through history, he has now begun to add a new dimension to his work by confronting the present with works that are truly contemporary in subject as well as theme.

Wilmeth: Since you were trained as an actor and director, why did you begin writing?

Linney: I was an actor and I went to Yale Drama School and then I was drafted. In the army I got interested in other things, Japanese theatre especially. And I came back and changed my major to direction. I went to New York as a director, though I couldn't function either as an actor or a director because of the theatre of the fifties, with so few Off-Broadway theatres and no Off-Off—it was very difficult, and I was a pretty messed up young man, with lots of psychological difficulties. So I would hole myself up in a room and begin to write—very badly, for as a writer I had to learn very painfully. I wrote two novels and they did okay. Then they got progressively more dramatic. The first novel in 1962, *Heathen Valley,* has sections of first-person narrative in it. The second novel, published in 1965, *Slowly, By Thy Hand Unfurled,* was a woman's diary, which was like a great long monologue. So the third thing I wrote was a play. Since then I've written only one other novel, *Jesus Tales,* in 1980. All the rest have been plays.

Wilmeth: You are invariably clear in your stage directions in terms of simplicity. Your settings seem to be down to essence.

Linney: I think ground plans as a playwright before I get going. I have to know where everything is and have to feel almost as if I'm directing while I'm writing. Many directors while reading my plays are put off by this, but I don't want to scotch the director's contribution. Sometimes people have taken the plays and done them in all kinds of different ways, and they worked out all right, so you never know. I do think you have to be trained as a director to direct. What a playwright will try to do if he directs his play is to get results too quickly. You have to know the actors' processes, and you have to be able to leave something alone and let it grow rather than force it.

Wilmeth: You feel that the training as a director gave you the detachment and the objectivity that you needed?

Linney: Yes, and it gave me the knowledge to see in a small beginning how an actor is going to grow and to leave him alone—because I acted a lot, and I knew that the directors who drove me crazy were the ones who would never let me alone.

Wilmeth: This is a hard lesson for directors to learn.

Linney: Especially in America, because American directors think they have to be like corporate executives—they have to take charge of people in the good old American way. And it doesn't need to be like that in the theatre, especially with sensitive and good actors. My productions, directorially, are extremely simple. I don't like to have anything onstage that isn't used, and I like everything to be consumed by the end of the play.

Wilmeth: Could you talk about some of the major influences on your writing—other writers?

Linney: While in the army, stationed in Hawaii, I went to Japan on a long leave. When I came back from Japan, I began to write. I was not a writer when I went to Japan. Somehow when I came back I was. And I believe it had something to do with the lesson I learned from the Japanese, that extremely humble and modest materials can be organized into something artistic. You stay at a poor little Japanese inn in the country, and you come into a room, and it's just old wood, but they have it arranged in such a way that you suddenly realize it's a beautiful place. I think the Ryoanji stone garden outside of Kyoto is the most beautiful work of art I've ever seen in my life. It was a cosmic experience when I walked out on the porch of the temple there. About six hours later I came to. So I figured, since I've never thought the materials I have to write about myself are of any great moment, immediate moment, and I don't mean to be falsely modest about this, for I write on grandiose subjects—Byron, Frederick the Great—and I'm perfectly willing to do so, but the approach is not grandiose, I don't think. In fact what I try to do is to be Japanese about it. To take the simple aspects and work them over and over. But that was the lesson I learned: you can combine simple materials—wood, stone, earth, flowers, whatever—and make something.

Wilmeth: Have you been influenced by any specific writers?

Linney: As a novelist I was a lot, more so than as a playwright. When I was learning to write, Faulkner, of course, explained my childhood to me long before analysis or therapy. He made me realize these things were not just in my head. A Swedish writer named Par Lagerkvist [1891–1974], also a playwright, at one point in my life was extremely important. Once again rather more like the Japanese, because Lagerkvist was a writer who uses extremely simple and spare means, as, of course, Faulkner does not—Faulkner can when he doesn't let his rhetoric go. Somehow mixing Lagerkvist and Faulkner together I learned to write novels. My thesis production at Yale was Eugene O'Neill's *Marco Millions,* and though temperamentally I am nothing like him, I did learn a great deal from directing this play. I wanted to make the play look as if I wrote it, and I was indeed a frustrated writer, trying to make a great man's play look as if I wrote it. O'Neill has a way of doing that. He knows what he wants and when you start fooling with his plays—you can't—when you're done you say, "Well, yes, this was nice, but he's better at this than I am." So I learned a great deal.

I also love fiction, and I love to teach fiction. At one time I read widely to find the people who really spoke to me. Now women writers, such as Jean Rhys, are superb. I always loved Katherine Anne Porter, Flannery O'Connor, and the southerners. There is a difference in being influenced as a novelist and as a playwright. As a novelist you are influenced by a book. As a playwright you are influenced not only by production and all the other elements that go into production, but you're also influenced by the weather, the air, because you see all kinds of dramatic things. So it's harder to know where your influences come from. I can speak quite clearly about my influences as a fiction writer, but as a playwright it is more mixed up.

Wilmeth: What about the themes and subjects of your plays? There are various strains in your work. History has clearly had its impact. You see other things in history. There is a good deal of autobiographical shadings in your plays, and there is a biblical influence.

Linney: Let's start with the history plays. My historical plays are not about history. They are about discovering in a great life something that I understand deeply.

When I read about Frederick the Great going to pieces as an old man when his dogs died—delicate, fragile little things, sort of like himself as a child—that tore me all apart, and I started crying. I was in a restaurant, and people looked at me as if I were a crazy man. Here was the king of Prussia, Hitler's hero, the man who created Prussian Germany, shut up in his room screaming in a paroxysm of grief about his dead dogs. This episode opened up a great many very personal things in my life that had to do with my father, who was a doctor in Tennessee but raised bird dogs. When I was a little boy, I used to go hunting with him and his friends, and I noticed, of course, the blissful, inestimable love that passed between these men and their bird dogs, a love that was denied to me as a child and was denied to their wives and denied to everybody. When I found out about this great German king that I knew a little about in college and what happened between him and his dogs, my authority of that understanding allowed me to do the research, which I did do for almost three years. I did all that, and I did it thoroughly. Even though I think the play is historically accurate, the basic core of the play is that emotional experience. Of course I discovered that the life of Frederick is really the study of a man and his father, which is where the very thoughts came from in the first place, so everything falls into place. Frederick is a man of titanic influence in the history of the world. I'm a modest playwright. I do know how that man felt about his dogs. The emotional connection comes first—then the history comes later. My history plays are like that. *Byron* is like that. *Sand Mountain* is really a history play because it comes out of the material that is in my novel *Jesus Tales,* which is about Jesus and St. Peter, as they are seen in New Testament apocrypha, which started not long after the death of Christ, and out of southern European folklore, which is a whole other kind of category. You mix the two together.

The point is that in a history play you don't write historical pageants but find something in the story that deeply has to do with you personally, and you lose yourself in this great life. And you have a kind of authority that allows you to investigate a great life with a kind of fearlessness about what it means because you know what it means. You may be wrong, of course, but you feel that you know. *Byron* is, I believe, an objective biography of Byron, but when I found other connections with the character, it became of greater interest. I got a theatre to commission a play on Byron because I had been going to see bits and pieces of Virgil Thomson's opera. I noticed that Virgil's idea of Byron was quite different from the cliché idea. He celebrated him. Byron was supposed to be this nasty man—Virgil didn't think so. So I began to study Byron, and I found out about his daughter. I discovered that my unconscious had led me to the one man who understood and put into words those incoherent feelings of a divorced father parted from his child. So that's what happens with history plays.

The religious play is not so much religion as it is a way of heightening my southern background. The play of mine that's done the most now is *Holy Ghosts,* which deals with southern Pentecostal snake handlers. It isn't religion itself—I'm profoundly uninterested in religion itself or philosophy—but that people under the stress of religion are brought to a pitch of human passion and emotion rather more quickly. There is almost nothing that makes people face themselves and all sorts of things more quickly than religious issues. And I grew up a little boy in the South and went to church. I didn't like church, but I loved it when an evangelist came to town in those days, before television evangelists. What I saw as a kid—the regular Sunday stuff was just social bullshit—was that these people needed some kind of strong support, and these evangelists gave it to them. Religion brings out in people very pure, unadulterated feelings. So there are plays about my southern background that do have religious tensions, but there are other things in them too. Religion and the South just go together in my mind.

Wilmeth: Why do you think southern writers invariably go back to the South for their subjects or at least for the texture in their writing?

Linney: I think "texture" is the right word. Paul Green, the playwright, a good friend when I was in the South, used to say, "You got to come back to North Carolina and write about the land and the people." "I love the land and I hate the people, and I'm not coming back," I would respond. "Don't say that, that's wrong." But my point was that when you grow up in the South—there is something about the humidity and the heat, the smell of the earth and all that stuff—whenever I go back there, it is the only place my body can really relax. The physical hold that the South has on you is really marvelous. I love to go back to southern beaches, but the values of the South are not mine. I feel as if I belong in every spot in the United States but in the South, where I feel alien, except that my body is at home.

Wilmeth: Could you focus a bit more on writing autobiographically?

Linney: If you are writing to do something about your parents—make them better or worse than they were—you'll get in trouble. You have to find the truth and let them fall as they go. I think that in different parts of your life you'll have different perceptions. One time in your life you may think that your father is a dreadful person, and you write a play in which he is the villain of the world. Another time maybe you might think quite differently of him. The basic difficulty in dealing with these frightening memories is to be as honest as you can.

Wilmeth: Do you work primarily from frightening memories?

Linney: I think that any unconscious memories—even ones that afford you great pleasure—may be frightening because they are unconscious, because you do not know where they come from or how they came to you, where they are. I think writing plays is frightening. If it isn't frightening, I'm not too interested in it. If it isn't dangerous and scary to me, I don't know that I want to do all the work necessary to finish it, to work it out. Tennessee Williams said that art lives in the unconscious, and I completely agree with him. So I think frightening is a good thing.

Wilmeth: Are you suggesting that only the strong emotional piece can come from familial relationships.

Linney: Well, there are also love affairs—but lovers become the family. That's prefamily existence, so plays are frequently about lovers. I think, if you look at the theatre of the world, that every play is about some form of a close family relationship, because only that emotionally holds the stage.

I think that the theatre depends on the basic core experience of people. That is why good theatre is able to unify a widely diverse audience. My play *Holy Ghosts* works really quite well when the audiences are sophisticated, such as in colleges. Or once I saw a Puerto Rican audience in New York, and they all came in speaking Spanish, and I thought, "I'm dead, what are they going to care about southern Pentecostal people?" Well, they understood it immediately. The same things go on in their churches, the same emotions, so they got it. But you have to be that basic in the theatre. Therefore, the writer who wishes to attach philosophical and political meanings to plays needs to express it through the basic family experiences, I would suggest.

Wilmeth: The Linney style seems very eclectic. You have several plays that are very linear and where the characters are quite conventional and very funny, *Laughing Stock,* for instance. Other plays have flashbacks and characters growing out of imaginations, with multiple characters. Could you comment on how you approach structure and form?

Linney: As suggested, I find the emotional experience first and then figure out how to tell the story. Although there are certain techniques that I return to frequently, I search for the best way to deal with a specific topic. For example, writing *Byron,* I found out early that I was going to write about Byron and his daughter, Ada. I discovered Ada's whole thing with the computer, and everything began to fall into place. I had two notebooks, and I had everything about the way I wanted it. But I did not know how I was going to begin that play or how I would shape it. There is a speech in which Ada talks about what she would do if she were in an old person's home. A line came out of nowhere that seemed right. Then somewhere the whole idea that she is drugged came into the play. And then I found the little poem that Byron speaks at the beginning of *Childe Byron,* which I got out of the first biography written about him. Then I decided that Byron had to just enter, I don't know how, I'll just bring him on. From that decision all the other things that happen in *Byron*—the change in the juxtaposition that the boy becomes the young Byron and then his homosexual lover and so forth—those things flowed out of that first decision, which came very late. I tried to brood over the emotional realities of the play and let the technical things just happen.

Wilmeth: Do you see moving in and out of a specific time frame as cinematic?

Linney: No, a lot of this comes out of my fiction experience. I think that when you have a play built in small scenes and flashbacks it doesn't make it cinematic. The difference between cinematic and theatrical technique is overwhelming. Movies to me are dreams—you can go from one scene to another scene the way you do in dreams; you can just cut the machine off—you can't do that in live theatre. You have to get to the bottom of a scene before you can go the next scene, and that scene has to be finished, and it has to point to the next scene before you can go on. Theatre is like chess, and movies are like checkers.

Wilmeth: You also write short plays. Don't you find this a difficult form?

Linney: I find writing them fascinating. A lot of my ideas are not workable in long form, but I could make short plays of them. I'm fascinated with the kind of kaleidoscope of short pieces that seem to be quite different but finally, when you put the evening together, are not. I like things that have an unseen and unified principle that is not at all what you think it is and is not obvious.

Wilmeth: You clearly do not write to be a commercially successful play-wright.

Linney: Goodness, no, but I think what is viable and acceptable is going to change. Notice what has happened to fiction. You notice how plays have gotten shorter and shorter. I think that soon short plays are going to have a vogue. They've always been around. I find it wonderfully sat-isfying to be able to do something instantly—there is a marvelous feel-ing of accomplishment. It has to do with all the stuff you are able to leave out. Hemingway was very good at that, and this was principle with him. His work is so alive because there was all that other stuff, and Hemingway just cut it all out. It is still there; it is there in the result.

Wilmeth: Do you see your use of language as having musicality about it?

Linney: Lots of people have said that they are trying to make my lines like music. I think that is a big mistake. I think that music is a great art form and that you shouldn't fool with it. Music is for musicians.

Wilmeth: In reading your plays I feel there is not a lot of movement. They are not static because you use a great deal of dramatic action, but the focus is not on traditional stage movement. Even though you don't see your language as musical, perhaps your plays are more language ori-ented or rhetorical.

Linney: I use language a lot, and I'm not afraid of it. Often people get in trouble with my plays when they think that the language is the most important element when it isn't. Dramatic actions and situations are the language of the theatre. What people say is secondary. I don't think the good plays have much physical action. If you have a play in short scenes, like a *Sorrows of Frederick,* which is structured like a Shakespearean play, there is a lot of movement, but the movement is just going from one scene to the next. That's where the movement is. Once you get into the scenes, it is static. Shakespeare is static. It flows, but what happens in the scene is relatively static.

The theatre deals with human situation, flesh and blood situations *and* actions. It is, of course, wonderful if out of those situations can come marvelous language that soars and stirs us and moves us, like Shakespeare's language, like O'Neill's finer passages. But the language will not by itself make the event happen. The basic structure of a play depends on situation, and I would suggest the language should just come. You must learn as a playwright to write in situations and then language. There are lots of plays in which the language is not very good but the situations are so wonderful that who cares. Compare it, for instance, to a stylistic novelist whose sense of language is so razor sharp. Every one of our great novelists has written a play. John Updike wrote a play. *Buchanan Dying* is not a very good play. The language is quite lovely, but forget it. Saul Bellow's play about the comedian, *The Last Analysis*, seems like a funny play, but it isn't because in the final analysis the situation doesn't work. A Pulitzer Prize–winning poet, Carolyn Kizer, my dear friend, writing now at the height of her power, a wonderful American poet—I go to her writings and I'm weeping, struck by the beauty of her language and the power of her conception. Carolyn wrote a play. We got actors together and read it. The language was marvelous, and you were interested for about ten minutes.

Wilmeth: You have gone back to some of your scripts and revised them several years after you first wrote them. How do you feel about revisions?

Linney: Sometimes this occurs because you get a chance to. When you get the opportunity, you look at a text and note things you didn't quite do to your satisfaction. I don't think plays are ever written but revised. You get a script up to a certain point, and you frequently have to go into production. Sometimes you do things then, because of deadlines, that you later regret. I don't think there is any play of mine that came to fruition that I'm not still interested in. Once a play of mine gets written, I'm probably going to keep thinking about it. Different plays are different in the degree to which they are ready after that first draft. A one-act play of mine called *F. M.,* which I think is one of the best plays I've ever written, just fell out. It had just one revision of one character. I worked very hard on *Byron;* I went through many revisions. The final script of *Byron* only came to be after the third production. The structure was always the same. I still have another version of *Frederick.*

Wilmeth: What is it like watching a play of yours onstage?

Linney: Theatre is like sex—you can't describe it. It is itself. And watching a play of yours work onstage is like good sex or something like that. Watching a bad production, is—just the reverse. A central question for a playwright is the extent to which you will change your plays to suit the exigencies of production. If you allow changes to be made against your better judgement, and they don't work and the play's a disaster, then you're really ripped off because you've betrayed yourself. If, on the other hand, you are a stubborn idiot who doesn't understand actors and their difficulties, and you're dumb that way, you're equally done in. The secret to being able to face your productions with equanimity is to feel that you did as absolutely well as you could with the business of being faithful to your conception and being a working partner with your other artists.

Wilmeth: What are your working habits?

Linney: I try to do something everyday, even when I'm traveling. The great thing today is that, with a computer, once you have the first draft done, you're in heaven. You can revise a play in a couple of days. I enjoy the writing now, and in part because I'm being produced and don't have all that anxiety. My pleasure now is more in the writing than in the production. This is a healthy way to feel, for it frees you to do a lot of things and allows you unlimited access to essential pleasures. You don't have to depend on anybody.

Wilmeth: Since 1986, when we initiated our first conversation, you have written a half-dozen major new plays, including *Three Poets, Unchanging Love, Ambrosio,* and, most recently, one that suggests a new direction in your work. Could you comment on this?

Linney: In 1987 I wrote the draft of *Unchanging Love,* based on a Chekhov novella, *In the Hollow,* which is Chekhov's story, the center of which is a baby murder. I also wrote *True Crime,* a play based on nineteenth-century chapbooks, and an Appalachian version of Tolstoy's *Power of Darkness,* also about a baby murder. Chekhov and Tolstoy had long been a strong influence on me, albeit an unarticulated one. Tolstoy condescended to Chekhov but still did not have the patience of Chekhov to revise and polish his work, which is a pity. But both have nevertheless gotten tangled in my work, and I decided to do my own baby murder play, with both writers somewhere in my unconsciousness.

In 1993, after a frustrating period in 1992, I began to move into a very productive period, culminating in drafts of four plays in a year. More importantly I think I'm moving into a time in which I'm looking at things I read and cared about from my youth and college in the same way that I deal with events in my psychological life. These past stimuli are like real visceral experiences. This creature from your unconscious comes back and nourishes you—not in the same form, but experiences tell you of other things that happened to you when they were happening. This is a phenomenon that seems to happen later in your life. History and one's own psychological life, or literature read and cared about, though different in reality, appear to you very much like the same events. This is of great interest to me now. This occurrence allowed me to write my first major play about modern people, called

Shotgun, a play that deals with the effect of divorce and reconciliation. An earlier short play, *April Snow,* a look at a world-weary older screenwriter who romances a youthful mental institution graduate, was anchored in the present, but now I believe I can write more plays like this, including longer, more developed efforts. This is a challenge that I've never been able to meet sufficiently—to write about people like myself. In the past I've filtered myself through historical characters, Appalachian people, or arms or soldiers from my past, rather than to explore contemporary people and the subtexts of their lives.

Wilmeth: You have two recent anthologies of your work. How do you feel about this?

Linney: I am very happy, especially to get my short plays together in the Smith and Kraus book. The TCG collection has three full and three one-act plays. These are older plays, but the two volumes together provide a major overview of my work to date.

Wilmeth: At the end of our first conversation you said you found more pleasure in the writing of your plays than in the production. Seven years later do you still feel this way?

Linney: I still love to direct, but as you get older, it is hard to direct and teach full time and to stay active as a writer. At the Signature Theatre in 1991 I codirected—James Houghton [artistic director] and I actually directed each other's scenes; we had complete trust and used each other's ideas. This was somewhat less strenuous and was certainly a unique working relationship. But I love to direct, and if I had nothing else to do, I would do more. But my writing is strong now. My work at Columbia is quite satisfying. I feel good about what I'm doing.

EMILY MANN

Leigh Buchanan Bienen

Emily Mann (courtesy of Emily Mann)

Since 1990 Emily Mann has been the artistic director of the McCarter Theatre in Princeton, New Jersey, which in 1994 was awarded the Tony Award for Excellence in regional theatre. At McCarter Mann has directed critically acclaimed productions of *Three Sisters* (1992), *Cat on a Hot Tin Roof* (1992), and *The Glass Menagerie* (1991). She adapted and directed Strindberg's *Miss Julie* (1993) and directed the rhythm-and-blues musical *Betsey Brown* (1991), which she cowrote with Ntozake Shange, with music by Baikida Carroll. In the spring of 1993 she directed the world premiere of Anna Deavere Smith's *Twilight: Los Angeles, 1992* at the Mark Taper Forum, which was hailed by *Newsweek* as "an American masterpiece," and in October of 1993 she directed its East Coast premiere at McCarter Theatre.

Mann began her professional career as a resident director for the Guthrie Theatre and the BAM Theater Company and subsequently has directed at leading regional theaters throughout the country, including the Mark Taper Forum, Actors Theatre of Louisville, the Goodman

Theatre, La Jolla Playhouse, the American Music Theatre Festival, and Hartford Stage Company. Mann's Broadway debut was as both playwright and director of *Execution of Justice* (1986), which was nominated for a Drama Desk Award for Outstanding New Play and received the Bay Area Theatre Critics Circle Award, the HBO/USA Award, and the 1986 Playwriting Award from the Women's Committee of the Dramatists Guild.

Her first play, *Annulla: An Autobiography* (1978), premiered at the Guthrie and was also produced in 1989 at the New Theatre of Brooklyn, featuring Linda Hunt. Her play *Still Life* (1980) premiered at the Goodman Theatre in Chicago and opened Off-Broadway at the American Place Theatre under her direction in 1981, winning six Obie awards, including distinguished playwriting, distinguished direction, and best production, as well as the Fringe First Award for Best Play at the Edinburgh festival. *Still Life* has been presented at major theaters throughout the United States and Europe.

In 1990 she completed a screenplay, *You Strike a Woman, You Strike a Rock: The Story of Winnie Mandela,* for Camille Cosby and Judith James. Mann has recently completed a new play, *Greensboro*, a documentary chronicle of the incident and trials arising from the Ku Klux Klan and the American Nazi Party's killing of five people and wounding of eight others in Greensboro, North Carolina, in 1979. It will remain at McCarter in 1996. Her numerous awards include the Helen Hayes Award, a Guggenheim, and a Playwright's Fellowship and Artistic Associate grant from the National Endowment for the Arts. An associate artist of Crossroads Theater and past vice-president of the board of the Theatre Communications Group, Emily Mann currently serves on the board of the Society of Stage Directors and Choreographers.

This interview was conducted at the McCarter Theatre in December of 1993.

Bienen: Is being the artistic director of a major regional theatre a logical progression in your professional development?
Mann: Absolutely. It's really rather interesting. Very few writers run theaters. Very few writers are also full-time directors, not just directing their own work, but actually having a career as a director. When I write plays, I write plays that break form, highly political and nonnaturalistic plays. Plays that are hyperreal, often based on nonfiction.
Bienen: As a director you have to get into somebody else's head in a way that is very different from what you do as a playwright.
Mann: Then when I produce, it is different again. Running a theatre is

about, yes, building a body of work for myself as a director and writer, but it also involves making an assessment of the state of the theatre. My vision of the theatre has to do with putting different artists together and helping others to create pieces, whether it's in the classical repertoire or new work. What I'm doing as an artistic director is putting together three parts of myself, plus a fourth part, which is community building.

This job is very political. I'm enjoying that side of it. Our theatre is community based. I have a community that I am responsible to. We are given state money, taxpayers' money, and it matters that we communicate to a diverse public. I want to put new plays into the literature that are by women and people of color. It's interesting. I'm not doing it because they're women or people of color, but what I'm really drawn to happens to be work that has social significance, and often that's who's creating it.

I'm constantly thinking about balancing the season. A great new work only is enhanced by looking at what came before it. The traditions that we came up and out of, the brilliant plays that have been written in the past, brought up to the present, with artists today reexamining them, that only enhances how we look at important new work.

Bienen: How do you see this audience? Where do you think they're coming from? What do they bring to the theatre?

Mann: They're smart. Tough-minded. Open to all different kinds of theatre. I was told that this audience was very conservative, very stuffy, very old, very white, very judgmental and Anglophile. And it's not! Or at least those folks have left since I arrived. The majority of people in this audience are rather substantial people, with some serious ideas in their heads, and they want to see themselves, their community, their world reflected or challenged on the stage. They're sick of the idiocy on television and in the mainstream movies coming out of Hollywood.

Bienen: Certainly if you get them hooked into you over a season, you can have a different kind of relationship with them. When you get people into the theatre, particularly with your own work now, what do you do?

Mann: The first challenge is to try and reach them, to try and get them immediately.

Bienen: Say it's a new play, and they don't know what to expect.

Mann: I've just been thinking about how I begin plays, both as a director and as a writer. People are coming from who knows where, with their own baggage, and they're in off a good day or a bad day from work or the kids, and how are we going to engage them?

Bienen: They're there. Now what?

Mann: You know that horrible Hollywood term "the grabber"? I realize that I do that in every single show I direct or write. For example, how I opened Williams's *Cat on a Hot Tin Roof.* I asked Baikida Carroll to compose a full minute and a half of music at the opening. Suki, the maid, enters. I wrote a silent scene. She sets the entire play. It is hot. A very high-class black woman, the maid, in an obviously white plantation home enters. Through her actions she sets up the story: that this a room where a man and woman sleep separately, no sex has taken place, someone's been drinking a lot. Somebody, the husband or the wife, has been sleeping on the couch. You see her stockings near the bed, and you see his pajamas on the couch. She sets the entire story in that minute and a half through music, a Delta blues, through sound, light, and action. I always end up doing that.

Execution of Justice, which I wrote and directed, opens with the Cop and Sister Boom-Boom, the two extremes of that city. The Cop was basically disgusted by homosexuals and what they're doing, in terms of the church and the morals of the country. He's revolted by all of that. On the opposite side of the stage there's a man dressed up in drag, as a nun, Sister Boom-Boom, making an inflammatory speech on the steps of city hall. The two are juxtaposed, the two are intercut. Almost like a prologue.

This morning I figured out how I want to open my new play about the Klan and the murder of five civil rights workers in Greensboro. Instead of looking at this material in terms of storytelling, I thought, "Okay, what do I want to say?" I'm starting it in the present, with white supremacists speaking out at a WAR [White Aryan Resistance] Conference. Out of three hours of tape I have culled probably seven minutes of the speeches of three white racists. Those speeches will be shaped. They'll form a sort of chorus, a prologue, that sets up this play about Greensboro.

You're hearing things that sound kind of logical, and then BANG! Right in the center of all of this is this horrible joke. One speaker says: " 'I have good news and bad news,' said the German commandant to the Jew. 'The good news is you're gonna see the best hotels in Europe. The bad news? You're gonna go as soap.' " This is when you realize the man talking about loving your own is a Nazi. You're hit with it in the belly. I was looking for a way to jolt people. It's not linear, it's suddenly visceral. All of a sudden the audience realizes, "Wait a minute. These people are for real. These people are out to kill; these people exist." And we, as a society, we let the Klan and the Nazis get away with murder. There's a national amnesia: "We don't know about it."

So I have set it up from the other side. Not from the victims' point of view, but from what they're up against, from the other side. Just like in *Cat on a Hot Tin Roof*. I don't start with Maggie the Cat. I don't set it up with Brick. I don't set it up with Big Daddy. I set it up with the maid. You've got tension with opposites, which reveal the bigger picture.

Bienen: Talking about the way in, especially for your new play about the Klan, people get drawn into this material, they start thinking, "This is something I understand."

Mann: Right. Then you keep reversing it on them.

Bienen: So the next reaction is, "This isn't something I understand."

Mann: The first reaction is, "I think I know all about this," and then you realize you don't know at all.

Bienen: So you create a kind of emotional and political and cultural and personal confusion, by surprising people. By confronting them with the fact that their preconceptions are limited or wrong or inaccurate.

Mann: Right. Exactly right.

Bienen: What's the next step?

Mann: A set of questions. Not, "Oh, I know this!" Because then the audience sits back. You've got to always have them sitting forward.

Bienen: Then the mood has to change at a certain point. You only have them for two hours. You get people hooked, you get people all riled up. You've got them confused. What happens next—

Mann: You've got them churning. Then you start to lay out the reason why you've done that to them, that there's a story you're telling. And you withhold as long as you can because they've got to be almost like people involved in solving a mystery or putting together the pieces for themselves. So there's a questioning active mind and heart going on at the same time, asking, "What happened?" It may be as simple as, "Well, what happened? Oh!" Then you think you know, because you've just heard one thing. Then, someone comes in with something else, and it's, "Oh! That's the opposite of what I thought." So you're keeping the audience actively searching, whatever it is you're putting together.

Bienen: That sounds a lot like teaching.

Mann: So that each time they thought they knew something, it's "Whoops! Wait a minute. There's something even more going on here that I didn't understand. And maybe this isn't just some weird thing that happened in North Carolina, but this is about me!" And you're going, "Oh my God this is happening now, right around the corner. It's *my* equal protection under the law that is at risk. These people could target me. Even though I'm not a 'Communist weirdo.'"

In the speech where he talks about tactics, the Klansman says: "Look at Joe Six-pack. If you show up with a handful of Klansmen and a hundred white screaming protesters, that doesn't show power. Joe Six-pack sits there, he's got nothing but contempt for the Klan. But we can win over Joe Six-pack with our ideology. He agrees with us."

Bienen: Joe Six-pack is your ordinary guy.

Mann: Right.

Bienen: So Joe Six-pack is the target audience.

Mann: Yes, the networks target Joe Six-pack too. The networks said to me, "Okay, how are you going to take Joe Six-pack, who's, you know, having his third beer and putting his feet up, how're you gonna keep him interested before the first commercial?" They say, "Show the massacre. He wants to watch a lot of blood!" This is why I do not want to do network television. I want to stay in the theatre.

Bienen: One thing that's striking about your work is that you cross the line of writing from the point of view of people who are clearly not yourself. It's so rare for a white writer to write from the point of view of blacks, not to mention the gender divisions, which are usually so apparent. Men write about the men they know, and women write about the women they know. But there seems to be almost a total absence of autobiography in your plays.

Mann: There's autobiography in *Annulla*. That was one of the premises of *Annulla*.

Bienen: That's the only one.

Mann: No! Everything I write about is all me. They're all me, all of them. In *Still Life* each one of those people, and especially each one of the women, was me. But especially the wife. I got into the wife totally, totally got her down. That was very personal. And of course the politics of that piece were very close to me. They're all very personal plays. That's the thing. It looks as if they're not because ostensibly they're all about other people and about public events. At first it seems they're not about me. But even the Greensboro play. There, but for the grace of God . . .

I am teaching a course at Princeton on documentary playwrighting in the spring of 1994. I find that if I can be very specific and simple with students, then I can be that way with myself, which means I know what I'm doing more and more. Teaching helps the craft of writing for me. And a lot of playwriting is craft. Inspiration is wonderful when it comes, but don't wait for it. It's really a question of slogging away at this . . . thing . . .

Bienen: Also it is good when you get a response, especially from young people. You know when you're getting them and when you're not.

Mann: Yes, but that can be false, too. I find that if I can get their work to transform itself and go up a notch before our very eyes, then I know I'm teaching well. Then when I go home, I'm clearer about my own work. Or even inspired. Sometimes they'll bring in stuff that is just great, and it sparks an idea for me. It's like a writers' workshop. I treat them like professional writers. I make them respond to each other's work, and sometimes their critiques are very good.

Through teaching I also have the opportunity to get hooked into young people's culture. I know the ten-year-old crowd because of my son, but I don't know the late teen–early twenties group anymore. That's often where the most exciting cultural things are happening. They are making popular culture. And they're in touch with it all. I just like to see what the women are wearing on their feet!

Bienen: What they're thinking about, how they talk, what they're listening to, what they're doing for fun, what they want—

Mann: I got in touch with that in Los Angeles when I was working on *Twilight,* basically with blacks and Latinos, but mostly blacks. I'm not very hopeful. Things are so bad that it is a miracle when anyone gets up from and out of places like South Central. The options are so few. The difference between what those people are dealing with and what the Princeton kids face is, as you can imagine, like being on different planets. Even when those kids do escape, they have to find a new way to think and feel and live. It's a dreadful situation. They're in a war zone. They're living in a war, and they've got all the stress syndromes of war victims. Some of them are incredible warriors. Some young people think there is a race war coming. When I listen to a white skinhead and a black gang member, I don't hear much difference.

Bienen: What about the blacks who do make it out of those neighborhoods, granted that they are few, there's nothing for them to go back to. What about the blacks who make it in the arts? How do they find their community?

Mann: This is such a complicated issue. The middle-class black communities are extremely strong, thriving and growing, getting bigger and bigger, and moving farther and farther away from that ghetto culture. The more that people leave, especially the more the middle class leaves, the more there are no leaders in that community. So the community degenerates further. When I was in Los Angeles what struck me, just visually, was that as you go down the main drag in South Central, every other block you see a liquor store, a gun store, and a funeral parlor, side by side.

Bienen: When they legalize drugs, you'll see the funeral parlor, the liquor store, the gun store, and the narcotics store.

Mann: It's a mess. I used to think that we all had good plans and a few answers. Now I don't see it. What's happened to a lot of very vital people who were working for social change is that they're tired. We're at a new point, and we aren't moving. We don't take action because we don't know the right action to take. So most people I know are now doing whatever they can in their own way, what Winne Mandela used to call a personal defiance campaign. Just every day do your bit: you do your work, you write your articles, you write your plays, you're good to people, you teach your kids to be good to people, you hope that when their friends come over, you teach those kids. I mean, you just do what you can in your own small world to make the world a better place, because that's all you can do.

Bienen: So that is the end of politics.

Mann: Maybe that is the real beginning of politics.

Bienen: What do you mean when you say you see yourself carrying on your father's work?

Mann: Well, he was a historian of America, and a great intellectual historian, a distinguished professor of American history at the University of Chicago. His expertise was ethnicity and race. He wrote a two-volume biography of New York City Mayor LaGuardia and another book titled *The One and the Many: Reflections on the American Identity.* He was brilliant on the subject.

I grew up thinking about these issues, discussing them, debating them, arguing about them. And I think these are still the key debates going on in the public today, in individual psyches as well as in public arenas. We Americans are obsessed with identity—ethnicity and race. *Twilight* is about that. Right after my father died, I started to work on *Twilight.* And I felt it was a way of continuing his work. Directly. And *Greensboro* is too, and so was *Betsey,* of course! Oh, did he love that show. Oh, God, he loved that show!

Bienen: In your references to him, in previous interviews, you often mention that you argued with him, you fought with him, but that the relationship had at its core what was clearly a very strong, intense, highly emotional exchange of ideas.

Mann: Yes.

Bienen: This relationship seems to have led you to the theatre. At each of the key points in your artistic life, there's an important, energizing interaction with your father, a kind of showdown. Were his political views very different from yours? It sounds as if they weren't. Didn't you come out of the same tradition?

Mann: Our political views were very different when I was younger.

Bienen: Give me an example.

Mann: I was against the war in Vietnam. My father was for the war in Vietnam. He said, "If you were a boy, I would not do what all these other people of privilege have done around here, which is get their kids out. You would have gone!" I said, "No. I would not have gone. You would have lost a son." That was one example. So I wrote *Still Life* as an answer to him. I couldn't write it from a liberal point of view. I had to show him from the Vietnam veteran's point of view. My central character was a man who had earned a Purple Heart in the war. Listen to him! Hear what he has to say about that war. That dialogue was with my father. At the end of that play my father said, "You've earned the right to have your own point of view. I don't agree with you. I will never agree with you. But I respect you."

Bienen: As the Vietnam War progressed, did he ever change his mind?

Mann: No.

Bienen: Where do you think this came from in him?

Mann: He was very idealistic about America. He was really part of that World War II generation. My father never talked about his experiences in the war. He thought it was very bad form to talk about the war. He hated seeing all these people come back and tell their war stories. He didn't do it. He wouldn't do it. His father came over as an immigrant with very little education, and his son, my father, went to Harvard on the G. I. Bill and became a professor. His father came over in the 1890s from Austria, and my father was born here in 1921. My father lived the American dream! If you worked hard and got an education and believed in this country, things came back to you. You could be the son of an immigrant with nothing and end up going to Harvard and becoming a professor!

Bienen: So what was the source of your ideological and political conflict with him?

Mann: We disagreed on Vietnam, we disagreed with each other on the politics of race in some ways.

Bienen: What about on sexual politics?

Mann: Well, he was a feminist. He was a big fan, a big supporter of women. He was one of the earliest academic feminists. Now I would say that in some ways he was right to have questioned my choices when I was young. I became increasingly radical. Early on he questioned the black/separatist, black/nationalist movement, thinking that it would lead to big problems. History has proved him right. But at the time I was very behind that and supported it. Now from this vantage point in time I see we were not that different, after all. We were in agreement about our goals, but I saw the need for more, for quicker change, more radical change than he thought would be lasting. He was an adult, and I was a kid. Toward the end of his life we both realized we were not that far apart ideologically.

Bienen: Did he feel that the model that worked for him would be all right for blacks?

Mann: He was very optimistic, you see, in the early years. My reflex is still to be very optimistic, but he became . . . less so. In the sixties he marched with his best friend, the acclaimed Negro historian John Hope Franklin, from Selma to Montgomery with Dr. King. They marched for change. The laws were going to change. Everyone was very optimistic. If we, people of good will, could get together, we could make it right, make the change. Remember there was this very strong black-Jewish alliance after the war. These two oppressed people saw great similarities between themselves, and they formed a strong political alliance that pushed for change. There were strong personal bonds, too.

We lived three doors down from Elijah Mohammed, now Louis Farrakhan's house, his palace. There began to be a great rift in the seventies, with the Muslim and Arab movement pushing to get Jews out of the civil rights movement. Especially in Chicago. There was a big black-Jewish split, politically. Black separatism came in, black anti-Semitism, and my father responded very personally to that.

Bienen: Where did he end on that issue?

Mann: In a lot of pain. You know, the seventies was a very sad time! A very sad time. So there was a lot of anger there, a lot of bitterness there. And I always fought that in him!

Bienen: I guess that's why it's good to have children.

Mann: I just said, "No, you don't get it!" It was always, *he* didn't get it. *He* didn't get it.

Bienen: So your political views were always, "In your face!"

Mann: In his face all the time about it all. But in fact he had his finger on things the way they were. He looked at the facts. He looked at things much more coldly than I do. And I'm beginning to see the wisdom in that. My father was saying things in the seventies that people are now saying in the nineties. They were too afraid to say these things in the seventies. He was a Cassandra, saying, "Look what's coming! This is bad news." But it was politically incorrect to say so, although no one used that term then.

We've been muzzled from saying a lot of important things recently. What the urban black kids said in response to *Twilight* was that they were grateful to see it. They were sick and tired of the fact that no one knew how to talk about race in this country. You couldn't just talk about color, they said, because there was a right way and a wrong way to talk. So people weren't really talking to each other. All the kids, black and nonblack, said this: "We're not talking to each other! How can we go further if we can't talk to each other?" The national disease is denial. If you repress all of these hatreds and scared feelings to the degree that we have, you are in a dangerous state. Then you start sounding sick and acting sick, like the Klan. I've heard it, from "good people,"

Bienen: Well, maybe your new play will get us talking about some of these things.

Mann: I hope so. Wouldn't that be nice?

NTOZAKE SHANGE
Neal A. Lester

Ntozake Shange (courtesy of Alan S.
Walker, Program Corporation of America)

Ntozake Shange is a black feminist. She is also a dancer, actor, director, author, lecturer, installation artist, poet, and playwright. Since the Broadway success of *for colored girls who have considered suicide / when the rainbow is enuf* (1976)—for which she received an Obie award, the Outer Critic's Award, and nominations for the Grammy, Tony, and Emmy awards—she has published four other theatre pieces in the tradition of the choreopoem genre: *spell #7* (1979); *a photograph: lovers in motion* (1979); *boogie woogie landscapes* (1979); and *From Okra to Greens / A Different Kinda Love Story: A Play / With Music & Dance* (1985). The collection *three pieces* (1981) comprises *spell, a photograph,* and *boogie.* Shange's one-act play *Daddy Says* appears in Woodie King, Jr.'s *New Plays for the Black Theatre* (1989). To her credit are two novels, *Sassafrass, Cypress & Indigo* (1982) and *Betsey Brown* (1985), as well as two novellas, *Sassafrass* (1976) and *Melissa & Smith: A Story* (1983). She has written six poetry collections: *Nappy Edges* (1978), *Some Men* (1983), *A Daughter's Geography* (1983), *Matrilineal Poems* (1983), *from okra to greens: poems* (1984), and *The Love Space Demands: A Continuing Saga* (1991), as well as a collection of critical essays, *See No Evil: Prefaces, Essays & Accounts* (1984). Her work also includes adaptations of Bertolt Brecht's *Mother Courage and Her Children* (1981) and Willy Russell's *Educating Rita* (1983). Her unpublished performance pieces include *Mouths: A Daughter's Geography* (1981), *Dreamed Dwellings: An Installation & Performance Piece* (1981), *Triptych & Bocas* (1982), and *Ridin' the Moon in Texas* (1986). Shange has also published a volume of prose and poetry entitled *Ridin' the Moon in Texas: Word Paintings* (1987) and is currently at work on a novel, *Little Rich Colored Boy*, and a play, *Three Views of Mt. Fugi*. Her novel *Betsey Brown* was recently transformed into a musical, produced in 1989 at the Forum Theatre in Philadelphia by the American Music Theater Festival, and her volume *The Love Space Demands* was dramatized in 1993 at both the Painted Bride Art Center in Philadelphia and the Crossroads Theater in New Jersey. Other shorter pieces include the "Fore/Play" [foreword] and "Pócame" in the anthology *Erotique Noire: Black Erotica* (1992), as well as "However You Come to Me" in the collection *Wild Women Don't Wear No Blues: Black Women Writers on Love, Men and Sex* (1993).

With a bachelor's degree in American studies from Barnard College (1970) and a master's degree in American studies from the University of Southern California (1973), Shange has taught courses in third-world poetry, women's studies, African-American drama, sociology of the black family, and humanities. At the time of this interview Shange was teaching playwriting and creative writing at the University of Houston.

Identifying herself as "a poet first and a playwright second," Shange has patented the choreopoem form as rooted in an African tradition of movement, song, music, and emotional catharsis. As a black person, as a black female, as a black feminist, as a black artist, and as a black female artist, Shange champions the woman of color specifically and people of color generally as they move toward optimal self-consciousness, positive self-identity, and unlimited self-realization in an oppressive and blatantly sexist and racist modern society. A crusader for race consciousness, preservation, and accurate documentation, Shange renounces the "redundancy of being sorry and colored at the same time in the modern world."

The following interview took place at Shange's home in Houston, Texas, in August 1986.

Lester: Did you assign the label "choreopoem" to your work, or is that a term the critics created?

Shange: I made it up because I knew I wasn't a [traditional] playwright.

My relation to theatre developed as a poet and a dancer, not as a person who was an actress or who was involved in theatre or the conventions of theatre as we know it, in whatever international framework you want to put it in. Also as a progeny of the black arts movement—almost a second generation of the black arts movement after Larry Neal and Imamu Amiri Baraka, and after the black fire issue in 1967—I was very concerned about and passionately committed to the idea of creating new rituals and new mythologies for people of color. I had two reasons for this. One was that the mythologies that were available to us were negative images, in James Baldwin's work or in Ralph Ellison's work, for instance, or in Claude McKay's. Their images of black people were not necessarily false images, but they were certainly images that were concerned with our relationship with the other (that is, white people), as opposed to our relationship with ourselves. Secondly I thought that one of the primary goals assigned young writers of color in the late 1960s was to direct our attentions inward, not so much introspectively, but in an actively introspective fashion, so that we could discern in our own communities which things were or were not functioning well for us. From what wellsprings could I draw things that might in fact envelop us in a sense of ourselves that was rooted to the earth, that was *not* rooted to the idea that white people had about us, that was *not* rooted to our relationship to white people, and that had solely to do with how we respond to being alive on the planet? I know from our experiences in the church, our experiences in black institutions, ranging from baseball teams to insurance companies to sororities and fraternities, and the like, that we're perfectly capable of creating our own social activities and our own elite motifs of occasions that are important to us. And I wanted my work to reflect this life of ours that had been up to that point, at least for me, articulated in vague ways, if realized at all.

If we go back to the idea of people organizing for Garvey, for instance, the idea of a public speaker or a person who approaches an audience and gives of himself or herself and then creates a sense of community was something I thought poets could do. I watched poets do it in California and on the lower East Side of New York. I watched communities of people, albeit in some instances communities of artists (for artists are *still* people), feeling a sort of belonging in a movement toward realization of self, in a collective sense that had been sorely missing in my youth but had probably been available to my parents because of travels by people like Paul Robeson and Langston Hughes, who went to public libraries and were available for people to see them. I didn't want to do just that. I wanted to use the forms that were available to us (that is, dance, music) that are used colloquially and in a vernacular art form to move those to another level, so that I could use the things that were endemically black in some cultural way as a further extrapolation of my understanding of our realities and our unconscious desires in both spheres. This also has to do with my information from women's studies: the significance of rituals is continually denied people of color and poor people. However, ritual is very important and is very satisfying, if it's done correctly. For example, some dance can be terribly ritualistic, just like some language and poetry. So I was interested in using that too. And as a woman I didn't and don't have any problems with the idea of women's perspectives—be they circular or nonvertical thinking or whatever you want to call it.

I get very bored with traditional black theatre in that it has vertical plays with vertical plots where the conflict is always with folks who are not in the house—"the white people"—who are not even there, either not there in the room or who are just some force that emanates off the stage and everybody knows "the white people." I thought that had to stop, and I didn't see black male writers doing it. Black men were continually having this battle with the white men, which I guess they have to have, but I thought it was interesting that, even though most black women worked at this point in time—before we had this incredible problem with the welfare system—we still did not continually focus all of our attention on the other. Our attention was in our community. It was not continually going outside even though we were having the same interfacing that the black men had, albeit in different ways. So I was working as a woman toward emphasizing in spoken and nonverbal ways the realities of women, as well as the realities and myths of people of color.

Lester: What do you feel are your greatest strengths as a playwright?

Shange: My strengths as a playwright would be the same as my strengths as a writer, and that, I think, is my intimate relationship with the language—a very peculiar ability to find legitimacy in sometimes aberrant or ordinary lives. It's very important to me to give us a sense of legitimacy, a validity, and to reinforce our capacity to imagine, not in the way the church does, where we will be rewarded after death. That is not interesting to me. In the here and now our dreams have substance; our nightmares have substance; our colloquial conversations are significant, especially if we hear them. With the demise of the black newspaper, a significant kind of cultural and political reinforcement was lost in our communities, and the information we got about ourselves no longer came from among ourselves but from white newspapers. That's a very dangerous situation when what we know about each other is gleaned from what is being reported by a community outside of us. It leads to all kinds of distortions and disruptions of relationships in our communities and of our responses to one another. The so-called isolation of the new so-called black middle class, I think, in large part is due to the fact that we are beginning to have so little to say to one another. If my characters don't do anything else, they talk to each other. And they talk to each other about their lives and what they want to do. No matter how crazy their talk is sometimes, what matters is that they're talking, that they're postulating their realities and their visions of the world.

Lester: How does language function in your works?

Shange: I knew that when we used to talk about using the oppressor's language, be it the king's English or the king's Portuguese or the king's French—I've had this discussion all over the Western hemisphere, and you can have it with any form of colonial people—we always get to a point where we say, or at least where I've said, "Is it possible that there are things that I simply cannot think because of the nature of the language that I use, thoughts that are simply unavailable to me? Is it possible that I can find a vocabulary through this nonverbal activity that would complement what I am able to struggle with in the language I have to speak?" It is very interesting to me that I have friends who are afraid to have Creole introduced as the language that their children were taught at the same time that we were struggling to have black English as an official language that we could teach children, at least to teach them how to read, in the United States. In Martinique it failed; it failed here. The French people won't translate my work because they say it can't be translated into French. So I say, "Well, put it in Creole." And they say, "Well, that's not French." And I say, "Well, I know that." And they say, "Who would read it?" And I say, "People who speak Creole!" But we are invisible as Creole speakers, just as we are invisible as black English speakers. June Jordan has an essay, "Nobody Mean More to Me Than You and the Future Life of Willie Jordan, July 1985" in her book *On Call: Political Essays* [1985], about teaching black English. She had some of her students retranslate into the king's English the first page of Alice Walker's *The Color Purple* (1982). It just disheveled the whole tenor of the novel. People who are not involved in the politics of language don't take it very seriously. But using words like *seems* or *alleged* or *is said to have* or using the passive tense all of the time in reference to people of color makes us spurious creatures at best and nonexistent creatures at worst.

And it's very scary to me as a woman that we're denied and defiled in language. That is a personal power to go from one language to another and continually find the same thing happening in romance languages and Germanic languages. It's really very scary. So, for me, the challenge was to kill off these things and to trip it and trick it and use it in ways that "they're" not expecting but in ways that people speaking the language I speak would receive and feel a sense of joy in. Language is a liberator, though not in the way that George Washington Carver thought that an education would free you. I don't mean that language will allow us to function more competently with people who use the king's English. I mean that language will allow us to function more competently and more wholly in a holistic sense as human beings, once we take hold of it and make it say what we want to say. Judy Grahn talks about "murdering" the king's English. That's a wonderful idea, because in murdering the king's English, we free ourselves. On the other side of that is something that one of my very favorite professors told me. I was taking a creative writing class once and was told by the professor that you can't detour from the king's English unless you do it on purpose. If you don't do it on purpose, then you're not in control of what you're doing, and you don't know what the implications are. That was a very important thing for me to learn, which is why I insist that my students and my colleagues do master the king's English or the king's French, because then it becomes the same thing that you do in military combat: you know your enemy so well that you're able to do something with his weapon.

I don't make mistakes when I write. I'm doing things on purpose, which puts me in control, and the most important thing is being in control. It *is* important for black kids to learn the king's English, and the king's French and the king's Portuguese, so that we can control it for ourselves. We are in fact being manipulated by the language when we make errors and don't know we're making errors. Then we're not doing these people or ourselves any good. We're being sloppy in our thinking because, when we make mistakes in language, we make mistakes in thinking. That's an efficient piece of thought. It is totally conceivable to me that having mastered the king's English, no one would ever want to speak it again. The last section of Jessica Hagedorn's poem "Song for my Father" from *Dangerous Music* [1975] reads: "my words change . . . / sometimes / i even forget english." That's because her experience in Manila had been so overwhelming and fulfilling that the king's English was inadequate for expressing the kinds of thoughts and feelings that she was having upon returning to her home in the states.

And I think that if we never really have a sense of "home," which is difficult for people of color in this country, at least there should be some solace in language. There should be some solace in communicating with others, which shouldn't create distance and shouldn't enclose us.

That's one of the things that has worried me about the street language of black people since the 1970s. I've noticed that as "the cause" becomes more intricate and clandestine, our street language is becoming more and more inarticulate. That's a very new occurrence and has happened in my lifetime. We've lost a very elaborate system of so-called slang words that was simply language for us. We renamed things and renamed circumstances and had a syntax that worked for that. I've been watching a whole people become inarticulate and silent by using repetitions of words like "well, you know, man," "hey, man," or "muthahfuckah" (or whatever the word is), and that one word takes on seventeen different meanings, so that no one knows what those meanings are because we haven't put any verbs in there. That's a new phenomenon, and I don't know if it's related to the absence of any exposure to people who talk or a lack of exposure to any kind of books or a lack of exposure to sophisticated thinkers of black newspapers that no longer exist. I don't know exactly what the problem is, but I do know that I have had experiences with people in prisons, people in universities, people in public and private schools, and almost straight across the board I have found an incredible inability to articulate thoughts in any form, in any kind of language—black English or "standard" English. We're not hitting a point. When I was at the University of Texas in Austin yesterday, I almost thought that the kids were afraid to say how they felt. They couldn't find the words to say how they felt. They think it's really going out on a limb to express their feelings. And I think that existentially it's very scary for people when they don't know how to say what they're feeling. I think they believe their feelings are illegitimate and that they can't find the words to express them without making themselves feel that way. They don't know what they're saying, and I think what they're feeling is something that they're afraid to think. So when you're afraid to think a thought, you repress it, and it starts coming out in these words that aren't connected to one another. And what's ironic about this is that these were supposed to be the brightest students in Texas. And I said to myself, "My God, yes, they're scared to death of something!" That's why language is so important.

Lester: In your work how is emotion or an emotional response, as opposed to an intellectual response, related to language?

Shange: First of all I don't think I could write an "intellectual" play where you had to go home and think about it. Ronnie [Ronald Reagan] tells you not only that you don't exist, but that if you do exist, you're worthless, or that if you do exist, you're not of any value. How can you then take yourself who is of no value and make yourself wonderful, or make the life of someone else, who is also of no value, wonderful? That's why it's so important to redirect our thinking from what's told to us to what *we* think—to clear away societal views that are damaging to us and replace them. It's a continuous uphill struggle.

In an "intellectual discussion" recently I talked about some people in Tomball [Texas] having a community association thing that they called "The Slave Auction." It was supposedly a fun neighbor-help-neighbor thing, where people would come and auction themselves off for a day's services. The black people of Tomball went crazy! So the association—which didn't have any black people in it, they also weren't selling black people—changed its name to "The Auction," which I felt was just as devastating. That's the ultimate conclusion of capitalism. Others thought there was nothing wrong with it since we weren't the only people who were slaves. I said that this had nothing to do with slaves. And the people of Tomball, whether they were intellectually aware of it or not, were simply responding to the idea that if people can use the words "slave auction" or even "the auction," it makes it much easier for an entire community to conceive of the idea of selling human beings as palatable. Therefore, it is dangerous and it must be stopped! On the other hand some were presenting this great internationalist's view that capitalism was capitalism, and if the people wanted to do this, it was really helpful, because suppose you couldn't clean your house for five days and someone can do it for you for five dollars. But I felt the point was that it was a sick idea! Then I suggested that they get a miniature Auschwitz to put outside because that was also "efficient," and it might help to remember just how "efficiently" things can work, which they thought was hitting below the belt. But it was the ultimate conclusion of what was said. That's just another illustration of how significant language can be. Even if the blacks didn't know why it was not okay to have this thing called "The Slave Auction"—I mean, they could go into Jungian and Freudian analysis of why this is societally dangerous—certain things hit certain kinds of chords that do make a group of people say, "I can't deal with this; this has got to stop!" And, thank God, they did! I also made another point about how interesting it was that Conroe, Tomball, and all the little towns outside of Houston were in fact full plantations at one time. Doesn't it say anything to you that the white people in places that were formerly plantations and that are named for former plantations were now "selling" each other? Doesn't that say anything? This is a very dangerous thing. They thought it was okay because they weren't selling any black people; they were just selling each other. Of course if they can sell white people, they sure as hell can sell us. [*Laughs*] But I do believe that we can respond to language that is oppressive to us, and I think that's a perfect example.

Lester: Would you say language functions pretty traditionally, though your vehicle is innovative?

Shange: Oh, definitely. I've never been able to understand why people would write something nobody else understood. I mean even if only black people understand what I write, that's fine. That's thirty million people. What's wrong with that? That seems to me a lot of people! That's adequate, *more* than adequate. It's remarkable! One of the nicest things that ever happened to me that made me think what I was doing was working came when I was asked to speak at two churches. To me that meant that I was ringing true in a tradition that black people, who don't necessarily like poets, understand. That's important. That would then give credence to the idea of poets as priests or seers—which could be pretty spiritual, although that's not why I was asked to speak in the church. The spiritual connection between being a poet and speaking in a church does not seem to be so far-fetched. And a lot of us are working toward that ideal of being able to address a congregation of people of shared values and people with a common mission, which always goes back to furthering the race. For me at this point it means maintaining certain kinds of institutions as inviolate. No matter what happens, people should always be able to find references in my work to my predecessors. Because if I don't do it and other writers of color don't do it, we'll lose them. We'll lose Langston Hughes. We'll lose Zora Neale Hurston. We'll lose Frederick Douglass. We'll lose the cadence and the rhythm and the passion, and we'll lose the historic foundation of our reality.

Lester: So language, and how it functions for us, is indeed the key to everything you're writing?

Shange: It's the key to everything we think. I hope there are some thoughts I can't think that I discover I can think in other languages. Speaking other languages is a very freeing reality because I can think things I can't think in English. It's amazing!

One of the things that was a freeing instinct for me as a child was not speaking English around white people when I didn't have to. If they bothered me, I could just not speak English, and then there was nothing they could do. Of course there was something they could do, but I had some power to control their influence on what was going on in my life. And then, of course, most of the other black people in the world who are intellectual don't necessarily speak English. And so it was another way to be involved in a greater community. It's also important to assist those of us who live in North America to understand that it is not our right to be monolingual; it is not a good state of affairs. And the identification with Anglo culture *solely* is not intelligent if we are not to feel totally isolated and, in our isolation, therefore feel less powerful and less capable of doing things about how we live and who we are and what total impact we're going to have on the world. We can't do that without analyzing what is going on around us. And being monolingual and having driving forces of energies that are created by other people for us certainly won't accomplish self-realization of a people, nor self-realization in a cultural and political arena.

Lester: In teaching *for colored girls* I have students attempt to do character analyses of the seven women. Should that be possible?

Shange: Actually, no. The women are indivisible. You can do that in the plays after *for colored girls* because those people have names. *for colored girls* was really a separate case. I divided the poems in *From Okra to Greens / A Different Kinda Love Story* into two voices, but they had names too. The indivisibility of *for colored girls* is due to the fact that they all had one voice, which I proceeded to divide. The same is true for the rest of my plays actually. They all started as poems, except *Ridin' the Moon in Texas,* which started as a long monologue that I divided. And it works divided up. What I discovered is that poems can work divided up. I didn't know that twelve years ago, but I can divide poems up so that other people can talk. So at a certain level all of my poems can become one voice if I'm dealing with a schizophrenic person. And in listening to colored people one finds that their other personalities do use language differently. They don't sound the same, and they don't use the same kinds of words.

What's not traditional about my character creation, I hope, at least in the plays I've done so far—except *Okra to Greens,* which is much like *for colored girls*—is that the people have access to their unconscious mind and can make that available to an audience. We're able to share with them their daydreams and their private reveries and/or fears and/or nightmares that usually aren't available to us. I haven't gotten that to the place where I absolutely want to have it yet. But it is something that is very important to me because I think that the richest area of human life—the part of living for years that was most enjoyable to me—was dream and daydream analysis and the incorporation of visual symbols and physical, nonverbal imagery into my persona. This makes the world very private and also very dense and comfortable when these things are assembled in such a way that one feels free about experiencing and expressing them.

Lester: In terms of your writing process, how do you start? Do you start with an idea, a situation, a message, or—

Shange: I never start with a message. It's very peculiar. Usually I know the last lines of things, or I know the last scene of something, and then I have to figure out how that happened.

Lester: Is it like writing an academic paper and having the conclusion and then working toward that?

Shange: Yes, except that I'm dealing with people, and I have to get them to the situation where this would have happened. Sometimes I don't know what's going to happen. All I know is who a character is. For instance, I wrote a lot of short stories about Cypress that had nothing to do with what eventually went on in the novel, just trying to figure out who she was and how she functioned. My process is essentially using whatever I can, either role playing or character studies or dance studies, to figure out who characters are and how they occupy their time and what they do with themselves and with other people.

Lester: What is the "average" person to make of all of the particular allusions in your work? Are you suggesting that what you write about should be part of a black person's experience?

Shange: I use allusions, just as other writers in the western European tradition do. They use metaphorical references to biblical activities and have done so for centuries. Their works have become annotated in and of themselves from one society to another and even from one continent to another. For example, a writer can use the same image of Job or refer to Faulkner or to Sartre or somebody else, and people will know what the writer is talking about. It's important for us, for people of color from societies that are not necessarily based on Western civilization, to be as familiar with our own mythologies and religions, so that we can pull on those same sorts of deep ancient roots for metaphorical images and know what we're talking about and recognize them in one another's work. That's why I think Ishmael Reed's work is *so* important. In a very contemporary way Ishmael uses non-European images and ideas that reintroduce and reinforce for us a reality that is not totally sustained by people that can't stand us. That's very important. In his earlier work LeRoi Jones did the same thing by going back to abolitionist images of black people. By moving from abolitionist to Indian to American and then to Asian references, he's able to pull us away from the quagmire of the European tradition that only allows us to have images of ourselves as golliwogs and/or "boys" in the colonial sense. That's important, and that's why a lot of us, I think, sometimes overuse or romanticize West African deities and religions and social systems, as they did during the Harlem Renaissance. Even if it is romanticized, it is still an alternative and is still properly our own, not in a proprietary sense but in an associational sense. In other words I wouldn't want to rip off, for instance, images of Shango from the Arubian writers in Nigeria. I don't need to do that. I can find enough references to Shango from the stuff in Carolina and from the Caribbean and Brazil to satisfy any needs that I have to make that a legitimate source for me. All that stuff takes historical research time, and it also takes time to feel comfortable in other cultures, when, in fact, they're not other cultures to feel comfortable in. They're societies where there is a significant non-white population into which we've been integrated very easily for the most part. Feeling comfortable with that makes it possible, at least for me, to introduce words and ideas and theories and deities and similar systems that are not necessarily associated with being a black North American, whatever that is, in the late twentieth century but can be very easily associated with being the fifth-generation descendant of diaspora in the Western hemisphere. It depends on whose history you're reading and where.

Lester: That's part of your mission, to lift black people from ignorance?

Shange: Hopefully. White people use their literature to maintain their culture. That's why you'll find references to Milton and Spenser and Shakespeare and Dostoyevsky in contemporary novels. Contemporary authors use whomever they come from to make sure that they're carrying the message of the names of western European culture into the next generations. I don't have to worry about writing about Spenser. Some white person will do that. And some white people try to write about us. Take Alice Adams's *Listening to Billie* [1978] for instance. My God! Our own characters are being appropriated. Brazilian writers, Columbian writers, Haitian writers, or Argentinean writers have the luxury of having their own countries' vastness of culture to use. We don't have that luxury. We have to make our culture right here.

My true sense of connection comes from other writers of color outside North America. I'm doing what they are doing, and my novels, I think, fit well in an international setting, as opposed to an Anglo-American setting. All of us, the Latinos and the French-speaking people and the Africans, are working in languages that have oppressed us, and we all seem to be aware that it is the Native Americans or aborigines or Africans who have supplied us with whatever kind of spiritual and intellectual strength we needed at this point in time. And the novels reflect that. This is true of Nicaraguans, of Panamanians, of every person I've met from the Western hemisphere, for the most part—the expedience of a culture that's in a cataclysmic collision with Western civilization.

Lester: What about your subject matter determines whether a piece will be poetry, fiction, or drama?

Shange: When I want to write something that I don't want to have constrain me in any way whatsoever, it should be a novel or a poem. A play or a short story has certain constraints. People can't go on and on about the weather. They can't talk about the color of the rocks forever because that doesn't necessarily move the story along. When people talk, it should move the story forward on the stage; it should go some place. A novel doesn't have to go anywhere. It can simply be, as Clarence Major says, about the adventure of writing or discovering a character who may not in fact be doing anything. And in order to get Liliane's story, the reader has to reconstruct it from information she gives. It's not just there to be used as she presents it, however. So I think novels and poems are the freest forms, for me at any rate. And when I don't exactly know what I want to have happen or when I just want to have a really good time and experience something as fully as possible, I'd write one of those. If it's a feeling I'm after or an incident, then I would probably write a short story. When I write things for the stage or change something for the stage, it's because the characters are alive and active enough to hold weight.

I do enjoy performance. In fact, I prefer to call things I do "performance work," but that gets confused with "performance art," which I also do. When I do performance art, I'm not responsible for the plot; I'm responsible for the method, for process. And that fits me all right, except that I'm too concerned with language to be a good performance artist. I like performance art because I can experiment with things. It doesn't have to work. For me it's important to try to find out what's wrong with something if it doesn't work, not the way you find out if a play works and then you want to fix it. What's exciting about performance art is seeing what the problem is. That is the adventure, not fixing it. I might not *ever* fix that. That is the dialectic, and I'm trying to present the dialectic. There it is. I can't fix it. I just want to demonstrate it, have it function in front of us so that it's unavoidable. I believe in things being unavoidable like that. Richard Wright had said that he

wanted Bigger Thomas in *Native Son* to be "relentlessly unredeeming."
I don't want to create a character who's relentlessly unredeeming. I do
want to create situations that unavoidably involve us in some way or
another, where we have to say, "Oh God, I can't deal with this!" or "I
can deal with this!"—something where the response is unavoidable, and
not to whether we like this material but to the emotional impact of
the imagery. We had two white technicians quit work on *spell #7*
[1979]. That was important. They couldn't handle what was going on
in the show. Emotionally that's fine. That meant it worked. They never
discussed the ideas. It just upset them. That's fine. That's incontrovertible
evidence that it does something to human beings. That's all I needed
to know. If they had been bored, that would have been different. That's
not working if people are bored. But anything aside from boredom will
work. Performance art gives me an opportunity to be involved with
process and to change things.

Lester: What, within a dramatic piece, determines whether a portion is
in verse or prose?

Shange: Some people don't talk. Some people talk in prose. Some people
really speak in poetry. And that's what some of my characters do. I don't
know what Liliane does. That girl's crazy! She's really funny. I have her
write all these chapters, and she has this big two-sentence that goes: "I
don't talk a lot. I see things." And I'm thinking, "My God! How can
I get her to keep going on and on about this if I've established that the
girl doesn't talk?" But that's true. She doesn't talk. She paints things. So
my editor said I could put drawings in there so that when she says,
"This is what I drew," or whatever, I can put the drawings there. I
have this strange situation of being in some ways a very noncommercial writer with a commercial press. Whereas it's expected of people
with noncommercial presses, like university presses, to do esoteric and
strange things, when I have a regular functioning capitalist press, they
think I'm going nuts.

Lester: So you still characterize yourself as a poet first and a playwright
second?

Shange: Yes.

Lester: So that hasn't changed since *for colored girls?*

Shange: No, because all of my work starts out that way. Even if I change
it to prose, it doesn't start out that way. If it's a narrative, it usually
started out as a narrative poem that I changed. In fact, whenever I consciously sit down to write a play, I can find the kernel of it in a poem
somewhere. Although I feel at home in other genres, the one that seems
intrinsic for me is poetry. The rest of them were acquired.

PART 4

CELEBRATING DIFFERENCE: THE AMERICAN THEATRE SINCE 1980

The 1980s and early 1990s advanced significantly a pluralistic American theatre attacking racial and ethnic prejudice and sexual discrimination. The Other triumphed. Beth Henley, Wendy Wasserstein, and Marsha Norman won Pulitzer Prizes; Harvey Fierstein, Terrence McNally, Tony Kushner, David Drake, and Paul Rudnick wrote plays with leading gay characters and predominately gay themes for a highly commercial theatre; ethnic plays as diverse as Herb Gardner's *Conversations with My Father* (1992) and John Leguizamo's *Spicorama* (1992) continued the American theatre's dedication to multiculturalism; and black playwrights such as August Wilson and George C. Wolfe, who won major theatre awards as well as the praise of theatregoers and critics alike, portrayed the black American's search for identity and dignity, whether in a 1927 scene from the life of legendary blues singer Ma Rainey (Wilson's *Ma Rainey's Black Bottom,* 1984), in a dramatic portrayal of Zora Neale Hurston's stories (Wolfe's *Spunk,* 1989), or through the life and music of Jelly Roll Morton (Wolfe's *Jelly's Last Jam,* 1992).

The rise, advancement, and continuing fascination with multiculturalism as a topic in the press, in the classroom, and in literary theory are succinctly articulated by C. W. E. Bigsby in his analysis of the diversity responsible for a "multiple" America: "We are all multiple selves as America is a multiple country, a kaleidoscope whose patterns change with every demographic tremor. No wonder that it has so often been in the theatre that this drama of national identity has been performed. . . . Certainly the theatre has always shown signs of that transforming energy as America has rediscovered the kinetic power of heterogeneity." [1] Such multiculturalism in the theatre, begun in earlier decades, continues breaking down hostile attitudes while at the same time celebrating America's diversity and artistic potential. In the 1980s and early 1990s various constituencies—blacks, Hispanics, and gays and lesbians—have been even more empowered to express themselves freely in a theatre that is listening to all voices.

This celebration of difference is largely responsible for Broadway's success in the 1990s and for the sustaining strengths of Off- and Off-Off-Broadway, as well as regional theatre. Harvey Fierstein's *Torch Song Trilogy* (1982) and Larry Kramer's *The Destiny of Me* (1992) portray gay Jewish family life; George C. Wolfe's *The Colored Museum* foregrounds black American history as a proud heritage while lampooning the pernicious stereotypes of black as well as white America; William Finn and James Lapine's *Falsettos* (1992) sets its climactic scene of a bar mitzvah celebration at a hospital bedside; and Jonathan Tolin's *The Twilight of the Golds* (1992) examines whether or not a Jewish couple will abort a fetus because testing has proven it to be gay.

In the 1980s women dramatists further provided important plays for the American and the world stage. Questioning the stereotypical roles expected of them, Beth Henley's heroines strive to know who they are and where they are going. In all of Henley's plays, in fact, women come to terms with a reality in which there are no absolutes as they learn to accept responsibility for their own lives. Consequently they must act on newly found beliefs, knowing their success at times can only be partial. In *Miss Firecracker Contest* (1980) Carnelle Scott escapes her "Miss Hot Tamale" past by casting off the bimbo stereotype and uncovering her true self; in *Crimes of the Heart* (1979) the MaGrath sisters—Lenny, Meg, and Babe—find strength in each other while facing gender, class, and racial assaults from within and without (Zachery's paternalism, Chick's Ladies Social League, and Hazlehurst's racism); and in *The Wake of Jamey Foster* (1982) Marshael Foster, estranged wife and widow of Jamey, asserts her independence by not attending her husband's burial. Each of these women vindicates her sense of self despite personal obstacles.

From her first success in the 1970s with *Uncommon Women* to her Pulitzer Prize–winning *The Heidi Chronicles* to her 1993 *The Sisters Rosensweig* (no other nonmusical production on Broadway has ever had more advance sales for seats), Wendy Wasserstein has turned her back on the consensus and paid tribute to individuality. Her protagonists are in every way proudly uncommon. In *The Heidi Chronicles,* Heidi Holland copes with handsome Peter Patrone, the man of her dreams who also happens to be gay; with arrogant and self-assured Scoop Rosenbaum, her on-and-off lover whose political ideologies and girlfriends blow with the wind; and with her sisters, who share her triumphs and disasters as they march together into the twenty-first century. At the end of the play, when she adopts a baby and becomes a single parent, she casts off selfishness and takes on the life of another, allowing her maternal instincts to mix with her professional life as a feminist art historian. Because of its confidence and commitment, Wasserstein's play may be the palimpsest for women in the 1990s.

Cultural differences define as well as celebrate ethnicity and sexuality for playwrights of the 1980s and 1990s. In *The Sisters Rosensweig* Wasserstein presents three middle-aged Jewish sisters who meet at Queen Anne's Gate in London to celebrate the fifty-fourth birthday of Sara, the eldest. Like Henley's heroines, their ethnic heritage brings them together in proclamation of sisterhood. All three have followed their drives, but their "successes" have been only partial: Sara, a brilliant banker and a divorced single mother, no longer sees the need for romance; Gorgeous, a suburban housewife and mother, has become a talk show personality; and Pfeni, a journalist and travel writer, longs to write her serious book on the women of Tajikistan. At the play's conclusion it is obvious that despite their differences the sisters are able to accept their eccentricities.

Regional theatre in the 1980s and early 1990s, as in the 1970s, continues to be the proving ground for a variety of plays not initially intended for the commercial Broadway stages, although some of them eventually soared there. As Alan Woods argues, Broadway theatre was neither ideologically daring nor terribly promising in the 1980s: "Many of the social issues facing the United States were conspicuous by their absence from Broadway stages. There was, for example, no mention of abortion at all in the commercial theatre's plays (and precious little of pregnancy apart from the 1983 musical, *Baby*). The problem of the homeless figured in the 1988 failure, *Eastern Standard*."[2] An obsession with money and the spectacle of riches dominated the Broadway stage during the Reagan years.

Meanwhile, regional theatre mounted new and more adventurous productions. For example, Tina Howe's *Painting Churches* (1983) premiered at the Second Stage at the South Street Theatre; August Wilson's *Fences* (1985) opened at the Yale Repertory Theatre; Lanford Wilson's *Burn This* (1987) came to the Mark Taper Forum in Los Angeles; and Tony Kushner's two-part *Angels in America,* comprising *Millennium Approaches* and *Perestroika* (1992), also was presented at the Mark Taper Forum. In addition to offering thought-provoking, politically sensitive productions, regional theatre remained even more accessible financially, far less expensive than a Broadway show. Regional theatre in the 1980s and 1990s also appealed to a wider audience, which included high school and college students, as well as the generation of aging yuppies and culture-seeking seniors. The last two audiences often sought to expand their horizons beyond the expensive Broadway shows.

Despite the high cost of tickets, Broadway also fared well in the early 1990s, as *American Theatre* documents:

> Broadway ticket sales reached a new high of $356 million for the 1993–94 season, according to figures released by the League of American Theatres and Producers. When combined with touring productions, receipts from admissions topped $1 billion for the first time. Broadway attendance during the same period was the highest in six years—a total of 8.1 million people throughout the season, up from 7.9 million the year before. Improved attendance and box-office statistics can be largely attributed to the increase in the number of shows running on Broadway, including 37 new productions (compared to last year's 33) for 1,061 total playing weeks.[3]

Broadway's success plus that of regional theatres augurs for a greater interest in American theatre for the rest of the millennium.

Like their predecessors, the playwrights of the 1980s and early 1990s explored ways of dramatizing national problems. With her anarchic wit Tina Howe not only celebrates the freedom of lunacy, but she also turns it into high art. In the foreword to *Three Plays by Tina Howe* her comments on art reveal the theatre's discomfort with the predictable politics of the 1980s: "I see terrible dangers in insisting on tidy parallels and meaningful departures," for they "drain away all mystery and delight." Instead each of her plays attempts to "burst the perimeters" of the play that went before.

> They share an absorption with the making and consuming of art, a fascination with food, a tendency to veer off into the primitive and neurotic, and of course a hopeless infatuation with the sight gag. Perhaps their oddest feature is how they shrink in physical dimension as they progress, moving from a crowded museum down to an intimate living room. Writers are supposed to start in their living rooms, not end up there. I did it all backwards and now have nowhere to go unless I jump down my throat and take on a whole new intestinal landscape.[4]

Another playwright of the 1980s who also explores new landscapes through the prism of another era is Joan Schenkar. Engaging in provocative historical research, Schenkar perverts events to publicize anew the horrors of history. *The Last of Hitler* (1982) isolates Hitler and Eva in the Jewish retirement section of Miami; *Between the Acts* (1984) is set in a large and exotic garden with talking plants and a gay male serpent; and her *Fire in the Future* (1988), a musical revision of the story of Joan of Arc, casts Marlene Dietrich as the saint who commands Joan to wear pants. Dealing with disturbing surreal landscapes of her "extremely complete and well-integrated unconscious," Schenkar sees "memory and history in relation to our psychic lives." In this respect she and playwright-director Emily Mann share a keen interest in and dramatic use of history. In its bold and experimental staging Schenkar's theatre is powerful and disturbing, darkly hilarious and brilliantly creepy as she deals with the familiar haunted by the unknown, attempting "to gain a shudder of recognition from the audience in the midst of their laughter." Emily Mann's plays also experiment with staging the horrors of the Holocaust, urban violence, and the Vietnam War. In some ways Schenkar and Mann carry on the legacy of Arthur Miller, Barrie Stavis, and Lawrence and Lee, who had earlier used historical events to purge and redeem our national consciousness.

Similarly in the collection of his first four plays, called *Broken Promises* (1983), David Henry Hwang focused on expressing one's identity while being surrounded by external pressures and prejudices. Hwang's plays concentrate on the difficulties and confusions of being of Asian ancestry in a land of unfulfilled dreams and broken promises. As he says in his interview included in this section, by being called "Chinese American," he becomes neither Chinese nor American. Elsewhere he explains: "I am interested in the dust that settles when worlds collide. Sometimes these worlds are cultural, as in my explorations of a Chinese past meeting in an American present. Sometimes they are spiritual, as in *Rich Relations,* where the gung-ho materialism of a California family struggles with its Christian mysticism. Most of the time I also try to walk the fine line between tragedy and comedy. I'm fascinated by America as a land of dreams—people pursue them and hope some day to own one."[5]

In *M. Butterfly* Hwang recasts the tragicomic tale of an East-West affair ending in a spy scandal. A collage of traditions, *M. Butterfly* uses a long flashback for the main action, combining pieces of music from Puccini's operas and Asian tradition, as well as drawing on Kabuki and Nōh traditions of Japanese drama. Hwang skillfully blends stylized acting, fantasy visions, and vernacular realism to create one of the most theatrically inventive plays of the late 1980s.

In *Angels in America* Tony Kushner also juxtaposes the visionary and the hallucinatory with stark realism as he confronts the AIDS crisis and human insensitivity, embracing along the way Mormons, blacks, Jews, and WASPs. With humor, pathos, and sometimes terror, Kushner explores religion and politics, sexuality and morality, as *Angels* moves from Washington to Moscow to the South Bronx to Salt Lake City, from earth to heaven and then back again. Kushner has been hailed as a prophet for the 1990s.

Preferring to keep his mind "oceanic and let books, people, events swim mistily where they will," Kenneth Bernard's Theatre of the Ridiculous sees literalness, "a puerile sense of representation," as "the disease of the American theatre establishment." Saying "No!" in thunder "to false pieties, to delusions, to systematic and technological mutilations of the human spirit," Bernard's *La Fin du Cirque* (1984) meditates on the human condition in terms of gravity (earthboundness) and weightlessness (the desire to soar). His *We Should . . . (A Lie)* (1992) explores Phaedra's reluctance to give voice to the enormous scream growing within her; as Bernard explains, "Articulation will not only bring down the curtain but it will also mediate the scream."

Before the late 1960s, and often into the 1970s, plays with gay themes were not considered commercially viable, and gay characters were frequently represented through outrageously ridiculous stereotypes. Camp dominated. Historically important, Robert Anderson's *Tea and Sympathy* in 1953 dared to deal with the subject of a boarding-school youth unjustly accused of being gay. The subject matter was so controversial that Robert Anderson had to stand up to the anger of various would-be censors. (In London the play had to be performed at a private playhouse with a membership fee required because the Lord Chamberlain had banned it from the public playhouses; similar problems confronted Williams and Miller.) Tennessee Williams successfully explored homosexual themes in *Cat on a Hot Tin Roof* (1955) through the frustrated relationship between best friends Skipper and Brick, as well as through Big Daddy's relationship with the previous owners of his southern plantation, Jack Straw and Peter Ochello, a gay couple who slept in the bed now occupied by Maggie and Brick. In 1968 Mart Crowley's successful Off-Broadway play *Boys in the Band,* exploring homosexual lifestyles, proved a landmark production, as gay theatre began being accepted in the mainstream. Between 1968 and 1982 plays with gay themes and characters received even greater acceptance. Harvey Fierstein's *Torch Song Trilogy* (1982), chronicling the love affairs of a drag queen, garnered rave reviews from both the *New York Times* and John Simon. Moving from a small house to the Actor's Playhouse, *Torch Song Trilogy* ran for three years, and then went to Broadway, where it won the Tony. In 1983 Fierstein adapted Poiret's play *La Cage aux Folles,* one of the most successful plays of the decade.

The growing danger of AIDS affected tremendously the development of the American theatre in the 1980s and 1990s. With the spread of this disease gay playwrights explored a subject that was of great interest to heterosexual audiences as well. Plays on AIDS were featured on Broadway as well as Off- and Off-Off-Broadway. AIDS has had an impact on everything we do in this part of the twentieth century. Larry Kramer's *Normal Heart* (1985) indicts the government, the media, and the public for refusing to deal with the great plague at the end of the twentieth century, as his play explored the powerful emotions of private lives caught up in the suffering and doom of an AIDS-threatened universe. Whether a subtext in *Frankie and Johnny in the Claire de Lune* (1987) or a central theme in *Lips Together, Teeth Apart* (1991) and *A Perfect Ganesh* (1992), Terrence McNally combats homophobia as "a virus in people that bubbles up somehow and that has to be dealt with." In McNally's most recent plays, gay relationships and individuals coming to terms with being gay contextualize the larger values of American cultural, religious, and political life. In William Finn and James Lapine's *Falsettos* (1992), which was able to recoup its expenses in less than six months and went on to be a huge success, gay characters and themes sold to mixed audiences as straights and gays alike flocked to enter its fictional world of "Round Tables Square Tables," where "Everyone Hates His Parents," where baseball games and chess matches are cultural determinants and where the "Miracle of Judaism" is not so miraculous. David Drake's *The Night Larry Kramer Kissed Me* (1992) and Paul Rudnik's *Jeffrey* (1993) arrived at the same time, drawing favorable reviews and large audiences who now seemed willing to tolerate everything from caustic verbal exchanges about AIDS to simulated acts of homosexual love.

There is every reason to believe that gay American theatre will continue to prosper throughout the 1990s. As far as theatre is concerned, it is once again the Gay Nineties. No playwright has shown this more clearly than Tony Kushner, who with his two-part epic *Angels in America* (*Part One: Millennium Approaches* and *Part Two: Perestroika*) presents "A Gay Fantasia on National Themes." Considered a cultural touchstone of the 1990s and earning Kushner a Pulitzer Prize and the Tony Award for Best Play in 1993 and 1994, *Angels* deals with the betrayal that infects society before the millennium: the betrayal of a wife by her gay husband; the betrayal, by his lover, of a gay man with AIDS; the betrayal of a nation by leaders and a populace who look the other way. Set in an America suffering from sexual, social, religious, and political tremors, *Angels* laments the inevitable loss (loss of a loved one, loss of ethical values, loss of cultural identity, loss of innocence) that results from the cataclysmic shock waves ripping premillennium America apart. The title of Kushner's second part of *Angels, Perestroika,* is a complex metaphor for human change: the revolutions of 1989, the fall of the Berlin Wall, the collapse of twelve years of Republican presidential policy, the breakup of the Soviet Union as a world superpower, the dissolution of old oligarchic ways, and the scientific advances into a dark future.

But at the heart of it all is a celebration of difference as an important part of change that will lead us into the twenty-first century. Phyllis Jane Rose quotes Audre Lorde in "Dear Heidi: An Open Letter to Dr. Holland": "Difference is that raw and powerful connection from which our personal power is forged."[6] As the plays of the 1990s demonstrate, the search for common ground can be painful when politics, race, and gender become battlefields. While there is no question that traditions are important, they are changing. What was once marginal is now major. As Jack Gelber announced in his interview in part two of this collection, the avant-garde of the 1960s has become the establishment of the 1990s. The American theatre celebrates changes, as these changes celebrate "the multiple selves as America," to end, as we began, with a quotation from C. W. E. Bigsby.

Notes

1. C. W. E. Bigsby, *Modern American Drama, 1945–1990* (Cambridge: Cambridge University Press, 1992), 341.

2. Alan Woods, "Consuming the Past: Commercial American Theatre in the Reagan Era," in *The American Stage: Social and Economic Issues from the Colonial Period to the Present,* ed. Ron Engle and Tice Miller (Cambridge: Cambridge University Press, 1992), 259.

3. "Briefly Noted," *American Theatre,* September 1994, 65.

4. Tina Howe, *Three Plays by Tina Howe: Museum, The Art of Dining, Painting Churches* (New York: Avon, 1984), vii.

5. K. A. Berney, ed., *Contemporary Dramatists,* 5th ed. (London: St. James Press, 1993), 325.

6. Phyllis Jane Rose, "Dear Heidi: An Open Letter to Dr. Holland," *American Theatre,* October 1989, 116.

KENNETH BERNARD

Joan Templeton

Kenneth Bernard (courtesy of Elena Rojas)

In *New American Dramatists, 1960–1980* (New York: Grove, 1982), Ruby Cohn characterized Kenneth Bernard this way: "A family man with an academic position, he has written the most outrageous plays of all" (134). The extreme superlative accurately characterizes reviewers' reactions, whether in praise or blame, to Bernard's exuberantly disgraceful and relentlessly disturbing dramas. Michael Feingold of the *Village Voice* described *La Justice; or, The Cock That Crew* as "a pure and perfectly terrifying creation, a sugar-coated fishhook" (29 October 1979) and in reviewing *Play with an Ending; or, Columbus Sets Out to Discover the New World* noted that "Bernard couldn't be adorable at gunpoint, and his lack of interest in pleasing commercial audiences is total" (1 May 1984). Glen Loney commented in *Educational Theater Journal* (vol. 20 [1968]) that *The Moke-Eater* makes "concentration camps seem tame," and Robert Skloot wrote in *The Darkness We Carry* (Madison: University of Wisconsin Press, 1988, 62), his book on holocaust drama, "Compared to the violence and graphic terror of this theatrical enactment of Nazi depravity and human suffering [*How We Danced While We*

Burned, 1973], the hell of Sartre's *No Exit* is benign and almost pleasant."

Bernard's dramatic career is inextricably linked to that of the turbulent director John Vaccaro, founder of the Play-house of the Ridiculous. During the season of 1967–68, Vaccaro expelled Charles Ludlam and most of the members of the Ridiculous Theatrical Company from his production of Ludlam's *The Conquest of the Universe.* Meanwhile, Bernard had seen the play, and although he could not understand many of the words (a continuing problem with Play-house performances), he was impressed by the company's extraordinary vitality. He mailed Vaccaro three plays, and when they met on a rainy November night, Vaccaro told Bernard that he wanted to produce *The Moke-Eater.* The meeting was as fortuitous for Vaccaro as for Bernard; the crisis in his company had made him think of retiring, and Bernard's play sparked him to start over. The autumn 1968 production of *The Moke-Eater,* performed upstairs in the Union Square restaurant Max's Kansas City, began, in Gerald Rabkin's phrase, "one of the most creative collaborations in experimental theater" (*Soho Weekly News,* 18 October 1979), and transformed the image of "Ridiculous Theatre" from one of campy titillation to serious, shocking confrontation. During the sixteen-year period from 1968 to 1984, Vaccaro directed eight Bernard plays, most of them at La Mama, including: *Night Club* (1970; *Night Club and Other Plays* [New York: Winter House, 1971]), which takes place in the metaphorical Bubi's Hideaway and is Bernard's most widely produced play; the short but infamous *Monkeys of the Organ Grinder* (1970; *Pyramid* 3 [1969]: 45–53), some of whose spectators fled (one presumes in horror); *The Magic Show of Dr. Ma-Gico* (1973; *Theater of the Ridiculous,* ed. Bonnie Marranca and Gautam Dasgupta [New York: Performing Arts Journal Press, 1979]), a play that pits the (sometimes demonic) power of art against the realm of political and worldly power; *La Justice; or, The Cock That Crew* (1979; *How We Danced While We Burned, La Justice* [Santa Monica, Calif.: Asylum Arts, 1990]), which treats the relation among justice, expediency, and power, an ambitious reflection that is often called Bernard's best play; and *La Fin du Cirque* (1984; *Grand Street* 2, no. 2 [1983]), a metaphorical meditation on gravity (earthboundedness) and weightlessness (the desire to soar).

Because of the Bernard-Vaccaro collaboration, Bernard has been classified, along with Charles Ludlam and Ronald Tavel, as a playwright of the Ridiculous. But although Bernard's plays exhibit some characteristics of Ludlam's travesties (flamboyance and camp humor) and one characteristic of Tavel's linguistic experiments (preoccupation with language), what are ends for Ludlam and Tavel are means for Bernard. Ludlam wishes to *épater le bourgeois;* Tavel, to invent elaborate word games. However, Bernard's subject, like that of his absurdist predecessors, is the human condition itself, and both the language and the spectacle of his violent plays function to dramatize a ferocious yet poetic vision of human life. Bernard's work, in fact, has fewer affinities with the "Theatre of the Ridiculous" than with Artaud's "Theatre of Cruelty," although Bernard wrote his first plays before reading Artaud.

One of Bernard's favorite plot devices is a theatrical framing action in which a master of ceremonies—Bubi in *Night Club,* the title character in *The Magic Show of Dr. Ma-Gico,* the Drag Queen in *The Sixty-Minute Queer Show,* the Judge in *La Justice,* the Commandant in *How We Danced While We Burned,* Theseus/Director of *We Should . . . (A Lie)*—directs a "show" composed of grotesque performances. The violent interaction both between the performers and the master and among the performers themselves dramatizes a power game of cruelty and desire whose pathos arises from the powerlessness of both players and director, locked into a ritualized persecution of terrible intensity. The members of the audience are voyeur-participants in the victimization that provides them with "entertainment." The ritualized mise-en-scène, whether it is the night club, the circus, the court room, or the rehearsal set, serves as an anchor for Bernard's destabilizing language and character and takes the place of a conventional "plot," providing at the same time a structure for ironic commentary. Bernard's language is both literary and antiliterary, a mixture of formal eloquence, schtick, and double entendres that at times achieves lyrical intensity. Bernard's plays are both theatrical spectacles and referential texts rife with allusion and wordplay, making him the heir both to Genet and to Beckett.

Bernard's plays have been performed in Europe, Canada, and Australia, as well as throughout the United States. *The Magic Show of Dr. Ma-Gico* and *The Sixty-Minute Queer Show* were put on at the Holland Festival, the former play in 1973, where it was filmed for Dutch television, and the latter in 1977. *Night Club* was performed in 1980 in Calgary, Canada, where it was termed by the *Calgary Albertan* as a "necessary step for theatre in Canada" (10 January 1980) and again in Toronto in 1986.

Three volumes of Bernard's plays have been published, and several plays have been anthologized. Bernard also writes poetry and fiction. The first third of his long poem *The Baboon in the Night Club* (Santa Monica, Calif.: Asylum Arts, 1994) won an Arvon Poetry Prize in En-

gland and was lauded by Ted Hughes and Seamus Heaney. In Richard
Kostelanetz's *Dictionary of the Avant-Gardes* (Pennington, N.J.: a capelle
books, 1993), where he is described as the "ultimate fringe writer,"
Bernard characterizes his fictions as "first-person narratives that contain inward-spiraling ironies," a description echoed by reviewers of
The Maldive Chronicles (New York: Performing Arts Journal Press,
1987) and *From the District File* (Boulder: Fiction Collective Two, 1992).
Bernard has received Guggenheim, Rockefeller, and National Endowment for the Arts grants and fellowships, among others.

The following interview took place on two successive days, 30–31
January 1992 in Manhattan, on the set of the Living Theater's premiere
production of *We Should . . . (A Lie),* the third play in Bernard's trilogy
Curse of Fool (Santa Maria, Calif.: Asylum Arts, 1992). Following his
custom, Bernard had been present at almost every rehearsal, quietly
watching and taking notes and conferring discreetly with the director
and cast.

Templeton: Why do you always make it such a point to be present during
rehearsals of your plays? Is it to make sure the director gets it right?
Bernard: I try to be a kind of resident force of conscience regarding the
text. I explain points of difficulty when they come up. The tendency
of actors and directors when they cannot "act" something or see the
"logic" of it is to discard it, change it, or to cut. My presence has rescued
text on many an occasion. In the end there are always mistakes in performance, even agreed-upon cuts or changes—rare, actually. But by
being there constantly, observing the tricky protocol of author, director, actor—a power-ego dynamic—I reach opening night having
done the best I could by the play.
Templeton: Your description of the dynamics of the rehearsal set sounds
rather like the power struggles you dramatize in your plays.
Bernard: I find the rehearsal situation a miniature world, much as I think
Melville saw a whaling ship. As such it is endlessly fascinating to me.
Of course personal history and interactions, etc., also manifest themselves. The three components—author, director, actor—come together
as strangers and work to create a difficult and strange community of
being onstage. It's hard work, fraught with human finitude. It's moving,
rewarding, and sad. We do, after all, go our separate ways, resume our
natural tracks, in the end.
Templeton: Your insistence on participating in the production of your
plays in order to safeguard the text suggests that you are suspicious of
the *auteur/directeur* theory. To paraphrase Stanley Fish, do you believe
that there really *is* a text in this theatre?

Bernard: In my own experience the cult of the director and the cult of the group have provoked a lot of thought, since they usually put me, as the supposed "producer" of a text, in an anomalous position. But if the director is substituted for the writer, all the criticisms directed at the autonomous writer can then be directed at the autonomous director. Traditionally the director nominally served the writer's text. In recent times the director has seen the text as raw material out of which he can create the "real text" onstage. There is nothing intrinsically wrong with this as long as both author and director agree to it. But often there is no agreement.

Templeton: I take it then that you do believe that there *is* a text in this theatre?

Bernard: Yes, although I confess that I often feel like one of Hawthorne's soul-probing villains who should probably apologize, if not disappear, for daring to promulgate a text in my own name.

Templeton: And what a text! I would like you to comment on what reviewers and critics have always emphasized in discussing your work: its cruelty, violence, sadism, the "worst side" of human nature. Rabkin titles his introduction to the volume *How We Danced While We Burned* and *La Justice* "The Unspeakable Theater of Kenneth Bernard."

Bernard: I have to say that I find all this a bit puzzling. By now we are well accustomed to daily doses of outrage to our sensibilities on television and in film, in magazines and books, in music, and most of all in real life—

Templeton: I want to break in here, Kenneth, to quote Michael Feingold: "Nothing is more revolting than a Kenneth Bernard play—except, of course, real life."

Bernard: Yes, I liked that. Anyway, the only thing I can conclude about this insistence on the outrageousness of my work is that it must shock and/or offend people because it has no mitigating parameters. An example of what I mean is that the violence and brutality, the manifold assaults on our lives, on our societies, on our planet, often come to us in an economic context: they are presented fundamentally as an "entertainment" to sell something. We are thus desensitized to their actuality. The advertising break for Mobil Oil in a TV documentary on the holocaust, for example, frames the event in good old America, where the sensitive corporation uses the holocaust to sell its image. How bad can anything be? I don't think I offer such mediation. My work, in that sense, is unredeeming. It is "nasty." I do not feel any inclination to make life appear easier than it is or to embellish blindness. I feel that I have a responsibility to say "No!" in thunder to false pieties, to delusions, to systematic and technological mutilations of the human spirit.

Templeton: What makes your plays problematic, I think, is that they *don't* seem to be saying "no"—or "yes," for that matter—to anything. Their dramatizations of torture and violence seem to be presented simply as "the way it is."

Bernard: That's true. I'm not particularly interested in answers. Answers are too often delusions, too often precede, and therefore frame, the questions. Of course we live within a scientific-rationalist tradition that places high value on answers and has devised elaborate methodologies to ascertain them. But our tendency is to screen out what does not lend itself to a neat formulation. All the enabling configurations of society, of course, do the same. The laundry, after all, must get done. But it is what is left out, what is tragically *di*sabling, that I am interested in.

Templeton: I find your holocaust play *How We Danced While We Burned* very moving in this respect. I know that people are afraid to produce it, and I wonder why it is that a play like *The Deputy* or films like Ophuls's *The Sorrow and the Pity* and Lanzmann's *Shoah* are acceptable—politically correct, as we now say—and *How We Danced While We Burned* is not. Is it acceptable to write "realistic" plays or make documentaries about the holocaust but unacceptable to dramatize its gratuitous executions within a metaphor of failed performances?

Bernard: I would say first that film documentaries are rather like photographs, and as Susan Sontag has suggested, a photograph immediately becomes history, that is, forgettable. It's something that has happened, that is finished, archival. We can look it up if we have to. A stage presentation, however, is immediate, uncomfortable—

Templeton: Especially a concentration camp with a prisoner commandant as master of ceremonies.

Bernard: Yes, and the camp exists again every night. With a full load of contingency. No expectation or anxiety can be alleviated or pacified in advance.

Templeton: So you would agree that *How We Danced While We Burned* is too "real" even for the Off-est Broadway.

Bernard: Evidently. Although it *was* put on at Antioch College, for the first and only time, in 1973.

Templeton: Did you go?

Bernard: Yes. I took a fourteen-hour bus ride. Beverly Grant, an old Andy Warhol "star" and a later associate of Vaccaro, directed. The audience and local papers were confused, caught between the abyss depicted and the students' rough-edged exuberance. When we tried to reproduce it the following summer Off-Off-Broadway, with much the same cast, I decided midway that it was turning out sacrilegious. I couldn't allow it to continue and canceled it.

Templeton: You are usually classified, as you know, as an author of the Ridiculous. This is the way you are referred to in the *Columbia Literary History of the United States,* for example. I find this unfortunate, in a sense, because the Ridiculous is often conceived of as simply "camp" theatre. Could you comment on the postabsurdist Ridiculous context in which most of your work has been performed?

Bernard: First of all the Ridiculous movement in theatre split very early. Charles Ludlam's Ridiculous was essentially a one-man show that became a titillation of the bourgeois through varieties of transvestism. Beneath that there were sometimes telling commentaries on sex, society, literature, and so on, but they were lost, except to a few commentators like Stefan Brecht. The public essentially conceived of Ludlam's Ridiculous as a place of easy laughs and campy thrills. John Vaccaro's Play-house of the Ridiculous was anything but that. John is a quirky, mad impressario-performer-director whom I never worked with without wanting at one point or another to throw him out the window. He worked with many writers and offered a variety of productions, some of them not very different from Ludlam's drag shows. But Vaccaro is really an intellectual who, in his quieter moments, likes to talk about Melville and who has very dark ideas about America. His brand of sexual ambivalence and anarchy is anything but safe or amusing. He genuinely offends. His gender ambivalence, for example, is disorienting rather than titillating; it blurs the focus. His stage is crowded and disequilibrious, and it destroys any possibility of conferring authority or authenticity. We began to work together because he found in my plays works that paralleled his ideas. I would like to say that in all the time I worked with him he never once gave a line reading that I felt was untrue. In all our work together he was scrupulous with the text without compromising his directorial integrity, except on one production.

Templeton: The near breakup over *The Sixty-Minute Queer Show?*

Bernard: Yes. He found it too harsh. Odd, for him. Stefan Brecht treats this very well in his book *Queer Theater,* by the way. In any case, about the Ridiculous and postabsurdist drama, I ended up in the Ridiculous camp because there was nowhere else for me to go. I don't think that in America the Ridiculous is seen as an extension of continental absurdist drama, by the way. Nor, although it undoubtedly is indebted to it, should it be. Absurdist theatre is best seen in the context of modernism, as part of the great assault on the values of bourgeois culture, but it retained a certain high purpose and elevated intellectual content despite its heritage of dadaism and surrealism.

Templeton: Well, that depends. I'm not sure about the "high purpose" of much of Ionesco's work, for example, and I would say that Genet's theatre is arguably nihilist.

Bernard: All right, but I would still say that the Ridiculous, with its embrace of low culture, its mixture of styles, its devotion to the amateur, the banal, the disgusting or offensive, its irreverence of all tradition—history, society—its total disregard of the techniques and conventions of acting and of theater, all this makes it postmodern before the term came into being. Unfortunately critics and public alike tended to see in it only its strong homosexual component, its circus brashness, its vulgarity, and thus dismissed it as "queer."

Templeton: This makes me think of that line in *The Sixty-Minute Queer Show:* "Queer is queerer than you think." I also like "Throw a queer a fish today." I think sometimes that people are so shocked by the violence in your plays that they don't hear the humor. And speaking of violence, the person most often mentioned as an influence on your work is Artaud. I've noticed that it is sometimes taken for granted that you are deliberately writing a theatre of cruelty. Could you comment on this?

Bernard: Derrida has a wonderful essay on Artaud in which he refers to the scream in humanity that articulation has frozen over, the repressed gestures in all speech, the "speech" anterior to words. All this interests me very much. My current production, *We Should . . . (A Lie),* whose situation is a group of actors rehearsing Racine's *Phèdre,* is very much about Phaedra's reluctance to give voice to the enormous scream growing within her. Articulation will not only bring down the curtain, but it will also mediate the scream. Artaud's undeviating promulgation of that excluded, mostly silent world that seethes beneath society's paradigmatic articulations is what he means by theatre of cruelty. I am drawn to that, and to his strategies, for example, of spectacle, ritual, and metaphor. I bought *The Theater and Its Double* in 1968, *after* I wrote *The Moke-Eater.* Artaud writes about giving words the power of dreams, a version of what he calls somewhere else, I think, the metaphysics of speech. When I have called my plays a "theatre of metaphor," I mean the same kind of thing.

Templeton: American productions of your plays have been well reviewed by European critics, and I suspect that this is because your work follows the nonrepresentational mode that has marked post–World War II European drama. Could you comment on this?

Bernard: I have always felt that Holland and Germany were good venues for my work. Not only is theatre more acceptable there as a literary as well as a dramatic form, but there is a greater interest in and support of experimental/avant-garde theatre. Artists like Robert Wilson and Richard Foreman were initially taken much more seriously in Europe than in the United States.

Templeton: Are you consciously aware of being influenced by any writer?

Bernard: No. At various times various writers have been important to me, of course. Right now I'm a great admirer of Isaiah Berlin. Some years ago Erich Heller's *The Disinherited Mind* struck me with some force. Isaac Babel and Robert Walser appeal to me very much. Beckett and Kafka, of course. I spend a lot of time reading things I don't understand and am a great believer in reading a book twice or three times. I feel enormously ignorant but don't find the condition uncomfortable. Assurance appalls me. I obviously spend a lot of my time quoting in one way or another Lothario's line from Rowe's *The Fair Penitent:* "It is the curse of fools to be secure." Although I practice coherence in much of my life—to pay the rent—I prefer to keep my mind oceanic and let books, people, events swim mistily where they will.

Templeton: This reminds me of Merleau-Ponty's *mot* about Cézanne's having led a bourgeois life and created schizoid art. In any case do you think there is any hope that serious plays, like or unlike yours, will ever again be put on, on Broadway?

Bernard: I'm very doubtful. Someone told me recently that Gore Vidal said he moved to Italy because America is a joke. I think Broadway's a joke. It has very little to do with art and everything to do with entertainment. It sells a product, and the bonus is confirmation of one's cultural status. All our cultural institutions are going the same way. It is all an elaborate swindle, something like Conrad's dancing monkeys over the abyss. Only catastrophe can change us, if we survive it.

Templeton: Do you see no hope, then, for American theatre or, for that matter, the world?

Bernard: That's difficult to answer. Temperamentally I'm inclined to pessimism. The postmodern breakdown of categories, the crises of legitimation and evaluation have clearly presented an opening to yesterday's marginalities, not only third world, but women, gays, the handicapped—the list continues to expand. And with this challenge to cultural pieties goes a parallel challenge of vast political and economic consequence. This aspect of postmodernism is sometimes subsumed under the aegis of multiculturalism and is either condemned as relativism and anarchy (that is, anything goes) or praised as a real hope for justice and equity. I certainly cannot say where it is all going to end. However, I have a lot of respect for Marcuse's observation about the power of consumer capitalism to co-opt even the most radical threats to its hegemony, when it cannot destroy them outright. Consumer capitalism seems to me to have a seamless capacity to convert radicalism into a processed waste product, while the world continues to collapse in on itself. I think the danger is in the desire *not* to remain the "other," the desire to be *inside*. My notion of salvation is to remain outside.

Templeton: As a woman I'm tired of being the other. Perhaps it is because you, as a white male, are normative, like it or not, that you can have the luxury of seeing a salvation in remaining the other. For me being the other means being the disenfranchised.

Bernard: When one considers the "muck"—Beckett's word—of being *inside,* perhaps one can see power *outside.* I don't mean to imply that "community" action in a just cause should not be undertaken, only that Edenic immersion in any utopian closure is a misperception of reality. Radicalism can best resist being co-opted and retaining its transforming potential by retaining its alien stance. It must question daily the format of its seeming success within any system. One can be co-opted in many ways. True believers are more often dangerous than not. When everyone is happily within *the* system, we will be hearing our death rattles.

Templeton: Richard Kostelanetz's characterization of you in *A Dictionary of the Avant-Gardes* as the "ultimate fringe writer" seems to confirm your own preference for being outside.

Bernard: Perhaps *edge* is better. I once wrote a poem entitled "The Pagurian," referring to the family of crustaceans that includes hermit crabs, for example, creatures that are tidal edge-dwellers, between land and sea. I write from that vantage point. I am extremely wary of attachment to any group that represents the power (and injustice) of history, tradition, and money, or any group, however "noble" its proclaimed goals, at the end of whose rhetoric I can see a gun pointed at me. Either way, as I say in a forthcoming symposium in *Performing Arts Journal,* there *is* a body count. Although it might be argued that one must make the leap of faith, of commitment, I prefer not to but rather to stay on the edge. This is perhaps irresponsible or cowardly. But I don't think so. There's a penalty for pagurians. And as I say, I don't like body counts, either way.

Templeton: That's all rather grim. Where does that leave us?

Bernard: I don't know. Obviously some things will never be the same again. There are major changes in process. I think, in the end, our human frailties will save us. Delusions of necessary order, justice, or grandeur, the constraints of political teleologies will finally take on their normal bloated look. Struggle will not vanish.

Templeton: And your plays, your fiction and poetry?

Bernard: Also, I think, on the edge. Maybe they will be washed away. Without conformity to marketplace or ideology they don't have much space. Vaccaro wants very much to do at least two new plays, but there are few venues and no money. Worse, there are few actors. The ones who might have sufficed—also edge-dwellers—are dead or living the good life. But perhaps there will be a new theatre at the edge.

Templeton: Let's hope so. Meanwhile, let me congratulate you on the January 29th rave review in the *Times,* which I've brought with me. Richard Bruckner ["Drama Review," *New York Times,* 29 January 1992] praised your wit, your original and intricate handling of the Phaedra myth, and your "unerring instinct for the dramatic possibilities in philosophical questions that have troubled people for thousands of years." Would you mind commenting on this?

Bernard: I could say a lot, but I'm sure there's no room. What I will say is that the play deals simultaneously with several issues: the insufficiency of language, the impossibility of knowing character (being), the conflict between living and observing life, that is, immersion and ignorance versus control and delusion, the dichotomy between life and theatre—

Templeton: As in *Night Club, La Justice, La Fin du Cirque,* and *How We Danced While We Burned?*

Bernard: Yes, and, here, the contrast between a theatre of rhetoric and metaphor and a theatre of rational articulation and representation. The imagery is dominated by the wheelchairs the main characters rest in, the legend of the labyrinth and the minotaur and the minotaur's lair, and the darkness of chaos from which the characters proceed and to which they return throughout, to a pounding, maddening music, representing, I would say, the Artaudian forces beneath the consciousness of civilized life, which probe and poke humanity, something like what Melville's Ahab intuited behind the pasteboard mask of reality. Theseus is spectacularly a man of the world as rationally constituted, and Phaedra is equally spectacularly a creature of the void, of silence and darkness. And as the actors rehearse and analyze Racine's version of the myth, they gradually create their own play, from which they cannot escape, except for the minor characters, who are free to enact a different kind of drama in a different kind of world.

Templeton: Kenneth, thanks for your time. I think we're out of space.

Bernard: You put it well.

BETH HENLEY

Mary Dellasega

Beth Henley (courtesy of Beth Henley; Rocky Schenck, photographer)

Beth Henley is a native of Jackson, Mississippi; born on 8 May 1952, she is the daughter of a lawyer and an actress and is the second oldest of four sisters. She attended Southern Methodist University, where she graduated with a bachelor of fine art's degree in theatre in 1974; for one year she worked toward a master's degree in acting at the University of Illinois. When she moved to Los Angeles, she intended to be an actress, not a playwright.

Henley's previous efforts had been one-act plays written as class assignments. One of these, *Am I Blue,* was produced at SMU, but the playwright was too shy to allow her name to be used on the program. In Los Angeles, frustrated with the lack of acting opportunities, she began writing her first full-length play, *Crimes of the Heart.* The play was written for one indoor set and six characters to make it more attractive to little theatres. When a friend in Louisville submitted the play to the Actors Theatre's third annual Festival of New American Plays, it was an immediate success. *Crimes* was produced at three other regional theatres before the Manhattan Theatre Club staged it in New York. Before moving to Broadway the play had won both the New York Drama Critics Circle Award and the 1981 Pulitzer Prize, making Henley the first woman to receive the award in twenty-three years. *Crimes* also won the Guggenheim award and a Tony nomination.

Crimes demonstrated a sense of comedy also seen in her subsequent plays: it is based not on one-liners, but on empathetic understanding of her characters' desperation. Frank Rich has observed that she "gets her laughs not because she tells sick jokes, but because she refuses to tell jokes at all. Her characters always stick to the unvarnished truth, at any price, never holding back a single gory detail. And the truth—when captured like lightning in a bottle—is far funnier than any invented wisecracks" (*New York Times,* 5 November 1981). Henley herself has noted in an interview, "I've always been attracted to split images . . . the grotesque combined with the innocent, a child walking with a cane; a kitten with a swollen head; a hunchback drinking a cup of fruit punch. Somehow these images are a metaphor for any view of life; they're colorful. . . . Southerners always bring out the grisly details in any event" (*Washington Post,* 12 December 1986).

Henley has often been compared with other southern writers, such as Flannery O'Connor and Eudora Welty, largely because of her penchant for writing about eccentric, colorful characters in southern settings. Most of her plays have been set in the South: *Crimes of the Heart* (1979), the story of the MaGrath sisters, takes place in Hazelhurst, Mississippi; *The Wake of Jamey Foster* (1982) centers on a family reunion in Canton, Mississippi, for the purpose of burying the title character, who has been kicked in the head by a cow; Carnelle Scott, who dreams of changing her image by winning *The Miss Firecracker Contest* (1984), lives in Brookhaven, Mississippi; the characters who dream of striking it rich with a dance hall called *The Lucky Spot* reside in Pigeon, Louisiana; and *The Debutante Ball,* which Henley calls, in the preface to a 1991 printed edition, "one of my stranger plays," in which the characters are "fighting to pluck and spray and shave away their true natures—adorning themselves with lies," is set in Hattiesburg, Mississippi.

Beth Henley has adapted two of her plays into screenplays. The film *Crimes of the Heart,* starring Jessica Lange, Diane Keaton, and Sissy Spacek, received an Academy Award nomination for best screenplay in 1986. Holly Hunter reprised her role as Carnelle Scott in the film version of *Miss Firecracker,* one of several projects on which she and Beth Henley have collaborated (Hunter has appeared in *The Debutante Ball, The Wake of Jamey Foster,* and *Control Freaks*). Henley also cowrote the screenplay for *True Stories* with musician David Byrne and actor-director Stephen Toblowsky, with whom Henley lived for several years (Toblowsky, who was in the cast of *Wake,* directed *The Debutante Ball, The Miss Firecracker Contest,* and *The Lucky Spot*).

In spite of their southernness Henley's plays have also been well received abroad, particularly in Britain, which has seen multiple productions of *Crimes of the Heart* and *The Miss Firecracker Contest,* as well as *The Lucky Spot* and *The Debutante Ball.* However, her latest plays move away from her familiar southern territory: *Abundance* (1989) is set in the late 1860s in Wyoming territory; *Control Freaks,* which opened in August of 1993 as her directorial debut, is set in Los Angeles, Henley's adopted home.

This interview took place 15 December 1993, when Henley was working on her new play, *Revelers.*

Dellasega: I know your mother, Lydy Caldwell, is an actress. Did she inspire you or influence you to work in the theatre? I believe you both acted at the New Stage Theatre in Jackson.

Henley: Yes. We worked at Jackson Little Theatre, and then later they had the New Stage Theatre, and she worked at both. So I really grew up around the theatre, and it absolutely did inspire me. My mother was often on the play selection committee and she had Samuel French versions of plays around, so I got into the habit of picking them up. I really enjoyed reading dialogue. I also loved going to see her act in plays and going backstage.

Dellasega: Is there anything in particular you remember that she did?

Henley: The Glass Menagerie. She played Laura, and she was so beautiful with all those little glass animals. She used to limp around when she went to the grocery store, trying to pick up cans that Laura would pick up. I coached her on her lines a lot. I know practically all the lines to *A Streetcar Named Desire* because she played Blanche.

Dellasega: And your mother still acts, I believe.

Henley: Yes, she was just in a play this last year, *Lend Me a Tenor.*

Dellasega: You originally moved from Mississippi to Los Angeles for an acting career. What changed your goal to playwriting and screenwriting?

Henley: I think, the fact that I could. [*Laughs*] You just have a pencil and paper and you can write, but you have to get an agent and get cast in something to act. I loved acting in college because I was always doing wonderful plays. But in the real world there are so few opportunities to do great pieces, and I found that very discouraging. Plus kind of horrifying, when I had to have pictures made of myself and send them out to strangers. I hated that.

Dellasega: I know people have told you that *Crimes of the Heart* reminded them of their relationships with their sisters. Did you see yourself or your sisters in the characters?

Henley: I think the relationships and the way sisters interact are definitely based on my family: people remembering little things for years on end, you know, and bringing them up at just the right moment to drive you crazy. [*Laughs*] I didn't think about it at the time, but I do also think they are all kind of different split visions of myself, the characters—different things I myself was grappling with.

Dellasega: I've heard that *Crimes* was submitted to the Actors Theatre without your knowing about it.

Henley: Well, that's sort of the glamorized version. My friend Fred Bailey, who had won the contest the year before, sent the script in and told me about it, so I knew it had gone there. When Jon Jory called me, he thought I didn't know about it, but that's just because I'm so shy. I was so nervous when I talked to him, I could hardly speak.

Dellasega: How did it feel to have the play performed in Louisville by professional actors?

Henley: It was so frightening. I had had a play done in college, *Am I Blue,* in 1973, but this was the first time people were paying to see it. It was January and it was freezing and it was snowing. I remember standing in the parking lot, and these people in fur coats were getting out of their cars. And I thought, "Oh, my God, they paid money, they hired babysitters, and they came out to see this," and I started crying. I was terrified that I was going to be arrested for fraud. [*Laughs*] It was really scary.

Dellasega: And you were pleased with the production?

Henley: Yes. Actually, it had two of the greatest actresses that have ever been around, Susan Kingsley and Kathy Bates, so I was very lucky.

Dellasega: I wanted to ask what inspired some of the changes made in translating *Crimes* and *Miss Firecracker* to the screen, for instance, the very interesting change in the character of Popeye, the seamstress who makes Carnelle's dress in *Miss Firecracker.*

Henley: You mean to make her black? Well, that was actually Tommy Schlamme's, the director's, idea, because we were looking for locations, and he said, "Gosh, there's such a discrepancy between where the black populations live in these towns; it literally is the other side of the tracks." And also what inspired me was his mention of Alfre Woodard, who is one of my favorite actresses. I wasn't as interested in changing it to a black actress as changing it to Alfre Woodard; I like her work so much. And also to bring in that world, which is so present—the black world, which is still fairly segregated from the white world—and to incorporate that world. However, this is something we did more in the original screenplay we talked about than in the eventual screenplay we did. There was a blues scene that we never got around to, for instance, because the budget couldn't incorporate it.

Dellasega: I was thinking, too, about the confrontation between the two women toward the end of the film, when Carnelle discovers Elain *did* bring the red dress but didn't give it to her to wear in the contest.

Henley: Yes, that's new. Actually that was inspired very much by Tommy, who thought they should have a confrontation, which they actually don't have in the play. But it was a tangible thing that could be discovered, that could symbolize their whole relationship, which was, I thought, very smart of him.

Dellasega: It was a very effective scene. And after that we see Carnelle alone, watching the fireworks, rather than with Popeye and Delmount.

Henley: Yes. That play really opened up. I think it was required. The play all takes place backstage, and it's very Greek, with people running on- and offstage saying what tragedies just happened, and that works in the theatre. But in a movie you want to see the contest. I got very excited at the idea of actually seeing all the scenes that had been in my mind, to actually get to see them. It just made more sense, sort of spiritually, for Carnelle to be wholly alone—wholly in the spiritual sense of the word—and for the lovers to be together, and for Elain to be in her own trap. So I liked how we were able to do that.

Dellasega: Many critics have commented on the eccentricity of your characters and the frequency of grotesque images and bizarre events. What is the connection between the southern locales and the vivid characters and situations? Do you yourself see the characters as strange?

Henley: I looked up that word—let's see, I have it here: [*drawing the word out*] "strange!" What does it mean? "Unusual or queer" or "new." Only in the sense that all human beings appear unusual to me. No stranger than anyone I know, certainly no stranger than people you see on the news. Or how about those police shows, now that they have those "reality" shows? Basically when I write I try to discover what I can strongly relate to about the characters. To write them I find what's the same about me that's the same about them. Things that I'm afraid of or things that I need or I can see people need or I've seen people dream of. I don't think I take them out of any sort of life I've observed or experienced.

Dellasega: Do you still go back to the South for inspiration?

Henley: It's always inspiring to go home, simply because people are such good storytellers. I don't know if it's my family particularly, but they always inspire me because they've always got so much life going on around them. I live a fairly secluded life, you know, being a writer, and they seem to be so much more out in the world and know what's going on. It's pretty exciting.

Dellasega: Is *The Debutante Ball* the first time you portrayed a lesbian relationship onstage?

Henley: Yes. I think one of the things that the play is really about is love and self-love and also seeing through facades. I wanted it to express that these women really connect on some essential level that doesn't have to do with the fact that one's from the country and one's from the city. It's just a need they both have, a desperate need to be loved and to be seen, and this need and acceptance of each other overcome other elements, such as that they're both women, or that one speaks French and one doesn't, or that one has probably never had a lover at all and the other one has had many. I wanted to illustrate something that many people would say wouldn't be right—and then turn it around because love is right.

Dellasega: I have a very beautiful edition of *The Debutante Ball* that was illustrated by Lynn Green Root. The two of you seem to share a wonderful tragicomic vision. How did this collaboration come about, and are you going to do it again?

Henley: I would very much love to work with Lynn again. I think this idea was from JoAnne Prichard, the woman who is an editor of the University Press of Mississippi. I've known Lynn since we were children. Actually I was ahead of her in school, but I knew *of* her. And I just loved her sketches when she sent them to me in her portfolio and got very excited. We had hoped to do a version of *Abundance*. We applied for a grant, but we didn't get it. So we would love to work together again, but it just hasn't worked out yet.

Dellasega: I would love to see that. That brings me to *Abundance*. Most of your plays have been set in the South and in fairly contemporary times. With *Abundance* you moved to the Wyoming territory and the mid-nineteenth century.

Henley: I think I have a sense that the first plays that I wrote, *Crimes of the Heart, The Miss Firecracker Contest, The Wake, The Debutante Ball,* were all set in Mississippi and vaguely in the past, more like in my childhood than in the eighties when I was writing. And then I went to *The Lucky Spot,* which took place in the thirties, and then I just kept going farther back. *The Lucky Spot* was set in Louisiana, and then I went farther west, to the Wyoming territory. But one thing that inspired *Abundance* was this book, *Wisconsin Death Trip.* I saw this book, and I was just stunned because of the harsh reality of the West it showed, which was not portrayed in the cowboy movies or the westerns of the time. I was fascinated with the specifics of everyday life and how brutal they were. They triggered my imagination, who these people actually were and their madness. People were eating the heads off matchsticks, and then they would print it up in the paper so matter of factly. And something about that book made me get interested also. After living in California for so many years, I like the idea of having the West symbolize hope and new things and danger—you know, you can move West and change things.

Dellasega: Often the women in your plays find support from other women more than they do from men. Does *Abundance* show a darker side of female relationships? The mail-order brides, Bess and Macon, swear eternal friendship and then seem to betray each other.

Henley: Yes, they do. Of course I don't see women being that great to each other throughout my plays. Elain's not that great to Carnelle. And Chick is just a horror. But I think I was dealing with what happens with people's dreams in *Abundance*—how people come out to California so full of hope to be an actress or to be in movies and slowly they find themselves working at Chicken Bob's, or they want to be great novelists and they're trying to write bad TV scripts. How do your dreams get chipped away? And these two women—one has a dream to find true love and the other has a dream to find her adventurous spirit and daring. And they each betray their own dreams, and that's betraying themselves, really. And I'm fascinated by the insidiousness of how this happens in life, how this is a process in which you're hardly to blame because it's so invisible how it seduces you. Suddenly Macon really wants that copper kettle instead of just taking off. So I think it was more an exploration of that, and at the end it wasn't an easy fix. But I think by looking at the darker aspects truthfully, there is something much deeper about the shaft of hope that *is* there at the end.

Dellasega: Bess wins a certain amount of autonomy by selling the story of her abduction, and yet to do so she gives her approval to the idea of the extermination of the Indians.

Henley: Yes. That to me shows how far she has gone away from her dream of true love because I feel that she did love Ottowa and her children. But she feels *he* betrayed *her,* and so that's her revenge. She agrees to that, and it's really kind of blood-curdling. It's amazing what people will do when they've been hurt, how they will strike out viciously. And it costs them so much, eventually, as far as their hearts go.

Dellasega: Would you discuss the recurrence and significance of women in your plays who are in or have been in relationships with men who are emotionally or physically abusive? Is it a comment on marriage that the married female characters so rarely seem happy? I was thinking of Catty in *Wake,* Jen in *The Debutante Ball,* Bess in *Abundance,* and Babe in *Crimes of the Heart.*

Henley: Yes. That's one side of the coin. You're leaving out the other side of the coin, though: Barnette and Babe and Pixrose and Leon have positive relationships, and Sue Jack and Hooker have a volatile romance, but at least they come together at the end. I think there are all aspects of human connections that I try to show in my plays. But I do very much believe that men and women have a hard row to hoe, connecting with each other, as do women and women and men and men. But I think because of the sexual thing, there's something a lot more volatile.

Dellasega: I know you've identified yourself as a feminist in previous interviews. How do you think your feminism is reflected in your plays and in your female characters?

Henley: I don't know. I cringe at that word, *feminist.* I always look that up. Okay, you're for female rights—well, of course! But I don't favor women over men characters when I write them. I try to understand each. I certainly like Delmount more than Chick, if you want to know the truth. I just try to look at people more than at just the sexes and hope that it'll be more a human point of view rather than having some sort of agenda to show that women are better, because I don't actually think they are. I think some women are better than some men. I know that sounds equivocating, but it's just true. And some men are better than some women. But to me it's not a question of better. My favorite characters are the ones that screw up most.

Dellasega: Which ones are you thinking of?

Henley: Well, I do love Meg, and she's insane, you know. And Sue Jack is a very destructive person. Boswell in *Signature* is awful, he's really conceited. I love and I understand Bess when she seeks revenge on Macon, but I understand Macon when she chains Bess up. I am so excited by people who are driven to extremes because of their passions.

Dellasega: That leads to my next question. You have often been compared with Chekhov, I think partly because you show your characters' flaws and foolishness without judging them, simply revealing them.

Henley: Well, I'm very complimented by that. I do try to track the characters' throughline, from their point of view, and try to understand, even if it makes no rational sense whatsoever, what is compelling them to behave the way they do.

Dellasega: Do you see your sense of comedy as being at all similar to Chekhov's or as an inspiration to you?

Henley: Definitely an inspiration. Very much. I always look at *Crimes of the Heart* as a real steal from *The Three Sisters. Crimes* is a much less brilliant and inspired version. But I always think they could be played in repertoire with Irina as Babe, Masha as Meg, Olga as Lenny, Natasha as Chick, and Vershinen as Doc.

Dellasega: That's a wonderful idea. I wanted to ask you about Holly Hunter, who's worked with you on six plays now?

Henley: Five, I think.

Dellasega: Do you see qualities in her that are particularly appropriate for your characters? Or by this time are you sometimes writing with her in mind, and how does this affect your writing?

Henley: Actually I wrote *Control Freaks* with her in mind, because I wrote it with four characters and on one set to do at our theatre here in L.A. But I just think anyone would want Holly in anything. She's extremely versatile and extremely brilliant.

Dellasega: Would you discuss your recent play, *Control Freaks?*

Henley: The plot of it? It's about this family that tries to open up Furniture World together, and they end up killing each other. It's got four characters: Carl and his sister, who's called Sister, and his new wife, Betty, and then Paul, who is kind of a guest whom they're buying the space from for Furniture World.

Dellasega: Would you call this play something of a departure for you?

Henley: Yes, because it takes place in L.A., and it's extremely expressionistic and theatrical rather than a more naturalistic story like *Crimes of the Heart.* I mean, the props are extreme—they have bubbles for breakfast in the frying pan, and there's flying onstage. It's a bit odd and more theatrical.

Dellasega: The language and the sexual situations are also something of a departure?

Henley: It's a play about incest, basically. That's one of the themes that is the darker side of the human spirit and passions. In that sense I think it's kind of the path I was on.

Dellasega: Do you think your vision has turned darker with your later plays?

Henley: I think they have a darker vision, but it's only because my vision is broader. I suppose I mean by that that I feel more able to embrace the endlessness of our mysteries and risk the darker waters without that paralyzing fear of drowning. Why I feel more able to do this, I don't know. Practice?

Dellasega: Will you be turning more to California or L.A. for inspiration now?

Henley: I don't know. I've got some notebooks, and I'm not sure where my next play is going to take place. The one I wrote after *Control Freaks* actually takes place around Lake Michigan and is entitled *Revelers. Revelers* is actually about going to sprinkle the ashes of a friend around Lake Michigan. And these characters all started working together at a theatre in Chicago when they were young and have taken divergent paths and are coming back for this ritual. It has a light touch to it. They do this performance for the deceased, and it's a bit *Midsummer Night's Dream*-y.

Dellasega: Your first time directing was for *Control Freaks*. What was the experience like?

Henley: Very challenging. And really sort of monumental for me because I had to take responsibility to communicate and to really go with a vision without leaning on a director and being able to leave when things got boring or heated. It was a big leap—but hard.

Dellasega: I read somewhere that you were working on a screenplay for *A Confederacy of Dunces.*

Henley: I've done a version of that, but as far as I know, that version is shelved.

Dellasega: What a shame.

Henley: Yes.

Dellasega: What was it like adapting another writer's work?

Henley: I just fell in love with John Kennedy Toole. It's a very sort of spiritual connection you have. I wanted so much to meet him.

TINA HOWE

Judith E. Barlow

Tina Howe (photo J. P. Laffont/Sygma)

Tina Howe began her playwriting career with *Closing Time* (1959), a one-acter performed at Sarah Lawrence College during her senior year. Her early plays include *The Nest* (1969), the first of Howe's works to revolve around her self-professed fascination with food, and *Birth and After Birth* (1973), a family comedy that clearly shows the playwright's links to the Absurdist writers she admires.

Museum (1976) premiered at the Los Angeles Actors' Theatre before moving to New York under the auspices of the New York Shakespeare Festival. A largely plotless play, *Museum* wittily satirizes the responses of visitors to a contemporary art exhibit. *The Art of Dining* (1979), co-produced by the Shakespeare Festival and the Kennedy Center, takes a trendy restaurant as its setting and alternates the action between the kitchen—where food is actually prepared onstage—and a dining room peopled by an eclectic assortment of patrons. Both of these works show the playwright's deftness with physical and verbal farce (witness the game of musical plates in *Dining*), as well as her deadly accuracy as a critic of pretentiousness (witness the mindless adoration of blank canvases in *Museum*). Howe centers the majority of her plays around artists, whom she considers the true heroes of our era. One of her most brilliant creations is *Dining*'s Elizabeth Barrow Colt, a writer with awesome imaginative powers and the social graces of a six-year-old.

Howe gained wide critical and popular acclaim in 1983 with *Painting Churches*, which premiered at New York's Second Stage, reopened the following year at the Lamb's Theatre, and was televised on *American Playhouse*. Returning to the favorite subject of the American playwright—the nuclear family—Howe uses her anarchic wit to explore the relationship between a young painter and her aging parents. *Churches* was the first of Howe's works to be directed by Carole Rothman, with whom she has established a continuing creative collaboration; the play garnered numerous citations, including an Outer Critics Circle Award. Three years later the Second Stage's production of *Coastal Disturbances* (1986) also enchanted critics. Once again choosing an unusual setting for her work, Howe places this comedy on a stage full of sand and proceeds to weave a web of love stories against a background of changing sea and sky. *Coastal Disturbances* added a Tony nomination to Howe's list of honors, which also comprises an Obie Award for Distinguished Playwriting, an Award in Literature from the American Academy of Arts and Letters, and a John Gassner Award, as well as grants from the Rockefeller Foundation and the National Endowment for the Arts.

Howe's two most recent works, *Approaching Zanzibar* (1989) and *One Shoe Off* (1993), were both produced by the Second Stage and met with mixed critical receptions. A "road play" that follows a family of four as they drive cross-country to Taos, New Mexico, *Zanzibar* has strong echoes of *Birth and After Birth*. Although clearly a comedy—including a hilarious parent-child role-reversal scene—*Zanzibar* probes even more deeply than the preceding plays into the frightening substratum that exists in all Howe's works, a substratum inhabited by our fears of death, abandonment, and loss of creative powers. These themes reemerge in *One Shoe Off*, in which two married couples and a charismatic movie director share dinner in a decaying farmhouse. As the wind whistles threateningly outside and vegetables and trees sprout *inside* the house, the characters strive to hang on to their integrity while healing the rifts in their relationships. In her preface to *Coastal Disturbances: Four Plays by Tina Howe* the playwright notes that her beloved Marx Brothers "didn't just celebrate lunacy, they turned it into a high art form." At their best Howe's own comedies achieve the very same goal.

The original interview took place on 9 January 1989, in Howe's apartment on the West Side of Manhattan. She was preparing to begin rehearsals the following month for *Approaching Zanzibar*. The followup questions about Howe's recent activities date from a visit she made to the State University of New York at Albany on 21 October 1993.

Barlow: You began writing plays your senior year in college. Why plays rather than novels or poems?

Howe: It was out of default or desperation. I was in a short story class—I always wanted to be a novelist and figured if I could learn how to write a short story then I could write a novel. So I was in this class of very gifted writers, and I was clearly the worst in the class, and my stories were pretty much of an embarrassment. And it came time for the spring, when you have to do a major project at the end of the year, which meant a story for me that would be worse than all the others. My work was just so self-conscious and purple and hopeless that out of frustration I began writing this little one-act play. And I didn't even know it was a play, and I didn't really even know what I was writing about. But I just started writing voices, a typical Sarah Lawrence work, being about the end of the world and kings and queens and pigeons and—oh God!—you don't even want to know about it. But there was something about it that was charming and elusive to me, probably because I didn't have to describe everything, probably because it was so disembodied, so I was able to write this little thing. It was about twenty pages; it was called *Closing Time,* and I showed it to my buddy Jane Alexander. And she loved it and said "Tina, we've got to put this on." It was this great hit. And everyone was yelling "Author! Author!" And I found myself rushing up to the stage and blowing kisses because I thought that was what you were supposed to do. But I think it was that I'd finally found a form where I could practice my imagination but not be bogged down by all those damn words. And then hearing that response, when for so many years there had just been this embarrassed silence when one of my stories was read in class, now all of a sudden there were all these rhapsodic faces.

Barlow: How do you get your inspiration for your plays?

Howe: Actually, each play inspires the next. I think any person, any writer or nonwriter, goes around with a certain number of stories and old complaints that you want to air and old fantasies you want to air. But actually, in terms of writing a play, I find that each play in some way is a response to the one that went before. It may not be obvious to the audience or to the scholar where a particular work came from, but it's very clear to me what has to be redressed in each case. If it wouldn't bore you to death, I could tell you exactly how each play that I wrote was an attempt to take care of unfinished business of the one that went before. It's all very logical. Of course, the surprise is that when you're actually writing a new play, you realize that the true reasons for doing it have nothing to do with this fancy aesthetic but they come from some darker, throbbing mystery within.

Barlow: When you begin a play, do you set out with a firm idea of how either the characters or the plot will develop, or do the characters and plot emerge as you work? Or does this vary from play to play?

Howe: It varies. I have the events more or less in mind, but. . . . With this new play [*Approaching Zanzibar*], in particular, I tried to stay as open as I could, because I was writing about stuff that really scared me, and I knew if I laid it in there and didn't let my fear carry me along, I knew that I'd be cheating myself and the audience and the actors and everybody involved. So, it's sort of a balance of trying to know what you're doing and being in control, so that you can create a work of art that has some design and proportion, but yet be brave enough to allow the irrational and the ugly and the frightening to overtake you. It varies from play to play. I had thought I was going to have a different ending, I had planned a totally different ending, and then I got this scene of the little girl and the old lady in bed together and I knew that was the heart of the play, that I had finally brought the little girl up against what she feared the most, and *that* was the issue, and *that* was where I was going to have to solve the play and resolve the play and give it its meaning. And so, in fact, the characters did tell me what to do.

Barlow: Do your plays change much in rehearsal? Your plays are so wonderfully physical. Do you create all of that movement in your head beforehand, or do you need to see the actors onstage?

Howe: Most of it I do in my head. I really do. If anything, I really shun readings and workshops before I go into rehearsal because I'm very afraid of being seduced by clever actors, and I feel that somehow it's the writer's responsibility to create the world, and I'm very selfish that way. I do want it to be my vision that we're exploring, and so I'm very cautious about letting the work out until it's done. And then of course, once we're in rehearsal, if something doesn't work, then I'll change it or I'll cut it. But most of the business and the events have been thought up by me, and my director Carole Rothman's genius is that she's not afraid of them.

Barlow: In recent years you've been working regularly with Carole Rothman. What are the advantages of having one individual direct several of your plays?

Howe: Oh, it's necessary to work with the same director. Most of the writers who have had any kind of long-standing career have realized the wisdom and importance of working with one director. Look at Marshall Mason and Lanford Wilson, Miller and Kazan, all of the people who work with one director. That's the key. For so long that was part of my problem, that I would be put with various directors who had various gifts of various kinds but with whom I didn't always see eye to eye, with whom I didn't always have this history of past productions. I get violent about this. You have to have one director, or it *helps* to have a director who is sympathetic to your work, because you have this shorthand, you understand each other, and for me it's been crucial to have Carole. And it's not just having the same person, but it's also having *her,* because she's really a unique person in many respects. It's this combination of her being tremendously fair and steady and yet creative at the same time. There's very little ego and game playing and conspiracy, which is the way so many directors work—through conspiracy and suspicion and innuendo. Carole is very forthright and very honest. But at the same time she's really inspired as a director. She has a vision, and she's daring, she understands about comedy, she understands about heartbreak, she understands about the dramatic gesture. And that combination of being rather earthbound in terms of the way she works and airbound in terms of her vision is really unusual. So I feel very fortunate in having been able to work with her.

Barlow: Do you ever feel that you may unconsciously be writing things that she would like, or are you conscious of her preferences as you write?

Howe: I think I am to a certain extent. One of the best things she ever directed was *How I Got That Story,* which was a road play that was set in many different locations. I was really exhilarated not only by the play but by the work she'd done on it, and I know that Carole is game for just about anything. And she loves the impossible, and that's sort of my tendency anyway, to try to take on the impossible, and knowing that she's responsive to that is a goad.

Barlow: When your work is translated into other media, of course, you have to work with different people. Did you like the television film [1986, *American Playhouse,* PBS] of *Painting Churches?*

Howe: I thought it was beautifully done. I found it a frustrating art form, though. And then when we watched it at home on the TV, I was terribly upset because there was no audience. I suddenly realized how important the audience is when you're watching a piece. I think that the *American Playhouse* version was very beautiful and very reverential, but

I did miss the madcap aspect of it. And I think, given the nature of the form, I never could have had it. I would like to try a movie, but in writing a movie, it wouldn't be a play. That's what I'm going to do next. I want to do a movie. I do, I do. Again, it's that visual thing. I want to pose luscious visual scenes with not much dialogue, just pose certain scenes and incredible situations you can only do in real life.

Barlow: You once said, "I can see myself writing a play with four words. Perhaps I'm becoming a choreographer in that sense." Yet it's obvious that you love language. I'm thinking, for example, of *Museum,* where Tink Solheim gives that wonderful account of going collecting with Agnes Vaag. Each of the plays has marvelous speeches like that.

Howe: Well, there are less and less. The new play has only one monologue, at the end. I was very worried, and I was saying to Carole as I was working on it—because I never show her anything until I feel it's done—and I would say to her periodically, "Carole, I'm concerned, there are *no* monologues." Because this was before I'd gotten to the end, and I think, because the new play is a road play and it's a family on the road, there simply wasn't time for any of these people to have a speech, because everything was going on at once. If you have two children involved, the parents don't have the luxury of ruminating about this, that, and the other. And the kids are always interrupting anyway, so that there really wasn't any long, great aria until the very end, and it was making me nervous. I was thinking, "Gosh, maybe this really is a movie. Maybe it isn't a play." Except that the conception is very theatrical. And even though the play takes place in specific geographical sites that are remarkable and beautiful in and of themselves, I think part of my responsibility as a playwright is to sort of bathe the audience in a heightened reality. And even though I'm writing about real places, I take great joy in creating an oversize space in a theatre, because I think movies and TV can handle reality much better anyway, so if one is going to write a play, at least go for size and don't worry about whether it's real or not.

But it is true that in this play there is a little less language, and it did make me nervous. And for a long time I thought, "I'll never write another play," because in a funny way, this play is the culmination of, pardon the expression, my career. This is the play, I mean of any play I've ever done, this is the one that I'm proudest of, that somehow says everything I've been trying to say all along. And I've been feeling that, working on it, that I probably won't be able to top myself. But then because there isn't that much language in it, and that does bother me, I suddenly realized, well, there is one thing that I haven't done yet as a playwright, and that is I haven't really written a vehicle for a star. I haven't written a really dense, intense play with tons of language and tons of emotional ups and downs for one or two characters, and that's probably what I'll do next. I will cram all of the space that I've been dealing with in the last two plays, I will try to condense it into the dramatic lives of one or two characters and really try to do a real virtuoso piece for one or two people to carry.

Barlow: It's evident from your plays that you're fascinated by the relationship between language and gesture. In *Coastal Disturbances,* for example, Leo literally sweeps Holly off her feet, literally makes her weak in the knees. The language comments on the gesture, and the relationship between movement and verbal expression is very important.

Howe: I'm a visual writer. I remember reading an interview with Marsha Norman saying that what kicks off her plays tends to be a fragment of dialogue, something overheard or something that she hears in her own mind, and it made me wonder, "Where do I get my inspiration?" And I must say that every play starts with the setting. The play's switch for me is something very visual; it's what the audience is looking at. It is true that I think what inspires me more than anything is what happens; it's not so much the words. I'm always flattered when people talk about my language, the beautiful language, the lyrical language, but when I'm working on a play, it's always the events that I'm thinking about and the behavior, and that always does come first.

Barlow: As you've frequently commented, all of your plays are about art, and in many cases about visual art and artists: Holly Dancer is a photographer; Mags Church, a painter; Agnes Vaag, a sculptor.

Howe: Well, one of the challenges that I gave myself with this new play was to see if I could stop doing that, if I could have a play reverberate emotionally. The key reverberations would be emotional rather than aesthetic. And, it's funny, there were a few givens that I started with when I began this play. One was to try to write about more ordinary people, write about life itself, not be so hung up on the aesthetic qualifications. I also wanted to see if I could end a play with a crescendo. I have been doing these silent dying falls now for too long—you know the wistful, fading smile on Leo's face in *Coastal,* the fading waltz at the end of *Painting Churches*—and I've been noticing that so many of the plays that are real smacking box office successes and that bring audiences to their feet are plays that end with a large, joyous sound, like August Wilson's *Fences,* when Gabriel is blowing on his horn. And I decided the time has come to see if I can do that, to create a loud, joyful noise at the end. So that was written into the intention.

Also, having written a play [*Coastal Disturbances*] where the children were very much on the periphery of the play and not really relating to the generations that were around them, I really wanted to try to write a play in which the children would relate directly to the generations in a very life-and-death way. I didn't want the children to be sort of charming accessories, but I wanted them to be the heart of the play. I used to think while watching performances of *Coastal* how wonderful it would have been if those little kids could have talked to the older couple on the beach. I was determined to have a scene between someone much older than either of those people and a child who would maybe be even younger than the children in *Coastal*. Because it seems that most of the plays that we see these days are about twenty-, thirty-, or forty-year-olds, and that you rarely see the extremes. And I love the extreme, and so in fact the key scenes in the play are between a nine-year-old girl and a ninety-one-year-old woman. And that was something that I was determined to try to do, and also to see if I could once and for all move out of one setting, because I've always been so dependent on mining one setting as fully as I could, whether it was a museum, a dining room, a beach, a townhouse. And I thought the time had come to be expansive and try something a little more daring and more spacious, so I was determined to see if I could do a road play. So that, in a funny way, I put all of these restrictions on myself before I even begin a project. But ironically it's those restrictions, of course, that release you to do your most daring work, and were it not for that very severe grid that one sets up, you couldn't begin to invent. It's a weird dynamic.

Barlow: Would you talk about your central concerns in *Approaching Zanzibar?* What engaged you most as you wrote the play?

Howe: It's about this little family, a mommy and daddy and two children—Pony, who's nine, and her brother, Turner, who's twelve—taking this trip across the country to visit Charlotte's aged aunt before she dies. The aunt is a sort of Georgia O'Keeffe character. Again, I seem to write about artists because for me artists are the closest we come to heroes in our society. If I were asked who do I perceive as the modern-day hero, I would again and again point to artists, whether they're visual artists or poets or whatever. So, many of the characters in the play are artists, but the actual trip and action of the play concerns life itself, and the things that happen are much more human and familial. We follow this family going on this trip from New York State to New Mexico and all of the adventures that they have along the way. And of course what pulls the play, the motor of the play, is the fear and the anxiety about (a) getting there on time, before Olivia dies and (b) what kind of shape is she going to be in when they get there. And I suppose the irony of the play—and for me the joy of the play—was putting the greatest fear in the youngest person, so that it's little Pony, who's nine years old, who is most terrified. It's that fear of what's going to be at the end of this long trip that pushes the action; and all of the scenes in the play, in one way or another, have to do with that fear.

Although it is a comedy—it's clearly a comic play full of all kinds of implausible events—it was harrowing to write. Because—I now can say this freely, I haven't been able to say it for a long time—I turned fifty last year, which I took very hard. I don't know, I suppose some of us take that harder than others. People say, "Think of the alternative, if you don't have that birthday," which is true, but you never think that you're going to suddenly be middle-aged, and I took it very hard. In conjunction with turning fifty I'd been watching various family members of mine die. There's also the reality of AIDS, which is ever-present in New York, which I find devastating and which I think about daily. And I wanted to try to write a play that in some way would deal with some of this pain, the bewilderment, turning fifty, death, people dying, survivors, how the survivors keep going. I think because I'm a mother and have my own children and have also reached the age when I won't have any more children, I posed it as this little play about the family. The mother in the family is herself going through menopause, and part of her anguish is realizing that she won't have children anymore. And she's on this odyssey to visit this wonderfully creative old woman before *she* dies, and they keep running into babies along the way, which are both life-affirming and cause for great joy, but which in an odd way catch the mother up and make her sad. So it's really acknowledging my fear of death but trying to celebrate life at the same time. I just feel that all of us, in one way or another, are in a period of mourning. And I want to give us survivors some hope, so that the play, for all of the fear in it and all of the darkness, is *wildly* uplifting at the end, and it does make a joyful sound, and I suppose that's why at the moment I feel strongly about it.

Barlow: Let me back up just a minute. You were saying that *Zanzibar* focuses on emotion rather than aesthetics. But haven't all the plays been emotional? Your artists are those who paint and take photographs because they *have* to; they have a great emotional investment in their work.

Howe: Yes, and then of course *Coastal Disturbances* was a love story, more than anything it was a story about a woman falling in love and being torn. I sort of wanted to get away from the WASPy artsy-fartsy thing, and I wanted to get away from the New England thing as well. And I've finally put some minorities into the play. I mean it's high time that I get away from all of these New England types, and I really wanted to have some Blacks and Hispanics and southerners and all kinds of different people in the play. I wanted to be less parochial and try to let in more of the world. Even though I may be a New England type myself, my sympathies go much further than that.

Barlow: You've been using children in your plays since *Birth and After Birth.* Until fairly recently there haven't been many young children in American plays.

Howe: I know. It's astonishing to me, because I think what children bring to a story is monumental, and when you think about it, most TV sitcoms are all about children, and so many of our movies, and the most successful movies and the most thrilling movies, are about children. We're so used to seeing them on film and on tape, but it is very rare to see them in the theatre. And I remember when I first saw Durang's *Sister Mary Ignatius* and that little boy walked on in that blue blazer and those little gray flannel slacks and had that first scene with the nun, I just thought that this was heaven, this is what we should all be doing. Before *Sister Mary* opened, I had written a play about a four-year-old [*Birth and After Birth*], but I just knew I could never cast a four-year-old, so in the stage directions I wrote that a grown, hairy man should play the part. But children have always figured very strongly in my life. Also, I have always seen myself as being a child, this very young person put inside of this very tall body, but that basically I've always felt that I'm emotionally sort of a nine-year-old. And just seeing the way the audience responded to those children in *Coastal,* they were swept away. Those kids could have done anything, and the audience would have been swept away. And so it wasn't lost on me: put the children in a life-and-death situation and *then* see what will happen. Well, it was just inevitable that I would write a play that would really push the children right out center stage. And I'm not that nervous about children being able to carry it. I'm convinced that they can because I've written real children's parts for them, not tons of language; I don't try to twist them into adult shapes or give them adult ideas or adult words.

And then the play does get more serious and scary, but I just found it incredibly liberating to write about children because I suppose in the end, as with most plays, you're really writing about yourself. And I feel that my work is autobiographical, though I'm not necessarily writing about my specific situation. And I think by finding this little nearsighted nine-year-old little girl, who's totally ignored by everyone . . .

she was a wonderful catalyst for me for finally getting out all of my own wild fantasies and my own hurts through the years. And she's, as a result, to me a very rich character, and I think I've tapped into something that's going to keep reverberating and reverberating. I mean I now have an idea for a movie, and I can't stop myself. Once you really go back, once you start going back, I think you open up more and more. I'll probably end up doing this fetus play in my sixties. That's where it will end. A fetus play. It'll all take place in an amniotic sac.

Barlow: Do you think one of the reasons there have been so few children on the American stage is because most of the plays have been written by men?

Howe: Absolutely. Absolutely. I keep saying to Carole, "Why don't playwrights write about children?" And she says, "Because they're not mommies." A lot of the men I know are truly gentle souls, but I think somehow there's the male mystique, which in some ways is just as pernicious as the female mystique. That men have to fulfill all this nonsense about being brutes and cruel and wanton. And in fact the baby scene, the scene with the newborn [in *Zanzibar*], the tender scene is between a father and his newborn baby, and I figure there won't be a dry eye in the house, because to me nothing is more poignant than male tenderness. I figure if the men aren't going to celebrate the tenderness of themselves, I'll do it for them.

Barlow: You've said that you see your plays as more European than American. Could you expand on that?

Howe: Yes. Well, I suppose because I love surrealism, and I think in a funny way—oh, this is going to sound so pretentious but . . . oh God, forgive me for sounding pretentious—but I think my concerns are rather existential, that I'm not so much concerned with relationships and the here and the now as I am with ephemeral matters. And my heroes have all been Europeans: Ionesco and Beckett and Pirandello and Virginia Woolf and Proust, the artists who have tried to pin down the ineffable and who have tried to give a name or to hold on to what's changing in front of their eyes. I think of that as being a sort of European preoccupation, and maybe it's simply because my models are of that sort that I consider myself, my work, more European in flavor. Of course, the irony is that my plays haven't been done much in Europe, and God knows the English have no patience with them because they don't think I'm American enough. But I've always had this wild hope that if I keep writing long enough and if I write enough plays, that sooner or later the Europeans will find me, because I've always been waiting for the French to discover *Museum* and *The Art of Dining.* I just have this feeling that put in the right hands, those plays would be lapped up over there. In fact, the Italians are doing *Painting Churches* in a couple of months, and I've already received the translation, which is hysterical. And you know, there's my sort of playfulness and my irreverence. I think that's more European, that I tend to turn things on their heads, that I'm not terribly into realistic, heartbreaking, the familiar in that sense. What thrills me is goofiness and the ephemeral and farce and the outrageous, and I guess I tend to think of those as being more European than American. I've never studied any of this, so in a certain way I'm just talking off the top of my hat.

Barlow: Are there any American playwrights whose work you particularly like?

Howe: I love Mamet's language, and I love Chris Durang's madness, but I guess I'm so firmly entrenched in the Absurdist tradition. I love Pinter. I must say I think *Betrayal* is a perfect play. I think *Betrayal* is absolutely gorgeous, although the writers that inspired me the most I'd have to say were Beckett and Ionesco. I always go back to the Absurdists, who I think were the real groundbreakers. I suppose I think my own short-comings have to do with the fact that I'm not nearly experimental enough, that given how much I respond to the avant-garde I should be much more daring than I am. I started out writing more daring plays, but I was so punished for it that I've sort of backed off as a reflex. But if I ever really came into my own, I think my responsibility in a way is to be more daring. That's what I criticize myself for the most, not being inventive enough, given the way I feel about the artists who really have been on the cutting edge.

Barlow: One notable aspect of your plays is that at the end there is— whether it's presented in a "dying fall" or the "crescendo" you talked about a few minutes ago—some sense of redemption. Isn't that more American than European? Do you find that in Beckett, or is there in European Absurdism generally a more nihilistic vision than you find in American works?

Howe: Yes, I guess that's true. I think I'm an optimist. I think that's part of it. But also to a certain extent a lot of my models are in terms of the novel, and I suppose if you ask me which writer I love the most it would be Virginia Woolf, who I think is deeply into the epiphany. And I think of Joyce and *The Dubliners*—each of those stories ends with an epiphany. And I suppose my true mentors in a funny way are those novelists. I've always viewed the novel as the highest of the literary art forms, as being of a much higher order than a play. If I could be Virginia Woolf or Tennessee Williams, I would choose Virginia Woolf in the flash of an eye. I suppose it's an academic argument and a ridiculous argument, but there's something about being able to sustain a whole work with only language, that you don't need lights and powders and costumes and actors and trickery but you can just do the whole thing through language. There's something in me that finds that extraordinary, and I wish with all my might and main that I could do that. And I suppose when I read literature and when I follow through a story that ends with an epiphany, I'm just swept away, and I suppose that's why I try to mimic that in my own work.

Barlow: Can you imagine yourself writing a play that isn't in some way comic? I'm assuming that you consider all of your plays so far to be comedies.

Howe: Yes, that's basic to my nature. I'll do almost anything for a laugh. I really will. It's disgusting. That'll never change. No, I'll always try to write comedies. Always.

Barlow: You said in an interview that you're beginning to face your own femininity, and that this is "tremendously dangerous." Can you expand on that a little bit?

Howe: I've always perceived women as being phenomenally powerful creatures, much more powerful than men. I've always had that view, probably because my mother towered a good foot above my father in size and in volume, and the women in my family have been very strong, dominating characters. And I started out going to these private girls schools in New York, and maybe it's just because children are cruel—I don't know whether children being cruel or little girls being cruel—but I certainly suffered terribly at the hands of little girls growing up. I've always been somewhat frightened of women and frightened of the woman in myself. As much as women are creators and nurturers, I've also seen them as being destroyers. I've always been very sensitive to that aspect, and I think of the great heroines of the theatre, the Lady Macbeths and the Amandas, and I think there is a prototype of the female as destroyer. And I know it exists in myself. Part of how I've gotten by is by playing the clown and playing the ingenue and the naif, but I know there's the "Tina the Destroyer" part of me and that that's part of being a woman, and I think that's the part that's frightening to me.

Barlow: I was wondering where this comes through in the plays.

Howe: I think I hide it. There's a lot that I haven't written about. I mean, I'm sort of waiting for my mature years. One thing that was always said about our family was that we were all late bloomers, which is true. I'm very young for my age, and I haven't really, as they would say, come into my own yet in many ways—emotionally, artistically. And there is a violent, jealous, nasty streak in me that I have gone to great pains to hide. I sometimes think that when the day comes when I'm really able to face that, my jealous side, which is very powerful, that that will be a real breakthrough of a kind. I have been daring; I think my plays have been relatively daring about a number of things, but there is a violent side that I haven't let out yet.

Barlow: To some extent you have, I think. There's jealousy and a certain emotional violence in Tink's speech about Agnes in *Museum,* for example. Tink is jealous of Agnes, and she paints a very ominous picture of her gathering—even licking—the dead creatures she uses in her sculptures. At the same time the picture is very comic, because Tink and Agnes are trotting through a park lugging suitcases.

Howe: That's what I mean, that I'm always sort of hedging my bets, that I tend to cover it up with the comic touch. Just at the most crunching moment of that speech, I have Bill Plaid say, "Go ahead . . . SMASH THE UGLY THING" [Agnes' sculpture], which brings a great laugh from the audience. I tend to do that. When I start getting ugly and upsetting, it makes me nervous and I know I've got to let the audience off the hook and make them laugh. So it's a matter of slowly, slowly, not being afraid of that, but on the other hand being somebody who's firmly wedded to the comic tradition. It's very tricky to be true to your darker self and still get laughs, to put it on its most vulgar level. But there is a lot more darkness and pain than I've been willing to show. That is certainly a fact. And I think of it as being a rather female darkness and a female pain, that I haven't been willing to explore that. Maybe I never will. It's interesting. In this new play, *Approaching Zanzibar,* I came the closest to setting up the equation so that I could do what I had to do, and there are certain issues that I simply refuse to go into because, I suppose, the play was posing other issues that were more pressing to me. One of the things that's frustrating about writing a play is that there are certain moments when you wish you could write about everything, but then in the interests of the play . . . I knew because it was so much about life and death that I couldn't go veering off into more arcane regions of my own—jealousy or anger or whatever.

Barlow: It may not be that comedy is a way of evading issues but rather that at some level what we fear most *is* comic. It may well be that the comic and the terrifying are inextricable.

Howe: Yes, and also if you're dealing with really ghastly stuff, you've got to be comic; otherwise it'll become so self-pitying and disgusting that the audience won't be able to stand it. So you have to soften it anyway, like the trick of Mags, who at times comes very close to being a creep and a pill. I had to be very careful to make her endearing and to give her some comic falls. Otherwise she just would have been revolting, and you would have wanted to step on her, because what right does she have to have that much arrogance in the face of her parents' packing up and going off to die? What right does she have? It is a tricky balance.

Barlow: You've said that *Painting Churches* was the most difficult play for you to write. Does *Zanzibar* replace it for that "honor"?

Howe: Part of the reason why *Painting Churches* was so hard was that I had the wrong metaphor. I had posed an impossible dramatic equation. Initially I wanted the girl to be a musician on the eve of her debut. I wanted her to be a nonverbal character, and I was trying to see if I could write a play in which I had a nonverbal character interacting with very verbal characters. It was just this obsession that I had to see if I could write a musical character in with a speaking character. I don't know why this was so important to me. And of course in draft after draft what emerged was just this very dull, mute person that had no feelings, nothing was going on in her, but I spent three years trying to make that work. Now maybe the reason it took three years wasn't because I was posing this impossible dramatic dilemma, but maybe it was because I was trying to write about something that was very close to me, and it would have taken me that amount of time anyway because there were certain things I didn't want to say.

I would say the new play was both very difficult to write and a joy to write. What made it extremely difficult was that I knew it would be under a lot of scrutiny. Because now people have certain expectations, and they're hoping that maybe I'm a playwright of some stature. People are hoping that maybe I'll write a really good play. And that was making me very nervous, thinking that—oh God—people are hoping I'm going to do something really wonderful this time. Of course when you're worrying about trying to write something really wonderful, you are totally hamstrung because you're trying to be wonderful all the time, and the minute you're trying to be consciously wonderful, everything is appalling. So that was very hard, to get over thinking that people were expecting me to write a wonderful play. And that's why I think I spent a year writing a ghastly version that I never showed to anybody. It was full of airless, virtuoso writing that meant nothing, and it was totally bad. And it took a lot of courage, I suppose, to face that, that I was writing garbage, trying to please this imaginary group of fans that I had. Because success has eluded me for so long, I've been very lucky.

Because my early plays were greeted with either disdain or horror or downright rage, I had a long period in which to grow as an artist, because I knew no matter what I did, I was going to be cut down. There was sort of a perverse luxury in that, of being able to find my voice. What made this play hard was feeling that somehow there were certain expectations on me. And I finally decided, well, I'm just going to do this for me, and it's not an issue of topping myself, it's an issue about writing about what I want to write about. And once I reached that stage, it really was a joy. I think because I was writing about matters that were of such crushing urgency for me, crushing urgency, the play—once I figured out the shape of it—it more or less wrote itself. It's very daring, it's very dark. It's all about my fears. And I think once I got to the point where I could bear to enunciate them, it's just shutting your eyes, and you just keep running.

[The following questions deal with Howe's work since 1989.]

Barlow: Tell me about the recent production of *One Shoe Off.*
Howe: There were problems with the first scene. There was always a problem because it was so labored and tragic. And then we had all these different endings. Samuel French [publishers] saw the play on a good night, I guess after we had opened—there was a week there when it was pretty elegant, although there were still problems—and French loved it, and they said "Oh, this play is going to play all over the country," so I sold it and then got the opportunity to do some work on the script. I made the first scene much warmer.
Barlow: What about the critical reception?
Howe: What distressed me in the reviews was that nobody got the point that it was a play about the theatre too as much as it was about survival and the meaning of love. But then I feel the only way *One Shoe Off* is going to get another chance is if I write an even better play, so I'm going to try to. I mean, this is what it is to be a writer, a playwright. You have your good years, and then you're shot down.
Barlow: You've said that you'd like your next play to open out of town rather than in New York.
Howe: Being a playwright is so difficult because we have such visibility. Whenever a play opens, it's reviewed in the *New York Times.* It's too intense. There's too much pressure. Nobody opens a new play in New York anymore.
Barlow: What do you think about opportunities for women playwrights at the moment?

Howe: It's a rough time for women playwrights. If you study the work by women that's been successful lately, it tends to be one-woman shows portraying women as victims. And they're wonderful and they're fascinating and full of life and invention, but for some reason the momentum we got going as dramatists in the eighties has slackened off. And my last two plays were very challenging because they took on the domestic scene, and I think that's always dangerous.

Barlow: Would you talk a little about the play you're working on now?

Howe: I am writing a new play. And it's strong. *One Shoe Off* was an inner landscape, an Absurdist piece about the randomness of life and the catastrophes and how one holds on. It's quite claustrophobic; it takes place in one evening in one house. It's very intense. So I knew that the next play I would do would be more spacious, and I wanted to get away from these darker themes and do something more entertaining, with more language, a big, lyrical, open piece, a toss of silk.

DAVID HENRY HWANG

Interview by Marty Moss-Coane
Edited with an Introduction
by John Timpane

David Henry Hwang (Courtesy of Writers and Artists Agency,
West 44th Street, Suite 1000, New York NY 10036)

David Henry Hwang has characterized himself as a "Chinese-Fili-
pino-American-born-again-Christian from suburban L.A." His
art, like his life, is a study of how cultures merge yet resist merger, how
identity endures yet constantly changes. Hwang was born in 1957 in
San Gabriel, California, a suburb just north of Los Angeles. His father,
an enthusiast of things American, had left mainland China for Taiwan
and then left Taiwan to study at the University of Southern California.
There he met Hwang's mother, a Chinese-Filipino concert pianist
seeking a career. The Hwangs were fundamentalist Christians who rejected Chinese ways yet retained strong elements of the Confucian culture they had left behind.

Hwang experimented with dramatic writing while an undergraduate at Stanford University in the late 1970s. He sought the advice of John L'Heureux, then the director of the creative writing program at Stanford. After giving Hwang some frank and bracing criticism, L'Heureux advised him to read and see as much drama as he could. Hwang attended the first Padua Hills Playwrights' Festival in 1978, where he studied with Sam Shepard and Maria Irene Fornes. He wrote his first theatrical success, *FOB* (1979), originally for performance in the Okada dormitory at Stanford University. He sent a manuscript of the play to the O'Neill Theater Center, and it came eventually to the attention of Joseph Papp, who produced it at the Public Theatre on Broadway in 1980. The reviews were good, and Hwang's career had begun.

That career has encompassed the éclat of an early success, a mixed reception for his next plays, *The Dance and the Railroad* (1981) and *Family Devotions* (1981), and a period of comparative writer's block in the mid-1980s when his purpose and goals as a writer were in transition. *The House of Sleeping Beauties* (1983) and *The Sound of a Voice* (1983) were followed by *Rich Relations* (1986). Then Hwang read of the French diplomat René Bouriscot and his wartime affair with the transvestite Chinese actor and spy Shi Peipu. He turned that story into *M. Butterfly* (1988), a massive success with both audiences and critics worldwide. His next plays were *Bondage* (1992) and *Face Value* (1993).

Since *M. Butterfly* Hwang has extended his dramatic writing into the realms of performance art, opera, and film. He collaborated with Philip Glass and Jerome Sirlin on the multimedia theatre piece *1,000 Airplanes on the Roof* (1988) and wrote the libretto for Glass's opera *The Voyage* (1992). There followed the screenplay for the movie version of *M. Butterfly* (1994), as well as an original screenplay for the film *Golden Gate* (1994).

M. Butterfly thrust Hwang into an international spotlight as "the" Asian American playwright. He has been both conscientious and ironic about this role—he is the only Asian American playwright most people know of, a fact that both amuses and embarrasses him. He has always stressed the diversity of ethnicities, aims, and purposes in the Asian American community, constantly reminding his readers that there is no single Asian American culture, or art, or drama. Nevertheless he does see much that makes Asian American experience and writing distinctive.

His plays explore the conflicts arising from that experience. Identity, both cultural and personal, has been the major theme uniting all of his plays. *M. Butterfly* explores identity on the sexual, cultural, and political levels simultaneously. *FOB* memorably studies the tensions between European American culture and Chinese American culture on the one hand, and between Chinese Americans and the Chinese who are FOB, "fresh off the boat," on the other. *Family Devotions* depicts a family much like Hwang's, which both rejects and retains a Chinese mentality, both embraces and transforms Western Christian culture.

For Hwang the Asian American is neither wholly Asian nor wholly American. Hwang's own literary evolution attests to this dilemma. Many critics have expected him to have a deep grounding in Asian drama, when in fact he has more often expressed his enthusiasm for the plays of Pinter, Chekhov, Shepard, and Shange (his interest in Chinese and Japanese theatre, opera, and film came later). In homage to Western psychology, Hwang has repeatedly emphasized that writing is a way for him to "access the unconscious"—to explore the unsuspected concerns and themes in his own work. Rather than seeking to create a drama that is exclusively and distinctively Asian, Hwang is building an interpersonal, intercultural body of work, American in tradition and Asian American in outlook.

The following is an edited transcript of an interview with Hwang on the program *Radio Times* over station WHYY, Philadelphia, and broadcast on National Public Radio. The interview was first aired on 29 November 1993.

Moss-Coane: M. Butterfly has been produced all over the world. Can you explain its popularity?

Hwang: It taps into a couple of themes people are currently interested in. First there's the shifting power balance between East and West. Second there's the idea of the French diplomat who deludes himself into thinking that he's having a powerful Western imperialist relationship with this submissive Oriental woman—only to discover that, if anything, it's he who is the actual butterfly and he who has been sacrificed for love. The Chinese spy would therefore be more like the character Pinkerton, the American explorer from the opera *Madame Butterfly.*

Also the play questions the role playing of men and women, and to the extent that those roles are starting to change and the construct of what it means to be male or female is being redefined, I think such questioning fascinates people as well. And then there's always the plus of having sort of a sensational plot. Some people have referred to the play as an intellectual striptease—and I suppose that doesn't hurt, either.

Moss-Coane: When you heard about this story, did you think, "Ah-ha! This really gives me a chance to explore some of the themes about East and West and men and women!"?

Hwang: When I heard the story, I had an ambivalent reaction. On the one hand, part of me felt this was an unlikely story. How could the Frenchman not know the sex of the Chinese spy? On the other hand, another part of me felt that this story was inherently credible, that it made sense. I write plays usually because there's a question I'm trying to answer, and the writing is a way to delve into my subconscious to find out what I really think about something. And I suppose that I wanted to try to use the opportunity of writing this play to reconcile my ambivalence about the actual story.

Moss-Coane: What's interesting about the story is that love affairs are often filled with lies, whether they are lies that people tell each other or lies that people tell to themselves, either about themselves or about the other.

Hwang: There are several axes the play turns on. One is the East-West theme, another is the male-female theme, and there is also the fantasy-reality axis. One of the things the play is about primarily is self-delusion. In the wake of the release of the film version of *M. Butterfly,* there was a lot of publicity about the actual case, and Barbara Walters went to France trying to find the real Bouriscot and interviewed the real Shi Peipu as well. These things are always advertised as if, "Now you're going to find out the real secret," that is, what were the physical mechanics? how did the Chinese spy do it? And I think that's not actually what the play is about. I don't think it's ultimately about what physical apparatus the Chinese spy did or did not have—it's about self-delusion, about the fact that the diplomat wanted to be deceived, and that therefore he was. I think many of us can relate to this, in the sense of having, for instance, a person who knows that his or her spouse is cheating but chooses not to know. Many of us wake up one morning, and we're in some relationship, and we say, "This person is not who I thought he/she was at all. He/she is exactly the opposite. How could I have fooled myself for so long?" The case of the French diplomat is a more extreme case, obviously, but it works from the same psychological principles.

Moss-Coane: Neil Jordan's film *The Crying Game* picks up on many of these themes. This confusion about gender and sexual orientation, and the confused sexual politics that most of us have to deal with—do you think this is now a widespread cultural concern?

Hwang: All one has to do is turn on the TV, whether to sitcoms or to afternoon talk shows, and people are really concerned or angry or furious or happy or any number of emotions about the way in which men and women are changing and the way in which our relationships are evolving. Something like *The Crying Game* testifies to the fact that sexual distinctions are actually becoming blurrier; therefore, the transvestite seems to serve as a metaphor for this process.

Things like gender and race exist in relation to someone else. I am a man, but I'm a man also because I'm not a woman. To the extent that the definition of woman is changing, my own identity as a man is called into question.

On the one hand, all the analysis of the plays and my characters feels redundant, like overkill. On the other hand, it feels flattering, a sign that people are interested. Sometimes I feel I've become a character in a Latin American novel who has created these characters, who now in turn play such a huge role in my life. I appreciate the analysis, although a lot of it doesn't have much to do with my impulses for creating the work. If people find themselves moved or interested enough to have a particular take that they want to bring to the subject, I think that's great and that's what art is supposed to do. Even from the first previews of the play in Washington, D.C., when nobody knew what they were seeing, people leaving the theatre tended to discuss the ideas rather than where they parked—and that's always been gratifying to me.

Moss-Coane: You wrote the screenplay for the movie version of *M. Butterfly.* How different is it to move from being a playwright to being a screenwriter?

Hwang: One of the things you learn quickly is that you're dealing with a visual rather than a literary medium. In the theatre most of the information is conveyed through the dialogue, and the visuals support that, whereas in a movie it's quite the opposite, and the information is supplied mostly visually. Therefore, as a screenwriter—and this is not a situation unique to me, but rather it probably applies to all screenwriters—you find yourself in a secondary position artistically to the director. I liked the movie of *M. Butterfly,* but it's very much director David Cronenberg's picture, in the sense that it focuses much more on the fantasy-reality aspect. And it's rather different from the screenplay I handed in. That's a situation very common to screenwriters: many of them feel that if they don't hate the picture that gets made from their script, they're happy.

I knew the movie was going to be different—it couldn't be exactly the same thing as the play, and I tried to find a filmic equivalence to the theatrical techniques used onstage. And I do think David has done a wonderful job with the picture, but since it's not really the picture I envisioned when I wrote it, I ended up feeling in a limbo-esque position: I enjoyed it, yet it's not completely my child.

Moss-Coane: Are you forced, then, to use different language for the screen as opposed to the stage?

Hwang: Certainly, the stage can tolerate a much more stylized kind of dialogue than the screen can. That's not the way people talk in real life. Dramatic characters tend to be extremely articulate or to talk in verse. What's more, the verisimilitude demanded in film demands a different approach. Theatre can tolerate metaphor more easily, tolerate discussion of ideas, because theatre itself is a metaphor. You walk into the theatre, you see the set, and you know it's a set and not, for example, a real drawing room. To that extent you're already collaborating with the theatrical artists in creating a metaphor. On film, by contrast, you're actually *in* China, you're actually *in* Seattle.

Moss-Coane: Does this experience make you think about directing a film, actually shaping the whole product yourself?

Hwang: I guess I've just been spoiled as a playwright, in terms of being able to articulate my own vision, of being the primary creative force. In the theatre the actors or directors can't change a single word of the text without the author's permission or approval. In film the studio essentially buys your copyright. That's why you see six or seven writers on a movie. The actors change dialogue on the set. Like many screenwriters, I feel, particularly for works I create from scratch—that is, works that are not adaptations—the need to get in the director's chair.

Moss-Coane: When did you begin to think about playwriting?

Hwang: I actually didn't start doing it until I was an undergraduate in college. The only real experience that I'd had prior to that was trying to compile a family history in a relatively long historical novel. Even my earliest impulses to write related to the desire to place myself into some sort of context, whether it was cultural or historical or familial. When I got to college, I had the desire to write plays and started doing it in my spare time in my sophomore year, and I found a professor who would take a look at them. He told me they were horrible, which they were. My problem was that I was writing in a vacuum. I had the desire to be a playwright, but I didn't actually know anything about the theatre. He ended up being a great adviser to me. So I spent the next couple of years trying to see and read as many plays as I could.

FOB, which was my first play to be done in New York, I originally wrote to be performed in my dorm at Stanford. We did it there in the spring of 1979, and then it went to something called the National Playwrights' Conference, which is held every year in Waterford, Connecticut. A dozen plays are worked on there, and many professionals come up from New York to see them. At that point *FOB* came to the attention of Joseph Papp, arguably the most influential theatre producer of the late twentieth century. He produced it, and I had a career.

Moss-Coane: That sounds so simple, as though it were relatively easy. There's none of the suffering of the artist trying to get the words on paper or the paint on canvas.

Hwang: I'm not a big advocate of the suffering theory, personally. One doesn't have to go looking for trouble to be an artist. The trouble will come to you, just in the regular course of life. It was a wonderful and relatively quick way to get out of the gate, but then, after that, I had a couple of years where I didn't feel I could write anything—and right now I'm still dealing with the aftermath of *M. Butterfly* and being so much associated with that play, and at the same time desiring to move on. I had a play earlier this year on Broadway, *Face Value,* that failed. So one's career has those ups and downs, and you just deal with them.

Moss-Coane: Are you saying that the success of *M. Butterfly* has made you self-conscious about your writing—that you have to meet this public and private expectation?

Hwang: For a long time before *Face Value* I felt intimidated by the fact that whatever I did next would likely be perceived as a disappointment relative to what I'd just done. Now having had that failure and gotten that out of my system, I feel liberated to write whatever I want. There is a certain burden a successful work carries with it, and that's a sort of suffering, if you will, which you don't have to go looking for—it'll come to you.

Moss-Coane: When you had such success at such a young age, did you say to yourself, "Wow! This is going to be easier than I thought"?

Hwang: I was surprised by it. When *FOB* was produced, I was twenty-three. That's young for an Off-Broadway playwright, and it left me feeling a little unclear about how much devotion this art took. In 1986 I had a play called *Rich Relations,* which failed Off-Broadway. In the wake of that I continued to think, "Writing is great. I'm glad I did it. I'm going to continue to do it." That's when I first realized that I was really going to be a writer my whole life—and that came from a failure. It was the feeling that I could do this and that I still loved doing it—and that it's not the failure or success of a particular work—though you'd rather have a success—that determines your love for the craft.

Moss-Coane: Your father came to this country from China and your mother from the Philippines, although she had grown up in China. When did they come to the states?

Hwang: They came in the early 1950s to attend the University of Southern California, which is where they met, and then they just stayed in Los Angeles and had their children.

Moss-Coane: Did they come because they were leaving something behind, because they wanted to get out of the political situation in China or the Philippines?

Hwang: Not so much in my mother's case. She came because she was a classical pianist and had decided to come to the states to study. My father's family had left China after the revolution and had come to Taiwan. Subsequently my father came to the states. He has always been very much an American assimilationist, if you will, and even as a child in China he'd seen American movies and had decided that America was where he wanted to be. He felt he didn't have much use for Chinese culture or Chinese ways. He jumped in feet first and fully embraced the American spirit as an immigrant.

Moss-Coane: Growing up in an Asian-American family, did you celebrate Asian holidays? Was there any reference to your Chinese past?

Hwang: Not really. We were raised pretty much as white European Americans in terms of the things we celebrated. There's an odd confluence in my family between a father who decided to turn away from things Chinese and a mother whose family had been converted to Christianity in China several generations back. Consequently between the two of them there was no particular desire for us to speak Chinese or celebrate Chinese holidays at all. I dated a Chinese girl when I was a senior in high school, and that was the first time I figured out when the Chinese New Year actually was!

Moss-Coane: Did you feel you were missing out on something?

Hwang: Not so much. As a child you're given a world, and you learn to live in it. It wasn't really until I was in college that I began to question some of this and think about roots. On the other hand, it's interesting that when I was in the seventh grade I chose to do a family history. That implies a desire for some connection to my roots, even though I wasn't consciously aware of it at the time.

Moss-Coane: How far did you get in that family history?

Hwang: About five generations.

Moss-Coane: Do you know what you were looking for?

Hwang: I think I was trying to figure out how I fit in. When I mentioned wanting to place myself in some sort of context, I suppose it implies a feeling of isolation, of not really knowing where one belongs. Many Asian Americans deal with the notion of being perpetual foreigners. One's family can have been in this country for several generations, and people will still say, "Oh, you speak really good English." It's a feeling of never quite being accepted as a "full" American—and at the same time not feeling connected to anything Chinese. In my case that created a certain amount of loneliness that I was trying to resolve by figuring out where I came from.

Moss-Coane: What kind of neighborhood did you grow up in?

Hwang: It was pretty multiethnic. I grew up in a suburb of Los Angeles called San Gabriel. It was mostly European American, Latino, some Asian, some African American. Fairly mixed.

Moss-Coane: Did you have to put up with teases and taunts because you were Asian American?

Hwang: I don't remember a whole lot of racism growing up. I don't actually remember people yelling things on the street—"Go back where you came from" or anything like that—I didn't experience that until I got to New York. But that might be because if you grow up in L.A., you're in the car most of the time, so people can't really yell things at you.

I was aware of a certain discomfort while watching Asian characters portrayed in film and television. Whether it was "the enemy" in Japanese, Korean, or Vietnam War movies or the obsequious figure—*Bonanza's* cook, Hop Sing, for instance—all of these people made me feel embarrassed, frankly. You could argue that that was the beginning of some impulse that led me to create my own Asian characters later in life.

Moss-Coane: Asian Americans have been described as the "model minority," the achievers, the people who do the best in school and contribute in very positive ways to the culture. Did you feel that kind of pressure?

Hwang: Pressure exists in at least two ways. Chinese society is built very much on the past—ancestor worship, for example—and even though my parents weren't consciously following these ideas, I think their mentality continued to be Chinese. Within the family there is a sense that whatever you do represents the group, whether it be your family, Chinese Americans in particular, or Asian Americans in general. So that exerts a strong internal pressure.

At the same time there is an external pressure, which wasn't quite as great when I was growing up, because people weren't as aware of Asian Americans as they are today. Even then there was beginning to be this notion of Asians being the "model minority." Ronald Takaki addresses the many ways the dominant American culture has used Asians as a club to show African Americans, as a means to say, "Look, they could do it, so you should be able to do it too. What's wrong with you?"

Moss-Coane: Do you feel that you've been used that way, as an example of immigrant success?

Hwang: Yes. I feel that way whenever *Time* or *Newsweek* does an article on "Asian American success." On the one hand, it's wonderful to have success, and it's important to celebrate it. On the other hand, there is an implied put-down of other minorities that haven't done "as well," and that put-down ignores the racism directed at, say, African Americans. Not to say that Asian Americans aren't the victims of racism too, but it's a different type of racism.

Moss-Coane: What type is it, exactly, and how do you experience it?

Hwang: This notion I mentioned earlier of being the perpetual foreigner has a lot to do with the particular type of racism that Asians encounter, the notion that you don't belong, the "go back to where you came from" idea. Coupled with the perception at this point in history that Asians are doing very well, there's a mentality that's somewhat traditional, in the sense that anti-Semitism is traditional, the sense that "they're taking over, they're doing so well that they must be doing something sneaky."

Asian Americans therefore end up being the scapegoats for a lot of tensions between the United States and Asia. Certainly in the 1980s, as trade tensions with Japan rose, so did violence against Asian Americans. There's a famous case in Detroit of a guy named Vincent Chin, who was clubbed to death by unemployed autoworkers who mistook him for a Japanese and were mad at Honda and Toyota. There's also the example of Japanese internment during World War II, which shows some of the dangerous effects of this notion of the perpetual foreigner.

Moss-Coane: I assume that people will think you're from Vietnam or from Japan or from China, or from anywhere except America.

Hwang: People generally don't make the distinction (a) between different Asian ethnic groups and (b) between Asians and Asian Americans. As an Asian American, I always feel a certain disjunction between my interior and my exterior. I can be walking down the street and people might think, "He's a Japanese businessman," or "He's from Vietnam," and when I open my mouth, there's a different reaction. Having that experience almost daily, you become very conscious of the difference between the external self and the internal self.

Moss-Coane: Do you feel then that you are or have been forced to be a spokesman, an ambassador for your race?

Hwang: I call it "the official Asian American syndrome." In the arts when there is a minority, like Asians, that haven't been exposed very much, when a member of that minority gains prominence, they then are asked or expected to represent the experience of the entire community, whether it's myself or Amy Tan or Maxine Hong Kingston—we've all dealt with this. Of course it's an unrealistic expectation. The views and experiences of the community are as divergent as are those of any other community. All an artist can do, all any individual can do, is speak for himself or herself.

Moss-Coane: It must be a double challenge to articulate experience that is your own and yet has resonance for others, not just Asian Americans, but other hyphenated Americans.

Hwang: To the extent that just about everyone in America comes from immigrant roots, my experience as the child of immigrants is a quintessentially American story, although it took place in cultural surroundings slightly different from those usually associated with the "immigrant experience." What we're all trying to do in talking about our lives and doing this type of art is to make those connections, to say that in art the universal transcends the specific. I can see one of August Wilson's plays in which there's an African American family, and I can feel I understand that family. In certain ways it's similar to the family I grew up in, even though the skin color of the characters is different. That's one of the functions art is able to perform.

Moss-Coane: Do you feel a pull from China? Have you gone back, say, to try to find family members? Are you still trying to complete that family history?

Hwang: Strangely, I've traveled a fair amount in Asia—Tibet, Japan, Singapore, Indonesia—but I've never actually been to China. That fact—well, if you believe Freud, nothing is accidental—may have to do with this conflict I feel. I think I'm afraid that if I like it, if I enjoy China, I'm going to feel more alienated from my life as an American, and if I don't like it, I'm going to feel more alienated from my genetic culture. It's a bridge I have yet to cross.

Moss-Coane: Do you have brothers and sisters?

Hwang: I have two younger sisters. My closer sister, Mimi or Margery, is a cellist, and my younger sister, Grace, teaches school in Los Angeles.

Moss-Coane: Do the three of you talk about these issues of culture and identity?

Hwang: We didn't for a long time. Because as you get older, you begin to ask some of these questions, and maybe because I tend to be closely identified professionally with some of these subjects, we have begun to talk about them more. And when we do, it's more an effort to ferret out what it is in our upbringing that seems to us to be a holdover from the Chinese mentality. Many of the Chinese influences we got were disguised.

Moss-Coane: Such as?

Hwang: Well, I have a lot of pastors in my family. They're evangelical born-again pastors. But because a lot of them are immigrants, what they did was take a Confucian mentality and graft it onto a Christian dogma. So you thought you were getting the specifics of the Christian experience, when actually you were getting the Chinese experience in disguise. It's a little difficult to pick out, now that we're adults, but that's what my sisters and I are doing.

Moss-Coane: Are you personally born-again?

Hwang: I'm not. At this point I'm dead-again, if anything. I stopped being associated with born-again religion when I was in college, which felt very momentous at the time, since so much of my growing up had had to do with that religion. But subsequently most of my immediate family has gotten relatively lax on the subject of religion, so maybe I've started something.

Moss-Coane: But when you rejected your religion, and certain parts of your family as well, you thought this was going to be a big deal?

Hwang: I thought so, yes. Later I found that it didn't end up destroying my relationship with anyone in my family, so it wasn't as momentous in that sense as I had expected. At family functions we usually do this thing called family devotions, which is also the title of one of my plays. We all kind of get up and witness. My grandmother tells the story of her grandfather, who was kidnapped by pirates and sold to a Chinese family that happened to be Christian. They bought him and dedicated him to God. So there is supposed to be this legacy, that we're all descended from someone who was dedicated to God, and that we're also dedicated to God. This is a really clear example of the meshing of the Christian ethic with the Confucian ancestor worship ethic. We are responsible for carrying out what my great-grandfather did, which is a Confucian idea. The specifics of what he did, however, had to do with the Christian religion and are therefore Western.

Moss-Coane: And it had to do with capitivity on top of that.

Hwang: With capitivity and with slavery, so there are a number of different power themes all meshed together.

Moss-Coane: You say you're "dead-again" in place of being born-again. That sounds very dark, very gloomy and pessimistic.

Hwang: Ex-fundamentalists, like ex-Catholics, always have this sense that they are going to go to hell. So I describe my outlook that way in an attempt to use humor to ward off the fear. In essence I feel that some of the most important decisions I've made in my life, and the ones of which I'm proudest, have to do with making my own way in terms of the religious issue, as well as deciding to become a writer.

Moss-Coane: How has writing your plays gotten you to think about the Asian American experience? Certainly that has been a theme you've been very much interested in.

Hwang: Writing for me tends to be closely bound up in the exploration of my identity as an Asian American. It has been my way of accessing the unconscious, and when I started doing so, many of the issues and concerns that emerged—racism, the cultural issue—were things that I didn't necessarily know that I was that concerned with.

Writing and exploration of identity are so closely interrelated that I can trace the evolution of my thinking on Asian American/ethnic issues through my work. There have been certain periods when I have been more isolationist/nationalist, and currently I tend to be more intercultural/internationalist, trying to find connections between different groups in our society, rather than separating them. And all that is reflected in the progression of the plays. I started out being fairly assimilationist, trying to pretend I was white. Then, as I mentioned, I got to a place where I was more isolationist/nationalist, wanting to work only with other Asians and not wanting to have that much to do with European American society. Now I'm more interculturalist, trying to make connections, talking about how all of us have a number of different identities. And these identities are not particularly static. It's not as though I decide I'm a Chinese American and that therefore defines me for the rest of my life. That, to me, is another form of fundamentalism, as insidious as the religious fundamentalism that I grew up with. It's important constantly to question and to change, and part of the experiment that's going on right now in America has to do with the question "Can we become a world culture?" Can all these different groups from around the world retain something of themselves and yet feel enough of a bond with one another that we feel that we're a country?

Moss-Coane: Do you feel optimistic about the resolution of that challenge? This is, of course, the challenge of America.

Hwang: I'm very interested in the challenge and think it's very worthwhile, and I'm doing my bit to try to advance it. Am I optimistic? It depends on what day you ask me.

Moss-Coane: You mentioned growing up with certain negative stereotypes of Asian or Asian American characters in films and on television. I'm curious whether, if you get more involved in Hollywood and making movies, you'll see it as part of your responsibility to humanize and give dimension to Asian and Asian American characters.

Hwang: There's no such thing as a good stereotype or a bad stereotype per se. It's merely that such a character presents someone who does not seem sufficiently human, whether it's Gunga Din, who is so obsequious and so helpful and so "good" that he seems not completely human, or the evil Fu Manchu. To me to write well is to battle stereotypes. To write well is to create three-dimensional characters that seem human, so that whether what they do is good or bad isn't really the issue. My responsibilities as an artist and a political person coincide in this case. They require me to do my best as a writer.

TONY KUSHNER
David Savran

Tony Kushner (The Joyce Ketay Agency)

Never before in the history of the American theatre has a play fascinated a Broadway audience for a seven-hour duration; amassed the Pulitzer, the Tony, and other prestigious awards; garnered academic respectability; and epitomized the zeitgeist so stunningly. This achievement is even more remarkable when one considers the fact that all five of its leading male characters are gay.

Tony Kushner's *Angels in America: A Gay Fantasia on National Themes* has become, arguably, the theatrical event of the 1990s. Its two parts, *Millennium Approaches* (1991) and *Perestroika* (1992), were first performed at the Eureka Theatre, the Mark Taper Forum, and the Royal National Theatre of Great Britain before finally reaching Broadway in 1993 in productions directed by George C. Wolfe. Bringing together Jews and Mormons, African Americans and European Americans, neoconservatives and leftists, closeted gay men and exemplars of the new queer politics, *Angels* writes a history of America in the age of Reagan and the age of AIDS. As if to confirm what activists have been asserting since the late 1960s, it demonstrates the mutual imbrication of the political and the personal by dramatizing the often tortuous connections between various ideological positions and a wide range of various sexual, racial, religious, and gendered identities. Drawing on Brecht, the innovations of the theatrical avant-garde, and a narrative tradition that stretches back to Eugene O'Neill and Tennessee Williams, it invents a kind of camp epic theatre—or in Kushner's phrase, a Theatre of the Fabulous. Spanning the earth and reaching into the heavens, interweaving multiple plots, mixing metaphysics and drag, the sacred and the profane, vengeful ghosts and Reagan's vicious henchmen, *Angels* demonstrates conclusively that what passes for reality is in fact deeply inflected by fantasy and dreams.

Angels in America's title and its preoccupation with the utopian potential inscribed in even the most appalling moments of history are derived from Marxist philosopher Walter Benjamin's extraordinary meditation, "Theses on the Philosophy of History," written in 1940 as he was vainly attempting to escape the Nazis. In this essay Benjamin uses Paul Klee's painting, *Angalus Novus,* to construct an allegory of progress in which the angel of history, his wings outspread, is caught between past and future, between the history of the world, which keeps piling wreckage at his feet, and a storm blowing from paradise, which propels him blindly and helplessly into an unknown future. For Kushner this allegory serves as a constant reminder both of catastrophe (AIDS, racism, and the pathologization of female and queer bodies, to name only the play's most obvious examples) and of the perpetual possibility of revolution, the expectation that, as Benjamin puts it, the continuum of history will be blasted open. This notion of messianic time ensures that the vehicle of enlightenment in *Angels*—the prophet who announces a new age—will be the play's most abject character, Prior Walter, a man born too soon and too late, suffering AIDS and the desertion of his lover. Moreover, in Kushner's reconceptualization of American history this concept of time is inextricably connected both to the extraordinary idealism that has characterized so much American political discourse and to the ever-deepening structural inequalities that continue to betray and mock that idealism.

It is hardly coincidental that *Angels in America* should capture the imagination of critics and theatregoers at a crucial moment in history, at the end of the cold war, as the United States, its economy and infrastructure deteriorating, is attempting to renegotiate its role as the number one player in the imperialist sweepstakes. More brazenly than any other recent play or film, *Angels* takes on questions of national mission and attempts to interrogate the various mythologies—from Mormonism to neoconservatism to multiculturalism—that have been constructed to consolidate an American identity. At the same time the play seems inextricably linked to the strategies of Queer Nation, a group whose founding in 1990 in fact postdated the writing of the play. Like the partisans of Queer Nation, it aims to subvert the distinctions between sexuality and politics, to undermine the category of the normal, to cross the borders of the licit and illicit, to refuse to be closeted, and to question the fixedness and stability of every and any sexual identity. Refashioning America, giving it a camp inflection, *Angels* announces: "We're here. We're queer. We're fabulous. Get used to it."

The following interview took place on a cold Sunday afternoon, 9 January 1994, in Kushner's upper West Side apartment in New York City.

Savran: How did you first get interested in theatre?

Kushner: My mother was a professional bassoonist, but when we moved down to Louisiana, she didn't have enough playing opportunities, so she channeled her creative energies into being an amateur actress. She was the local tragedienne and played Linda Loman and Anne Frank's mother. She also played Anna O in *A Far Country,* her first play, and I had vivid homoerotic dreams about her being carried around by this hot young man who played Sigmund Freud—you can make all sorts of things about that!—and I have very strong memories of her power and the effect she had on people. I remember her very much in *Death of a Salesman,* everybody weeping at the end of the play. She was really very, very good in those parts. So I think it had something to do with being a mother-defined gay man [*laughs*] and an identification with her participation.

And then there were other obvious things. I grew up very, very closeted, and I'm sure that the disguise of theatre, the doubleness, and all that slightly tawdry stuff interested me. I acted a little bit when I was a kid, but because most of the people who hung around the theatre in town were gay men, I was afraid of getting caught up in that. I had decided at a very early age that I would become heterosexual. So I became a debater instead. And then when I got to New York, I started seeing every play.

Savran: When was that?

Kushner: 1974. I arrived at a pretty great time. Broadway had not died completely. So you could still see some interesting Broadway-type shows: *The Royal Family, Absurd Person Singular,* things that were sort of trashy but really well done, with actors like Rosemary Harris and Larry

Blyden. Musicals were already dead, but there was something that re-
sembled excitement: *Equus, Amadeus,* and all that shit, which I knew
wasn't good but at least had energy. And at the same time there was all
this stuff going on downtown. I saw the last two performances of
Richard Schechner's *Mother Courage,* and then I watched as the Performance Group disintegrated and became the Wooster Group. I saw
Spalding Gray's first performance pieces and *Three Places in Rhode Island,* Lee Breuer's *Animations* and JoAnne Akalaitis's *Dressed Like an
Egg.* And I saw one piece by Foreman, I think it was *Rhoda in Potatoland,*
but I didn't understand it. It was the first piece of experimental theatre
I'd ever seen, and I was horrified and fascinated. My first real experience
with Foreman was his *Threepenny Opera,* which I saw about ninety-five
times and which is one of my great theatre experiences.

When I was in college, I was beginning to read Marx. As a freshman
I had read Ernest Fisher's *The Necessity of Art* and was very upset and
freaked out by it. The notion of the social responsibility of artists was
very exciting and upsetting for me.

Savran: Why upsetting?

Kushner: I arrived from Louisiana with fairly standard liberal politics. I
was ardently Zionist, and where I grew up, the enemy was still classic
American anti-Semitism. It was a big shock to discover all these people
on the left at Columbia who were critical of Israel. My father is very
intelligent in politics but very much a child of the Krushchev era, the
great disillusionment with Stalinism. I guess I just believed that Marxism was essentially totalitarianism, and I could hear in Fisher, and then
in Arnold Hauser, a notion of responsibility that is antithetical to the
individualist ideology that I hadn't yet started to question.

And there were two things that changed my understanding of theatre. One was reading Brecht. I saw *Threepenny Opera* in '76 and thought
it was the most exciting theatre I'd ever seen. It seemed to me to combine the extraordinary visual sense that I had seen downtown with a
narrative theatre tradition that I felt more comfortable with. And there
was also the amazing experience of the performance. When Brecht is
done well, it is both a sensual delight and extremely unpleasant. And
Foreman got that as almost nothing I've ever seen. It was excoriating,
and you left singing the songs. So I read the "Short Organum" and
Mother Courage—which I still think is the greatest play ever written—
and began to get a sense of a politically engaged theatre. When I first
came to Columbia, I was very involved in trying to get amnesty for
draft evaders, and I did a library sit-in in '75, which was a big experience for me. It was the first successful political action I'd ever been

involved in. And I met all these people from the Weather Underground who were still hanging out in Morningside Heights, and I got very deeply into the mythology of radical politics. And in Brecht I think I understood Marx for the first time. I understood materialism, the idea of the impact of the means of production, which in Brecht is an issue of theatrical production. I started to understand the way that labor disappears into the commodity form, the black magic of capitalism: the real forces operating in the world, the forces of the economy and commodity production are underneath the apparent order of things.

Because of Brecht I started to think of a career in the theatre. It seemed the kind of thing one could do and still retain some dignity as a person engaged in society. I didn't think that you could just be a theatre artist. That's when I first read Benjamin's *Understanding Brecht* and decided I wanted to do theatre. Before that I was going to become a medieval studies professor.

Savran: Why?

Kushner: I loved the Middle Ages, and I think there's something very appealing about its art, literature, and architecture, but I was slowly getting convinced that it was of no relevance to anything.

Savran: What about the Middle Ages? The connection between art and religion?

Kushner: I have a fantastical, spiritual side. And when I got to Columbia, I was very impressionable. The first class I took was a course in expository writing taught by a graduate assistant who was getting her Ph.D. in Anglo-Saxon literature. So we did *Beowulf.* I found the magic and the darkness of it very appealing, and I was very, very moved by—and I still am—being able to read something nine hundred years old, or two thousand years old in the case of the Greeks, and to realize that it isn't in any way primitive. And you also realize—although I don't believe in universal human truths—that there are certain human concerns that go as far back as Euripides or Aeschylus.

Savran: And of course medieval art and culture predates the development of bourgeois individualism—

Kushner: Exactly.

Savran: Which you go to great pains to critique.

Kushner: And it's extraordinary to see that great richness can come from societies that aren't individuated in that way. The anonymity of the art is terrifying to a modern person. It's not until very late, really until the beginning of the Renaissance, that you start to have artists identifying themselves. You realize these human beings had a profoundly different sense of the social.

At the same time I started to get very excited about Shakespeare and Ben Jonson. I directed Jonson's *Bartholomew Fair* as my first production at Columbia, and it was horrible.

Savran: It's a very difficult play.

Kushner: Yes, I know. I didn't start easy—thirty-six parts. I couldn't even find thirty-six actors. One of them didn't speak English, and we had to teach him syllabically. And you can't understand most of it anyway because of the references to things that have long since disappeared. But I had fun doing it and decided at that point—although I'd tried writing a couple of things—that I would become a director because I didn't think that I'd ever write anything of significance. I was also attempting to follow in the footsteps of people I really admired, like Foreman, Akalaitis, and Liz LeCompte. I thought that the best thing to do was to write the text as a director. And so I spent two years answering switchboards at a hotel and two years teaching at a school for gifted children in Louisiana. I directed several things there to get over my fear of directing, *The Tempest, Midsummer Night's Dream,* and I did my first take at *The Baden-Baden Play for Learning,* which I'm beginning to think is, next to *Mother Courage,* the best thing Brecht ever wrote. And then I applied to NYU graduate school in directing because I wanted to work with Carl Weber because he had worked with Brecht—and he looked like Brecht. And at my second attempt—George Wolfe and I just discovered that we were rejected by him in the same year—I got in.

Savran: You mention *Bartholomew Fair,* with its multiple plot lines, like your own work, and you also speak of the American narrative tradition with which your writing certainly is engaged.

Kushner: I think it's completely of that tradition.

Savran: What impact have Miller, Williams, and O'Neill had on your writing?

Kushner: Miller, none. I do actually admire *Death of a Salesman.* I think it really is kind of powerful. And I can see how, in its time, it had an immense impact. And it's still hard to watch without sobbing at the end. But some of it is a cheat. It's melodramatic, and it has that awful, fifties kind of Herman Wouk–ish sexual morality that's disgusting and irritating. And unfortunately Miller went around talking about what a tragedy it is, the little man and all that. But it really isn't, it's incredibly pathetic, or bathetic.

I sneered at O'Neill for a long time, but I'm beginning to realize that two or three of his plays—not just *Long Day's Journey into Night*—are amazing. I went back and reread *Long Day's Journey* and found it so complicated and theatrical—it's about theatre in ways that the tradition doesn't allow for.

I've always loved Williams. The first time I read *Streetcar,* I was annihilated. I read as much Williams as I could get my hands on, until the late plays started getting embarrassingly bad, although there are some that are much more interesting than I realized. But I loved *Night of the Iguana.* And I've always thought *Orpheus Descending* is a fascinating play, much more fascinating than the Broadway production directed by that Tory weasel, Peter Hall, which I thought was just awful. I'm really influenced by Williams, but I'm awestruck by O'Neill. I don't feel that he's much of an influence because he's from a very different tradition with a very different sensibility.

Savran: On the other hand I'm always struck by the utopian longings in *Long Day's Journey,* Edmund's dreams of the sea, which, I think, tie into your work.

Kushner: But O'Neill's utopian longings are inseparable from death. He's a Catholic who doesn't believe in redemption, but in death instead. I was so struck by that in *Moon for the Misbegotten:* the only thing that you've got to look forward to is to rest in peace. Josie's wishing Jamie a quiet time in the grave. It's horrendously bleak and very Irish, isn't it? It's also very New England, the fog people. I don't feel that I'm a fog person. I think I'm a lot more sappy than he is. Even Williams, eating the unwashed grape, "as blue as my first lover's eyes," that whole vision that Blanche has of dying at sea, has more space and possibility and hope than O'Neill.

I've become very influenced by John Guare, whom I think is a very important writer. I have to admit to not being nuts about *Six Degrees of Separation,* which I am confused by, but I think *Landscape of the Body,* the Lydie Breeze plays, *House of Blue Leaves* are amazing. Like Williams, he's figured out a way for Americans to do a kind of stage poetry. He's discovered a lyrical voice that doesn't sound horrendously twee and forced and phony. There are astonishingly beautiful things scattered throughout his work.

Savran: As I was watching *Perestroika,* I also thought about Robert Wilson.

Kushner: Hollow grandiosity (*laughs*).

Savran: But the opening tableau, the spectacle, the angel.

Kushner: I saw *Einstein on the Beach* at the Met in '76 and was maddened and deeply impressed by it. I'm very ambivalent about Wilson. The best I've ever seen him do, the piece I loved the most, was *Hamletmachine.* I was horrified by what I saw of *Civil Wars.* It really seemed like Nuremberg time—done for Reagan's Hitler Olympics. And what he does to history—and I'm not alone in making this criticism. This notion of Ulysses S. Grant and Clytemnestra and owls and Kachina dancers—excuse me, but what is this? What's going on here?

Savran: So you see a complete dehistoricization?

Kushner: Absolutely. And to what end? What are we saying about history? Because these figures are not neutral, they're not decorative. You do see ghosts of ideas floating through, but it just feels profoundly aestheticist in the worst, creepiest way, something with fascist potential. Also the loudest voice is the voice of capital: this cost so much money, and you've spent so much money, and it's so expensive. There's a really unholy synthesis going on of what is supposed to be resistant, critical, and marginal, marrying big money and big corporate support. He's an amazing artist, but it disturbs me. I've always felt much more drawn to Foreman and early Akalaitis. JoAnne did some very interesting things with *Dead End Kids.* And with Foreman, even if you're completely awash in some phenomenological sea, you absolutely believe there's a stern, terrifying moral center, and so much blood and heart in it. What I like about Wilson, and I felt this watching *Hamletmachine,* is: this is such tough theatre, this is hard work. I was always afraid of making the audience work.

Savran: Your work does bring together so many of these things: Brecht, the American narrative tradition, downtown theatre, Caryl Churchill—

Kushner: I left out Maria Irene Fornes. She's very, very important to me. I got to watch her go from really experimental stuff like *The Diary of Evelyn Brown,* a pioneer woman who lived on the plains and made endless, tedious lists of what she did during the day. And Fornes just staged them. It was monumentally boring and extraordinary. Every once in a while this pioneer woman would do a little clog dance. You saw the monumental tediousness of women's work, and that it was at the same time exalted, thrilling, and mesmerizing. And then she moved into plays like *Conduct of Life* and *Mud.* I think she's a great writer, and the extent to which she's not appreciated here or in England is an incredible crime and an act of racism. And she's the only master playwright who's actually trained another generation, so many wonderful writers like José Rivera, and Migdalia Cruz and Eduardo Machado. And she's a great director.

And then Churchill is like . . . God. The greatest living English-language playwright and, in my opinion, the most important English-language playwright since Williams. There's nothing like *Fen* or *Top Girls.*

She came to see *Angels* at the National, and I felt hideously embarrassed. Suddenly it sounded like this huge Caryl Churchill ripoff. She's a very big and obvious influence. One of the things that I'm happy about with *Perestroika* is that it's bigger and messier. I found a voice, and it doesn't sound as much influenced by Churchill as *Millennium*. The important thing about the British socialist writers, even the ones that I find irritating, is that that style comes out of the Berliner Ensemble touring through Britain. They have a strong Marxist tradition they're not at war with, and they've found a way—Bond, of course, did it first—to write Marxist, socialist theatre that has a connection with English-language antecedents. So it was very important for me to read Brenton, Churchill, Hare, and Edgar. During the late seventies, when there was nothing coming out of this country, they seemed to be writing all the good plays.

Savran: Whenever I teach *Angels in America,* I start by noting how important it is that it *queers* America, the idea of America. As the subtitle makes plain, this is a play that deals with national themes and identities and recognizes that gay men have been at the center of that. Although Queer Nation had not yet been formed when you started working on the play, I still see the play connected to its politics. How do you see *Angels* in relation to the development of queer politics?

Kushner: I'm in my late thirties now and of the generation that made ACT UP and then Queer Nation, a generation stuck between the people that made the sixties and their children. I see traces of the Stonewall generation, of Larry Kramer and even to a certain extent Harvey Fierstein, but also the generation of Greg Araki and David Drake, that totally Queer Nation, Boy Bar kind of thing—I have problems with both of them, I didn't like *The Living End* at all. But I feel that I'm part of a group of people, Holly Hughes, David Greenspan—

Savran: Paula Vogel.

Kushner: And Paula. I told Don Shewey in the *Voice* that I think of it as a change from the Theatre of the Ridiculous to the Theatre of the Fabulous. The Queer Nation chant—"We're here. We're queer. We're fabulous. Get used to it"—uses fabulous in two senses. First there's fabulous as opposed to ridiculous. It's amazing in *The Beautiful Room Is Empty* when Edmund White writes about Stonewall being a ridiculous thing for these people. That's the essence of the ridiculous. It's a political gesture, what Wayne Koestenbaum calls "retaliatory self-invention," a gesture of defiance. And the drag gesture is still not completely capable of taking itself seriously. I don't want to talk in a judgmental way, but there's still a very heavy weight of self-loathing, I think, that's caught up in it. You couldn't say that Charles Ludlam was self-loathing. But there is a sense in which the masochism—I'm sounding like Louis now—and the flashes of really intense misogyny, when another victim of oppression is sneered at and despised because of her weakness, come from the fact that one hates one's own weakness. There's a certain embracing of weakness and powerlessness in the whole Ridiculous.

Savran: John Waters, too, is such a good example of that.

Kushner: Yes. And there's also an incompatibility with direct political discourse. How can you be that kind of queer and talk politics? And of course what AIDS forced on the community was the absolute necessity of doing that, of not becoming a drab old lefty, or old new lefty, of maintaining a queer identity and still being able to talk seriously about treatment protocols and oppression.

So there's fabulous in the sense of an evolutionary advance over the notion of being ridiculous, and fabulous also in the sense of being fabled, having a history. That's very important, that we now have a consciousness about where we come from in a way that John Vacarro and Charles Ludlam, when they were making it, pre-Stonewall, didn't have. Think back to Jack Smith, that whole tradition of which he was the most gorgeous and accomplished incarnation. Ludlam died before ACT UP started. Had he lived, there's no question but that he would have had no problem with it. I knew nothing about his theoretical writings when he was alive; I just knew he was the funniest man I'd ever seen. But he was working through a very strong politics and theory of the theatre, and I'm sure the times would have made many amazing changes in his art. So I feel we're another step along the road now. It's incumbent upon us to examine history and be aware of history, of where we've come from and what has given us the freedom to talk the way we do now. We're the generation that grew up when homophobia wasn't axiomatic and universal and when the closet wasn't nailed shut and had to be kicked open.

Savran: The progress narrative you're constructing here makes me think that *Perestroika's* idea of history is not only rooted in dialectical materialism but also in your belief in the possibility of progress and enlightenment.

Kushner: As Walter Benjamin wrote, you have to be constantly looking back at the rubble of history. The most dangerous thing is to become set upon some notion of the future that isn't rooted in the bleakest, most terrifying idea of what's piled up behind you. Scattered through my plays is stuff from Tennessee Williams, Robert Patrick, all the gay writers that came before. When I started *Angels,* I started it, following

Brecht, who always did this, as an answer: you find a play that makes you mad—either you love that it makes you mad or you think it's abominable—and needs to be responded to. I had seen *As Is,* which I really hated—I hated the production even more than the play. I had seen so much bad gay theatre that all seemed so horrendously domestic. And it's even in *Torch Song,* although I really love *Torch Song,* which, obviously, is an important antecedent. When Arnold, who desires to be straight, turns to his mother and says, "I only want what you had," there's something that's really getting missed here.

When I started coming out of the closet in the early eighties and was going to the Coalition for Lesbian and Gay Rights meetings, it was so bourgeois and completely devoid of any kind of left political critique. There was no sense of community with any other oppressed groups, just "Let's get the gay rights bill passed in New York and have brunches and go to the gym." It was astonishing to discover that only ten years before there had been the Gay Activist's Alliance and the Lavender Left and hippie gay people, and I thought, "What happened? Where did they go?" And of course they went with the sixties. But ACT UP changed all of that. Now it's hard for people to remember that there was a time before ACT UP, and that it burst violently and rapidly on the scene.

Savran: It seems to me that this development of queer politics has in part prepared for the success of *Angels in America.*

Kushner: Absolutely. It kicked down the last door. The notion of acting up, much more than outing, is what really blew out liberal gay politics. I mean, you depend upon the work that's done by the slightly assimilationist but hardworking libertarian civil rights groups, like the NAACP, but then at some point you need the Panthers. You need a group that says, "Enough of this shit. This is going too slow. And if we don't see some big changes now, we're going to cause trouble. We really are here. Get used to it." Up until that point the American majority—if there is such a thing—fantasizes that the noise will just go away, that it's a trend. The way the play talks, and its complete lack of apology for that kind of fogginess, is something that would not have made sense before.

Savran: Unlike *Torch Song,* in which Arnold just wants to be normal, *Angels in America,* along with queer theory and politics, calls into question the category of the normal.

Kushner: Right.

Savran: This is what I mean by queering America: there is no such thing in this text as a natural sexuality.

Kushner: When I met you at TCG [Theatre Communications Group] and was so stupid about Eve Sedgwick's *Between Men,* you suggested I go back and look at it again. And I did. And then *Epistemology of the Closet* came out, and what she's saying is true for all oppressed groups in this country. This project of pushing the margin to the center is really the defining project, not just for her, but for bell hooks and Cornel West and so many feminist writers. Creating the fiction of the white, normal, straight male center has been the defining project of American history. I'm working on a play about slavery and reading eighteenth-century texts, and it has been the central preoccupation in American politics for the entire time during which this land has been trying to make itself into a country. The founding fathers weren't getting up and arguing about making homosexuality legal, but it's been an ongoing issue. And in this century, as you point out in your book, it's been an obsession during various times of crisis. It always seems to me to be the case that in the concerns of any group called a minority and called oppressed can be found the biggest problems and the central identity issues that the country is facing. Also, because of Brecht, when I was writing *Bright Room* and reading the history of the collapse of the Weimar Republic, I realized that the key is the solidarity of the oppressed for the oppressed—being able to see the connecting lines—which is one of the things that AIDS has done, because it's made disenfranchisement incredibly clear across color lines and gender lines.

Savran: Which is why the play also goes in a sense beyond the identity politics of the 1970s. Or rather it's interrogating identity politics and attempting to valorize coalition politics.

Kushner: I think that's a good way to put it. There's still a lot to be explored in identity politics, and for me one of the big questions in *Perestroika* is: what exactly does a community mean, and what kind of threat does somebody like Roy Cohn pose to the notion of identity politics?

Savran: One scene that I found very interesting in regard to that is the one in which Louis confronts Joe about his legal briefs and broaches the idea of lesbians and gays as a class.

Kushner: There's an amazing term in constitutional law: suspect class. It isn't a community of like-minded people with similar material interests, as in the working class, but rather a group that has been formed, to a certain degree, by hostility from without. From the point of view of the Constitution the forces that shape the group into a class are suspect, rather than the people in the class. I find that a fascinating idea. In America you can always talk about social justice but never economic justice. There is no such thing, supposedly, as economic class in this country. So there's a community that seems to be incredibly clear at times and then at other moments, depending on which way the light is striking, disappears completely.

Savran: You were talking before about Brecht and the importance of a materialist analysis. In your work, however, there's a much more indirect relationship between culture and the workings of capitalism.

Kushner: We're in a different time. And of course the clearer Brecht gets, the more trouble he gets into. The closer he is to Trotsky and the further away he is from Lenin, the better he is.

There's also a question in Brecht of historical agency and subjectivity: are we the subjects of history, or are we completely subject to history? do we make it, or are we made by it? That's not certainty. And with *Arturo Ui* it's a miracle that in the middle of it he could see it all happening so clearly. But finally it's unsatisfying because Hitler was in many cases supported by the proletariat, so something else was going on. And now we're in a period of such profound confusion, it's certainly impossible to be a Marxist now. It's almost impossible even to be a socialist.

Savran: Why do you think it's impossible to be a Marxist now?

Kushner: I don't want to start sounding like the more right-wing perestroikans from Russia, but I do think that we really have to ask questions about the notion of violent revolution as the locomotive of history. And that is in Marx. Of course being a Marxist is an odd idea to start with. Was Luxemburg a Marxist or a communist or a socialist, or was she a . . . Luxemburgan? And you read people like Luxemburg and Benjamin and the weirdos and rejects, and those are the people who speak now, even Trotsky in his exile days. Although there are things in Marx that are still of incalculable value.

Savran: It seems to me that it's useful to distinguish between Marxism as a political program and Marxism as a mode of analysis. Isn't the latter indispensable?

Kushner: Yes, if you mean dialectical materialism. I think that rigorous, classical dialectical materialism is probably of great value. But any method of analysis that becomes Jesuitical is problematic. And consider that some of the most powerful political movements of the twentieth century have been led by people who were not materialists. Martin Luther King was not a materialist. He was a Baptist minister. Liberation theology is in some ways a materialist interpretation of the Gospels, but in other ways it's founded on notions of sacrifice, for instance, that are profoundly lacking in Marx.

It's difficult to separate out the political Marx from the theoretical Marx. In the parts of *Capital* that I've read and in some of the early Marx, he talks about things that are not purely materialist forces. He actually uses words like "magic," "spirit," and "soul" in *The Economic and Philosophic Manuscripts.* So a Marxist Leninism that rejects the spiritual world is something we have to be very skeptical about. Take Yugoslavia. There must be a way of analyzing what's happening in the Balkans in a historical materialist fashion. But I also can't help but think—and maybe it's just because I'm sloppy—that there's something else going on. You start to think in a kind of new age-y way about energies in the world. Brecht did, and you can see that in his poetry. There's injustice everywhere and no rebellion. I think Adorno was really wrong: after Auschwitz we need poetry all the more, because you can't talk about these things except by recourse to forms of expression that are profoundly unscientific.

Savran: That really ties in with Benjamin and the conjunction between the political and religious, Marxism and Judaism. His politicization of messianic time as utopia is absolutely crucial to your project.

Kushner: And his sense of utopianism is also so profoundly apocalyptic: a teleology, but not a guarantee. Or a guarantee that utopia will be as fraught and as infected with history. It's not pie in the sky at all.

Savran: I keep thinking of that line from the *Angelus Novus:* "Where we perceive a chain of events, [the angel] sees one single catastrophe which keeps piling wreckage upon wreckage and hurls it in front of his feet." The scene in heaven in *Perestroika* really took my breath away, seeing the wreckage behind the scrim.

Kushner: And there's a whole scene that we didn't perform because it just didn't play: they're listening on an ancient radio to the first report of the disaster at Chernobyl. And these are very Benjaminian, Rilkean angels. I think that is also a very American trope. In *The American Religion* Harold Bloom keeps referring to this country as the evening land, where the promise of utopia is so impossibly remote that it brings one almost to grieving and despair. Seeing what heaven looks like from the depths of hell. It's the most excruciating pain, and even as one is murdering and rampaging and slashing and burning to achieve utopia, one is aware that the possibility of attaining utopia is being irreparably damaged. People in this country knew somewhere what they were doing, but as we moved into this century we began to develop a mechanism for repressing that knowledge. There's a sense of progress, but at tremendous cost. What will never be.

Savran: And it's Prior who carries the burden of that in *Angels.*

Kushner: Yes.

Savran: And of course embedded even in his name is the sense that he's out of step with time, both too soon and belated, connected to the past and future, to ancestors and what's to come.

Kushner: He's also connected to Walter Benjamin. I've written about my friend Kimberly [Flynn], who is a profound influence on me. And she and I were talking about this utopian thing that we share—she's the person who introduced me to that side of Walter Benjamin. The line that he wrote that's most important to her, and is so true, is, "Even the dead will not be safe if the enemy wins." She said jokingly that at times she felt such an extraordinary kinship with him that she thought she was Walter Benjamin reincarnated. And so at one point in the conversation, when I was coming up with names for my characters, I said, "I had to look up something in Benjamin—not you, but the prior Walter." That's where the name came from. I had been looking for one of those WASP names that nobody gets called anymore.

Savran: Despite all these utopian longings, at the center of both *Bright Room* and *Angels* are characters, Agnes and Louis, who are, in one way or another, liberals. I realize that *Angels* is not about Louis, but structurally he is at the center; he's the one who ties all the characters together. Not that his viewpoint is the prevailing one.

Kushner: Right.

Savran: So in both plays you've foregrounded well-intentioned liberals whose actions are at an extraordinary remove from their intentions. And of course we know from Brecht, among others, that ethics are always defined by action. Why did you put these characters at the center?

Kushner: I've never thought of Louis and Agnes as a pair, but they really are. I think they're very American. American radicalism has always been anarchic, as opposed to socialist. The socialist tradition in this country is so despised and has been blamed so much on immigrants. It's been constructed as a Jewish, alien thing, which is not the way socialism is perceived anywhere else in the world, where there is a native sense of *communitas* that we don't share. What we have is a native tradition of anarchism. And that's such a fraught, problematic tradition, because Ronald Reagan is as much the true heir as Abbie Hoffman. Abbie Hoffman was an anarcho-communist and Ronald Reagan is an ego-anarchist. But they're both anarchists. And anarchism is a tradition I have a lot of trouble with.

The strain in the American character that I feel the most affection for and that I feel has the most potential for growth is American liberalism, which is incredibly short of what it needs to be and incredibly limited and exclusionary and predicated on all sorts of racist, sexist, homophobic, and classist prerogatives. And yet, as Louis asks, why has democracy succeeded in America? And why does it have this potential, as I believe it does? I really believe that there is the potential for radical democracy in this country, one of the few places on earth where I see it as a strong possibility. It doesn't seem to be happening in Russia. There is a tradition of liberalism, of a kind of social justice, fair play, and tolerance, and each of these things is problematic and can certainly be played upon in the most horrid ways. Reagan kept the most hair-raising anarchist aspects of his agenda hidden and presented himself as a good old-fashioned liberal who kept invoking FDR. It may just be sentimentalism on my part, because I am the child of liberal-pinko parents, but I do believe in it—as much as I often find it despicable. It's sort of like the Democratic National Convention every four years: it's horrendous, and you can feel it sucking all the energy from progressive movements in this country, with everybody pinning their hopes on this sleazy bunch of guys. But you do have Jesse Jackson getting up and calling the Virgin Mary a single mother. And on an emotional level, and I hope also on a more practical level, I do believe that these are the people in whom to have hope. I mean, I don't want to get paternalistic about it either. And Agnes is, as her name says, an egg. She is unformed, while Louis is a much more . . . the characters are very different. But I feel that these are the people whom the left either can hook onto and mobilize, or not.

I feel that in Germany in the late twenties, these were the group of people who came out and voted communist in that one election before Hindenburg blew it for everybody. Their genuine good nature, their fear, lack of insight, and weakness were played upon, and the left did not find a way to speak to them. Louis is a gay version of that, whom ACT UP could have enrolled and then radicalized. And I do feel that ACT UP did that. Now we'll see how lasting it is.

Savran: Although none of the characters is involved with mass movement politics.

Kushner: But the play is set—and I think this is very important—when there's no such thing in the United States for generally progressive people. For someone like Belize, there isn't anything. The Rainbow Coalition has started to waffle and fall apart. And there is nothing in the gay community. There's the Gay Pride parade, and GMHC [Gay Men's Health Crisis], and going up every year and getting humiliated at the city council in Newark. Nineteen eighty-four through 1985 was a horrible, horrible time. It really seemed like the maniacs had won for good. What Martin says in *Millennium* now seems like a joke that we can all snigger at, but at the time I just wrote what I thought was most accurate. The Republicans had lost the Senate but would eventually get that back because the South would go Republican. There would never be a Democratic president again because Mondale was the best answer we could make to Ronald Reagan, the most popular president we've ever had. So none of these people had anything they could hook into, which is the history of the left. When the moment comes, when the break happens and history can be made, do we step in and make it, or do we flubber and fail? As much as I am horrified by what Clinton does—and we could have had someone better—we didn't completely blow it this time.

Savran: I'm interested in father-son relationships in the play, the way that Roy is set up as the son of a bad father, Joseph McCarthy, and how he in turn is a bad father to Joe. And the scene between Roy and Joe is juxtaposed against the S&M scene between Louis and the Man in the Park. But isn't that S&M dynamic really crucial for mapping so many of the relationships in the play? Both Louis and Harper seem amazingly masochistic in very different ways.

Kushner: I hope that the two scenes speak to each other in the right balance. I don't know it you've read Dale Peck's book *Martin and John.* It's extraordinary. He's one of the few gay writers I've read who really deals with the issue of the father in gay life, as opposed to the mother. A lot of what he does is to play variations on father-son relationships, the father as a sexualized identity. There are things that I wanted to tackle with that, though. I want to explore S&M more because I feel that it's an enormously pervasive dynamic, that it's inextricably wound up with issues of patriarchy, and that there are ways in which it plays through every aspect of life. I think it's something that needs to be understood, thought about, and spoken about more openly.

Savran: I agree, that's why I've been writing about the relationship between masculinity and masochism in our culture.

Kushner: We subjects of capitalist societies have to talk about the ways in which we are constructed to eroticize and cathect pain, as well as the way pain is transformed into pleasure, and self-destruction into self-creation. What price must we finally pay for that? I'm glad you're writing about it. Until now there's been a kind of dumb liberation politics: all forms of sexual practice are off-limits for analysis and GSMA [Gay S/M Alliance] is fine; we just leave it in the bedroom. But of course it's not just the kind of S&M that's acted out that needs to concern us. I think that sexuality should still be subject to analysis, including the question of why we're gay instead of straight, which I think has nothing to do with the hypothalmus or interstitial brain cells, but has to do with trauma.

Savran: But isn't all sexuality rooted in trauma?

Kushner: We're just good Freudians. Yes, it's all trauma and loss, and the question is, are there specific forms of trauma? I believe that there is an etiology of sexuality that's traceable if anybody wants to spend the money on an analyst. Oedipus is still legitimate grounds for exploration and inquiry. And I think that the notion of the cultural formation of personalities is of tremendous importance. In another sense I really feel that it was incredibly important that Roy's generation of gay men have that kind of deeply patriarchal, gender-enforced notion of the seduction of youth, the ephebe and the elder man. Unbelievably, we still see that popping up in the plays of certain people whose names I won't mention. All the older gay man wants is the younger gay man. That comes down from the Greeks, homosexuality being a form of tutelage, of transmission, of dominance and submission. It felt to me that that would absolutely be part of Roy's repressed, ardent desire for Joe. And then what you see replicated in the blessing scene is a form of love that has to flow through inherited structures of hierarchical power.

These are some of the oldest questions with which we've been torturing ourselves. What is the relationship between sexuality and power? And is sexuality merely an expression of power? And is there even such a thing as a sexuality? Do we all want to end up like John Stoltenberg, married to Andrea Dworkin? Is male sexuality always aggressive? What do we make of the phallus? And then what's to be made of notions like the lesbian phallus? And how do we escape it? Any inquiry into that speaks to the larger questions, which for me are really the most exciting, interesting, and difficult ones. If we buy into the notion of the construction of these forms of behavior, and the construction of personalities that engage in these behaviors, do we believe in the deconstruction of these forms? What is that deconstruction? There's the issue of reforming the personality to become a socialist subject, starting with the trash that capitalism has made of us. And people who are formed in the image of the individual ego, how do we remake that ego in a way that isn't itself masochistic? Is there a form of unmaking that isn't destructive?

This is why I'm so fascinated by Brecht's *lehrstück* plays, the *Baden-Badan* play. By what process, that isn't submission, does the individual ego become part of a collective? All that Brecht can arrive at is death and submission. It's that very experimental form he was working in before he had to leave Germany and decided to become Brecht the genius writer of canonical literature instead. A pilot and a group of mechanics are flying, and their plane crashes in the desert, and they're perched between life and death. They ask a chorus of learned Marxist Leninists—who are the audience—should they live or should they die? And there is a series of illustrations asking, does man help his fellow man? And the mechanics, who represent the working class, consent to being part of the necessity of history and live because of their consent. That is, they die and are reborn. But the pilot, who is an individual, is destroyed. He's dismantled. He refuses to die, and so they have to kill him over and over again. The repetition is kind of creepy Stalinist, but what he's getting at is the absolute refusal, the marvelousness of the individual ego, and the pain and torment with which we imagine taking it apart. Is there a process other than revolution, other than bloodshed, agony, and pain—which is fundamentally masochistic—by which we can transform ourselves into socialist subjects? That's a big question, and it turns you toward things like Zen.

Savran: That's the question of the play: what is there beyond pain? Is utopia even imaginable?

Kushner: And the loss. It's the thing that I don't understand at all, which I think is undertheorized and underrepresented in the problematics of the left. If our lives are in fact shaped by trauma and loss—and as I get older it seems to me that life is very, very profoundly shaped by loss and death—how do you address that? And how does one progress in the face of that? That's the question that the AIDS epidemic has asked. Because there is nothing more optimistic than America, in the most awful way—like Up with People! It makes so many people queasy, and it's the subject of so much sarcasm because it seems so dumb. But identity is shaped, even racial identity. If there weren't bigots, there wouldn't be a politics of race. That there has to be a politics of difference speaks to the presence of enormous oppression and violence and terror. What do we do? It's an interesting thing, because the more we know about history, the more we realize—and this is an important thing about sadomasochism—that it really does return, it never ends. You can just see in our present moment a thousand future Sarajevos. You just know that when you're ninety, if you live so long, they'll still be fighting. Even after the holocaust the monsters are still among us. And can you forgive? That's why I ask this question of forgiveness, because its possibility is also, I think, undertheorized and underexpressed.

Savran: Relating to the question of forgiveness, why do you use Mormons in the play, along with Jews? Because the angels are so clearly Old

Testament angels, angels of the vengeful God. How does that tie in with the Mormon religion?

Kushner: There are interesting similarities between Mormonism and Judaism. They both have a very elusive notion of damnation. It's always been unclear to me, as a Jew, what happens if you don't do good things. Presumably you don't go to paradise. There is a hell, but even among the Orthodox there isn't an enormous body of literature about it—it's not like Catholicism. Mormonism has a hell, but it has three layers of heaven, four actually, that I know of. Also Mormonism is a diasporic religion. And as far as I'm concerned, the most interesting thing about Judaism is the whole diasporic, secular culture.

Mormonism is of the book. It draws its strength very much from the literal, physical volume, which isn't sacred like the Torah, but it's all about the discovery of a book. They say that Joseph Smith had a Hebrew teacher who was a rabbi. Also, Judaism, like Mormonism, is not a religion about redemption based on being sorry for what you've done and asking for forgiveness. The hallmark of Mormonism is, "By deeds ye shall be known." As you said, ethics are defined by action. And that is also true in Judaism. Your intentions make very little difference to God. What counts is what you do and whether you're righteous in your life. That appeals to me. It also feels very American. I wanted to have an orthodox religion that someone was having a lot of trouble with, but I didn't want Orthodox Judaism. And I wanted something American.

I started the play with an image of an angel crashing through a bedroom ceiling, and I knew that this play would have a connection to American themes. So the title, *Angels in America,* came from that. And I think the title, as much as anything else, suggested Mormons, because the prototypical American angel is the angel Moroni. It's of this continent, the place that Jesus visited after he was crucified. It's like Blake and the New Jerusalem. Christ was here, and this continent does have some tendrils snaking back into biblical mythology. It's a great story—not the Book of Mormon, which, as Mark Twain said, is chloroform in print—but the story of Joseph Smith's life and the trek, the gathering of Zion. That's so American. The idea of inventing a complete cosmology out of a personal vision is something I can't imagine a European doing. I guess Swedenborg and Blake sort of did that, but it didn't become this theocratic empire. And unlike Swedenborg, which is rather elegant and beautiful, and Blake, which is extraordinarily beautiful but mostly incomprehensible, it's so dumb. It's so naive and disingenuous. It's like Grandma Moses, the celestial and the terrestrial heavens, with all this masonry incorporated into it. It's so American gothic. I wanted Mormons in this play. I find their immense industry, diligence, and faith moving. The symbol of Utah and of the Mormon kingdom of God is a beehive, which is, in its own way, a socialist, communist image. And there were a lot of experiments in Utah of communally owned property, which is what Joseph Smith originally dictated, with wealth held in common and experiments with controlled economies. Their social experiments were independent of, but similar to, European socialist, communal notions of the nineteenth century.

Now they're so right-wing and horrible. Although the Mormons I've met I've actually sort of liked. I've found something dear and nice about them—they have good strong families, with all the horror that that implies. But I think, as with Judaism, there's not an enormously high incidence of grotesque abuses of patriarchal power, incest or wife beating, for example. So they come out as nice people with centers, while most conservatives are so horrendous. When I was working on Joe, I wanted to write a conservative man that I actually liked. I didn't finally succeed [*laughs*]. Although I feel that he gets somewhere and will ultimately be redeemable, in *Angels,* part three.

Along with bits and pieces of Mormonism, I used the cabala for the angels. They're mostly from Holy Scripture and the cabala, except in their method of delivering the epistle—purely Mormon. The idea of a man who gets a set of spectacles from an angel—only in America. *The Fly* as theology.

Savran: And you're working with Robert Altman now?

Kushner: Yes, to turn *Angels* into an Altman movie.

Savran: You're writing the screenplay.

Kushner: Yes.

Savran: After seeing *Short Cuts,* I realized why.

Kushner: Nashville had a profound impact on me, the extraordinary interweaving of stories. I wanted somebody whom I respected and whom I knew would make it very unlike the stage play. And I'm completely confident of that [*laughs*]. He allows a certain kind of messiness to be a part of his aesthetic, which appeals to me a lot. He's the first filmmaker, years before Woody Allen, to go for that hand-held camera, documentary look. When I first approached him about it, I hoped that he might be interested in doing it for television, but he felt that was chicken shit [*laughs*]. And I'm sure he's the only person in Hollywood who said immediately that we have to do two films.

I hope that I can get him to deal with the difficult question of gay sexuality. He hasn't always been great about that. But I can't believe that he'd want to do this without being aware that there are going to be men naked in bed together or in the park. I really want him not to get silly about that, because I'll just die if this is another one of those films with two men lying in bed with the bedsheet pulled up against their pecs. I think it will be very important, given the way that he improvises, that he has some gay actors in the cast. I don't want to see a lot of straight people trying to figure out what it's like.

Savran: And you're working on another play?

Kushner: I haven't completely committed myself to what the next big one is going to be. But I have two that are cooking. One is about Vermeer. It's sort of a history of capitalism. And the other is a play about a slave named Henry Box Brown, who mailed himself out of slavery in a box to Philadelphia. Then I discovered in a fluke that Henry Box Brown wound up in England and toured English textile towns trying to get them to boycott southern cotton before the war. When I was working on *Millennium* at the National Theatre, I went to one of the towns, and I've just unearthed this whole treasure chest of amazing characters from the industrial revolution.

It's the international character of capital, that slavery was made profitable because the British imported eight hundred million tons of cotton a year for the biggest textile mills in the world. When the blockade was set up, the textile towns were hit with a famine, the likes of which Britain had never seen before. It was total economic devastation because of the American Civil War. A great evil does not exist in the world independent of support.

When I visited the town, I went to research the man who had owned the biggest textile mill in all of England. He was also a liberal in Parliament and passed the first labor laws in Britain. And he had a whole family of what sound like great bleeding-heart liberals that made millions of pounds off of cotton. One of them even married a mill girl. So she's shown all over the town standing on ears of corn, and he built her a castle on a hill, which is now in ruins. And I found my way into the castle, and in the central hall are roundels over each door in which are bas-relief depictions of cotton being grown in America—horrendous scenes of white men whipping black people and black people in chains, all in the most damning detail. And his wife became an outrageous alcoholic, embarrassed him for years, and finally drank herself to death. That great little tragedy has also been mixed into the play. And George [Wolfe] is going to direct it both here and at the National, probably with British white actors and African American actors.

Savran: So you remain committed to writing history plays.

Kushner: I'm a little nervous about it, because I think that *Angels* is my best play because I started writing about my world. But there's a kind of safety in writing a history play—you can make up everything. And it insulates you to a certain extent from the assault of everyday life. But I've also decided to write more *Angels in America* plays, and those may be the only ones in which I deal with contemporary reality.

When I was writing *Perestroika* this summer, I got very, very angry at the characters. At first I thought it was because I was sick of them, but now I've come to realize that I hated the idea of not being able to work on them anymore. I want to know what happens to them. I already have most of the plot of part three in my head. It won't be continuous, but I could have a cycle of nine or ten plays by the time I'm done. The characters will get older as I got older. I'll be bringing in new ones and letting characters like Roy go. So I'm excited about that. I think it's harder to write that kind of play than a history play.

Savran: Although I think of *Angels in America* as a history play.

Kushner: In a sense it is. Although when I started writing it, it wasn't. But it receded into the past. As it gets older, it will become increasingly about a period of history. There is a danger for me of writing too much out of books, because I'm sort of socially awkward and not much of an adventurer. I don't want to write only about the past. Brecht never wrote anything about his contemporaries. Did he?

Savran: Arturo Ui.

Kushner: Except it's set in Chicago, and they're speaking in a very different way.

Savran: What about the learning plays?

Kushner: But again they're drowned in pseudo-Confucian poetry and set in China and other places.

Savran: But in all of his work he was historicizing his particular moment.

Kushner: Exactly. That's all you can ever do.

KAREN MALPEDE
Richard E. Kramer

Karen Malpede (photo © Sandra-Lee Phipps)

Though often drawing on ancient myths or mythologized historical events, Karen Malpede's plays always focus on the plight of ordinary people and the nobility of the human spirit—or at least the potential for nobility. She is committed to social action and political protest, but her work encompasses the poetic language and rhythms of the Greeks, the theatricality of the Living Theatre and Open Theater, and the philosophy of Bertolt Brecht. Her plays reflect a search for an aesthetic she calls "compassion and hope," which led her to compile a collection of the writings of theatre women in *Women in Theatre: Compassion & Hope* (1983). Malpede, whom Judith Malina of the Living Theatre called "one of the most consistently coherent of contemporary women playwrights," is unapologetic about calling her work "feminist," and insofar as it concentrates on women characters, it is. But at their base her plays are about all of us who, at one time or another, for one reason or another, find ourselves on the outside facing the forces of a power elite.

To Malpede art is a powerful force itself. In a letter published as the preface to her first book, *People's Theatre in Amerika* (1972), she wrote, "POLITICS ARE NO LONGER SEPARATE FROM ESTHETICS. They do not seem any longer to be two separate things." In fact for her they are not separate. In a February 1992 interview Malpede declared, "I believe that the theatre is a political, moral, spiritual voice for our time . . . ," and she challenges her audience with both her themes and her theatricality. This can confuse and frighten some segments of her audience, and mainstream critics have been frequently unkind to her plays, accusing her of being anti-theatrical, of making the audience "study, rationalize, deduce and define," of putting too many ideas and themes into her work, of wordiness and pretentiousness. In contrast others have appreciated her "fluid and sophisticated weave of drama, movement and music," her "strong and resonant" language, and her "absorbing and unusual" vision. Malpede describes her own work as "plays with lots of ideas, lots of words, lots of characters—many-layered images—but also very theatrical plays."

If theatre is a political force for Malpede, it is also a catalyst for enlightenment. "I think theatre can surprise people . . . ," she has said. "It surprises you into your own depth of feeling—that through image and word and power and beauty of the stage event, you, yourself, are changed. The audience is opened—literally opened—opened to their own deeper selves. The theatre is, therefore, a transformative event." Malpede picked up this notion from her observation of the Open Theater, the subject of her second book, *Three Works by the Open Theater* (1974), and the Living Theatre. She subsequently put it into practice at the New Cycle Theater, a politically oriented company founded with Burl Hash in Brooklyn in 1976 and dedicated to making "the poetry of dialogue, characters, and deep psychological exchanges . . . part of the theatre again."

Poetry and theatricality are the two common components of Malpede's dramaturgy, which she devotes to a condemnation of violence and alienation and a pursuit of "intimacy, trust, and tenderness." Her past plays are *A Lament for Three Women* (1974), *Rebeccah* (1976), *The End of War* (1977), *Making Peace: A Fantasy* (1979), *A Monster Has Stolen the Sun* (1981), *Sappho and Aphrodite* (1983), *Us* (1988, directed by Judith Malina), *Better People* (1990), and *Blue Heaven* (1992). Her recent works include *Kassandra*, a stage adaptation of Christa Wolf's novel, which debuted in 1993 at New York University under the direction of renowned Greek actress Lydia Koniordou, and *The Beekeeper's Daughter*, which had its world premiere at the 1994 Dionysia World Festival of Contemporary Drama in Veroli, Italy, with Malpede directing. Malpede also contributed texts for *Collateral Damage: The Private Life of the New World Order (Meditations on the Wars)*, a Gulf War protest collage in June 1991, assembled by Leonardo Shapiro, artistic director of The Shaliko Company, and *Roadkill,* a street event conceived by Shapiro for the finale of Theater for the New City's First Annual Eco-Festival in May 1992. In March 1992, WBAI Radio in New York City broadcast an early version of her play *Blue Heaven,* then called *Going to Iraq,* which subsequently premiered at Theater for the New City in September and October. *Blue Heaven* was originally planned as a coproduction with Shaliko under Shapiro's direction, but Malpede and Shapiro developed serious differences near the end of the rehearsal period, and he withdrew as director but remained credited for his production design. (At the time of this interview, in August 1992, Malpede expressed great respect for Shapiro as an artist, but she has since declared that she no longer holds her former high opinion of him. She later restored the play's title to *Going to Iraq.*)

In her 1989 biography included in *Contemporary Authors,* Malpede lists her politics as "Anarchist" and her religion as "Nonviolence," both underlying precepts of her art. Her father was Italian American and her mother Jewish, an ethnic conflict that also figures in her work. Malpede's father was a passionate man, but he was also abusive and neglectful until he died of cancer at forty-two; domestic violence and such losses as those she and her family experienced appear in her plays. She is the twin sister of performance artist John Malpede and includes in her plays many images of paired opposites (living–dying, birth–death, dreams–deeds, vulnerability–strength, freedom–oppression, tenderness–violence, peace–war); she is also the mother of Carrie Sophia Malpede-Hash, whose birth in 1980 has been an important influence in her work. It would be correct to deduce from this that Malpede's art is not only political but remarkably personal as well. But then, "politics is personal" is a feminist tenet.

Karen Malpede was born in Texas and grew up in Illinois. She has a bachelor of science with honors from the University of Wisconsin, Madison, and a master of fine arts in theatre history and criticism from Columbia University. Featured in *Interviews with Contemporary Women Playwrights* (1987), she is the recipient of the 1994–95 National McKnight Playwright Fellowship. Malpede has taught at Norwich University, Smith College, and John Jay College of the City University of New York and is currently an assistant professor in the department of undergraduate drama in New York University's Tisch School of the Arts. Her play *Us* was published in *Women on the Verge: Seven Avant-Garde Plays* (1994), edited by Rosette Lamont for Applause Books, and

The Beekeeper's Daughter was produced in New York in January 1995 by the Florence Mission Project, which Malpede has recently launched with actress-choreographer Lee Nagrin and actor-producer George Bartenieff, cofounder and former codirector of Theater for the New City.

Kramer: Your degree from Columbia University is in theatre history and criticism, and you started out to be a critic.

Malpede: I didn't actually start out to do that, but that's how it turned out. I had always known that I was going to be a writer from the time I was ten years old. But, then, what to write became progressively narrowed as I became more educated—in traditional education—as I came to believe that women didn't write plays, you see, because I had never read a play by a woman. The first thing I wanted to write was novels because that's what I read. But something happened to me as I became more and more educated: I lost faith in my own voice. So I kept narrowing down what it was that I was going to write, and it ended up finally being theatre criticism.

On the other hand, I've always been glad that I didn't study playwriting and that I did study plays—that my education was based on reading plays and reading a lot of them very, very closely. It ultimately became more interesting to me to study Shakespeare with Bernard Beckerman at Columbia than to study playwriting with Jack Gelber and Arthur Kopit, not only because Shakespeare is a more interesting playwright to study, but also because of the attitude toward women students and women playwrights that was around at that time—and much more around at that time, although it still is quite pervasive now—which is this sort of unspoken—or spoken—assumption that women can't write plays, or, if they do, their plays aren't as good—they aren't real plays.

Kramer: But you did start out as a writer about theatre. How did you come to writing plays?

Malpede: I came to writing plays because I noticed that the plays that I wanted to see weren't being written. So, I spent some time trying to convince other people to write them. Quite specifically, the end of the Open Theater was the time that I wrote my first play, *Lament for Three Women,* in 1974. At that time, Joe Chaikin had invited a group of us to sit around and talk about what the theatre should be like, and what kind of work we thought should be done, and what kind of work we were doing. And the more that I listened to everybody, and the more that I talked to myself, the more that it became clear to me that in order to have happen what I wanted to have happen in the theatre, I would have to write those plays. In other words, I knew what I wanted to do, and no one else could logically be expected to do it. That's not the critic's position. The critic's position—the literary critic, I'm not talking about reviewers—is that someone else is doing it to your satisfaction and you want to comment on it, and elucidate it, and illuminate it, and leave a record of it, and dialogue with it. Suddenly I wasn't in that position anymore. Nobody else was doing what I thought should be done, and it dawned on me that I would have to do it.

So, Jean-Claude van Itallie said, after I gave a rather long talk about how I thought plays should be, "It's easier to talk about it than to do it"—which is certainly true—and suddenly I was forced back to what had been my original project all along, which was writing fiction. And that was able to happen because of a couple of things. One was that the woman's movement had started, and there was suddenly a woman's community that had formed to support women's work. The other thing that I think happened was that I had also stopped writing fiction when my father died when I was eighteen. It was a very complex situation, and there was really nobody to discuss it with. There was no way to work it through, so I think I simply shut down the part of my feelings that is used to create fiction for those years. I think *Lament* and *Us* deal with a character like my father or the situation like the situation I was in with my father, although both of them are fictionalized. And again, what I think allowed those feelings to be dealt with and processed was the woman's movement.

With me, and I guess with art in general, there's what you know and what you don't know. What I knew consciously was that I had all these ideas about how plays should be, and I didn't see them anywhere. What I didn't know was that I had, in fact, stopped writing fiction—when I went to college and when my father died, which happened at the same time. I didn't know how to process the complex web of feelings around that death, and the more that I read male literature and the more that I studied male literature. . . . When I went to college, I had only one female teacher, who was the graduate assistant teaching the writer's workshop for freshmen, and otherwise I didn't see a female face. In graduate school I had one woman teacher as well, and nobody taught women's plays. The assumption was—and during those years Kate Millet wrote *Sexual Politics,* which is not about women's writing, it's about men's writing—you were not experienced with women's writing. That doesn't mean women didn't write. Women have always written. Women have always written plays, as I came to find out much later when I started looking for women's plays. But it does have an effect on women writers that they have very few models. That's why a lot of the work of women who came out of the feminist movement who stayed in teaching has been to put women's work into the curriculum. I find today when I'm teaching at NYU—I teach a course on women in theatre—that none of the women in the class—a few men were in the class, too—had read any of the plays. And they were all knocked out at the beauty and magnificence of these plays and totally inspired in their own work and inspired to go look for women's plays and do women's plays.

Kramer: Who were some of the writers in the course who have been discovered?

Malpede: Well, Gertrude Stein, Marguerite Duras, Susan Glaspell. Then they go up to the newer writers. Gertrude Stein's plays are not in print, so even though most educated people know who Gertrude Stein is, most educated people haven't read her plays. You might know who Susan Glaspell was, or you might have read *Trifles,* but you haven't read *The Verge,* which is her best play and which is out of print in this country. People know Caryl Churchill; they know the obvious American playwrights, but they don't know the less obvious, even to the point of Adrienne Kennedy, or Ntozake Shange, not *for colored girls* but some of her other work. Or Aishah Rahman. Or even Alice Childress—*The Wedding Band.* Or Augusta Gregory.

Kramer: In the introduction to your first book, *People's Theatre in Amerika,* you said, "Politics are no longer separate from esthetics. They do not seem any longer to be two separate things." How is it for you that politics and art are so inextricably connected?

Malpede: In many ways I'm an extremely unpolitical person, in the ways that the word *politics* is usually used—and I probably wouldn't use that word any longer. What I still do believe is that the worldview of the playwright comes through in the plays that the playwright writes. This is true of Neil Simon, and it's true of Mac Wellman, and it's true of me. A worldview has a lot to do with how people relate to one another— how people could relate to one another; how people do relate to one another; how people should relate to one another; how people might relate to one another; how people want to relate to one another, but can't; how people think they're relating to one another, but aren't.

To me, what's interesting when I write a play are those relationships and also the relationship with self, because how you relate to yourself has a lot to do with how you relate to other people, and how characters relate to themselves—how much they know about themselves, and how much time they spend wondering about themselves—has to do with how much they know about other people and how much time they spend wondering about other people. Every play in that sense is political, since the worldview of the playwright takes place in the social-relational world. So, Wendy Wasserstein is as political a playwright as I am. Her politics are different, or shall I say her worldview is different—her concerns are different, her sense of what's possible is different, even where she casts her eye to look at what's interesting is different—but it's every bit as political as mine.

I think that there's a set of politics implicit in *The Heidi Chronicles,* for instance—a set of feelings and a sense of how the world is that asks certain questions and doesn't ask others. For instance, if you were to go out and adopt a child tomorrow, there's a whole set of interesting questions—moral, ethical questions—that arise. Where does that child come from? Whose child was that to begin with? Why is the person who's giving up that child giving up that child? Where do you have to go to get the child? Do you have to leave the country, or do you not leave the country? Do you pay money, or do you not pay money? Whom do you pay money to? What kind of life are you going to provide for the child? Why is it better for the child to be adopted by you than to stay with its birth mother? I'm bringing this up because this is how *Heidi Chronicles* ends—the woman adopts a child—but none of this is ever addressed. The audience doesn't know where the child came from at all. It makes a sociopolitical statement that it doesn't matter where you get the child. If you want a child, you go out and get one. It doesn't matter what kind of life the birth mother of the child had because you want the child. That seems to me to be a very concrete statement about how the world ought to operate, which goes along with capitalism essentially: if you have the money and you want a thing, you go out and get it. Other questions are not interesting. Kathy Tolan wrote a play called *Approximating Mother,* about a woman who adopted a child. She had a different sociopolitical-moral interest in the question from [that of] Wendy Wasserstein, so she double-plotted it so you saw the life of the birth mother and you saw the life of the woman who adopted the child.

Kramer: The matter of how much you know about yourself and learning about yourself is in all your plays. *Sappho and Aphrodite* is all about discovering yourself. In *A Monster Has Stolen the Sun,* the one who most significantly learns about himself is Conor, the young boy, who actually makes a flip-flop.

Malpede: As a playwright, I am very interested in this inner journey for the characters. Whatever the shapes it takes, people tend to change in my plays. I think that they change perhaps in the way that Conor changes, which is that they become more what they were really anyway. Conor's dilemma is that he wants the love of his father, which I think is something that we all want. Certainly men have this dilemma. Then he's literally turned into a hunter by his father. That scene is also the link between Conor's relationship to nature and his relationship to women because he wasn't a killer of birds; he was a very innocent and lovely young man, and then he gets turned into a killer of birds and becomes a conqueror of women. Then he comes back to himself.

I think another person who really changes in the play is Owain, Conor's father. In the cave scene, assisted by the young Etain, Owain suddenly contacts his own grief, and at the moment he contacts his own grief [over the death of his wife, Queen Etain], he contacts his own love for his son. Then in the fight, he puts down his weapons; he disarms in front of his son, who's come to kill him. His son's murderous rage at the father who has never loved him in the way that a child has to be loved disappears.

Kramer: Conor was going to live out that traditional scenario in which the prince kills the king and becomes the king, and his son will ultimately overthrow him in one way or another.

Malpede: That's right. But the prince can only kill the king and become the king if the king continues to be the king. What Owain does is de-king himself and become the father. Owain, in the second scene of the play, is transformed by Brigit into a father, but it's in a dream, and he wakes from the dream. It's very startling in production, because the actor actually gives birth, so it's hard to forget. But it's also a scene that's out of time. In other words, it's not yet Owain's time to be able to become the father that he does at the end of the play sixteen years later, by which I mean the nurturing, caring man. Internally, he can't yet work the change, so he snaps back into being the sort of macho king. But there's that hint at the beginning that it's there, waiting to be released, waiting to be fulfilled, waiting to be found.

Kramer: You wrote in a 1985 essay about your conflicted ethnic background, and you said that coming from "two despised peoples," meaning Italians and Jews, you really belonged to no group. You have dealt with that kind of inner dichotomy in at least two plays: *Us* and *Blue Heaven,* where Aria is an Israeli and a Palestinian at the same time. Palestinians and Jews have for generations been peoples who have warred against one another, and here in this one character is a person who is both at the same time. Is that a way of dramatizing the problem of living nonviolently in a world made up of differences?

Malpede: Yes, sure. Everywhere right now we hear a lot about ethnicity and multiculturalism and diversity. What has happened because of diversity and waves of successive immigration is that many of us are, indeed, half or less of different peoples. I happen to be half Italian and half Jewish; my daughter happens to be a quarter Italian, a quarter Eastern European Jewish and half French Huguenot, and on and on. In effect we don't belong to any one group either by how we grew up, because often what happens is that parents who make this kind of match leave their ethnic group and live somewhere else. I didn't grow up with Jews or Italians, I grew up in the Midwest with Protestants—Anglo-Saxons.

But to get back to Aria: the reason that I did that was that it's so easy to blame someone else for every problem, and it seemed to me that that was exactly what was going on with the war in the Persian Gulf. A lot of the people followed the government and decided that, not only was Saddam Hussein Hitler or the devil, but that the Iraqis are not to be considered as human beings and therefore all right to kill. It seemed to me that it's much harder to do that if you hold the warring factions inside yourself, which is Aria's dilemma. She can't hate the Israelis or the Palestinians because she is half Israeli and half Palestinian, and she has to work it out somehow. This seemed to me a much more interesting dilemma than to decide that all people who were not me are bad—or that specific different people are bad.

Kramer: Whereas Sada takes the more traditional view; not having that conflict, she has no problem getting behind the war.

Malpede: Sada's also a contradiction, actually, as all the characters in the play are. I think what's interesting about people are their contradictions, not their seamless oneness. Again, it's what they don't know about themselves and what they do know about themselves that gets in the way or affects their actions. Sada's a big contradiction because Sada is the one who feeds everyone, and Sada is the one who feeds *on* everyone. Her view of herself is that she is probably one of the best people in the world. The reality is that she is a kind of nurturing vampire.

Sada is also trapped in a historical set of circumstances that give her her emotions. She's trapped in two ways. She is not herself a Holocaust survivor, but she has a very strong memory of the Holocaust. She's an Eastern European Jew whose family was split, and her sister [Aria's mother] ended up in Israel and she ended up here. So she has strong fears. And she's also trapped in a past incest life that she hasn't dealt with. That's why she projects onto [Aria's daughter] Sierra. But Sada's emotional life in the present is determined by what happened in the past, which she has not dealt with.

Kramer: This is the "knowing yourself" question, and she doesn't. She essentially refuses to; she's shut it down.

Malpede: Yes, she's shut it down because it's too painful and it's also temperamentally easier for her to manipulate other people than to look inside herself. That's why she also never moves in the play, except one time, and she gets fatter and fatter.

Kramer: What brought you to *Blue Heaven?* Can you connect the dots for me?

Malpede: The same thing brings me to every play, which is some kind of emotional connection to the material, some kind of passion. With *Better People,* it was a passionate concern about Mary Beth Whitehead, about surrogate motherhood. I was very involved in the feminist defense of Mary Beth Whitehead, and people kept saying to me, "Why don't you write a play about it?" And I kept on saying, "I don't really write single-issue plays," which I don't—my plays are layered. That's why in eighteen years I've written only nine plays; it's a play every two years. It takes me a long time to write a play because they're complex plays. I think it does take time to put everything together in what is a very condensed form: a play.

But *Better People* didn't just come out of the Mary Beth Whitehead case, it came out of a passionate feeling that the reproductive rights of women were under attack, and not only by the prolife people, as they call themselves, but also by the reproductive technology people. That in turn led to a larger concern with Western science as a way of looking at the world—with mechanistic science, of which genetic engineering is the latest manifestation. Nuclear power was a slightly earlier manifestation. We all know now that nuclear power is maybe not such a good idea, and how you put the genie back in the bottle is one of the problems. Well, genetic engineering is right at the point where it's being released from the bottle. My guess is that in twenty or thirty years we will be faced with the same problem of how we contain this thing that we've unleashed that has done so much damage. Right now it hasn't quite yet been unleashed, but it's been deregulated, and everybody's going ahead with it. So, from a very specific connection with a very specific woman, Mary Beth Whitehead, and her dilemma, and a very specific issue, surrogate motherhood, *Better People* became a whole meditation on what's wrong with Western science. It also tried, as all my plays do, not just to expose what's wrong but to offer another vision of science—of how science might be practiced.

The same situation led me to *Blue Heaven,* which was two things. One was a very personal connection to the murder of [artist] Ana

Mendieta, which had to do with the plight of the woman artist in 1980/1990s New York City. I was working on that story in the fall of 1990 as the buildup to the war began, and then I felt a very real emotional connection of terrible grief and sorrow and rage and upset about the war in the Persian Gulf. So those two things led me to *Blue Heaven.*

For me, it was impossible not to write about that war, although while the war was going on, I put the play away. Now, it's as if that war never happened; it's been repressed—like all traumatic events. Just like a rape or an incest story that you can't deal with as a child, you forget that it ever happened. That's what the American people have done with that war, led by their leaders in both parties. Something that's ambiguous, something that's confusing, doesn't make good politics, but it makes great art. Ambiguity is the heart of art. So, the political leaders can't talk about the [Gulf] War because politics can't be ambiguous. It has to be absolutely one-dimensional. But art has to be ambiguous, and the fact that the same administration that fought that war is trying to defund the arts is no coincidence.

Kramer: Especially the arm of the arts that would deal with this and probably would deal with it critically.

Malpede: Well, I don't know of any such creature as a prowar play. There might be some jingoist plays, but there's a whole body of plays that most people would consider fine plays that are pretty much antiwar plays. I'm not talking about movies. Certainly modern plays when they deal with war tend to be antiwar plays because modern playwrights have tended to be horrified by modern war. It's the playwright's role to deal with what the society can't deal with. I don't know what it means to do a play about the Persian Gulf War now. It'll be interesting to find out.

Kramer: But *Blue Heaven's* not only about the Persian Gulf War; it's about this need to beat people up.

Malpede: Why do we do things, too, that we have to forget so fast? In that sense it's about trauma—about collective trauma. It's also, on the flip side, about art and community and people's ability to heal. Leo [Shapiro, founder of the Shaliko Company] is fond of saying that everybody in the play is a wounded healer, and I think that's true. One reason we changed the title [from *Going to Iraq*] was to address the deeper issues that the play is about, and not just to focus people's minds on a war that is too easy for them to dismiss. We wanted to make it more difficult to dismiss that war by opening up the field of vision and call the play *Blue Heaven.* It has to do with the song as the quintessential version of make-believe America.

What also led me to *Blue Heaven* is that, since *Us*, I have been writing plays with a particular actor in mind—George Bartenieff. One of the things I was dealing with in *Blue Heaven* was not only writing a part for George, which is the Herbie-Hermes part, but also dealing with the particular relationship in that play of a Hermes-like character who releases in Aria her own art and her own self. In other words, it's a particular relationship between a man and a woman, which in the play is not sexual, and it's not at all a relationship based on any kind of power dynamic. It's a relationship based on a kind of muse dynamic, where he sees in her things about her that she doesn't see or doesn't believe yet in herself, and his seeing allows her to be. That's something I think I dealt with in *Sappho and Aphrodite,* too, in a community of women where being seen by someone allowed you to become yourself.

Beyond that, I was very interested in creating in Aria a character who was torn in as many directions as I could tear her. So, she's Palestinian and Israeli; and that's not enough, so she's the mistress of a man who's married; and that's not enough, so the married man whose mistress she is actually kills his wife; and she's a wanderer, a homeless person, coming from nowhere with no place to call her own; she's a mother; she's an artist; she's a lover; she's blocked. In as many different ways as I could pull her apart, I wanted to pull her apart because I do feel that that's not only my situation often, but it is a woman's situation—that we are many, many things. And those many, many things are very complex. Unless you make a choice, as somebody like [author] Camille Paglia does, to live a celibate, solitary life and devote your entire energy to your intellectual production, you are likely, if you are a woman artist, to be torn in about fifty or sixty directions.

Kramer: Blue Heaven is your most nearly realistic play. It's also the closest to ordinary speech; your other plays, except *Better People*, are unequivocally poetry.

Malpede: Yes, my earlier plays are more clearly nonrealistic because they're set in myth. You know, I'm a Mediterranean person. It's only since I've had the opportunity to travel to Italy and recently to Greece that I realized that English is only my language because my grandparents and great-grandparents settled in this country. My emotional language is that of the Mediterranean—one that is an *emotional* language. English happens to be the language I write in; but it's not exactly the language of my self. So, I think what I've done with English is heighten it.

A lot of my plays, including *Blue Heaven,* have music in them. *Sappho and Aphrodite* was almost an opera—it was almost all song when we did it. These are plays that take place in an emotional terrain. They don't take place in the living room. Although, you're right, *Blue Heaven* takes place in a café, and it was somewhat intentional to set this play in what looks like a realistic setting.

Kramer: In various comments over the years you've characterized men, at least symbolically, as the embodiment of wrong-thinking. You have made the statement, for instance, that "The men who were the central figures in the [avant-garde] movement were either scared of the new insights [of feminists] and so blocked them out, or they continued to believe . . . that women's lives are of so little consequence that they could not possibly affect so august a form as the theater." Earlier, you made the same comment about the rejection of women writers—the assumption that they can't write or don't write real plays. At the same time, you've worked very, very closely with a number of men who have been very important to you: George Bartenieff, who's been in most of your recent plays [and is now a partner in the Florence Mission Project]; Leonardo Shapiro, for whom you have considerable respect as an artist; Burl Hash, with whom you cofounded the New Cycle Theater; Ned Ryerson, who supported your early work; and, of course, Joe Chaikin and Julian Beck, who were early inspirers of your principles.

Malpede: What you're saying is that I have been a harsh critic of patriarchy, which is true, but I have worked with, admired, and loved individual men. There's a difference between a social system and individual people within the social system.

Kramer: An awful lot of the male characters in your plays are representative of this patriarchy.

Malpede: An awful lot of men in the world are representative of the patriarchy.

Kramer: But then there are some, you say, who don't buy into the system.

Malpede: And there are some in my plays who don't buy into the system.

Kramer: As there apparently are women who essentially buy into a patriarchy for whatever reason.

Malpede: Sure. The New Cycle Theater was probably the only theatre that called itself a feminist theatre that was not separatist. On the other hand, I've done many projects just with women. I have actually a twin brother, and it's quite in me from the womb on—womb to tomb—that I would have intimate relationships with men as I spent my first nine months wrapped around this twin. My experience in the world is that there's a great deal of violence which is perpetrated by men against the rest of us—meaning women, children, animals, and other men—much of which has become institutionalized. Shakespeare's plays are virtually made of men who are, as you say, wrong-thinking—men who do horrible things. Nobody notices this because the situation is not being critiqued; it's not being held up to notice. There are also a lot of good people in the world—interesting people, caring people—who are men and women, and that's what I try to get at in my plays. One thing I have noticed about violence is that women are expected to write nonthreatening plays. In fact, they're rewarded for writing nonthreatening plays. If they don't, they're not rewarded, and it's also seen to be somewhat suspicious that they have pointed up the fact that patriarchy is a violent system.

I feel that playwrights do say things that are deeply unsettling. That's the tradition that I see myself in—of people who actually wrote *plays,* not boulevard comedies or commercial works, but works of literature and art and heart and imagination. I don't care if people are upset. My plays are strong; that's why I love the theatre, and that's why I persist in writing plays. I do feel that plays are powerful vehicles for speaking a truth—your personal truth—and that personal truth often has elements of social truth in it. That's what plays do; that's what they're supposed to do. That's why you can discuss the entire psychological history of the Western world by talking about *Oedipus, Hamlet, The Master Builder.*

Kramer: It has to do with the journey of discovery not for an individual but for a society. Artists—playwrights in particular, but artists in general—have to open these painful wounds so that we can learn what they mean to us rather than burying them.

Malpede: Self-discovery or self-reflection would be meaningless if it didn't have to do with living in the world. But it does have to do with living in the world. As we used to say in the feminist movement of the seventies, the personal *is* political.

Kramer: Of course, the fact that your plays are disturbing, to a great extent, makes critics reject the work. You've said that many establishment critics are uncomfortable when they're made to feel things.

Malpede: To tell a critic story: [*New Yorker* critic] Brendan Gill was invited to see *A Monster Has Stolen the Sun.* The producer who called him explained that the play had a scene in which a pregnant woman wrestles with a man. That piqued his interest enough so that he wanted to come. I stood in the balcony and watched him literally kick the pew in front of him—it was done in a church space—in rage during that scene. I surmised that it had never occurred to him that she would win this fight. In fact, the incidence of wife beating goes way up when the women are pregnant—this is a documented, sociological fact—and most of the blows are aimed directly at the abdomen of the woman.

That contemporary historical fact is being dealt with in this mythic play, but it's being dealt with in such a way that the woman is victorious.

We did that play in Trenton, New Jersey, as part of a street fair. The Passage Theatre Company wanted to produce the play, but they didn't have enough money to do the whole play at that moment, so they excerpted pieces of it. We walked through the fair, and we went into a performance space and threw the doors open, and the audience followed in. The audience was multiracial, multiclass—women pushed baby carriages in, dogs came in; it was just a street-fair crowd. The woman who played Macha was actually seven months pregnant, and when it came time for the wrestling match, Macha took off her dress and there was a real pregnant belly there. They wrestled and she won, and the women in the audience were hooting and hollering and cheering in approval, and saying, "That's the way it is! That's the way it is!" It was this very volatile, wonderful theatrical experience. In fact, George, who played Owain, had been uncertain about the play; he thought it was a historical play and mythic and poeticized and wouldn't really reach people—until that experience when he saw that it was more direct than anything could be.

After that experience, the Passage Theatre dropped their plans to do a full production of the play. One reason that I could figure out was that these two performances had had such strong reactions. They told me that certain people on their board came up to them and asked them if they intended to do that feminist play. The response was incredibly positive, but it was strong. The thing is, you're not supposed to say these things.

When we were doing *Us* at Theater for the New City, it was mobbed every night—standing room only. The set was sixty feet long and eighteen feet high and three feet wide, so it was this great, huge, long expanse of the wall. The way that Judith Malina staged the incest scene, where the father's in bed with the mother and the baby and he's rolling over on one and then the other—it's a very brutal scene and a very heightened piece of the reality of incest, which is that oftentimes the mother says that she doesn't know and in this case the mother's right in the same bed and she doesn't seem to know, and the father often goes between the daughter and the mother. The bed was perpendicular so that the actors were standing up and the audience was looking as if they were looking down on the bed. Every night the people who were sitting right under that scene walked out; but they walked out in a particular way: the man pulled the woman out. She wanted to stay, and she kept looking at the scene. They had to walk across the whole sixty-foot expanse, and it became almost a part of the production. It's too disturbing to tell the truth about certain things, or to experience the emotional truth about certain things. It's not that *Us,* for instance, dramatizes violence; it's the way in which *Us* dramatizes violence that's upsetting—that it dramatizes violence from the point of view of the victim, that it shows the emotional upset of the perpetrator.

Kramer: Except that it's acceptable when it's on TV. If this were a TV movie, nobody'd object so strenuously. Yet, when you put it on stage, it raises hackles.

Malpede: First of all, I think that there's a difference in the way TV movies do things. For instance, the language in *Us* is very much unlike any kind of TV movie.

Kramer: I think the liveness has something to do with it, too, just by itself. There are people up there. It may be a fictional event, but you're watching live people, not an image on a screen.

Malpede: Yes, I agree, but it's also the writing of TV movies. TV writing is, shall I say, not literature. There's something about doing it as literature, coupled with the liveness, that gives the theatre particular power. Imagistic writing, emotional writing, has enormous power.

It always sounds so serious when I talk about my work, but most of the plays have humorous moments to them, with the exception of *Lament* and *Us.* Actually *Sappho and Aphrodite* and *Better People* are very funny. *Blue Heaven* is funny in parts.

Kramer: In 1981, you wrote, "We require an *impassioned criticism . . .* which presupposes critics who are brave enough to make themselves vulnerable before a work of art, and so be profoundly moved." What is "impassioned criticism," and how do we get it?

Malpede: I have no idea how we get it. Let me just say that I don't have a problem with audiences. I do have a problem with critics. How we get an impassioned criticism—how we get anything—is by having the idea of it, first of all.

Kramer: Well, what do you mean by "impassioned criticism"?

Malpede: I mean a criticism where the critic is willing to be passionately involved with the experience of the work. That means, of course, that the critic is writing literature himself, or herself. So often you read theatre reviews in the daily papers that talk about what bad writing they'd just seen on the stage, and the review is so badly written that it's just laughable that somebody who wrote like that would dare to say that somebody else doesn't know how to write. It's just silly.

The bigger problem is that theatre is not a capitalist endeavor. The daily critics are working within the parameters of capitalism, and the theatre is working outside the parameters of capitalism. It doesn't work. Theatre's never worked within capitalism. It needs patrons, it needs funding. I'm talking about the real theatre, not the boulevard—not the commercial plays.

I'm really interested in doing my work. I would love to have better reviews because I would love to have more money to do my work with. My plays really ask for wonderful actors, and there are wonderful actors who do them, but they have to do them with financial sacrifices.

My other hope is that we'll persevere and that things will change. But they may not change. Most of the best plays from the past are totally unknown, as I said earlier. In a way you have to press on without any sense that you will get results. So it's not so much about pressing on. I think it's about the pleasure in the work itself. It's what sustains you. If you didn't take a great deal of pleasure in actually doing the work, you wouldn't write plays.

I'm very ambivalent about the critics, because I'm not a person who likes to be seen. I'd prefer to be invisible. I have always felt that it's been, in a way, a luxury not to be understood, because it left me totally free to keep on experimenting with each play, and to work in a kind of absolute freedom, which I don't think you have, or I think would be a lot harder to come by, if one were an immediate success. After writing plays for almost twenty years, I think I could easily tolerate success, but I think that it's suited my character to have this kind of difficult critical go because it left me very free.

Kramer: You said in 1987, "Every age has its own obsessive question, one that becomes the central dramatic action of its plays." What are the "central questions" for the 1990s?

Malpede: The question that I have, in fact, been obsessed with through all the plays is the one of violence and nonviolence and looking at how it is that we might live together on this planet in a nonviolent way. I do think that's the central question of our time; I think more and more people are getting it. I think the ecological crisis is making it very clear that we're not only violent to one another, but we're violent to the very life that supports us and sustains us. That is the obsessive question: how do we live together in a world of many different kinds of people and many different kinds of species and not destroy each other—and not destroy ourselves.

Kramer: You link this violence, which, in dramatic terms, is the *agon,* the struggle in which the tragedy always ends in death, to the patriarchal system. In your alternative aesthetic, the conflict doesn't have to be a violent one ending in death. The development of this nonpatriarchal aesthetic results from "the love women have recently openly expressed for women," which you assert was the genesis of the rise of so many new women playwrights. Do you think that men, who don't generally express such affection for one another, can and therefore ought also to be working in this kind of aesthetic? Or do we need this bifurcated kind of aesthetic?

Malpede: I don't think there's much to be gained by violence as the inevitable way to go anymore because the world is threatened by humanity's own violence, not by anything else. Nature is still working to sustain life, and people are working to destroy life. The theatre rose historically in the West with patriarchy—after patriarchy, but to reify it—to solidify it in the minds of people. The *Orsteia* is the great statement of father rite. I think we're at another turning point, another nexus of two worlds where we have to move into a world that is based on nonviolent principles.

Kramer: It would be interesting to imagine the kind of art men would produce under your aesthetic.

Malpede: Well, Leo and George are going to do that. They haven't written any plays, but they're going to do *Blue Heaven*. It's an interesting aside that George and I are a creative team and now Leo has joined that creative team, but that it's not the actress being directed and written by the playwright, as has happened in the past with Olga Knipper and Chekhov and Eleanora Duse and Gabriele D'Annunzio. It's a female voice and a male actor who realizes that voice in quite an extraordinary way.

Kramer: I think it's more than just interesting. It's possibly a glimpse into that future. Up till very recently, dramatists were essentially writing plays about women based on the same aesthetic as men. We seem to be getting this Linda Hamilton-Sigourney Weaver kind of feminism, or *Thelma and Louise*—male myths with female bodies put on them.

Malpede: And what I'm trying to do are gynocentric myths that include men—because they do include men—and have major women and major men characters.

Kramer: And some of the female characters have been essentially patriarchal. Some of them have been rather dichotomous: Brigit, for instance, in *Monster,* is not always right.

Malpede: Well, nobody is always right. It's not so interesting to see a character who's always right. I have never been touted by the feminist critics, either. My plays don't sit well with people who have a certain agenda; they only sit well with people who are open to the artistic experience. Art is more complex than an agenda.

TERRENCE MCNALLY

Steven Drukman

Terrence McNally (William Morris Agency)

Terrence McNally was born in St. Petersburg, Florida, on 3 November 1939, was raised in Corpus Cristi, Texas, and received his bachelor's degree in English from Columbia University in 1960. His most recent plays are *A Perfect Ganesh* (1992), *Lips Together, Teeth Apart* (1991), and *Frankie and Johnny in the Claire de Lune* (1987). *Lips Together* has been produced in a record-breaking number of regional theatres throughout the United States, including the recent controversial staging in Marietta, Georgia, where conservatives, in a mind-boggling mixture of illogic and ignorance, boycotted the production because of its threat to "traditional family values." McNally won the 1993 Tony award for best book of a musical for his adaptation of Manuel Puig's *Kiss of the Spider Woman,* which is still playing to sold-out houses on Broadway. Other plays include *The Lisbon Traviata* (1985), *The Ritz* (1975), *Bad Habits* (1973), *Where Has Tommy Flowers Gone?* (1971), and *Next* (1967). McNally won an Emmy award for *Andre's Mother* (1990, for American Playhouse) and has received two Guggenheim fellowships, a Rockefeller grant, and a citation from the American Academy of Arts and Letters. He has been vice-president of the Dramatists Guild since 1981.

It was my good fortune to meet and talk with McNally in his Chelsea brownstone in late October 1993. I could hardly be unaware of the timeliness of this interview. After having won the Tony the previous June, McNally was perhaps the "hottest" dramatist in New York at the moment (*Time* magazine had recently dubbed him "the height of hot"). At the time of the interview, he had not one but two eagerly awaited world premieres coming up: *L'Age d'Or* at Circle Repertory and *Love! Valor! Compassion!* at Manhattan Theatre Club. He was busily making the lecture circuit while in the preliminary stages of writing a biography of Tennessee Williams. He teaches playwriting at Juilliard and has also taught at New York University.

What's more, McNally seems at present to be in a period of creative regeneration and artistic maturation. Ever since *The Lisbon Traviata* in 1985 (although, in this interview, McNally marks the turning point as 1982, with *It's Only a Play*), his voice has become more serious. His incursions into his characters' psyches seem richer now, and he has learned to orchestrate their discordant souls to produce sonorous, and often unsettling, drama. All these later plays have shared the same dramatic motif: despite yearning for intimacy, human beings have myriad ways of building barriers between one another, denying and evading emotion, and keeping their distance. "Only connect," E. M. Forster's oft-quoted dictum, hangs onimously, unheeded, in the salt air of *Lips Together, Teeth Apart*, so, too, in *The Lisbon Traviata, Andre's Mother*, and *A Perfect Ganesh*.

This is not to give short shrift to his early satires. Plays like *Whiskey, Bad Habits*, and *It's Only a Play* drew up scathing parodies of American theatre folk, in the tradition of Noël Coward. Still, McNally is very much a "man of the theatre," as demonstrated in this interview. He was most passionate in his musings about the practical side of the business— the prohibitive economics of New York theatre and the "suburbanization" of its audience—rather than the vagaries of literary analyses of his drama. It was refreshing to hear a playwright calling for *more* critics (to diffuse the power of the *New York Times* as sole arbiter) as well as his concern for actively rebuilding the atrophied young audience in the theatre.

Finally these two themes that I have chosen to extract—the world of the theatre and the complicated negotiations of intimacy—sadly make the subject of AIDS almost an inevitability in McNally's work. AIDS has, of course, robbed our community in so many ways, and

McNally's plays (since *Frankie and Johnny*) have responded in kind. He spoke of the issue candidly in this interview.

Drukman: First of all, congratulations are in order for your Tony award. I'm wondering if these awards mean that much to you.

McNally: Oh, yes, of course. They're dessert, they're icing on the dessert even, but they're very nice. I don't think you write things to win Tony awards, but it's nice to have that kind of acknowledgment, and there are days when you wonder if your work means anything to anybody. That's what an award means to me: an affirmation that you've been heard, as opposed to "you are better than" anybody else. I don't see them as contests in that way. I see them as kind of recognitions, and I think anybody who wins any kind of prize, it's also for what's come before it. It's not *just* for *Spider Woman,* it's for a body of work.

Drukman: Although it's not surprising that you did win for *Spider Woman,* a musical, because music seems to play such a major role, both thematically and structurally, in your plays. I'm wondering how that translates into compositional strategies. Do you "score" a play? Do you hear the music or the rhythms of certain characters and try to get that down first?

McNally: Well, you're right, music *is* important in my work. I'm not a trained musician, and I don't read music or play an instrument, so it's kind of intuitive, and most of my plays have a musical tonality to them. Often when I write a play, I will play the works of a composer all the time, even while I'm *writing* sometimes, and it's sort of a subliminal influence. For example, when I wrote *The Ritz,* I played only Rossini overtures, and when I wrote the second act of *Lisbon Traviata,* I remember I played *Pagliacci* and *Cavelleria Rusticana* and other verismo operas a lot. I forget what I played when I wrote the first act of *Lisbon Traviata*—I think maybe Maria Callas.

But I think listening to music without being able to talk about it technically has given me a sense of structure. But it's very hard to talk about it; it's something I *feel* more than I can define how I do it. But I do know about creating themes, developing themes, bringing them all together, resolution, and I think listening to chamber music is obviously very helpful there. The characters also obviously have their own musicality. That's sort of a separate issue, though. That's really in building a character, learning to listen to how they really speak and express themselves, so that your characters don't sound like each other, which I think is terribly important. There the best example, I think, is Shakespeare. Hamlet never once sounds like Othello, who never once sounds like

Lear, who never once sounds like Ariel. So Shakespeare is the real model there, when you want to be reminded how important it is that characters have their own rhythm, vocabulary, accent, tonality.

Drukman: One of your more musical characters, Googie Gomez, first appears in *Bad Habits,* only to reappear as a major character in *The Ritz.* Have you ever created characters that you thought either so exemplary or so appealing that you wanted to write other plays around them, something along the lines of Lanford Wilson's Talley plays?

McNally: It hasn't occurred to me yet. The only character I'd like to do another play about is Mendy in *Lisbon Traviata.* Audiences love him, I love him, and I want to call it *Mendy in Love,* which I think is a wonderful title. But to answer your question, "Do I want to write a bunch of plays where people are connected?" I don't know, that was kind of an "in" joke, the Googie Gomez. It's funny you ask that. I've already tried some cross-referencing of characters once or twice, and usually it goes out in previews because it's so self-conscious. It's like you're nudging the audience: "Remember *Bad Habits?* Remember *The Ritz?*" I think in all these Lanford Wilson plays people really related, and they're about the same people. But I do want to write *Mendy in Love.*

Drukman: Speaking of Mendy, you're known around town as an opera aficionado. Would you ever like to write a libretto?

McNally: No, because I think librettos are really the work of poets. I think opera needs really strong plot, and I'm very minimalist when it comes to plot, so I think that would be a very bad combination. But I don't know why contemporary composers don't go to playwrights and people who have a sense of drama to write librettos. Most of these librettos are written by people who are *not* of the theatre, and I think you have to be of the theatre to write a really strong libretto.

Drukman: What about directing one of your plays?

McNally: No, no interest, none. Because I don't have the patience or concentration to direct. You really have to be at every rehearsal, and you have to care about everything: the acting, the script, the lighting, what color shoes the leading lady is wearing. I like to go to rehearsal when I'm working on the script. I don't enjoy rehearsals unless I'm really fixing a scene.

Drukman: And yet you have clearly made a home for yourself in the New York theatre. In fact a list of your plays' dedications reads like a who's who of American theatre. Leonard Melfi, Lynne Meadow, Elaine May, James Coco—

McNally: Well, Elaine May directed my first successful play, which was a play I wrote for Jimmy Coco. They weren't "Elaine May" and "James

Coco" then, if you know what I mean. Elaine was somebody who was trying to figure out what to do with her life after the breakup of Nichols and May. She was a very successful comic performer, but this was her first directing that I know of—I think she might have done some things when they were students in Chicago—but Elaine hadn't directed in a long while.

Of course I don't dedicate them to well-known people just to flatter them!

Drukman: Oh, no, I'm not suggesting that. In fact your plays don't always draw the most flattering renderings of theatre people. Does this reflect an ambivalence about the community of which you've been such an important part for decades?

McNally: Actually, I think that the main play I've written about "the theatre," *It's Only a Play,* is a very positive piece. When people talk about it as bitchy comedy about the theatre, I really don't think they've understood what the play's about. People in the theatre say desperate and bitchy things just like anybody does. *It's Only a Play* is a very positive portrait of the theatre. I think the only negative theatre people I've invented are the Pitts in *Bad Habits,* that overweening-ego kind of couple, which was a, perhaps not so affectionate, jibe at Ron Leibman and Linda Lavin. It was no secret that that's who that couple was based on. They weren't terribly thrilled. I thought it was more affectionate than they did, so they were kind of unhappy with me for a while. But we've made it up, and we've all gone on to other things.

Still, all my characters are me as much as they're anybody else, so I also have the same ego as the Pitts in *Bad Habits.* I never make up a character one hundred percent. I don't believe you can write a character unless you've experienced the emotion that that character portrays. So everything that is petty and desperate and ambitious about the Pitts has to be in me too, or I couldn't have written it. Just as everything that's loving and tender in another character has to be in there. I don't think you can write feelings you've never had. So, to say that those characters were based *only* on "real people" is a little false. It's not *really* about Ron and Linda; I didn't know them that well. But I think you write about characters you recognize yourself in, elements of yourself. And then you perhaps build that up.

But I think in my work a character is usually about thirty-three percent me, thirty-three percent somebody else I've observed, and thirty-three percent by the grace of God, or inspiration or creativity. I'm not of the school of playwriting where you list ten characteristic traits about each person so that they're different. That's for an actor—to chew gum or play with his ear, or stutter—let *him* characterize. The playwright must simply *listen* to how they talk, and *see* what they're doing. That's the main thing Elaine May taught me. She'd say, "What are your characters doing? I don't care what they're saying." And I still fall into the same trap. I write a thirty-page scene, it's brilliant writing, but no one's *doing* anything. That's the biggest problem I find, in my own work still (I'm fifty-four), and from my students at Juilliard who are in their twenties. They are writing reams of dialogue, but no one's doing anything. It's the hardest thing to get through our heads: *playwriting is recording behavior, not dialogue.* Dialogue is something people do while they're doing something. You talk a different way when the turkey's burning in the oven than you do sitting in a hammock on a cool summer day. So that's what I got from Elaine, which is why you dedicate a play to someone like Elaine. She taught me more about playwriting than anyone. I'm also a self-taught playwright. I did not take any playwriting courses in college. I was an English major.

Drukman: Right. At Columbia?

McNally: Yes.

Drukman: And after graduation you took off for Mexico to write the Great American Novel.

McNally: (Laughs) Ah, well.

Drukman: So how did you drift into the theatre?

McNally: Well, I'd always liked it, and when I came to Columbia, I started going to the theatre practically every night. And then when I was off in Mexico, I wrote this play called *This Side of the Door.* I don't even think I still have a copy of it! It was autobiographical in a way that made me uncomfortable, and I thought, "If you can't enjoy watching your own plays, that's not good." But I sent it off to Actors' Studio, and I was asked to join the playwrights' unit and also to work there as a stage manager, by Mollie Kazan, who ran it. So I learned a lot by observing other actors and directors, and I saw some very exciting projects done there for the first time. *Zoo Story* was done there for the first time! *Night of the Iguana* was done there for the first time! It was kind of the height of the studio. It was wall-to-wall famous actors doing scenes, and Marilyn Monroe was sitting there with no makeup, and Olivier was doing Beckett. It was a very intense place to be.

Drukman: My favorite of your plays from this period is the absurdist *Bringing It All Back Home.* Handy comparisons of this play can be made to Edward Albee's *American Dream.* Was he one of your major influences?

McNally: Oh, he was an influence on any writer of my generation. Had to be. His stories were this startling explosion of language. The only performance of *Bringing It All Back Home* I've ever seen was given on the back of a truck in Central Park at a Vietnam demonstration, and you couldn't hear any dialogue. It was written for Vietnam moratorium day, one of those events. But Edward certainly was an influence on *Things That Go Bump in the Night.* I think one way Edward influenced a lot of writers is just by subject matter. In comparison to what was going on, the norm in Edward's theatre seemed rude and impolite. Because Tennessee Williams did always seem gothic and southern and somewhat poetic, whereas Edward's voice was, "This is how we're living in New York City right now." As much as I revere Tennessee Williams, there's that feeling of watching a poem, and that kind of wasn't *really* about life on the IRT and Morningside Heights and all that. Whereas Edward's work, I think, had that kind of energy. Tennessee Williams is kind of a dead end as a stylistic writer. It's southern, and he's pretty much cornered that territory, and I think you'd have to be very foolhardy to get into that milieu after he's been there.

Drukman: What about *Cuba Si* [1968]?

McNally: Wow, yes, that was another very specific piece, in terms of intention. That was written for a benefit reading for Melina Mercouri to do at Madison Square Garden. They were raising money for the Greek junta. A lot of Greeks, she and [Irene] Papas, they were all living here in exile. And then it was picked up by Viveca Lindfors, who did it quite a bit.

Drukman: Cuba Si can almost be thought of as a proto-*Perfect Ganesh,* in its tackling the issue of white bourgeois complacency. Of course 1968 was a very different time.

McNally: It's funny, you're talking about some of my work that I really have forgotten. You're right about that. I had hoped to expand it, and maybe I did, in a sense, through *Ganesh.* But what I remember best about that play is Melina. She had that kind of larger-than-life style, which *I* respond to. I was never *totally* at home with Actors' Studio style of acting. I mean, I'll take Olivier over Marlon Brando any day, or Zoe Caldwell over Kim Stanley. It's just my taste.

Drukman: Although your work became more concerned with the psychological in *Bad Habits,* a play about two different paths to fulfillment and ways of forming a cohesive "identity." Act one in Ravenswood presents a hedonistic, follow-your-bliss approach, and act two in Dunelawn prescribes a self-abnegating, fasting from pleasure. Any new thoughts on this topic, in the age of AIDS?

McNally: That's very interesting, but a hard question to answer. I think people will always follow the anything-you-do-is-okay route, even in the age of AIDS. And the second approach, that vigorous self-abnegation, starving yourself, well, we know people still pursue that. Consider the millions of people just battling with their waistlines—that becomes so important, that they be able to wear a size six or four dress. It will never go away, this "we're not good enough." In both plays people really aren't accepting who they are. But I think our bad habits, you could also say, define who we are. Everybody would end up all the same if all the bad habits in the world were eradicated. AIDS hasn't changed that.

But I think that play is more properly understood as my having fun with psychotherapy, which seemed to be very, very big twenty years ago, and maybe a little annoying, since all my friends were busy being analyzed more than anything else. Some were of the school of therapy "I'm OK, you're OK," and others were "Let's go back and look at everything" and discover where our personalities went "askew." I think *Bad Habits* is probably the blackest play I've ever written. I think it's *very* negative about what it says about human change and endeavor. In act one, the woman has totally changed her life by the end, and the man still doesn't love her, and her only recourse is a kind of sedation. In the second act, I think the couples accept that we often end up with partners because nobody else in the world would put up with our particular foibles. So I don't think either message is *positive,* and I think it's pessimistic about true change. Not like my later plays.

Drukman: AIDS, as you know, has had a tremendous impact in the theatre community, and so many of your plays seem a well-considered response to this. While other playwrights, for example, Larry Kramer, have written polemical works around the subject, your work again documents the private and often agonizing responses to a plague in late twentieth-century America. It's intriguing that AIDS, as the acronym, as the word, isn't even really mentioned in *Lisbon Traviata*—I think Stephen refers to it obliquely. I don't know if you mention it at all in *Andre's Mother . . .* once, maybe.

McNally: I don't know either, but it's pretty clear . . . I think actually the word is there once, I'm not sure; I'd have to look at the text. I think AIDS affects everything we do, in this part of the twentieth century. We don't talk about it all the time, but it's like something sitting there on the table. The men in *Lisbon Traviata* don't *have* to talk about AIDS. They allude to it, certainly, but, you're absolutely right, I don't think the word AIDS is said there, but it's everywhere. Certainly it permeates *Lips Together.* And I guess it's in *Ganesh,* too. I don't see how you can write a play today—if you're writing about contemporary life—and, if not mention it, have it as a subtext in the play. It was certainly a subtext in *Frankie and Johnny* without ever discussing it overtly. And even if you're writing a period play today, I think it would still somehow get into it—it'd be like a time when it was easier, freer, or there wasn't a specter hanging over people. Any writer who's really seriously dealing with our society must contend with AIDS. I'm trying to think of serious plays that don't, and I guess I'd be hard-pressed. In a play like *Lips*, it's a response to the situation that would never have been created without AIDS. If her brother hadn't died, they wouldn't be in that house. So, it's the way it's affected everybody's lives. And the mother in *Ganesh* who dreads her son calling to say, "I have AIDS"—the biggest fear of her life—instead gets a call that he's been murdered, sacrificed to another kind of homophobia. In fact, one of the plays I'm writing right now, *Love! Valor! Compassion!*, is about seven gay men—they're not talking about AIDS so far, but it's there. It's there if you say, "Were you at so-and-so's memorial?" There's a line in *Lips* when Sally, calling across from the deck, asks, "Were you there? Yes, wasn't it lovely?" I'm sure everyone in the audience knows she means her brother's memorial service. You don't have to *say*, "AIDS." That's what I mean, that it permeates everything.

Drukman: Well, it certainly does permeate *Lips Together, Teeth Apart,* a play about the demarcations drawn between ourselves and other people, as well as our inner and outer selves. This makes the response in Cobb County, Georgia, all the more ironic, doesn't it? Does all this controversy around this play surprise you?

McNally: Yes, mainly because the play has been done so many times without even a ripple. As usual, of course, the man that started all of this hasn't even seen the play, only heard about it. I think it's somebody who's looking to make an issue down there, heard there was a gay play, and decided to make the issue without even bothering to see the play. And you know, he's getting support. But it's such a misreading of the play that it's bizarre. Ironically, some gay critics have accused the play of being homophobic, because it's about four uneasy people. The people in that play are homophobic, but I don't think they go around in the streets yelling, "Faggot," and loosening goon squads out to beat up gay men and women. No, they're homophobic the way I think a lot of people are. It's in that when-they-see-something-they-don't-like, under-their-breath way. But when his wife says, "John's been terrific—there's somebody on the faculty with AIDS," I believe that. I think he's probably been wonderful, despite his uneasiness. So homophobia is like a virus in them that bubbles up sometimes, and that's what I'm dealing with. I would never want to write a play about four homophobic people; that wouldn't interest me. The people who are doing this in Cobb County, I wouldn't know *how* to write a play about them, because I would hate them so much, and you can't really write characters you hate. So, to answer your question, it's a crazy play to cause this commotion. If they were doing *Lisbon Traviata,* I would've certainly disagreed with the issues at large, but I would've understood it. This seems bizarre, to accuse this play of promoting a gay lifestyle. I just don't get it. But, as I said, the guy hadn't seen the play, so he's really a jerk in my opinion.

Drukman: This theme—building barriers through granting people the status of the "other"—is carried over into *A Perfect Ganesh,* and again the terror of AIDS is shown to evoke this response from "civilized" people. That telling line, something like, "You held an angel, and you didn't even know it."

McNally: Yes, her own son, yes. And she's also holding an Indian child at that point. "Foolish woman," I think it was, "you held a god in your arms, and you didn't know it." I do believe there is a divinity in all of us, and we all are perfect in a way. It's such a change from what I wrote about in *Bad Habits.* I think we all are divine and perfect, but we set up so many rules. I talk about that a lot in *Frankie and Johnny.* Because give me another five minutes and I'll think of a million things I don't like about you, the way you hold a pencil, the way you cross your legs. It's so *easy* to find what separates us, and we're so frightened of what connects us, and it's so easy to say, "He's a Jew, he's a faggot, he's a nigger." I think it's out of terror of one another and of intimacy that we become racist and homophobic and sexist and all these things. Likewise I think men are terrified of the intimacy women seem to want to offer them, so they relegate them and keep them apart.

It's really become a very big theme in my writing, which I wasn't aware of, but now you're having me look back, and it's in all the plays. When Margaret has a chance in *Ganesh* to reveal that she also has lost an infant, and she *doesn't,* some people have pointed out that they didn't understand *why* she didn't. In fact, one fellow playwright said, "You must rewrite one scene, then you've got a big hit: that scene on the train when she says, 'Well, there's one thing that we'll never have in common; I lost a son.' And the other one has the chance where she can tell her that *she too lost a son,* and then they become friends." He completely missed the point of what I was trying to do, that Margaret respected the other woman's grief and privacy too much to sort of one-up her.

I think maybe one day she does tell her, when they get back to Connecticut, but to have told her there would have been on the order of, "Oh, you think you have a bad life!" That was what was so wonderful about Margaret. She didn't have the need at that point to *top* her. She's allowing Catherine her grief.

I think that that issue, the barriers between people, and why they stay there, will always interest me. I don't know what AIDS, being fifty-four, this society, have to do with it all. I think so many forces impinge on us and make us write the things we do. And I think it's after the work is done that people start tracing themes in your writing. I know there are writers who start out with "themes." My plays usually begin about people that interest me, and a journey, and I've gotten more and more interested in using the theatre. I thought it was very *theatrical* of me not to have the gay men onstage—I could've put them on so easily—and then to read that the play is homophobic, when the gays are reduced to offstage characters, it *completely* misses the point of what I was trying to do. In *Ganesh* I suddenly got interested in masks and more of an expressionistic kind of play, and I feel less and less need for scenery. I like more of an acting space to work in.

A lot of my early plays are either satirical or have an element of satire in them. That interests me very little at the moment, because satire always implies a certain kind of condescension to your characters, as in *Bad Habits.* I think the turning point play for me, in terms of where I am now, was *It's Only a Play,* which is part satiric and part heartfelt. And that's the intention. I've seen productions of it where the balance was not captured, and there should be some really touching moments in *It's Only a Play,* if it's done well, and that's what I intended. And I have seen some productions where it was just silly all evening.

Drukman: In *It's Only a Play,* a producer, director, actress, playwright are all awaiting Frank Rich's verdict in the *New York Times.* Now that Rich is handing over the reins—and one might say "reign"—to someone else, would you care to comment on his role in the development of New York, and, by extension, American, theatre in the past decade?

McNally: I would feel free to even if he weren't. It's very hard to talk . . . because you end up talking about Frank Rich, and the issue is that we have one newspaper, and somehow, through tradition, people worry about what New York papers say about a play. They don't worry about what New York papers say about a movie or a TV show. Thousands of movies become big hits without the approval of the *New York Times.* TV shows that the *New York Times* hated entertain fifty million people every night. But when I first came to New York, there were about eight daily newspapers, so we're really not talking about Frank Rich, we're talking about the *Times*. I think we've got to find a way to change that.

If we found a way to develop dialogue about theatre so it wasn't just, "What did Frank Rich say?" . . . we're all very aware when Frank Rich does not give you an enthusiastic review. For a play like *Ganesh*, his less-than-enthusiastic review made it very hard for us. Every performance was like a victory! But we can't blame the *New York Times*. It's our fault! We have empowered that paper. If they give us a good review, we take a full-page ad out. If every producer in New York said, "We're never going to advertise in the *New York Times*," signed a solid pact, and the only way you could find out even when a play began or what was opening that week was to buy an independent journal, and [if the journal were to] hire twenty critics, twenty opinions on each play, and it costs fifty cents a week or a dollar a week, I think people would buy that paper. I think there should be *more* newspapers, *more* critics! Everybody's a critic, after all.

It's not going to change overnight. But we have done this to ourselves. And we have not done anything to develop theatregoing as a habit in which you go to hear various and opposed viewpoints about the way we live today expressed. To me that's what a theatre is; it's a public forum for what's going on in our society. And it's become like the flavor of the month, "This is the hit, that's the hit," and it's like there's only room for one hit at a time. And I think we should do one performance a week free for anyone under eighteen, just to see what happens. Maybe no one would even show up, which is really scary, because they're all at the movies or playing video games. There aren't many young "stage-struck" people, the way I was. Theatre is something their parents or people my age do. Theatre sounds boring to most young people.

Drukman: You're teaching young people now. Do you find that many of them want to start writing for film and television?

McNally: Well, if they do, they wouldn't dare tell me, because that's a no-no of the class. You're supposed to be committed to being a playwright. But it is obviously what's happening. A lot of gifted writers are quickly snatched up by Hollywood. I think maybe they say, "How'm I ever gonna get produced or get established in New York?"

So I say to all my students at Juilliard, "Start your own theatres; it's the only way you're gonna have a theatre." You know, Caffe Cino and La Mama have been romanticized a lot. But it was really hard working in those theatres in the sixties. People forget that these plays by Lanford

Wilson and John Guare, Sam Shepard—plays now regarded as contemporary classics—*all* started this way. It was hard. It was fun, but it was hard. Now La Mama's sort of a big deal, with a budget and international prestige and everything. It wasn't then. When I was getting started, *anyone* could have their work done at La Mama. That's not true now. Practically everyone they do now is an established writer.

Drukman: Yes, but critics have a hand in establishing these writers. Given the power of the critical apparatus of the *New York Times,* how has Frank Rich—considering his taste, his critical prejudices as well as his insights—shaped American drama for the last ten years?

McNally: I actually think Frank Rich, who has been good and bad to me, all told, has been a positive critic for the new writers, and I think he cares about theatre. I think he's stage-struck and really cares about it. Sure, I wished he liked *Ganesh* more, but he loved *Lips Together* and *Frankie and Johnny.* I just wish, at this stage in my life, there were enough people who would be interested in any play I wrote that I wouldn't have to go through that again, that there was like a McNally audience. You know, by the time Tennessee Williams died, there wasn't even a Tennessee Williams audience left, and that's kind of a sad comment on the falling-off of the loyal theatregoers.

Drukman: Tell me about this biography of Tennesse Williams you will be working on.

McNally: Marty Duberman has been asked to publish and edit a series of books written for young readers, ages fourteen to eighteen, presenting gay people in a style accessible to a young gay audience. My contribution is more a long essay on Tennessee Williams, what he's meant to me, and why I think his work is so important and lasting. And I hope that a young person will read this and feel encouraged. For a whole generation such as mine, there were no positive gay role models. Even Oscar Wilde, in my high school, you didn't know who he was. I think this is potentially a very important series. It's an appreciation of Tennessee Williams, written from the viewpoint of another gay playwright. And things have changed, obviously, about being "out" since he worked. Whenever I hear young people critical of Tennessee Williams for not being "out," I just think, "Well, you're too young, you don't know what it was like, and he was pretty terrific, what he did." His plays were really considered shocking in their day, and it's hard, I guess, for someone who's twenty-five to know that *Cat on a Hot Tin Roof* was considered shocking, or in *Suddenly Last Summer,* that homosexuality was even *acknowledged* as a subject. And Tennessee Williams wrote some gay characters in the last few plays of his life, and the plays were not very successful. They were done Off-Off-Off-Broadway, and many people have never even *heard* of them, but they were done. Most people think of them nowadays as never having been performed, because he had sort of really fallen out of favor. People just weren't interested in his work anymore. *Not interested in Tennessee Williams!* And I don't know how that can happen to an artist that's given so much.

Drukman: Well, I look forward to your book.

McNally: (*Laughs*) Me, too. But I'm a *long way* from writing it, and all I can think of is my new play at the moment. So, we'll just wait and see when it happens.

MARK MEDOFF

Mimi Reisel Gladstein

Mark Medoff (photo by R. Sterling
Trantham, courtesy of Mark Medoff)

A forty-minute drive up the Rio Grande valley, through fields of chili and cotton and groves of pecan trees, brought me to Mesilla Park, New Mexico, where Mark Medoff, his wife, Stephanie, and two of their three daughters reside. The interview took place in the Medoff hacienda, a capacious, beautifully appointed, and warmly welcoming home, set on five acres of land. My host greeted me dressed in shorts and a T-shirt, ready for a postinterview golf game.

Medoff is a prize-winning playwright, having received an Obie for *When You Comin Back, Red Ryder?,* which also garnered the Outer Circle Critics Award for best playwriting of the 1973–74 season. *Children of a Lesser God* won the 1980 Tony award, and Medoff was also nominated for an Oscar for cowriting the film adaptation of his play. Among his early successes is *The Wager,* which had a successful Off-Broadway run in 1974.

Many of Medoff's plays are dominated by explosive and aggressive male characters, characters who challenge the self-satisfaction or naively smug assumptions of not only the other characters in the play but also the audience. The playwright uses these characters to create an atmosphere of almost palpable tension, one of his theatrical fortes; his plays resonate with incipient violence. In the words of one writer, Medoff's creative voice is that of "moralist-turned-metaphysical desperado." The violence-inspired tension is especially evident in the early plays, *The Kramer, The Wager,* and *When You Comin Back, Red Ryder?,* though not in the Red Ryder sequel, *The Heart Outright,* or in *Children of a Lesser God.* It reappears in the more recent, unpublished play *Stumps,* which vibrates with so much psychological and physical terrorism that a calming aftermath scene was added to allow attendees' heartbeats to return to normal before they exit the theatre. The play is a theatrical tour de force, but so far its violence has deterred other productions.

Beginning with his enlargement of the role of Sarah in *Children of a Lesser God* and evident especially in *Stumps,* where the heroine more or less single-handedly defeats the villain, who has physically and mentally bullied all the other characters, Medoff has begun creating fuller and more interesting female roles than in his early works. His recent female characters, in works as diverse as *The Homage That Follows, Clara's Knee,* and the just-published novel, are assertive of their rights and represent a growing feminism in Medoff's ouevre.

Medoff is a multitalented theatrical force. Besides his considerable talents as a playwright, he also functions successfully as actor, director, or administrator. His powerful performance as Teddy in *When You Comin Back, Red Ryder?* was acknowledged with the Jefferson Award. Audiences in the Southwest have applauded him in such roles as the psychiatrist in *Equus,* as Marat in Peter Weiss's *Marat/Sade,* as Sherlock Holmes, and as characters in productions of his own plays. He also has numerous directorial credits, sometimes directing his own work, but often interpreting the work of other playwrights. Recently he has written a number of screenplays, notably *Clara's Heart,* which starred Whoopi Goldberg, and *City of Joy,* which featured Patrick Swayze in a dramatic departure from his usual romantic roles. Until 1987, when he took a leave of absence to spend six months in Hawaii writing a novel, he was theatre arts department head at New Mexico State University, as well as artistic director of the American Southwest Theatre Company, an organization he midwifed into existence. The company has contributed appreciably to the cultural milieu of the New Mexico/Texas border community, not only as a showcase for Medoff's works in progress, but also by setting a high standard for community theatre in hiring professional actors and directors to work with under-graduate students and local actors. In 1992 the appearance of his first novel, *Dreams of Long Lasting,* published by Warner Books, demonstrates still another of Mark Medoff's numerous creative talents.

Gladstein: Can I begin by asking you when you first knew you wanted to be a playwright.

Medoff: Well, I knew I wanted to be a writer from about the time I was fifteen years old. My teacher, Pat Samuelson, asked the class to write a short story. I found out, a week or so later, that mine was better than everybody else's, and I had no idea that I had this ability, but he really set me on a course that I have been on for a long time, thirty-five to forty years. Then when I got out of graduate school at Stanford and came to New Mexico State to teach English, among the first people I met and among the first two who befriended me were a couple of people who had just become involved in a community theatre here in Las Cruces. And one of them suggested to me one day that I should write a play and that they'd put it on. When I came here, I came here as a prose writer. I was trying to write a novel at that time, and so it happened that I found myself writing a short story in my first semester here that was virtually nothing but dialogue, and I thought, "Well, why not try a play?" So I turned this into a play. And in fact they did do it. It was a long one-act play with ten scenes, ran about an hour. Over the next eight years I rewrote the play assiduously sixteen times, sixteen different productions, and it finally became the second play that I had in New York, *The Wager.* During that eight years I wrote a number of other plays, among which were *The Kramer,* which was the second play I had done in a professional venue, by ACT in San Francisco and in the Mark Taper Forum, and *When You Comin Back, Red Ryder?,* which then really became the first play I had on in New York, even though it was the third play I wrote.

Gladstein: So you weren't a great theatre lover as a child?

Medoff: Yeah, you know, one of the fondest memories I have as a little boy is going to the theatre in Chicago and seeing Mary Martin in *Annie Get Your Gun.* And we were sitting in the fifth or sixth row, and I got to sit on the aisle, and we were there . . . for some reason we were there very early. And while the band, the orchestra, was warming up, the drummer waved me forward and let me come into the orchestra pit and hit his base drum. And, I'm not sure, some combination of his letting me hit the drum and my being mesmerized by all these kids spilling out of the train cars in one scene did in fact infuse me with an interest in theatre. And I did a lot of acting from the time I was a little kid until I was well into high school, at which time I became consumed by athletics and girls. And I never really got interested in the theatre again until I came here.

Gladstein: Do you think your interest in athletics has affected your writing?

Medoff: Oh, yeah. I think that we can probably do an entire interview on how important sports have been to me. Both in terms of what I write about and the fact that I have come, over the years, to recognize the consequence to me personally of exercising every day and how daily exercise enhances my work. And I have gotten into a very, very rigid routine over the years, where I start writing very early in the morning, usually between five and six in the morning, and quit usually between ten and eleven and then invariably, invariably, go exercise. And for many years I played tennis. Then I played racquetball and tennis. This was after my legs got so bad I had to quit playing things like football and basketball. And now, over the past three years, I've become obsessed with playing golf. Of course one of the nice things about golf is that you're outdoors in green pastures. You walk a great distance if you play eighteen holes of golf. You're walking four to five miles. And I've never seen an ugly golf course. They tend to be great Walden Ponds, if you will, out in the middle of beautiful countryside. So I find it enormously stimulating mentally to go out on the golf course, and I almost prefer going by myself. I do have friends that I enjoy playing with, but they know that I don't want to go for four hours and chitchat. I really don't. I want to scream profanities at my inadequacies on the golf course, and I wanna just think.

Gladstein: Do you think there is any connection between your interest in things athletic and, say, the amount of violence in some of the shows that you write.

Medoff: I don't . . . well, I was going to say I don't think so, but I guess I do. There certainly is a great appeal to me in violent sports. Now, I was taught as a kid that I was not to start fights with people. I was not to express the violence that I think lives in most of us by arbitrarily picking fights with people, which was probably a good idea, because I was not ever a real large person. I mean, I was six-feet tall in high school, but I weighed about 125 pounds. But my father told me I could express any violence I wanted to through sports with rules. So as a kid I did some boxing, and I didn't really like that because I didn't really want to have my face moved around. So I loved the violence of football. *I loved the violence of football.* And I played quarterback in high school, and I also loved playing defense, because I loved to hit people and it was perfectly legal to do. So in that sense, yeah, I think that the violence of sports like tennis and racquetball, even the violence of golf, the controlled violence in golf, where you are allowed to swing hard at something and make it fly through the air, is very satisfying. But I really think the violence that is in my plays comes from some wellspring of anger at the world. And over the years I have come to realize there was nothing really terribly unpleasant about my childhood. So it's not a violence that came from any kind of abuse or rejection within my family. And I have come to feel over the years that it was really something that came more from observation, a frustration with the world as it is, and from reading a great deal of literature, starting at a very young age. I was an avid reader as a kid, and I started reading rather serious books at a young age. And of course most good literature tends to have a very negative feel to its greater body, and then at the end of most great literature the lesser body is a kind of denouement or resolution that tends to put things in a somewhat more positive light.

Gladstein: Well, I wanted to interject something personal here. In my observation of, for example, your character Teddy, I find him to be more of a psychologically violent person than he is purely physically violent. I think the terror comes from his psychological manipulation. I've seen three actors "do" Teddy: Marjoe Gortner, Kim McCallum in one production here, and you. And no one even approached your interpretation of Teddy.

Medoff: What was the difference?

Gladstein: Well, yours was a mesmerizing characterization. I mean, it absolutely sent vibrations of the intensity of the rage off the walls of the . . . I think it was the Old Fountain Theatre. I sat in that performance and I thought, "My gosh, he does that so well." I just wondered where all of that rage came from.

Medoff: I really think it's something, as I say, that comes from observation, and certainly there's an element that comes from my own dissatisfaction with myself. And perhaps, like many artists, I have a rather negative view of myself as a human being, and I think many artists view themselves rather askew and unpleasantly. But that perhaps gives us the license then to comment on the value of other people. I'm not positive that's right, but I do know that as I've grown older, I don't view myself as an awful human being. I do think that the feelings of inadequacy, from wherever they came as a kid and a young man, did help fuel that violence.

Gladstein: Do you remember that performance, do you remember how that performance felt?

Medoff: Oh yeah, oh sure. And I got to do it a lot. I did it in Chicago for several months, and I did it in New York for several months before I came back and did it here. And I've told people many, many times that though I see myself as all the characters I write that, really, given my background, I should've played the husband in the play, and that it was a great treat to be able to play Teddy and to expiate every night for two hours all those feelings that he had. It was certainly one of the great ongoing epiphanies of my life to be able to do that eight times a week in Chicago and New York for months.

Gladstein: I'm interested in the development of that character. Did you get to act the part on the way to finishing the play, or had you finished the play before you had acted the part?

Medoff: No, no, it had been on for quite a while. It had been playing in New York for a year or so already.

Gladstein: So acting the part didn't contribute to your writing the part. The part was complete when you acted it.

Medoff: Like many writers and many playwrights, I think that I imagine myself playing certain roles in my plays, and I think that as a young man I wrote such male-dominated plays because I imagined myself playing the most interesting male roles in my own plays. I think it's that simple. And it really was not until I came to write *Children of a Lesser God* . . . and Gordon Davidson literally locked me in a room one day with himself and several of his hench guys present. And they ripped me apart and said, "You proved that you could write these plays with these very glib, angry male protagonists. Why don't you now expand your horizons and write some decent women?" And, really, feeling that I had been ripped apart with good reason, I determined, on my way to the L.A. airport to fly back here to Las Cruces, that he was absolutely right, and that I really needed to invest that deaf woman with the same passion, give her the same scope, the same amount of time onstage as I had given to that hearing/speech teacher. So I called him from the airport, and I told him that I was going to cut five characters out of the play, since he was, at that time, casting. And he was quiet for a moment. And he said, "Then, in other words, I should stop casting those roles." And I said, "Yes," and I went home and in a couple of weeks rewrote that play. And it was a seminal moment in my life in that that became the first play I wrote where, in truth, by the time I was finished, I felt I had successfully become female. And I think one of the things about the heterosexual writers of my generation is that, with growing up in the fifties, there was a real negative feeling to ever being considered in any way feminine or effete. And it took me a long time to realize that as a writer I really had to be androgynous—I didn't need to be homosexual, but I did need to be androgynous in my head—and that I couldn't be afraid of the female parts of me. And since that time I have consciously set out to write large female roles. And in the novel that just came out, I think, among the nicest compliments I've had have been from women who have complimented me on the women I wrote. I know I can write men, but to be able to write women whom women will respond to is a great piece of growth.

Gladstein: I like the woman in *Stumps,* particularly your heroine, the Asian woman.

Medoff: I wrote a play called *The Homage That Follows.* I don't know if you saw that or not.

Gladstein: Yes, I saw that.

Medoff: I just started working on that again. I did that, I think, two years before I did *Stumps,* and it's about a female English teacher in her forties or fifties. And that's about to be workshopped in New York this summer, so I went back to it and got very interested in it again, and I purposely picked a female director to do it. And again the nicest compliment she gave me the other day when I sent her the rewrite was how strongly she related to this one. And I am this one. When I sit down to write, I am that woman.

Gladstein: I think Hortense Calisher [a contemporary writer and critic, well known among feminists] once said that the male generation of writers of the forties and fifties got caught up in Hemingway's jockstrap.

Medoff: Yeah, I guess that's true. Yeah, I guess for me it was some of that Hemingway, idiotic, macho quality. But I'm really happy to be past that or to feel that I could be both.

Gladstein: I want to get back for a minute to the character of Stephen Rider. What interested you enough to put him in a number of different plays?

Medoff: Well, the truth is that back in the early seventies my wife, Stephanie, and I were in Albuquerque, where one of my very early plays was being done. And the morning we were leaving to drive back, we went to a Toddle House up on Central Avenue above the University of New Mexico. And there were these two kids in there, and their names were Stephen and Nancy, and they were very much as I described them in the beginning of the play. And they were playing out this illusive love affair in this little Toddle House. And I whispered to Stephanie, after we were there a couple of minutes, I said that I would try to remember everything I could because I knew they were in a play I was going to write. And in fact on the way home she wrote down, on a section in *Parade Magazine* in the *Albuquerque Journal,* everything we could remember, and even as we were driving, I started adding things. Things just started to perk; they just seemed so rich as characters and so utterly alien to me, this young, Jewish, college professor/writer from an affluent family in Miami Beach, Florida, via Stanford University, who was really an alien in New Mexico at that time. And I wrote a one-act play about them, basically, and about Stephanie and me in a different guise walking in, and about a crippled young man who happened to be sitting in a booth that day, who then turned into Lyle Striker, the gas station attendant. And I finished the play, and I didn't think it was something to be done yet, and I put it away. And it was a year later that Teddy walked out of my head and walked into that diner, and I knew what the play was about, because at that time I had a lot of students who went to Vietnam and came back, and I had one particular friend who went and didn't come back. And some combination of the people who came back—especially Stephanie's twin brother, who came back carrying a lot of baggage, mental baggage, anguish— and the death of this friend of mine exploded in my head somehow, and Teddy emerged from some amalgamation of them, me, and all the feelings I had about the American heroic myth, which is essentially centered in old cowboy heroes and war heroes, formerly heroes.

Gladstein: I find him Byronic.

Medoff: Stephen or Teddy?

Gladstein: No, no, Teddy.

Medoff: We're trying to talk about Stephen.

Gladstein: Yeah, but Teddy is so fascinating to me because he is the disillusioned idealist. You're talking about the American dream, the hero, and he is, of course, the character that dominates that play. So I wonder . . . he walks off into the sunset, and you come back to Stephen. You come back to Stephen twice, don't you?

Medoff: I come back to Stephen, I think, because, of all the characters I have created, somehow he's my favorite, and I think he's my favorite because I think he is the most normal, not normal in the sense that he is well balanced as a human being but that he is the most like all of us, really, in the sense that he is an extremely basic, living human. Stephanie and I went to Africa some years ago to ride around and look at animals and savannahs and all that. And we were driving around, and Stephen literally started talking to me one day, in my head, he just started talking. He was talking about the movies, and I truly started writing what I heard him saying in my head, and that became the first act of *The Heart Outright,* which was a monologue.

Gladstein: That's a wonderful monologue.

Medoff: I really like it, and I understand now that lots and lots of kids do parts of that monologue at speech festivals and auditions. People would ask me, over the years, what happened to Teddy and to Stephen and Angel, and I always said, "I know that Teddy was killed that day and that Stephen and Angel met ten years later." And so approximately ten years later I find myself writing *The Heart Outright*. And I have just found that I love them a lot and that I am very happy to be with them again.

Gladstein: What is happening to *The Heart Outright?*

Medoff: That's kept track of in Florida, and so I don't know who's done it or how many times it gets done or if it gets done. It was done in New York, Off-Broadway, off-off-Broadway actually, a couple of years ago with Kim McCallum and David Andrews, who did it here, and Kevin O'Conner right before he died, and Anjanette Comer—wonderful cast, wonderful cast—and it ran for, I don't remember, a month or so, and I didn't really think it had commercial viability, so it didn't get moved or anything.

Gladstein: And *Stumps,* what's happened to it?

Medoff: *Stumps* is the only play I've ever written that got unified good reviews, granted they were out here in New Mexico. I can't get anybody to do it the way it is. I've had so many theatres tell me how well written it is and how offensive they find it. And I don't understand it. So I suspect I will do what I do with all my plays, that I will go back to it when it calls me back, and in its own good time it will wend its way into various theatres.

Gladstein: It's very cinematic. Have you ever thought of writing the screenplay?

Medoff: Yeah, but not enough to want to do it yet.

Gladstein: Oh, it was wonderful.

Medoff: Thanks, I liked it a lot, and I know that I inevitably rewrite everything I write. And I would like to go back to it and work on it again. Because I've been busy doing other things, I haven't felt compelled to do it. At some point I'll feel compelled to do it and will.

Gladstein: What brought you back to the novel? I read some place that your master's thesis was a novel.

Medoff: Yeah, my master's thesis was a novel called *The Savior,* which turned into my second play, *The Kramer,* which I don't think is a very good play. I think it's got some interesting things in it for anybody trying to figure out what was eating me and where I was coming from to get where I've gone. You could look at that and see a hominid of a character I've created a number of times. Actually both Stephen and Teddy exist in that play in different forms. I literally quit writing prose when I started writing for the theatre, and it wasn't until about five years ago, after I had been doing a lot of screenwriting and turning out a play every year or so, that I felt that the collaborative process in both those media is going to make me crazy if I didn't get away from it. I just was sick of working with other people, and I didn't hate either process, but I was just really tired of the enormous amount of input that you'd have to listen to even if you don't accept it. You have to learn to listen to it in both screenwriting and playwriting. And I decided that I was going to go away for half a year, get away from the telephone and away from both the theatre and the film, and that I was going to write them up. And I had pieces of this book in my head for a very long time. Parts of it are in the play *The Majestic Kid;* parts of it had gotten thrown out. And I kind of collected them, and from that something kind of just started to build, and I loved going back to prose writing again—I just loved it. It was wonderful to be all by myself during the times, the intense times, that I spent writing that book.

Gladstein: I was wondering if you cared to comment on the different kinds of artistic expression in your repertoire. I know you're all these things: an actor, a director, a playwright, a teacher.

Medoff: Well, I never thought I would enjoy being a teacher. I thought I was going to become a teacher because—

Gladstein: You believe that's an art also?

Medoff: Oh, absolutely. I became a teacher because my mentor from the University of Miami, Fred Shaw, told me initially that the only way I could make a decent living and have time to write was to become a college professor. And so I was working in Washington, D.C., in a normal job at a technical institute as a publications director, and I hated it. I went to graduate school, and I came here to teach because Fred had taught here as a young man. He kind of pushed me here. And I really didn't want to go teach anywhere, but he insisted that I come and start teaching, because he said, "That's the way you're going to develop as a writer." I wanted to go off to Europe and bum around. I probably actually wanted to go to Paris and pretend to be either Sartre or Hemingway. So I came here, and I thought the first day I walked into class that I was going to die of fear. And by the time I left my first class, I was in love. It was extraordinary. I have never had such an instant transformation in my life. Walking into my first classroom and seeing twenty-five faces staring at me, eighteen-year-old kids waiting for me to dispense information to them and to lead them somewhere, was absolutely stunning in terms of how quickly it turned me into a responsible adult. And I have never once not loved walking into a classroom since then, twenty-six years ago. And it very definitely is an art form.

Gladstein: What did you teach then?

Medoff: I was teaching freshman composition. I started by teaching four sections of freshman composition. That's a rigorous job, and I'm glad I don't have to do that anymore. Then I started teaching creative writing, though I didn't really think I was truly qualified yet, but I think I did a pretty decent job of it, because I'd learned a lot from Fred Shaw about how you conduct a writing workshop.

Gladstein: Did you take creative writing at Stanford?

Medoff: Yeah, I was in the writing center there.

Gladstein: Who were your professors there?

Medoff: Stegner, Richard Scowcroft were my two principal teachers. But I think that Fred Shaw told me the best and most important things about writing, the most useful, among which was that nobody could teach you to write. The only way you learn to write is you read and you write. He said, "If you are committed to it and you have a modicum of talent necessary to begin with, then it's about discipline, and then it will take you about ten years of doing it every day before anybody will appreciate anything you write. The rest of it will be crap, but it will be good, educational crap."

Gladstein: And who do you read?

Medoff: Well, I can plow through three or four books a week if I get on the streak, and I will read virtually anything from mysteries to nonfiction. I spent a couple of years reading books about physics and mathematics because they both frightened me. And so I set out to write *The Homage That Follows.* It's about a mathematician because it's an area that scared me. So I like things about the universe; I liked Hawkings's book. But I tend to fall back on the people I grew up loving, like Faulkner, who I guess is my favorite of all writers. I still love reading Philip Roth, John Updike, Saul Bellow, William Styron, and Carson McCullers and Eudora Welty. The first time I read *The Golden Apples,* it was absolutely one of the most extraordinary experiences I think I ever had, and I'm not even sure why, to tell you the truth. Charlotte, I mean, Emily Brontë, had an enormous effect on me as a young writer when I first read *Wuthering Heights,* just in terms of the way she structured the book. It taught me so much about structure.

Gladstein: I notice you're not mentioning any playwrights.

Medoff: Oh, I never read playwrights. No, and I still don't. I can't stand reading plays. I hate reading plays. Truthfully—this is a horrible thing to say—when I go to New York, I don't go to the theatre a lot. I don't really want to know what everybody else is doing. I don't want to be influenced in any way. I can't even tell you why, but generally I don't like going to the theatre because it seems to me that its so blatantly artificial somehow, most theatre. And I'm sure if I didn't know me and I went and saw my plays, I'd feel the same way. I would truthfully rather read a book or even go to a movie.

Gladstein: Now let's get back to the original question.

Medoff: What was it?

Gladstein: We were talking about the differences among being an artist as a teacher, an actor, a director, and a playwright, especially since you just finished saying you don't like going to the theatre.

Medoff: Acting is something that I enjoyed doing in my twenties and thirties and into my forties. I did really enjoy it, but it was really like . . . it was a little diversion. And I enjoyed the rehearsal process a whole lot. I liked the exploratory process. I liked working with other people. I liked being able to be a kid for a change and have a director who got to be the parent, because I'm so often the parent. But the fact is that acting is not of any great consequence to me. I could easily do without it. In fact, through the last three, four years, I've had no desire whatsoever to get onstage. I've been asked to do things, and it's just not important.

Gladstein: And directing?

Medoff: Directing is different. Directing is very important. I love being able to be an interpreter occasionally, rather than the source. I like interpreting other people's work. I've been as happy directing Shakespeare as directing any of my contemporaries.

Gladstein: Speaking of directing Shakespeare, I was a great fan of the *Macbeth* that you did.

Medoff: I'm glad.

Gladstein: I thought it was very effective.

Medoff: Thank you.

Gladstein: I have acted in *Macbeth* three different times, and I felt so challenged by your interpretation. Where did you get the idea of directing it in that futuristic— [Medoff's *Macbeth* was set in some future time among what appear to be Castro-like insurrection leaders, dressed in fatigues and combat boots. The witches are punk-rock groupies on roller skates, who put together their brew of hallucinogens and herbs in a Cuisinart, which acts as their cauldron. There are three television sets projecting the action. Both Duncan and Malcolm are women. Duncan and Banquo are romantically involved, which serves as a motivation for Macbeth's concern that Banquo will react aversely if he kills the king.]

Medoff: I'm not even sure except that I started thinking, at some point, I think, erroneously, that I didn't really like Shakespeare. And so I decided I really should do something. And going back to high school . . . I mean, I remembered in high school being very taken by *Macbeth.* And of course in high school you had to memorize all those monologues in *Macbeth,* and I can still remember them all. So I decided I'd do *Macbeth,* and I had Kim McCallum here at that time, an actor I liked a great deal and whom I knew was a fearless, fearless actor. So we decided we were going to do *Macbeth.* And I'm not quite sure where it came from, out of my head, to do it that way, but I know I had a great, great time, and the fact that you liked it is very satisfying. We had a wonderful, wonderful time, because what I found, of course, is what I guess anybody who does Shakespeare finds: that he spans the ages and you can't kill him. You can beat him, you can beat him to a pulp, which I think we did, but you can't kill him. The work just shines through. It's luminous.

Gladstein: But it worked perfectly well; I mean Duncan could be a female ruler, the king be a woman, and the language worked perfectly.

Medoff: It was great. It was great. But, anyway, I do, I really do, like directing and would like to do some film directing, though I'm at an age now where it's not mandatory. If the opportunity arises . . . and I do have several projects that, if they happen, I would end up directing. I would like to direct a movie. I have a feeling that that would allow me to amalgamate what talents I do possess. Because I think I do write pretty well, and I know I interpret pretty well, and I know I manage people pretty well, and that's what a film director has to do.

Gladstein: You once said that you make your living writing movies but satisfy your soul doing theatre. Do you still feel that way?

Medoff: I still pretty much feel that way. To tell you the truth, I would much rather, right now, just go and write another book. And I think part of that has to do with the fact that the movie business is pretty oppressive, in that the screenwriter is ultimately of so little consequence and gets so little credit and is usually the person who spends the longest time working on the project. And the reason I'm a little bit down on the theatre is that I think that the economic exigencies of our society now are adversely affecting the energy of playwrights. I don't any longer feel what I felt ten years ago, when I was confident that anything I wrote would have any number of venues. There is very little confidence that anything I write will ever get into any type of commercial venue because there is so little of what we would call "straight theatre" making its way into New York. I was talking to someone on the phone the other day—and I don't know how the subject came up, oh, I remember what it was, it was for this workshop that is being done this summer of *The Homage That Follows*—and the producer said, "Who shall I invite? Are there people you want to invite?" I said, "I don't have any idea who the producers in the commercial theatre are any more." And she said, "There are hardly any left." So I guess I would be just as happy to stay home and write another book and spend years doing it. And hope that some thousands of people would read the book.

Gladstein: Are you still happy being a professor at New Mexico State University?

Medoff: Yeah. I don't teach a whole lot any more. I usually teach one course a semester, and I teach in four-week blocks where I meet a small class every day for twice the normal amount of time. It's a very intense relationship, and I like that a lot. I can no longer teach a class where I have to be here a couple of times a week for sixteen weeks, and I don't like turning the class over to someone else. So the way I teach now is that way, in intensive blocks. The best teaching I do now, frankly, is with high school kids, when I go out and do three- to five-day workshops around the country. I really, really like doing that.

Gladstein: And the workshops are about writing?

Medoff: They're writing and acting, where I get writing and acting students together with high school drama and English teachers, and we lock ourselves up somewhere for three to five days. And I've worked out a method of operation. It's great fun, and it allows me to give back, because I've gotten a great deal from students and teachers myself. So I feel that I just don't want to close myself off here on the ranch and become a hermit, but if I'm going to teach, I want to do it effectively, and the only way I can do it effectively anymore is in short, intense doses.

Gladstein: Or with innocent students?

Medoff: Well, I think it's not only the innocence. I don't think of it that way, though you're probably right. But I feel that adolescents need this kind of encouragement, the kind of encouragement I can bring to them. And their teachers need someone like me to come in and corroborate that, indeed, the teachers are trying to lead them down an appropriate path. So I can, in effect, lift the spirits of the teachers and both impart to the students a certain amount of knowledge I've accrued and tell those of them with real talent that they have real talent and know that they will believe me.

Gladstein: I want to ask another question about your writing, your screenwriting. What you've done in the case of *City of Joy* and *Clara's Heart* is adapt someone else's work to the screen. Would you like to talk about that?

Medoff: On the one hand, when I first started writing screenplays, I did a lot of original stuff, and I thought at several points that it would be a lot easier to work on someone else's book. And then of course the opportunities began to arise, and in adapting both those books, in fact, there was nothing easy about them. *Clara's Heart* was somewhat easier because at least there were wonderfully full-fleshed characters in the book, but what I think every screenwriter finds in adapting a book, even screenwriters who adapt their own work, is that an apple is simply not an orange. They're both fruit, but they're different. The demands of the screen invariably force you to do exactly what you've been hired to do, to take the work literally, that is, to adapt something. That is, you take it from one form and turn it into a different form. *City of Joy* was a five-year-long process, and it was very, very challenging. And I've come to the point now—and I began with that thought—where I want to pick things to do in film because I know I'm going to end up irritated more often than satisfied, things that challenge me and things I have to learn that I don't know anything about. So going to India for five years in my head was a great challenge, and dealing with Dominique Lapierre's extraordinary book, which had hundreds of characters and hundreds and hundreds of vignettes, was a great challenge, because I had to figure out how to compress that into two and a half hours. In general, screenwriting is very frustrating, because, as I suggested earlier, the screenwriter gets very little credit and spends a lot of time working on material over which he has no control ultimately. So it's tough, but you make a great deal of money. And I think it's almost like surgery. After surgery you think, "I'm never going to go through this again. I'd rather be dead." And after a movie of mine comes out, I think, "I'm never going to do another screenplay. I'd just rather live off my retirement." But, as with surgery, you forget about it after a while and go back and do it again, because hope does beat eternally in the human breast. And each time I set out to write a movie, I think this will be a great experience. I've just started to write an original screenplay about hostage-taking in the Middle East, which I am writing for Tri-Star, which I will direct if they do it. And I'm about to start a movie about high school basketball and two boys, black and white, that I'm really looking forward to. In both cases it is going to push me into certain arenas. In the case of the hostage-taking, I've been immersed in reading the history of the Middle East, immersed for months. With the basketball thing, obviously I know a lot about sports and have a lot of impulses about boys who play basketball and want to play sports. But I think, because racism is so clearly rearing its ugly, ugly, head well above the horizon again, that it will be very good for me to have to get inside x-number of black characters and spend a lot of time trying to feel what that feels like for them to deal with it.

Gladstein: Would you like to comment about the nature of your unhappiness with the film version of *Children of a Lesser God?*

Medoff: Well, it came down to something very simple, well, two very simple things. One, they replaced me, because we didn't agree about what it should be, which I think was a horrible, horrible thing to do. It was an extremely uncomfortable predicament to be in. And the second thing was that essentially what they did was alter, adapt, the second part of my screenplay and reduce what I thought of as the political aspect of the play, having to do with Sarah Norman's EEOC suit against her school, to something that I thought was terribly oversimplified, where her sea-change to activist came about by virtue of meeting a deaf woman who was having some success in the hearing world. And although I thought it was a very lovely scene in the movie, I did not think that it created the impetus for the horrific thing that James Leeds does to her when he forces her to speak. I didn't think that we got where we needed to go, and to me it diminished the size of the movie enormously. And I was put in the ridiculous predicament of not wanting to win an Academy Award, for which I had been nominated, because I hated the experience and because I did not like the movie as well as I thought I could have and should have. So it's that simple. On *City of Joy* I had a wonderful experience with Roland Joffe, where we fought and made up. We became brothers of the soul, and the movie didn't get nearly the kind of reviews that *Children* did, but I liked it better because I thought it was a much more shared experience. But that, of course, is a very personal, personal point of view.

Gladstein: Have you ever thought about what a wonderful professional opportunity your movie created for Marlee Matlin?

Medoff: Yeah, sure. She's a very nice woman, a very sharp woman. I regretted at the time that Phyllis Frelich didn't get to do the movie role, but the one thing, the one thing that I begged them when I sold the movie rights was that they give deaf people those roles, because, given the nature of Hollywood, to put it in a positive sense, it is an extraordinarily large business, extremely business oriented. The bottom line has much more to do with commerce than it does with art. As someone joked once, "They don't call it show art, they call it show business." So they were, of course, thinking about some of our leading female hearing actresses to play that role. So if nothing else, I was gratified that there was a hearing-impaired actor in that role and in all the other hearing-impaired roles. But, you know, you don't, or I don't, not since I was nineteen or so, I don't think about what I do as earthshaking. I remember when I was nineteen, when I thought I was going to change the world, save the world by virtue of what I was going to write. I remember my mother telling me that if I ever affected one human being, ever changed or educated one person, I should consider that adequate compensation for my life as an artist. And I screamed at her that if that was all I could look forward to, I would quit writing and become a doctor, as I was supposed to. And of course we learn as we grow older, parents are so often right about what they tell us. Somewhere along the line I realized that my mother was absolutely right, and I stopped trying to write philosophy or politics or to educate a readership or a viewership. I started writing about behavior. Literature is about behavior. Literature is about characters, and I realized that in order to be effective, I had to write about behavior. I had to become all of my characters, and I had to care about all my characters equally. And if I did that decently, then what I wrote would suggest thought of one sort or another, would suggest politics of one sort or another. So when I set out to write *Children of a Lesser God,* I set out simply to write a love story. At that time in my life I simply wanted to write a boy-girl love story. I wanted it to be rough. I wanted them to go through a crucible of some size. And I knew at that time that I wanted to write for Phyllis Frelich, who was and is and probably always will be profoundly deaf. So I knew that the female character was going to be deaf, and that's all I knew when I started. But I certainly didn't set out to expropriate the deaf as one of the last available minorities or to change the way the world viewed deaf people.

Gladstein: Do you think that the fact that you have three daughters has affected your desire to develop the female part of you?

Medoff: Absolutely, absolutely. There is no question that living in a house full of women has, I guess you can say, either exacerbated or enhanced the need to confront the female.

Gladstein: You said once, "I put people through hell; I try to." Are you still trying to punish your audience?

Medoff: I don't think so. I think it varies. I still think it is very important to jolt people, because "the world is too much with us." It is so staggering in its fearsomeness and its brutality that it is hard to startle people. And so I think I have felt that a kind of selective violence can still do that. And I do try to make people squirm a bit, yes. But at the same time I'm very conscious about wanting to write things that speak to my children, that speak to the need to put things into a perspective where as individuals we try to live the best lives we can live. I think partly that is why I went back to Stephen Rider, especially in *Stumps,* where I wanted him to confront the need to live as good a life as he could, to make boldly correct decisions. So I think I try to do that consciously. At the same time I've written several what I think of as family plays over the last few years. *Kringle's Window,* which is a children's play, that's being done quite a bit. *Stephanie Hero,* which was the last play I wrote, which I set out to write really with my children in my head.

Gladstein: Do you think that it's helped your playwriting career that you have a theatre at your disposal, more or less. You have a place where your plays can be done, where you can experiment with them.

Medoff: There was a time when I thought that I really should have moved to New York, when I first started to have success in the theatre, because I felt as if I was one of the few playwrights of some repute who really didn't have a home. And though I've done several plays at the Manhatten Theatre Club, three at the Mark Taper, I did feel a little homeless. But I didn't want to move, so the thing I gained, I suppose, was my connection to New Mexico State University, where, in fact, I could workshop my work. And then as time went on and Andrew Shay developed the New Mexico Rep, then he and I became partners of a sort. He ran the New Mexico Rep for seven or eight years, and all but one year either he or I had a new play on there, and that way I didn't have to leave home. That was my idea of a good time. And I had also reached the point, after *Children of a Lesser God,* where I no longer felt it incumbent on me to have every play I wrote make it to New York. I was not totally satisfied, but I was sufficiently satisfied to do good work and to be able to stay home. And as it happens, most of those plays wended their way to New York. So I think, really, it has helped me to be an academic, just in terms of the breadth of knowledge I have been allowed or forced, depending on how you want to look at it, to immerse myself in. I think there is no question that as a screenwriter I am vastly overeducated, because so many screenwriters are badly educated. They come out of film schools where they learn virtually nothing about literature and a whole lot about the mechanics of filmmaking. And it's a little scary when you start talking to young filmmakers, especially about literature, because there's not a great background there; there's not a great frame of reference from which to work.

Gladstein: There aren't a lot of Faulkners screenwriting in Hollywood anymore.

Medoff: No, well, there are quite a few writers like myself. There are a lot of educated older writers who come from the world of the novel or of the theatre who do come to Los Angeles. But again, even with young theatre people, they don't read as much as we used to. They come from much more visual backgrounds, much less verbal.

Gladstein: Even in creative writing schools in English departments, they talk about the fact that students don't read.

Medoff: Yeah, there's no question.

Gladstein: Well, do you care to tell our reading audience about what you have in mind for your next play?

Medoff: Well, I know the next play I write will be about my mother and father, and I'm not sure when I'll write it. But I know the basic ingredients. I know the first line. I know it will span, oh, some several decades. I think it will entail two sets of actors, one set playing them in their twenties and thirties and the other playing them in middle age. I know it's going to be very difficult to write. I have a feeling it will be the best thing I'll ever write. And I'm not sure that I'm ready to write it yet, but I know that that's sitting there. And I know that the gestation period for me for a play can be anywhere from a year or two, to four, five, or six.

Gladstein: Are you going to be in the play?

Medoff: No. No, I really—

Gladstein: You're going to write about your mother and father, but not include yourself?

Medoff: Oh, will I be in it, you say? Oh, well, maybe as some kind of secondary character. But I don't have any desire to write about myself, and I want the play to gestate sufficiently because I want to be able to fictionalize them. I don't want to think I am writing a biographical play. There are certain things I want to write about them, more than about my brother and me.

JOAN SCHENKAR
Vivian M. Patraka

Joan Schenkar (photo by David Scribner)

J oan Schenkar's theatre work has been produced throughout North
America, England, and Western Europe at experimental theatres, universities, theatre festivals, and theatre conferences. She is the recipient
of more than thirty-five grants, fellowships, and awards for playwriting
(including seven National Endowment for the Arts grants) and has been
reviewed in every major newspaper in the United States.

Schenkar's published plays include: *Signs of Life* (recipient of a CAPS
grant and an NEA fellowship) and *Cabin Fever* (nominated for an Obie
award), both published by Samuel French; *The Universal Wolf,* published
by both the *Kenyon Review* and Applause Books; *Family Pride in the 50's,*
published by the *Kenyon Review;* and *Fulfilling Koch's Postulate* and *The
Last of Hitler,* excerpted by the *Drama Review.* She has had more than
two hundred productions of her work on stage, radio, and video, including: *Signs of Life* (1979), *Cabin Fever* (1980), *Mr. Monster* (1981), *The
Last of Hitler* (1982), *Bucks and Does* (1983), *Fulfilling Koch's Postulate*
(1985), *Hunting Down the Sexes* (1986), *Family Pride in the 50's* (1987),
The Lodger (1988), *Fire in the Future* (1988), *Between the Acts* (1989), *The*

Universal Wolf (1991, 1993), *Murder in the Kitchen* (1993), and *Burning Desires* (1994). Current works in progress include *The Viennese Oyster* and *Big Bad Brain.*

Schenkar has been playwright in residence at artists' colonies throughout the United States and with such experimental companies as Joseph Chaikin's Winter Project, the Polish Laboratory Theatre, and the Minnesota Opera New Music Theatre Ensemble. She is an alumna of New Dramatists and a current member of PEN, the Dramatists' Guild, the League of Professional Theatre Women, the Women's Project, the Brontë Society, and Société des auteurs et compositeurs dramatiques. She is artistic director of Force Majeure Productions in New York City, and the London production company Signs of Life Theatre is named after her play. She has directed five of her own works in full productions and is invited to speak about her work at colleges and theatre conferences throughout North America.

Joan Schenkar is best known for her "comedies of menace for the mental stage," and critics have frequently praised her "powerful, disturbing theatre," for its "unorthodox and bold experimental staging," "its echoing, austere, and dazzling language," and its "darkly hilarious and brilliantly creepy" comedy that challenges and provokes while giving no quarter to easy answers or mass popularity. Using an embroidered tapestry of the real and the invented and a lyrical, witty language that is skewed and repetitive, Schenkar's plays create disturbing, surreal landscapes of collective mind. The insistence in the plays on a community of obsessions, motives, and nightmares conveys the unconscious as a complex, entangling web among the characters created in collaboration with the culture they inhabit. Schenkar is fascinated by epistemology, by how people know what they know, and when they know it, and what they do with it. Tracking this knowledge by means of condensed, unusual theatrical metaphors drawn from cannibalism and cooking, from pathology and freakishness, from gardening and comic strips, and from performance and ritual, Schenkar's theatre creates a continuing exploration of gender politics and sexuality, fascism and violence, language and invention, and memory and history in relation to our psychic lives. The world of these plays is, as one critic described it, "the familiar haunted by the unknown," a world that elicits "a shudder of recognition" from audiences in the midst of their laughter.

This interview represents part of the continuing dialogue between Joan Schenkar and myself that began in the eighties and continues into the present of 1994.

Patraka: What prompted you to write your first play?

Schenkar: Before I was disinherited, I was a remittance relative for quite a while. And my father bribed me with this huge farm to get out of the Chelsea Hotel, where I was having a hell of a good time but perhaps not the good time my parents had designed for me. So I went up to Vermont, and I started talking to myself. I'd always talked to myself, but this time I began to write down what I was saying. Since I had no name for the things I was writing, I called them "conversations." I had no idea the "conversations" would turn into the play *Cabin Fever,* or that I would turn into a playwright. It was a terrible shock.

Patraka: Could you tell me about what the process of writing a play is like now and for the plays that followed *Cabin Fever?*

Schenkar: I hear a voice six inches behind my left ear. I have some dark dream fifteen minutes before daybreak. I see a place in which I think something interesting might happen. And suddenly things that have been unconsciously brewing for years amass a gigantic precipitation and rain down on my head all at once. And then one day, one terrifying day, I sit down with lots of notes—I do enormous historical research so I can completely pervert facts and skew visions toward my own obsessions—I sit down with these notes to find the form in which that particular precipitation is expressed. I knew the counters I was working with in *Signs of Life,* but until I invented that tea table, with those two men drinking blood in their teacups and eating the crushed bones of women in their biscuits, I had no way to structure all the information I had invented and gathered. Once I've found the form, I am released into the play.

Patraka: Can you think of structures like that for other plays as well?

Schenkar: For *Family Pride in the 50's,* it was when I sat those people down at the dinner table. For *The Last of Hitler,* I invented the radio announcers and split the stage. It's always a formalistic problem, and frequently it's tied to a physical positioning. In *Cabin Fever* those three old things sitting on their porch just appeared whole. The fact that I could not get them up out of their chairs completely determined what happened in the play. The determining form of *Fulfilling Koch's Postulate* was the frame of a comic book. I imagined a split stage, which represented an infected throat. On one side of the uvula was the laboratory, on the other the kitchen. I have an extremely complete and well-integrated unconscious intelligence, which does most of my work for me, and it's totally tied to the binary brain and my own rather ambivalent personality. I think that's why most of my plays work themselves out in some form of split stage, physically or metaphorically. When I'm writing, I go to bed at nine o'clock. From nine o'clock at night to five o'clock in the morning, I dream, and that's my nine-to-five workday. Marguerite Yourcenar has this notion of the writer being her own secretary, that in fact you are your own amanuensis, and all you are doing is taking dictation from what I presume to be a deeper self. The best writing is always automatic writing in the psychological sense. It's transferring. That's why I write at five o'clock in the morning, when I'm just up out of dreams.

Patraka: You were once quoted as saying the naturalistic play in America is the curse of theatre. What did you mean by that?

Schenkar: It's like a relationship that starts in the middle of a surreal and very interesting night and ends in the bright, boring, naturalistic light of a living room. American plays go through this dreadful, conscious, rewrite program, these frightful workshops, these endless readings, and they get closer and closer to the surface, closer to the living room, and farther from the deeper, darker, *bedroom* self that initiated them. Almost no other kind of writing is subjected to the editing that plays are subjected to. And so the kind of curse I'm talking about is a curse of both language and attitude, engendered by the idea that the language and attitude you should use in theatre is the same language and attitude you use in people's living rooms. Theatre is a special room in itself. It's in fact on a different physical level, on another plane from the audience, and requires another way to approach it. So let us not pretend that we are sitting in a living room on the same level with the audience, but let's make that language higher or lower, on a different metaphorical and stylistic plane. "Curse" is a quick word to use about naturalism. I meant something much more pernicious, more like a cellular disease that spreads and spreads and has really "televisionized" all of theatre.

Patraka: If you had to sort out your plays in terms of their levels of language, which play would go where?

Schenkar: All my plays have their own lives. They're like living things, in that they have an aesthetic, they have a physical body, they have an amatory life, they have a spiritual life, and they have a linguistic life, a metaphorical one, so that the language in each play is constructed around the vernacular particular to the kind of social circumstances I am investigating. For instance, in *Fulfilling Koch's Postulate,* I tried to construct a vernacular that sounded as if it were translated from low Bavarian and had a vocabulary of maybe three hundred words, because I was trying to invoke the comic book structures of the Katzenjammer kids. For *Signs of Life,* I had to invent a theatrical late Victorian speech that would work on the stage. In *Family Pride in the 50's,* my chief concern was displacing the adverbs so they would unbalance the sentences enough to suggest that odd, tilted 1950s TV-talk speech. Of course, I hope that the vernacular in that play is much more interesting than fifties TV-talk, but the idea was to give the theatrical feeling of that, which is different from the naturalistic feeling. I don't want people to think they're seeing real people from these eras but rather to be very aware that they're seeing a theatrical representation of some important ideas about each of these eras. In *The Lodger,* I tried to use a very ironic imitation of translations from Greek tragedies—Euripidean language, very simple. I used stichomythia and deliberately set the tone as a kind of mock-Attic. And in *The Last of Hitler,* I went for various vernaculars and accents that all dissolved into a kind of Yiddish.

Patraka: I've heard you say that the characters in a play are all part of a central ganglion, of a play's central consciousness. How does this work with a character's individual metaphorical life?

Schenkar: All the characters in any play of mine share certain assumptions or even contradictions, and each one contributes to this effect, which is why I don't even like calling them characters. They're parts of this artistic whole that I'm trying to make, and just because they don't have the same simple metaphorical construct, they share a much larger one. Frequently, for instance, the same phrase will appear in the mouths of everybody in the play, but as it passes from mouth to mouth, it's altered slightly. I do use a lot of repetition, but it's never the same, it's always changed by the circumstance of its having been repeated, its aspect rotated slightly by the fact of its passing through yet another constructed being.

Patraka: Why do so many of your plays contain doctor characters?

Schenkar: One of my obsessive and recurrent themes is some form of medical practice put on stage. Any client/patient relationship, any of those conditions in which someone has control over someone else, is a highly theatrical situation for me. And, of course, one of the easiest ways to access that situation is "the doctor." The professions in general are some of my favorite targets. I'm writing a play called *The Viennese Oyster,* in which finally, after a thousand years of therapy, I'm taking on Sigmund Freud and the boys. He's the doctor I've been after all these years, and I think I'll have a good time doing it. I'll set it around 1912 to 1922, when psychoanalysis was in its early phases and at its most interesting. I like to set things very specifically and never in the present. You trivialize yourself horribly in the present. You're forced to use a vocabulary that is not yet, to me, interesting, made up of slang rather than argot, real vernacular, and you can't use it as a prism through which to look at present-day things.

Patraka: When I talked to you years ago about *Signs of Life,* you said that you would never write a play that hopeless again.

Schenkar: Silly me. I was in a particularly good mood when I wrote *Signs of Life,* so I think what I was saying was that you caught me at a time when I thought I would never be in that good a mood again. I hope to write something even blacker this next year. *Between the Acts* is incredibly, presumptively cheerful, and I was just in a foul mood when I wrote it. The better the mood I'm in, the more of the black arts I can practice. You know how planets have these asteroids and dark moons that circle them? And there are these magnificent eruptions that they have, and they throw off these bodies and then circle them forever? Well, that's how I think about my plays. I've got all these black moons and hunks of asteroids swirling around me that I've pitched off in these wonderful eruptions of climate and temperature and high fever and fantastic metaphorical explosions. I'm always looking forward to writing something tremendously upsetting.

Patraka: If a work is upsetting for an audience, what does that mean?

Schenkar: Well, it makes me very happy certainly. Let me back up a bit, because I've been thinking about this lately. The inherent tragedy of being a writer, where what you do is constructed on the page, is that while you are always shooting for the eternal, trying to encompass an ambient eternity, you are confined to laying out these sempiternal thoughts like railway lines, like linear yardsticks, with beginnings, middles, and ends, dependent clauses, and punctuation. And people have to read them on the page, one after another. And if what you're trying for is polyphony, this polyphonic effect, where you create this universe, this *inescapable* universe for me—I'm interested in no escape, in really imprisoning the audience in a way and forcing them to enter these nightmares—to do this with these sentences is to use a pitifully poor tool. So what I try to do with these sentences is make at least two things happen at once: keep this humor going so people are laughing and, underneath it, keep this dreadful subtext going in which the thing at which the people are laughing is too awful for words. You access the dark world with this kind of laughter, which, in its final implications, has to be demonic, because think what you're laughing at. I mean, in the best of all possible productions I've made you laugh at something dreadful.

Patraka: What makes *Between the Acts* so cheerful?

Schenkar: All of it's about money, which I find just an hysterical subject, speaking as somebody who was disinherited and found that her final, real, response to that had to be laughter, laughter and tears being kissing cousins. Everybody in *Between the Acts* has money, whether they've been disinherited or not, and one thing that money does is to enable you to be cut off from the consequences of your actions, and this provides large opportunities for humor.

Actually, my most recent piece, which is a play for both stage and screen, *Burning Desires,* is also incredibly cheerful. I mean, Joan of Arc is saved from burning, and her evil father—a lobotomist, naturally, for if Joan of Arc were alive in the 1950s, it wouldn't be an Inquisition she'd be subjected to, it would be a sanity hearing—is confined to a halfway house in a kind of twilight sleep of testosterone. Plus the city of Seattle is sick, as Thebes was sick. Salmon are swimming backward, trees grow upside down, Girl Scouts start fires all over town, and all that actually gets healed. The only thing that saves my self-respect, saves me from thinking I've gone all downy and tufted and chenille-like, is that the play is full of vicious children and weird adults, funny in an uncomfortable way and motored by an absolutely inexplicable sexuality. Otherwise the thought of being responsible for a wholly cheerful work would be more than I could bear.

Patraka: Who would you identify as important influences on your work?

Schenkar: Emily Brontë, Emily Dickinson, Christopher Marlowe, Samuel Beckett, Shakespeare's *Troilus and Cressida,* Djuna Barnes, the painter Francis Bacon, rock and roll, any number of composers, Julia Child, Maria Callas, Janis Joplin, Henry James, and selected lovers. Every writer I've read and liked has influenced me, because I love repetition and I reread my favorites so often. And in all my works you can hear deliberate echoes and misappropriations of certain of their phrases.

Patraka: What does it mean to be a metaphorical writer?

Schenkar: For me metaphor is only as interesting as the form that encloses it. It's like watching people make love under bedclothes: you don't know who's under that duvet cover, but you can certainly see them thrashing around, making different shapes. So I'm interested, as a metaphorical writer, in the French lace that covers the act and the apparent deathlike struggle that's going on underneath it. The very formal structure of the sentence contains the metaphor, and then the metaphor itself contains the terrible tragic truth at its heart. The metaphor is the decoration, the frosting on the prison cake, which of course is yet another expression of what's at the heart of that cake, which might be the hacksaw that gets you out of prison, if you're very lucky.

Patraka: What difference is there between the kind of metaphor one finds in novels and theatrical metaphor?

Schenkar: In theatre you "dimensionalize" it, and certainly designers I work with are always reflecting it in lighting, in costumes, in sets. I thought that enormous twenty-foot-high radio of the 1920s in *The Last of Hitler* was a knockout. Whenever you set one of my plays and really take the metaphors literally, that has always seemed to me a delightful contradiction in terms, one that works very well on the stage. The stage as 1950s TV set in *Family Pride in the 50's* was wonderful. The infected throat in which the Typhoid Mary play [*Fulfilling Koch's Postulate*] was set was very funny. I tend to think visually, dimensionally, myself, so my plays are highly notated as to movement and to the way the thing looks. For *Between the Acts,* with a 120-page script, probably 40 pages are simple set design and are about the way in which the visual metaphors have to catch, reflect, comment on what's going on under those erotic plants at the center of that play.

Patraka: As a playwright what do you make of the current elevation of performance art?

Schenkar: Well, I see a lot of performance art, and I think its elevation is due to three things: infection by late-night television, the shortening of the Standard American Attention Span, and the complete undermining of fiscal architectures for the arts in this country. There is also a kind of fin-de-siècle collapsed quality about performance art, which is quite à la mode, along with a community-access-cable-station aspect to it, which is rather democratic. I mean, I like that a lot of it feels like a primary school party and sounds like a garage band. And I like less that its more formal and fashionable manifestations include my generation's obsession with objects, with visual appropriations, and with the disintegration of meanings. Performance art is also just easier—it's easier to produce, easier to consume, easier to forget—and in a country obsessed with ease, this is no small thing. Of course when it's good, it's very good indeed, but when it's one breath less than good, it's horrid.

At worst I think playwrighting is to performance art what acting is to acting out. However, since playwriting is more or less about ventriloquism, and performance is increasingly about assuming one's own voice, there's no reason that the forms couldn't conjugate in an interesting way. In fact I've tried to combine them myself in an opera-cabaret called *Murder in the Kitchen.*

Patraka: What do you think the function of critics is for playwrights?

Schenkar: Since you last asked me this question, I did a piece for *The Village Voice* ["Read My Scripts," 12 March 1991, 86] on theatre artists and critics, a kind of "modest proposal" for their future relations. This is the opening paragraph:

> It's very important to tell the truth about relations between theatre artists and theatre critics just now—and that truth is an ugly one. As anyone who has spent fifteen minutes listening to gossip in a dressing room knows, theatre artists are locked in a nightmarish dependency cycle with theatre critics. We hate you when you pan us, love you when you praise us, can't live with you, can't live without you, need you all the same and know it. The truth is (one of the truths is), theatre criticism has the same problem of definition and recognition that playwrighting does. It's the bastard child of its genre—courted and reviled by the same community it purports to define, and inextricably linked to the power structures that contribute to its devaluation.

Patraka: You decided to direct some of your plays yourself. Why, and what's it like?

Schenkar: Once again I'd like to retreat into something I've written—that's, anyway, the safest place for a writer. I've written a chapter for a book called *Upstaging Big Daddy,* about the motives that might prompt a playwright to direct her own work. I think I cited envy, competitiveness, and the desire to control one's own work as three of the most useful motives for prompting self-direction. Here's a paragraph from that chapter:

> As a writer, I think like a director. My mise-en-scènes are so elaborate and completely notated that they encompass lights, sets, sounds, movements, and even the pitch of voices. As a director, I am only a writer trying to make my work walk and talk. I do not identify as a director (I don't want to direct anyone's work but my own—and that only occasionally). I don't feel I have any great talent for directing, don't feel badly if I'm critically attacked for my directing, don't, in short, suffer any of the puncture wounds and body blows that bad writing about my language can deliver. (Nathalie Sarraute, 93 years old and celebrated on three continents, once told me that the only reviews of her work she remembers are the bad ones.) My chief concern as the occasional director of my work is not to limit the damage that the work can and must do to the assumptions of its audience. Sometimes I fail in this endeavor, but the failure is for the most part within my control and somehow far less galling than seeing the work

directed by someone who cannot realize its inherently dangerous qualities or by someone, more horribly, who deliberately neutralizes its possible effects. [From Schenkar's "A New Way to Pay Old Debts: The Playwright Directs Her Own," in *Upstaging Big Daddy: Directing Theater As If Race and Gender Mattered,* eds. E. Donkin and S. Clement (Ann Arbor: University of Michigan Press, 1993), 253–62]

Patraka: Given the fact that it's so hard to continue to make theatre, to continue to write plays, what keeps you going on?

Schenkar: Once you've entered the world with your work, taken a certain responsibility for it, there's really no going back to that place where you just sit and write and don't even think about whether a play will be produced or not. You can never really reclaim your innocence, "revirginize" yourself, when it comes to the world of theatre. And I'm not just a professional writer, I'm an obsessional writer. I'll never be happy unless I'm thinking in terms of some linguistic structure that can be uttered in a theatre or staged in a brain. I have no choice in the matter. Beckett, as usual, put the dilemma perfectly: "I must go on, I can't go on."

Patraka: You've begun to write for film. What's it like to extend your imagination to another genre?

Schenkar: Actually, I began to imagine other forms some years ago when I started to write for music theatre. My opera, *Fire in the Future,* was so delicious a subject for me—including, as it did, those two great war heroines, Joan of Arc and Marlene Dietrich—that I extended its possibilities into cinema. It just seemed the next place to go. Of course I turned the film frame into a kind of proscenium and wrote a cameo for the screenwriter Joan Schenkar, which appears under the opening credits. I continue my interest in making the writer's voice, as in both my play *The Universal Wolf* and my opera-cabaret *Murder in the Kitchen,* separate and distinct from the writer's stories. The screenplay, by the way, is called *Burning Desires,* and it explores the possible reappearance of Joan of Arc in the 1950s in Seattle, a city far too wet to burn her in. In this work I do exactly what I do in my plays, though in a much different way. I retrieve, I rescue, I quarry out from the limestone beds of history the lives of women, and some men, and return them to audiences, circumstances altered, psychological truths intact and extended, even enhanced, by the new forms I find for their stories.

Patraka: If I think of you as a feminist playwright, how do you respond?

Schenkar: I'm a feminist who *is* a playwright. I consider myself a . . . I don't like to use the word *revolutionary* because it implies an army, and

unlike my namesake, Joan of Arc, I'm not militaristic. But I do feel that
I'm always going against things. That's just my nature. And I think that's
very funny. I don't consider it a tragic position or necessarily a political
one; I consider it a wonderful condition for humor. The intention of
my plays is to invade people's dreams. In that sense, I've always seen
myself as a social terrorist, somebody who, instead of throwing a bomb
at the diplomats' ball, tries to write things that have the effect of terrorist activities, that really do explode the conventions in front of you.
Linguistic bombs, I guess you'd call them.

Patraka: Does your sexual orientation influence your playwriting?

Schenkar: I think it's the other way around. I think language influenced
my sexual orientation. Like Emma Bovary's, my imagination was seduced by what I read, and at a very early age too. Not to mention the
fact that my middle name is after Marlene Dietrich, a woman whose
richly varied sexual life I was always aware of. The inclusiveness of my
own sexuality has gone through my work, as Emily Brontë might say,
like wine through water. Its suppleness allows me to stand in many
places on the mental and emotional stage. And although I've never seen
any reason to reduce something as spiritual and mysterious as sexual
attraction to a politic, the tyranny of the times—but times are always
tyrannous—compels my imagination toward transgression.

Patraka: How does being Jewish affect your writing?

Schenkar: As Samuel Beckett said about life on earth, there's no cure
for it. Jews are historically, genetically, People of the Book. It's the
only religion I know of that forces literacy (that is, to be bat or bar
mitzvahed, you have to be able to read from the Torah) and that exag-
gerates respect for books (if you drop a sacred text, you're supposed to
kiss it). I don't think, however, you'd find me kissing the text that in-
structs Jewish males to thank Yaweh every morning for not having been
born a woman. Like most artist-Jews my age, I love the people, identify
with the culture, and have divorced the religion. I've prayed all my life;
I just don't quite know who I'm talking to. I see I haven't answered
your question.

Patraka: What about your attraction to French culture?

Schenkar: Living in another language is always interesting. I certainly
dreamt in the French language before I spoke it. My mother's background was French, so I have French manners. And I think those manners leak into the formalistic structure of my work. Many of my plays
could be called tragedies of manners or comedies of bad manners.
Manners are only interesting insofar as they're violated, and violations
of anything produce theatrical effects. So the terribly good manners of

the doctor and Henry James in *Signs of Life,* the elaborate courtesy of Monsieur Wolf in *The Universal Wolf,* the careful explanations of Dr. Dark in *Burning Desires* are all contrasted with what they're doing or contemplating, which is the slow, inexorable murder, the draining of life, of their women. In fact each play I write comes with its own inherent sense of manners.

Speaking of my attraction to French culture and the violation of manners, *The Universal Wolf,* my new, revisionist version of "Little Red Riding Hood," attempts to do violence to both the French Academy and the male-heroic nature of fairy tales. The play features a Reader who creates the voices of all the French writers represented—there are something like twelve of them, from Jacques Lacan to Pierre Louys—and who also embodies stage directions that the actors can't, won't, or don't do. The piece also sports competing narratives and a very risky moment where Monsieur Wolf insists that the house lights be turned up and the audience must read the brutal Perrault version of Little Red Riding Hood's demise. It's printed in their programs, and to my astonishment they do read it. I mean the play stops right in the middle for three minutes while the entire audience violates its structure and dutifully reads these four or five paragraphs I've placed in their programs. Its astonishing. A triumph of language over the baser appetites, if you ask me.

Patraka: There is something flamboyant and compelling about your dangerous characters, the ones with a lot of freedom, and yet I find nothing erotic about them, feel that you've taken pains to de-eroticize them.

Schenkar: I have to completely disagree with you. I find Gilles De Rais and Dr. Sloper and Monsieur Wolf and Dr. Reich extremely attractive because of the unlimited qualities of their imaginations. They're real madmen. I have yet to make a woman as mad as they are; I don't know if a woman can go mad in that way. I suppose I put up onstage what I find seductive. I don't find cruelty necessarily seductive or erotic. I do find the limitless imagination and the ability to speak that imagination one of the most erotic things in the world. Of course the fact that I've put dreadful deeds within their purview just speaks to me again of the contradiction. Everything lives to meet in its opposite, always, especially in the theatre. Contradictions, things yoked together by violence, are what interest me.

Patraka: You make the words *tragedy* and *comedy* seem interchangeable.

Schenkar: I don't see much difference. I mean the definitions have switched, haven't they? Something that ends in a marriage is almost always a cause for weeping, and something that ends in a death is frequently funny. I have an extremely tragic vision of life and a highly comic vision of living, and those two things coexist in a kind of uneasy entente cordiale. They inform and reflect and infect each other always. If you have to think dimensionally, the comedy is on top, the tragedy underneath. And I think they enhance each other, since the best comedy is really tragedy viewed at a distance.

Patraka: How do you think wit works in your plays?

Schenkar: Wit is like having an extra chromosome. It's an orientation much like sexual orientation is. It's not chosen, and it can't be taught. It's an ability to compress, a talent for succinctness, for seeing the world from a very odd angle. My wit manifests itself in a binary impulse, the impulse to yoke together by violence that which ordinarily would not be joined and to offer that contrast to an audience. Wit is really a worldview. You have to be exogamous, outside the tribe to be witty—it doesn't matter what tribe. And wit, I think, is best expressed in conversation. A playwright rehearses in conversation.

Patraka: Are we rehearsing now?

Schenkar: I have always regarded the interview as a performance.

Patraka: What would you say about the state of women's theatre in America, of playwriting by women?

Schenkar: Not enough is being produced, as usual. I don't know if the figures from over ten years ago have changed that much. In the known study done then, seven percent of the plays produced in the United States were written by women. About every fifty years there's a huge conflagration, and wonderful things by women flame up and then burn down to ashes. The system is too much for us. The social terrorists get tired. But in the last fifteen years we've experienced that again, and all this wonderful stuff has come up, and some of it has even made good art. News is being brought back from nerve endings, and that news is in sounds and shapes that we've not seen or heard before. And I do think, in all modesty, because the work has now completely its own life, that my play *Signs of Life* was one of the first to carry some of that news.

What we forget—and that act of bad memory does particular disservice to women because we get far fewer productions than men—is that all theatre begins with an act of writing and continues with an act of reading. No production is going to ensure the life of a play. Unfortunately in the United States you have to have productions, and productions of a certain sort, at least a long Off-Broadway run, before you can get your play published. It's backward and particularly damaging, as I said, to women playwrights, who don't get the publications because they don't get the productions. Things should be published and *then* produced. You can't make any decisions, know what the writer's intention is, until you've read a play, because so many minds go into a production. Who knows what devious direction the director has taken with the play? An actor having an off-night can throw the balance of a production. A badly lit play can sink under the weight of darkness. And by the way, many of the women writers you've heard of began by self-publishing and ended by self-publishing. The Brontë sisters had a legacy from a dead aunt. The first thing they did was take that legacy and publish their collected poems under, I'm sorry to say, rather neutered names. They didn't use it to spring themselves from hard labor as governesses. Gertrude Stein sold a Picasso and began Plain Editions. Virginia Woolf's legacy from an aunt helped start Hogarth Press. You would never know the names of these women if they hadn't published their own work.

Patraka: If you had any advice to give to a young woman who wanted to be a playwright, what would it be?

Schenkar: If you mean on the writing level, I really can't give any advice, because everything comes out of listening to yourself. I do think most good work comes out of silence. And if I were giving personal advice, the last thing I'd advise anyone to do is to go to the theatre for inspiration. I'd say stay home and read. Then, on the production level, I'd say be everywhere with your work. It's the exact opposite of the writer's level. Make sure everybody sees your work, knows about it, knows your name. Because theatre is a word-of-mouth business, where people need to know your name and associate that name with work. This is contradictory advice, and being a playwright is a very contradictory profession. Writing is a life sentence to solitude. Theatre is a life sentence to performing in public. Writers for the theatre are doomed to lives of eternal torment because of those two absolutely contradictory conditions—which must be maintained if your work is going to continue to live in the world.

WENDY WASSERSTEIN

Jan Balakian

Wendy Wasserstein (photo by James Hamilton, courtesy of Royce Carlton Inc.)

Wendy Wasserstein often jokes about the fact that, having a clear sense of her direction in life, she applied simultaneously to Columbia Business School and to the Yale School of Drama. The daughter of a prosperous textile manufacturer and of a housewife with a passionate interest in dance and theatre who took her to weekly dancing lessons at the prestigious June Taylor School of Dance, the sister of siblings who all became successful in the business world, Wendy rebelled against her family's more conventional values. When she began writing plays, her mother was concerned that her youngest daughter, a Mount Holyoke graduate, was neither a lawyer nor married to a lawyer. So it makes sense that Wasserstein's plays focus on women struggling to define themselves in a "postfeminist" America that still suffers from the backlash of sexism, homophobia, and traditional values. Not only does her writing reflect her interest in women, but it also reveals the fact that she is Jewish and a New Yorker.

Her first plays all grapple with the predicament of single women in

New York, women struggling to have fulfilled personal and professional lives. These plays include: *Any Woman Can't* (1973), produced Off-Broadway at Playwrights Horizons; *Uncommon Women and Others,* first produced in 1975 as her thesis at Yale, then presented at the Phoenix Theatre in New York in 1977, later televised for public television's Great Performances series in 1978, and finally revived in the fall of 1994 at the Lucille Lortel Theatre in New York with an updated ending; *Isn't it Romantic* (1979), presented by Playwrights Horizons in New York in 1983; and her Pulitzer Prize–winning play, *The Heidi Chronicles,* produced by the Seattle Repertory Theatre and Playwrights Horizons in 1988 and then produced as a television movie for TNT in winter of 1995. Her recent teleplay, *Kiss, Kiss Dahlings,* starring Blythe Danner, Nancy Marchand, Cynthia Nixon, and Charlie Rose, humorously depicts three generations of women actresses, two of which sell out to popular culture. In a slightly different key, her 1983 one-act play, *Tender Offer,* produced Off-Off-Broadway at the Ensemble Studio Theatre, poignantly explores the relationship between a young daughter and her father.

Although she resists being labeled a "feminist" playwright, arguing that men are not subject to such labels, she is seriously troubled by the double standards that she sees in American society, by the unjust inequities based on gender. Consequently women continue to interest her as the subject of her work. Her most recent work, however, depicts men more generously than her earlier work did. Indeed, Wasserstein is quick to point out that she owes a great deal to two men who have played important roles in launching her career: the artistic director of Lincoln Center, André Bishop, the former artistic director of Playwrights Horizons who produced her early plays; and the director Dan Sullivan.

Comedy is Wasserstein's trademark and her favorite genre. In addition to the above comedies she has written comedy sketches for the CBS television series *Comedy Zone* in 1984; *Happy Birthday, Montpelier Pizz-zazz,* about the social maneuvers at a college party, produced in New Haven, Connecticut, in 1974; a comedy with Christopher Durang called *When Dinah Shore Ruled the Earth,* a mockery of a beauty pageant, produced in New Haven at the Yale Cabaret Theater in 1975; and a comedy for public television called *"Drive," She Said,* about learning to drive in middle age.

Wasserstein greeted me graciously with a warm smile in the lobby of the Stanhope Hotel in Manhattan. In a salon in the back she spoke to me excitedly, even after a long day packed with appointments, about the receptive opening in Norfolk, Virginia, of her current Broadway hit, *The Sisters Rosensweig,* a comedy about three Jewish sisters from Brooklyn who meet at the eldest sister's London apartment to celebrate her fifty-fourth birthday. The play, which moved from the Greenwich Theatre in London to the Old Vic in the fall of 1994, reminds Wasserstein of the Broadway shows she grew up seeing as a little girl in New York. While *The Sisters Rosensweig* is not a musical, it is no surprise that in 1986 she wrote her own musical called *Miami,* about vacationing in Miami Beach in the fifties.

Wasserstein acknowledges the impact of Chekhov on her imagination, most noticeably in *The Sisters Rosensweig.* Chekhov's ability to capture the quotidian aspect of our lives as he balances humor and sorrow particularly appeals to Wasserstein's sensibility. In fact she adapted Chekhov's short story "The Man in a Case" to a one-act play, which was produced Off-Broadway at the Lucille Lortel Theater in 1986.

Well attuned to American popular culture, Wasserstein has also experimented with screenwriting. Her most recent screenplay, not yet produced, *The Object of My Affection* (1993), adapted from the novel by Stephen McCauley, boldly redefines the nuclear family. In addition, her screenplay *The Maids* exposes class conflict in a wealthy community, as did her 1979 teleplay *The Sorrows of Gin,* adapted from John Cheever's short story. With Christopher Durang, Wasserstein adapted Charles McGrath's short story "Husbands," originally published in *The New Yorker,* to a screenplay called *House of Husbands.* In many ways Wasserstein is a writer of the comedy of manners.

Most recently she has devised a new story outline for *The Nutcracker* for the American Ballet Theater, in collaboration with choreographer Kevin McKenzie. Their ballet, about changing seasons and emotions, reached New York during the company's 1994 May season at the Metropolitan Opera House.

Wasserstein has also been a prolific writer of prose. Her collected essays and articles, which originally appeared in *Esquire,* the *New York Times, New York Woman,* and *Harpers Bazaar,* have been collected in *Bachelor Girls,* published by Vintage in 1990. She currently has a column called "The Wendy Chronicles" in *Harpers Bazaar.* She began as a columnist for *New Woman* magazine in the fall of 1994.

Balakian: How did the production of *The Sisters Rosensweig* go in Norfolk, Virginia?
Wasserstein: It went very well. It's funny; I was in Norfolk eight years ago when the Dramatist's Guild and CBS gave a grant to the Virginia Stage Company, so I've actually been there before. The town is full of

empty office buildings, and I thought, "Who is going to come to this play?" It's a navy town. It was funny; it was like being in *All About Eve;* it truly, really felt like being on the road. Andre Bishop said to me, "If this show had not been in New York, and we were just on the road with this show, we would think we really had something." Mariette Hartley was really excellent. And the rest of the cast was quite good. It was nice because it felt very much in a theatrical tradition. I didn't know if this play would work outside New York because of the New York and Jewish references.

Balakian: I wanted to know if there was a big difference in the audience reception outside of New York.

Wasserstein: That's what was interesting, because it made me realize that the play worked. We got a standing ovation on the opening night. Caroline Aaron, a Virginian, told me that it was amazing to her that it went over really well. But I think it has to do with the fact that *Rosensweig* is a well-structured play that tells a story, and that ultimately the play is about three sisters who tell stories. That's when you really know if your play is working—if it's away from the place that it's about. It's like, as things age and . . . watching them again and seeing what works, aside the references. In a way *The Sisters Rosensweig,* unlike *The Heidi Chronicles,* is not really a period piece, except that it takes place in 1989 and has to do with the Soviet coup and in a way a fin-de-siècle sort of thing.

Balakian: I wanted to ask you about the influence of Chekhov on your work, because it struck me that Chekhov's *Three Sisters* must have influenced *The Sisters Rosensweig.*

Wasserstein: Chekhov has always been my favorite. I was amazed when we first read *The Three Sisters* in drama school because I didn't really know it until I got there. I wasn't a theatre major; I was a history major, so I didn't know that much theatre. When I read it, I thought, "Boy, this is really good. This is what plays should be."

Balakian: When I teach Chekhov, my students often say, "This is so dull! Nothing happens. They say they're going to go to Moscow, and they don't even go!"

Wasserstein: No, that's why in *Uncommon Women* when they say, "When we're thirty we'll be amazing, when we're thirty-five we'll be amazing," it's sort of a Chekovian thing. I think that the idea of finding moments in peoples' lives when they could turn to the right or turn to the left, or why they don't turn at all, is fascinating. I've often wondered if Chekhov were writing right now, whether he would be successful or not.

Balakian: Although his work continues to be done.

Wasserstein: It's interesting. They are not plays that call attention to the playwright; they are plays that call attention to the players, to the people within the play. And that's really interesting to me. And the use of the comedy and the melancholy is interesting to me.

Balakian: That's a combination that you use. On the one hand you're writing comedy, but on the other hand there is a serious undertone.

Wasserstein: There is a serious undertone, and there is a wistfulness in my plays. These are not tragic lives. Returning a Chanel suit is not the saddest thing one ever has to do, but in a way that's a very Chekhovian note, because it has to do with daily life. There are tragedies in life, God knows. Daily life in Sarajevo is about deep horribleness. But daily life here is about sadnesses and happinesses.

Balakian: And actually in the play Gorgeous's husband is out of work, and she is making a bold decision by cashing in the Chanel suit to send her son to school.

Wasserstein: Right. It's what she can do within her own world. But she's obviously a very courageous woman on some level. She's a survivor.

Balakian: So it's the combination of melancholy and humor in Chekhov that influenced you, although people don't often think of Chekhov as being a humorous writer.

Wasserstein: Isn't *The Cherry Orchard* called a comedy?

Balakian: Yes, and Chekhov said that he was misunderstood, that his work should be done more comically.

Wasserstein: I think if you can really capture human nature of a certain sort, bourgeois human nature, I think there's something comedic there because it has to do with surviving. Otherwise, if you really took it all seriously, ultimately there's death *(laughs loudly)*.

Balakian: The Beckett worldview. When I teach Chekhov, I talk about him as the predecessor to Beckett in the immobility and stasis of his characters.

What really strikes me about your work is the sense that you are a New York, Jewish writer. It's apparent in *Uncommon Women, Isn't it Romantic,* and *The Sisters Rosensweig.* There is the whole issue of assimilation in *The Sisters Rosensweig,* which I found really fascinating, because I grew up in New Jersey, but I am Armenian. I was sitting in the audience thinking, "Wow, this is how I've always felt, being this Jersey kid, yet having all of this rich and tragic Armenian past." Would you talk about the importance of being Jewish to your writing?

Wasserstein: The Sisters Rosensweig is about being Jewish.

Balakian: Absolutely.

Wasserstein: The Heidi Chronicles actually is not. But Scoop Rosenbaum is Jewish. If someone who wasn't Jewish wrote that play, I don't know that people would say, "Oh boy, what a Jewish play." In fact, people have assumed that Heidi is Jewish.

Balakian: I didn't feel that Heidi was Jewish.

Wasserstein: She's not. I wrote a musical call *Miami,* which is very much about being Jewish. It's about going to Miami Beach in 1959. I had the idea for *The Sisters Rosensweig* while I was living in London, writing *The Heidi Chronicles.* I guess that while I was there I felt very much American and very much Jewish and ethnic. And a lot of my life—going to Mount Holyoke and Yale—has been sort of being a Jew within . . . an outsider. What has interested me is that both *The Heidi Chronicles* and *Uncommon Women* are not per se about being Jewish. There is a Jewish character in *Uncommon Women.*

Balakian: What about *Isn't it Romantic?*

Wasserstein: You do have the Jewish mother and daughter paralleling the lives of a non-Jewish mother and daughter. *The Sisters* had to do with coming to terms with one's self, and in this case coming to terms with one's religion and one's heritage, and in that case coming to terms with Judaism, which is a very complicated issue. When a friend of mine saw *The Sisters Rosensweig,* he said to me that it was interesting because Sara is a self-loathing Jew, Gorgeous is a practicing Jew, Pheni is a wandering Jew. Someone was telling me the other day that they thought one of the problems with the American musical is that people don't grow up going to temple hearing cantors. I think in many ways my idea of show business comes from temple, not that I really practice, but also that sense of community and melancholy and spirituality is there. My folks used to travel every year to Miami, twice a year, Christmas and New Year's, and to San Juan, and the entertainment that I knew was the Jewish comics. And I'm a New Yorker, so I grew up going to the Broadway theatre. *The Sisters Rosensweig* reminds me a lot of the plays I grew up seeing: you laugh, you cry, stars, beautiful set, a fulfilling afternoon. It's definitely a play, not a movie.

Balakian: So finally in *Sisters* are you conveying the idea that, as much as Sara Goode wants to efface her Jewishness, she can't? She realizes the importance of it.

Wasserstein: At the end of the play she says, "My name is Sara Rosensweig." She has begun a process. I don't think you can run from who you are. I mean, I think you can. Who's going to stop you? But why? It's interesting that in those Woody Allen movies, for all the Jewishness, Woody always falls in love with the shiksa. It's always Mia Farrow or

Diane Keaton. And then you think, "Oh, I see. Why? Why is the thin, blond girl more valuable than the girl with the brown curly hair?

Balakian: Exactly.

Wasserstein: It makes no sense. The only thing is that it's ingrained into the girl with the brown curly hair. It's not saying that one is more valuable than the other, it's just that that's who you are. In a way Merv is right: "If it doesn't exist, why are you working so hard to make it go away? What is it about it that's so embarrassing?" But I also think it has to do with being an American too.

Balakian: I grew up with the feeling that "we're not really Armenian; we're American." So your play really rang true for me.

You also write about WASPs, and I'm interested in how you perceive the difference between the WASP and Jewish sensibilities.

Wasserstein: You can't really make that distinction. There's no one as WASPy as a WASPy Jew. Sara Goode would out-WASP a WASP.

Balakian: (*Laughs*) That's a good point. But what are those WASPy qualities?

Wasserstein: It's hard to categorize.

Balakian: Why have you chosen to write comic plays rather than tragic ones?

Wasserstein: I think it has to do with one's voice. I'm beginning to write a new play now, which is a pretty serious play. It's how you hear people, how they speak to you. Also you can take things a little deeper with a comic release, and then you can go in even further. I love the scene in *The Heidi Chronicles* in the pediatric hospital, when Heidi comes with all of her things.

Balakian: I love that scene too.

Wasserstein: It's a very sad scene, but there are funny moments. When she brings over all those books, and he says, "Thank you, we don't have any of these." She has brought over *The Secret Life of Salvador Dalí.* But it's very poignant, I think.

Balakian: I also love the moment when they are sitting in those little kids' chairs in the children's waiting room. It's as though they are being kids, and yet they are talking about serious stuff. After all he's treating kids with AIDS, his former lover has AIDS, and Heidi is about to leave town.

Wasserstein: It's the transition from naïveté. I have great respect for the craft of writing comedy. To make that work is *really* hard. I have great respect for Larry Gelbart, Neil Simon. They know how to build something. I've been on the David Letterman show four times, and whenever I talk to him, I have great respect for him. People think comedy is just one-liners. First of all if it's revealing character, it's not one-liners. It's like when Gorgeous in *Sisters Rosensweig* says to Pfeni, "I know you can't judge a book by it's cover—"

Balakian and Wasserstein: "But you're in the wrong library!"

Balakian: I laughed really hard at that line.

Wasserstein: It's a great line, but it works because she's talking about Pfeni's gay boyfriend. And also only Gorgeous would say something like that. And it works with sisters. You would go home and call your mother or friends and say, "You wouldn't believe what this woman said to me." And what's irritating about it is that she's right. So it works on a multiplicity of levels. Often people say, "It's sitcom writing." It's very different from that. But also it's just hard to get people to laugh.

Balakian: Things always seem to work out at the end of your plays. There's always a kind of affirmation at the end.

Wasserstein: Someone else could tell you that in *Isn't it Romantic,* she's alone in the end.

Balakian: But she made the right choice in not marrying that Jewish doctor at Mount Sinai!

Wasserstein: She did make the right choice. One of the reasons I wrote *The Sisters Rosensweig* is that I wanted somebody . . . in my plays most of the women end up alone. In *Heidi* she's with the baby, but she's alone. But Sara Rosensweig is at the beginning of a relationship. I don't know what kind of relationship it will be.

Balakian: I thought it was implicit that she and Merv would not end up together.

Wasserstein: They won't get married, but they'll see each other. He'll call her.

Balakian: What can comedy do that tragedy can't?

Wasserstein: There are different kinds of comedy.

Balakian: Your kind of comedy.

Wasserstein: It's a form of release, a form of nonpretentiousness. It's a form of sharing, a form of creating a community with the audience. It's a form of nonindulgence.

Balakian: But tragedy also creates a community with the audience.

Wasserstein: A different kind of community.

Balakian: Laughing together is different from crying together.

Wasserstein: They're both a release.

Balakian: Does your comic sensibility have to do with being Jewish? I'm thinking of Woody Allen and how much he makes me laugh. One of my students last semester came to class saying, "Wasserstein is a riot. She's like Woody Allen with a skirt on."

Wasserstein: I think Woody is a wonderful writer. Woody Allen's obsessions are being neurotic and Jewish.

Balakian: Totally.

Wasserstein: In my plays that's not the case. The obsessions tend to be more about women, and the traps of being an intelligent, well-educated woman. They're very much of their times. Sara is very much a woman who came of age in the fifties and is trapped in that. Certainly *The Heidi Chronicles* is all about that. Woody Allen's and my works are about very different things. Also he's a filmmaker. But he's wonderful. I love his work.

Balakian: Nearly all of your plays explore the predicament of being a single woman in New York, trying to have both career and family. I'm thinking of Heidi, Janie, Chris in your first play, *Any Woman Can't,* Nina in your new screenplay, *The Object of My Affection,* Heidi, who tells Scoop that talented women, or any woman, should not devote their lives to making tuna sandwiches for their husbands and children, and Scoop says, "Well, no one should do that." Would you talk about this idea of "having it all." Are we women doomed to frustration because of that idea that we're supposed to be bionic in our careers and as wives as well as mothers?

Wasserstein: The other day there was an editorial in the *Times* about a woman who was fifty-nine years old and had a baby. It's perfectly fine for fifty-nine-year-old men to have babies, but suddenly there's this fifty-nine-year-old woman and that's a terrible thing! The whole idea of "having it all" is a crazy notion, because it's all about being acquisitive. It's all about "I have this, this, and that." I think there are wonderfully energetic people who manage to have children and careers. I've always thought that you do different things at different times in your life. But I think there's always been this pressure on women that you have to have children, a family, a career, a really good body; you have to stay young forever.

Balakian: That reminds me of Heidi's monologue in the women's locker room before her aerobics class.

Wasserstein: Exactly. And I always think, "I don't know men who have that pressure." Men have different pressures and difficulties. I think women are very assuming, so they're very generous in some sense. They'll take on their own pressure and all the men's pressure as well. It's like, "I can bear it; I can take it." Also the thing about my plays and being single is that a lot of those plays have to do with choice.

Balakian: Arthur Miller says, "Where choice begins, paradise ends."

Wasserstein: When you make that choice to marry or not to marry, is it about passion, is it not about passion? Or is it what Harriet says, "Life is negotiation." Is it saying, "No, it isn't"? Is it childish or naive to say, "No, it isn't"? Who allows themselves to fall in love and who doesn't? Is it an illusion? Why does Sara allow herself to have an affair with Merv? Who knows. Is the choice of Geoffrey [Pfeni's gay boyfriend] a really bad choice? Are you better off with Marty Sterling [the Jewish doctor in *Isn't it Romantic*]? It's interesting to figure it out because it has to do with how you live your life. And then people are products of the time in which they came of age. I know that to be true. In my plays these women are very much of their times. What's interesting about the Rosensweigs is that here are these three people who lead vastly different lives, who are from the same place.

Balakian: At times they seem as though they couldn't have emerged from the same womb.

Wasserstein: And yet in some ways they have a great deal in common. At the end when they toast Rita [their mother], and this is what I felt in Norfolk, these are three impressive people.

Balakian: In their own right.

Wasserstein: They are people of dignity. In terms of talking about single women it's so easy in magazines to say, "This poor pathetic [*laughs*] creature." I thought, "No, they are very interesting lives." Women still interest me a lot.

Balakian: So you see yourself continuing to write about women.

Wasserstein: It's interesting to look at the two men in *The Sisters Rosensweig,* as opposed to the two men in *Isn't it Romantic,* because they're much nicer men. They're more catalysts for the action. Merv is a fuller guy than Dr. Marty in *Isn't it Romantic.* Janie is right not to be with Dr. Marty. She'd never be happy.

Balakian: He goes off and gets an apartment without telling her. He doesn't seem like a great catch to me.

Wasserstein: No.

Balakian: What's your definition of feminism?

Wasserstein: When I was in the car this morning, someone was talking about feminists and Mrs. Bobbitt. You know, women want to cut off men's penises. But as Heidi says, "We all have a right to fulfill our potential." I truly believe that it's just like racism or anything else. It's amazing to me that . . . there are limitations in life, biological ones, such as women can have babies and men can't, but probably in twenty years men will have babies—but to say that there are limitations on someone's life based on their gender is shocking to me. And it's all made up. I was talking to a man the other day, and he said, "Well, you know, a woman's window of opportunity ends at thirty-two. You really have to maximize between twenty-eight and thirty-two to marry, because women in their forties, or women with children, it's a dime a dozen." I thought, "Who the hell are you?" *Who* said that men who are forty-eight and successful are extremely desirable, and that women who are forty-eight and successful are scary and threatening? Men who are single and at your dinner party are desirable, and women who are single are sad. *Why?!* Who made that up? And I think in terms of feminism those things that are inequitable . . . the inequalities in life that are based on gender, both externally and internally, and what you grow up with as a girl . . . it's almost like there are women's problems, and that's shunted aside, whereas men's problems are all of our problems.

Balakian: It often seems that way.

There has been a lot of controversy among feminist critics in academia—

Wasserstein: I know that a lot of them did not like *The Heidi Chronicles* because Heidi adopts a baby.

Balakian: That's what I want to ask you about. What's your response to them?

Wasserstein: That there should be more plays by women, and in some plays the woman should adopt the baby, and in some she won't. One play can't stand for everything. And furthermore, plays are about the character in the play. If this were really Heidi's life, which the life of a play is, how can they say, "We find the choice in your life politically incorrect. Give your baby back." Also what happens is that feminism or anything becomes ghettoized, and you turn in on yourself, and you want to say, "Hey, honey, David Mamet is out there writing *Oleanna.* Why don't you go to see that play! Go see what's in the movies!" I thought feminism was turning against itself. Though I appreciated the criticism of my play; at least there's a dialogue going on about it. But I'm sure that always happens. I'm sure there are gay critics who don't like *Angels in America,* who like Terrence McNally's plays or don't like them. It's interesting that there has not been feminist criticism against *The Sisters Rosensweig,* although there has been larger criticism saying it's just comedic or it's unimportant.

Balakian: Feminist critics argue that Heidi succumbs to the status quo because she can't live without a baby. It's not the kind of subversive feminist play that they would have liked to have seen. And your response is that that decision is consistent with her character.

Wasserstein: Right. She's a woman who wants a baby. I think it takes enormous courage to do what she does.

Balakian: Absolutely. I was thinking of Dr. Marty in *Isn't it Romantic.* He says to Janie about his sister-in law, "She'll go back to work in something nice. She'll teach or work with the elderly. She won't conquer the world, but she'll have a nice life." I just cringed when I read that.

Wasserstein: That's a good reason not to marry Marty.

Balakian: Yes! Do you think that point of view is really representative of guys in the nineties, or is that a statement of that period?

Wasserstein: Of that period. Guys in the nineties wouldn't say that; they'd be scared to. But they might think it.

Balakian: The crucial question is whether they think it.

Wasserstein: Maybe because of economics they can't think it anymore.

Balakian: Is Heidi's sadness the result of the collapse of the idealism behind the feminist movement?

Wasserstein: That's what Heidi would say. Heidi is a good girl. She's a serious, good person. And I think her sadness surprises her, because she's very earnest and not very self-indulgent. Heidi plays by the rules. And life doesn't necessarily work by the rules. Other things come into play.

Balakian: I was wondering whether her sadness stems in part from the fact that she's single. Is that a source of melancholy for her?

Wasserstein: I think her melancholy is a lack of connection. Yes, it could be that she's single, or it could be that she's isolated. You have to go back to character. Heidi is an observer. And in life when you're slightly removed, it gives you a point of view, but the removal can give you a sense of sadness. When it's comfortable, the distance can allow you to be a critic or an academic or whatever, but when the gap becomes too large, you feel out of touch, out of time. That's what happens to Heidi. In some ways you can see it in her even at the high school dance. She's sitting on the side with Peter; she's not Miss Dance. That's a reflective, sensitive girl. Who at a high school dance goes and meets [*laughs*] Peter Patrone?! Tonni Little is not doing that at the high school dance. And even if the high school dances aren't fun anymore, there's still the person on the side, and there's still the person dancing.

Balakian: In one of her art history lectures Heidi identifies the "uniquely female" quality as being "slightly removed from the occasion at hand," like an art historian who is "a highly informed spectator."

Wasserstein: In Kenneth Burke's literary criticism he talks about the participants as spectators and observers. It was taught in a class I took at Amherst, and I was very taken with it. Heidi isn't someone who leads marches. She goes between being an observer and a spectator.

Balakian: And she also says that quality is female.

Wasserstein: Yes. Like Lilly Martin Spenser. She eases the way for others.

Balakian: So are you saying that being the outsider is being female?

Wasserstein: Not being the outsider, but I think the way one has traditionally, until this century, eased the way for others—make the family, make a home, make it possible for others to grow—the nurturer in some way.

Balakian: I'm interested in Heidi's wonderful monologue, which she gives as an alumna speech to her high school, about her observations of the women in the locker room before aerobics class. Is her sadness also because of the warped values that she sees?

Wasserstein: Heidi is one of these people, and I'm one of these people, who always remember what someone said to me yesterday. I can't remember the name, but I remember exactly what they said. Maybe it's because I'm not a great reader.

Balakian: It's because you're a playwright.

Wasserstein: Heidi is like that too. She's trying to put things together. She is thinking, "Wait a minute. Susie was a shepherdess last week, and now she's in Hollywood." There are people like that, who go with the flow. And I think that's hard to put together. And I think her sadness is noticing that she stayed the same in some way.

Balakian: She's a romantic.

Wasserstein: Yes. I think she's very romantic. The values seem to be that people are all sort of kidding themselves. It has nothing to do with being smart or not smart. Scoop Rosenbaum is very, very smart.

Wendy generously offered to continue our conversation at another time because she had to rush off to a dinner engagement. And so we parted at the Stanhope Hotel, which struck me as an appropriate place to meet a playwright who is such a keen observer of wealthy New Yorkers. While we were talking, well-dressed doctors, lawyers, and Wall Street people were sipping drinks, talking about their patients, their cases, and their latest deals. This is the social class of Wasserstein's dramatic world, but her protagonists are always searching for more substantive values as they struggle to work out their relationships, their careers, and their identities.

CONTRIBUTORS

Jan Balakian is an Assistant Professor of English at Kean College of New Jersey. She has published interviews with Arthur Miller, Wendy Wasserstein, and Eugene Ionesco, and articles on Zona Gale and Arthur Miller. She is also the author of a play, *The Ceiling Will Open,* which won Cornell University's playwriting award. Currently she is working on a book about Wendy Wasserstein's plays.

Judith E. Barlow is Associate Professor of English and Women's Studies at the University of Albany, State University of New York. She is the author of *Final Acts: The Creation of Three Late O'Neill Plays* as well as editor of *Plays By American Women, 1900–1930* and *Plays By American Women, 1930–1960.* Barlow has written and lectured widely on modern drama.

Leigh Buchanan Bienen is a Senior Lecturer at the Northwestern University School of Law in Chicago. Her current research interests in the law include homicide, capital punishment, sex crimes, women and the law, and jurors. Recently she directed an empirical study of all homicide cases in New Jersey since the reimposition of capital punishment. A graduate of Cornell University, the University of Iowa Writers' Workshop, and the Rutgers-Newark School of Law, she has been published in a variety of journals, including the *Harvard Law Review* and *The O'Henry Prize Stories.* A short play of hers was in *Winters' Tales 1994,* the McCarter Theatre's New Play Festival.

Jackson R. Bryer is Professor of English at the University of Maryland. He is editor of *The Playwright's Art: Conversations With Contemporary American Dramatists* (1995), *Lanford Wilson: A Casebook* (1994), *Conversations with Thornton Wilder* (1992), *Conversations with Lillian Hellman* (1988), and *The Theatre We Worked For: The Letters of Eugene O'Neill to Kenneth Macgowan* (1982).

Una Chaudhuri is Chair of the Department of Drama, Tisch School of the Arts at New York University. She is the author of *No Man's Stage: A Semiotic Study of Jean Genet's Plays* (1986) and *Staging Place: The Geography of Modern Drama* (1995). Her articles and essays have appeared in numerous books and journals, including *Modern Drama, Theater,* and *Theatre Journal.*

Marty Moss-Coane is the host of the radio talk show *Radio Times,* which airs Mondays through Fridays on WHYY in Philadelphia and is broadcast nationwide on many National Public Radio stations.

Nena Couch is Curator of the Library of the Jerome Lawrence and Robert E. Lee Theatre Research Institute at Ohio State University. She has an M.M. in Music from George Peabody College and an M.L.S. from Vanderbilt University. She is co-editor of and contributor to *The Humanities and the Library* (2nd ed., 1993) and the author of "Dance Collections" in *Managing Performing Arts Collections in Academic and Public Libraries* (1994). She is a member of the Theatre Library Association and the William Inge Festival Boards.

Mary Dellasega has taught Theatre at the University of Cincinnati, Augustana College (Rock Island), and Capital University in Columbus, Ohio, where she has directed the work of more than twenty-five playwrights, including Beth Henley's *Crimes of the Heart* and *The Miss Firecracker Contest.* In the fall of 1994, she presented a paper on suffragette playwright Cicely Hamilton for the Women and Theatre Conference at Hofstra University. Currently, Dellasega is a dramaturg for the Jane Doe Theatre, Seattle's only feminist theatre, and a member of The Alice B. Theatre's Laboratory program, which will soon present her work in progress, a play depicting the life of Hildegard of Bingen.

Elin Diamond is Associate Professor of English at Rutgers University. Author of *Pinter's Comic Play,* she has written articles on feminist and theater theory for *TDR, ELH, Theatre Journal, Modern Drama, Kenyon Review,* and *Art and Cinema.* She is completing her book *Unmasking Mimesis* and an anthology of criticism, *Performance and Cultural Politics,* both for Routledge.

John Louis DiGaetani is Professor of English at Hofstra University. His most recent books include: *A Search for a Postmodern Theater: Interviews with Contemporary Playwrights* (1991), *A Companion to Pirandello Studies* (1991),

An Invitation to the Opera (1991), *Penetrating Wagner's Ring: An Anthology* (1983), and *Money: Lure, Lore and Literature* (1994).

Steven Drukman teaches in the Department of Drama at New York University. His criticism appears regularly in *American Theatre* and *The Village Voice* as well as in many other magazines. He has published work in *Theatre Topics, TDR, Women and Performance, A Queer Romance,* and *Terrence McNally: A Casebook* (1995).

Mimi Reisel Gladstein is Director of the Western Cultural Heritage Program at the University of Texas at El Paso where she is a Professor in Theatre Arts and English. She has chaired the English Department twice and served as Director of Women's Studies. She is the author of *The Indestructible Woman in Faulkner, Hemingway, and Steinbeck, The Ayn Rand Companion,* and numerous articles in anthologies and professional journals.

Jeffrey Goldman is a freelance critic and reviewer living in Hollywood.

Alexis Greene has published widely on modern and contemporary American theatre. Her essay on Jean-Claude van Itallie appears in *American Playwrights Since 1945: A Guide to Scholarship, Criticism, and Performance* (1989); her reviews and essays frequently are published in *American Theatre, Theatre,* and *Theater Week.*

Philip C. Kolin, Professor of English at the University of Southern Mississippi and Co-Editor of *Studies in American Drama, 1945–Present,* has written or edited twenty books and published more than 100 articles on Shakespeare, American drama, folklore, and linguistics. His most recent books include *David Rabe: A Stage History and A Primary and Secondary Bibliography* (1988); *American Playwrights Since 1945: A Guide to Scholarship, Criticism, and Performance* (1989); *Feminist Criticism of Shakespeare's Plays: An Annotated Bibliography and A Commentary* (1991); *Confronting Tennessee Williams's* A Streetcar Named Desire: *Essays in Critical Pluralism* (1993); *Successful Writing at Work* (4th ed., 1994); and *Titus Andronicus: Critical Essays* (1995). Kolin is also the General Editor for the Garland Shakespeare Criticism Series and the author of a book of poems, *Roses for Sharron* (1993).

Richard E. Kramer, former editor of the newsletters *Directors Notes* and *Program Notes,* has written for *The Drama Review, Performance Studies, Studies in American Drama, 1945–Present, Theatre Studies, TheatreInsight, ATHE News,* and *The Village Voice.* His reviews have appeared in *Stages* and the *New York Native,* and he has contributed articles to *The Cambridge Guide to World*

Theatre and *The Cambridge Guide to American Theatre*. He has taught theatre and acting at Rutgers University's Douglass College, the Rockbridge Fine Arts Workshop (Lexington, Virginia), the Packer Collegiate Institute (Brooklyn, New York), the State University of New York College at Oneonta, and the Process Studio Theatre (New York City), as well as writing and composition at New York University and Felician College. Kramer is a professional actor, director, and dramaturg as well.

Colby H. Kullman is Associate Professor of English at the University of Mississippi and Co-Editor of *Studies in American Drama, 1945–Present*. He has published extensively in eighteenth-century studies and modern American drama. A regular presenter at the William Inge Festival, Kullman has written frequently on Miller, Inge, Williams, and Beth Henley. He was editor-in-chief of the two-volume *Theatre Companies of the World* (1986), which won an award from *Library Journal* for being a major research tool. His articles have appeared in such journals as *Kansas English, Odyssey: A Journal of the Humanities, 1650–1850, The South Carolina Review, The Southern Register, Studies in Contemporary Satire, Studies in the Humanities, Studies on Voltaire and the Eighteenth Century,* and *Theatre Journal*.

Neal A. Lester, Associate Professor of English, teaches African American literature at the University of Alabama. Lester has published in *African American Review, Journal of Popular Culture, The Oxford Companion to Women's Writing in the United States,* and *Diversity: A Journal of Multicultural Issues.* His book, *Ntozake Shange: A Critical Study of the Plays* (1995), is the first comprehensive examination of Shange's drama.

Felicia Hardison Londré is Curators' Professor of Theatre at the University of Missouri-Kansas City and Dramaturg for Missouri Repertory Theatre. She has also served as dramaturg for Nebraska Shakespeare Festival, Heart of America Shakespeare Festival, and Great Lakes Theatre Festival. She has published several books including volumes on Tennessee Williams, Tom Stoppard, and Federico Lorca. Her *History of World Theatre: From the Restoration to the Present* (1991) was a *Choice* Outstanding Academic Book. She has published articles in *Theatre History Studies, Journal of Dramatic Theory and Criticism, Theatre Journal,* and *Studies in Popular Culture.* She has also written an opera *Dusead D'Annuzio.*

Vivian M. Patraka, Professor of English at Bowling Green State University, has published in journals, including *Theatre Journal, Modern Drama, Discourse, The Drama Review, The Journal of Dramatic Theory and Criticism, Women & Performance, The Michigan Quarterly Review,* and *The Kenyon Review.*

Completing a book entitled "Spectacular Suffering: Theatrical Representations of the Holocaust and Fascism" for Indiana University Press, she also currently serves as Vice-President for Research and Publications for the Association for Theatre in Higher Education.

Matthew C. Roudané is Professor of English at Georgia State University in Atlanta, where he serves as Associate Chair of the English Department and as Editor of the *South Atlantic Review*. He has published extensively on American drama including *Conversations with Arthur Miller* (1987), *Understanding Edward Albee* (1987), and most recently *American Drama, 1960–Present: A Critical History* (1995).

David Savran has published widely on post–World War II American theatre and culture. He is the author of *Breaking the Rules: The Wooster Group* (1988), *In Their Own Words: Contemporary American Playwrights* (1988), and *Cowboys, Communists, and Queers: The Politics of Masculinity in the Work of Arthur Miller and Tennessee Williams* (1992). He is professor of English at Brown University.

David Sedevie is working on his Ph.D. in the Department of Theatre at Louisiana State University and has written on Jack Gelber and the Living Theatre's production of *The Connection*. His work has appeared in the *New England Theatre Journal* and *Theatre Survey*.

Susan Harris Smith is Associate Professor of English at the University of Pittsburgh. The author of *Masks in Modern Drama* (1984), she has just completed *Disciplining American Drama*. Her work has appeared in *American Quarterly, Journal of Dramatic Theory and Criticism, Theatre Journal, Modern Drama, The Dada/Surrealism Review, Women and Literature, Studies in American Drama, 1945–Present, Public Issues/Private Tensions,* and *Approaches to Teaching "Death of a Salesman."*

Joan Templeton, who teaches drama at Long Island University, Brooklyn, edits *Ibsen News and Comment,* and has published frequently on Ibsen and other modern dramatists in *PMLA, Scandinavian Studies, Modern Drama,* and elsewhere; she has also edited a collection of feminist criticism, *Reconsidered Spheres* (1994). She has received NEH and Fulbright awards and held Visiting Professorships at the Sorbonne, the University of Tours, and the University of Limoges.

John Timpane, a Lecturer in English at Lafayette College, has published essays on English Renaissance literature and contemporary American drama and (with Nancy Huddleston Packer) is the coauthor of *Writing Worth Reading* (1989), a composition textbook. He is currently completing *The Renaissance Laugh,* a book about humor in sixteenth-century England.

Don B. Wilmeth is Professor of English and former Chair of the Department of Theatre, Speech and Dance at Brown University. He is the author, editor, or co-editor of a dozen books, including the recent *Cambridge Guide to American Theatre* (1993) and the Hewitt Award-winning biography, *George Fredrick Cooke: Machiavel of the Stage.* He is the editor of the series, Studies in American Theatre and Drama, and is co-editing a three-volume history of the American theatre (both for Cambridge University Press). He was the past President of the American Society for Theatre Research and was a Guggenheim Fellow in 1982; in 1995 he became Dean-Elect of the College of Fellows of the American Theatre.

INDEX

812.5409 Speaking on stage.
SPE

41547

$29.95

DATE			
JUN 0 2 1997			